OLD TRAILS AND NEW ROADS

in South Dakota History

OLD TRAILS AND NEW ROADS *in* South Dakota History

Edited by Jon K. Lauck

THE CENTER FOR WESTERN STUDIES
Augustana University
2023

Publication made possible with funding by the Anne King Publications Endowment and Ronald R. Nelson Publications Endowment in the Center for Western Studies and by the National Endowment for the Humanities. The publisher wishes to acknowledge the assistance of Liz Cisar, Kari Mahowald, Kamryn Miller, Ana Olivier, Hal Thompson, Ronelle Thompson, and Laurel Trautwein.

ISBN: 978-0-931170-94-2
Library of Congress Control Number: 2022938434

The Center for Western Studies (CWS) at Augustana University preserves and interprets the history and cultures of the Northern Plains and seeks to improve the quality of social and cultural life in the region, achieve a better understanding of the region, its heritage, and its resources, and stimulate interest in the solution to regional problems. The Center promotes understanding of the region through its archives, library, museum and art exhibitions, publications, courses, internships, and public affairs programming. It is committed, ultimately, to defining the contribution of the Northern Plains to American civilization.

Visit the Fantle Building for The Center for Western Studies
Augustana University, 2121 S. Summit Avenue,
Sioux Falls, South Dakota

605-274-4007 • cws@augie.edu • www.augie.edu/cws •
Facebook • Twitter

Cover image: *Tasunka Oyate-Horse Nation*, 2022, by Donald F. Montileaux (Oglala Lakota). Prisma color pencil on ledger page dated 1907.

Designed by Anundsen Publishing Company

For
John E. Miller,
Scholar and Gentleman

Contents

Foreword

A certain irony exists when two history aficionados meet through an exclusively twenty-first century medium–Facebook. I met Jon Lauck, this book's editor, through a Friend request. I hoped that he would see a list of our mutual Facebook friends. He did, and he accepted my invitation. I had read a local newspaper article about the death of another friend, John Miller, Professor of History at South Dakota State University, and found out about Miller and Lauck's desire to create a new volume of South Dakota essays, but the project didn't get off the ground before Miller's death. When I showed interest, Lauck introduced me to Harry Thompson, Executive Director of the Center for Western Studies at Augustana University, who in agreeing to publish the work became another friend. I was able to offer financial support, and we were on our way.

I can hardly say enough about Jon Lauck's editorial qualifications. He not only is a history professor himself (at the University of South Dakota) and a proven author and editor, but he knows the most qualified individuals to write the essays. Local and regional experts as well as a further-flung professor at Oxford in the UK make the volume not only a good read but also a resource for educational institutions in South Dakota and undoubtedly throughout the Midwest.

My take on history is that we perceive it through the lens of human perspective encompassing memory, fact, emotion, and finally, analysis.

For example, I remember well the winter of 1969, mentioned in Chris Laingen's excellent essay, "The Extremes of South Dakota's Weather." I know facts about that winter, found in my diary from 53 years ago: how over 100 inches of snow fell in eastern South Dakota, how my dairy farmer father dumped milk on the ground because the milk truck couldn't get through the snowdrifts, how school was often disrupted by another blizzard, and how my family's church burned to the ground during a blizzard on January 26, 1969.

But I could also add my own emotional perspective: how I hated the milky ice rink in our Holstein yard, how I shivered as my siblings and I trudged over snowbanks on blocked roads to meet the school bus a mile and a half away for a blizzard-shortened school day, or how I was touched by the *Brookings Register*'s description of the church fire, "Spectators said the steeple was the last thing to go. . . . Almost as if it were a symbol, it towered over the fire until the very end. . . ." And using the analytical skills of my 15-year-old self, I compared my snow experiences to those of Laura Ingalls Wilder's in *The Long Winter* of 1880-1881. History is always a combination of memory, fact, emotion, and analysis.

These are the qualities that make the historical word so dynamic. I invite you, our readers, to form your own analysis as you compare your personal experiences to factual events and to the memories and emotions of the people brought alive by our essayists. And Jon and Harry, I value not only your historical perspectives but also your friendships.

Janet Hovey Johnson
Retired Instructor of English, Mount Marty University
Owner with husband, David, and sons Reid and Ethan, Reliabank

Acknowledgments

The Center for Western Studies at Augustana University, the publisher, wishes to take this opportunity to express appreciation to Jan Johnson and Reliabank for their generous financial support of this project, spearheaded by Jon Lauck and carried out by the thirteen authors whose research and writing constitute new perspectives on the history of South Dakota.

This is an especially appropriate publication for the Center. In 2005 we published the first new history of the state in over forty years, *A New South Dakota History* (2d ed., 2009), for which I served as project director and editor. Among the sixteen authors represented in that volume was John E. Miller, who contributed the chapter "Politics Since Statehood" and the essay "Small Towns: Image and Reality." He was joined in that endeavor by Herbert T. Hoover, long-time Professor of History at the University of South Dakota, along with several other historians and writers. Now is the time for the current generation of historians to offer a new and more inclusive interpretation of the past for the present. History (or the interpretation of the past) reflects the concerns and perspectives of those living today—and teachers, students, and the general public deserve nothing less. We believe this collection of essays is a step in that direction, along "old trails and new roads."

The Center for Western Studies would also like to acknowledge the following individuals for their matching gifts: Joseph Fenstermacher; Tony and Anne Haga; Stephanie Herseth Sandlin and Max Sandlin; Pastor Dave and Glenice Johnson; Richard Muller; F. Bert and Cindy Olson; Ann Smith; Elizabeth Soladay and Mary Soladay Wipf, in memory of Glenn E. and Lois Soladay; James and Penny Volin; and others.

Harry F. Thompson
Executive Director

INTRODUCTION
FINDING THE HISTORY OF SOUTH DAKOTA

Jon K. Lauck
University of South Dakota

On the morning of May 1, 2020, the great historian of South Dakota John E. Miller died in his kitchen in Brookings. He was 75 years old. Miller had anchored the unsung enterprise of writing state history in South Dakota for decades. He was a constant presence at history conferences, a frequent speaker at service clubs, and a regular commentator on public radio. His books about South Dakota and his articles and editorials about historical figures in the state were read by the civically-inclined and historically conscious. He also trained hundreds of history majors at the state's largest university, South Dakota State University, where he taught for three decades. Miller taught upper level courses on South Dakota history and on the "Methods and Philosophy of History." All history majors were required to take the latter, and the major requirement of the course was to write a research paper based upon original research. Some of those history majors went on to earn a Ph.D. in history and to write about South Dakota and the Midwest and Great Plains, just like Miller. As soon as he was eligible, Miller retired and devoted all his time to researching and writing history. His early death was recognized by many as a great blow to the collective historical consciousness of our fair state.[1]

Enter Jan Johnson. In early May 2020, Johnson read a remembrance of Miller that I had written for the Brookings newspaper.[2] The next day she sent me a message via Facebook and said she agreed with some of the points in my article about Miller. I had noted all of Miller's books and historical contributions, but also highlighted the need for more and better work on South Dakota's history. Miller had often said he was a "guerilla scholar," acting alone, without support, cut-off from the deep pockets of coastal research foundations, scrounging for time and resources, living off the land, and battling against the currents of historiography and the literary world, which showed little interest in Miller's work, especially his research on the small towns of the Midwest. Jan Johnson said she recognized the problem. She said she had also been a friend of Miller and shared a love of local history and had worked together with Miller on the Bruce, South Dakota, centennial back in the 1980s. Johnson said she had recently retired from years of teaching English composition classes at the Mount Marty University campus in Watertown, South Dakota, and that she wanted to aid the effort to recognize Miller and get more South Dakota history published. Naturally, I could not have agreed more and said that Miller would have loved this story of collaboration and organizing (he had even published a book about the dynamics underlying the creative process).[3] I suggested a new book, dedicated to the memory of John Miller, which explored various angles on South Dakota history—and Johnson was enthused.

My next call went to Harry Thompson, the executive director of the Center for Western Studies at Augustana University in Sioux Falls. Thompson was a great supporter of books about South Dakota and the region and the Center had become known as a publisher of impressive works of history, literature, and art. Thompson was working to complete a new history of the Center and all its contributions to cultural life in the region and thought the book idea fit the Center's mission perfectly.[4] In short order, the three of us met and mapped out a plan to recruit authors and finance the project with the generous support of Johnson and her family.

The working assumption behind this book was the belief that we needed more historical research into the story of South Dakota. Unlike other states, South Dakota enjoys no comprehensive multi-volume treatment of its history. The state's standard monographic history was written by University of South Dakota professor Herbert Schell in the 1950s (Miller added a few chapters to a new addition of the Schell book released in the 1990s). South Dakota does not have large history departments at its universities which employ scholars who spend their research time on South Dakota topics. Unlike every other state, South Dakota does not have a Ph.D. program in history spinning off theses and dissertations and other basic research that later become books. South Dakota also has no university press (by way of comparison, the University of Nebraska Press, south of the border, publishes 150 new titles a year; Michigan benefits from being home to three university presses). In the broader historical profession, the topic of South Dakota history provides little allure. To a large extent, we are on our own in South Dakota, where we rely on guerilla scholars like John Miller to fight the twilight struggle to keep South Dakota history alive. It takes generous people like Jan Johnson and homegrown institutions like the Center for Western Studies to advance the cause of promoting historical awareness of our state.

The Center is one of two main drivers of history in South Dakota. The origins of the Center lie with its intellectual godfather, the writer Herbert Krause, a Minnesotan who earned his Ph.D. at the University of Iowa and grounded the Center's mission in a broader Midwestern regionalist movement.[5] The Center now hosts the annual Dakota Conference, which began in Madison, South Dakota, at Dakota State College in the 1970s. This annual conference brings together dozens of scholars each year who hold an interest in state and regional history. The Center also publishes important books such as its study of the border between the agrarian Midwest and the more arid high plains and the first-ever history of the Big Sioux River Valley, which was central to the settlement of South Dakota.[6] Through such endeavors, the small staff of the Center maintains the vision of Krause and keeps the flame of South Dakota history burning.

The other driver of South Dakota history is the South Dakota State Historical Society in Pierre, first organized by the regionalist

Doane Robinson. In recent years, the Society struck gold by publishing the unpublished memoirs of Laura Ingalls Wilder.[7] This book, along with a publishing program which has come to life in recent years, have contributed to what John Miller saw, before his death, as a flowering of literary activity in the state.[8] The Society now has a new leader, Ben Jones, an entrepreneurial retired Air Force colonel, and a generous state appropriation for a new facility and is entering into a more active era of promoting the history of South Dakota.[9] The Society is even planning a new history of the state of South Dakota to finally replace Schell's old classic. The Center and the Society do great and crucial work, but they need reinforcements, more active scholars like John Miller joining the cause, and more books—like this volume—which add to the corpus of South Dakota history and inject vibrancy into this field of study. Despite this victory for the cause, the effort to build the field will likely remain a struggle. It is a permanent condition, part of the eternal mission of interior regionalists to tilt the coastal gaze, to generate more than passing attention, to alter the cultural dynamics over "who gets paid attention to and receives access to resources," to preserve "fragile gains in visibility and institutional support," and to escape chronic marginality.[10] Until a future of generous support and a more elaborate institutional infrastructure and more scholarly reinforcements arrive, the Center and the Society, aided by guerilla scholars and generous donors like Jan Johnson, will keep the flame of South Dakota history burning through works such as this one.

The organizational logic of this volume is double-sided. Since South Dakota's history is relatively impoverished vis-a-vis other states, we do not believe that some basic elements of life in South Dakota have been properly or thoroughly explored. That is why we sought out authors to research and explain some fundamental components of South Dakota history such as how the Sioux came to live in the Dakotas and the building of South Dakota's railroads. Also in this category are straightforward matters such as how South Dakota's borders came to be and the weather, which is often extreme and unpredictable and a major force in a state of farmers and outdoorspeople. These are Old Trails that some historians have traveled down in the past but they represent critical topics that need fresh eyes to remind us how important they are to our state. We also sought to explore some topics that have not been frequently taken up by historians. These New Roads lead us to matters such as popular culture in the form of movies about South Dakota, the history of food production and consumption in the state, the state's obsession with sports and hunting, and the environmental history of South Dakota's landscapes.

In chapter one, Pekka Hämäläinen, a Finnish scholar who is now the Rhodes Professor of American History at the University of Oxford in England, explores South Dakota's early Native American history. Specifically, Hämäläinen traces the rise of the Lakota nation and the larger Sioux alliance, the Očhéthi Sakówiŋ, the Sioux Indian Confederacy of Seven Council Fires. He shows how the Lakotas gradually moved from the western Great Lakes into the great continental grasslands in the Trans-Missouri West. The Lakotas and their Dakota allies responded to the dramatic transformations brought by the European newcomers: the introduction of horses, gunpowder, lead, diseases, cloth, and new ways of being in the world. Hämäläinen's chapter "In the Heart of the Continent" shows how the Lakotas carved out a vast domain in the Trans-Missouri West through systematic expansion. They did so by forging alliances with numerous peoples, both European and Indigenous. In the early eighteenth century, four Lakota oyátes—Oglalas, Sicangus, Minneconjous, Sihasapas, and Saones—launched a concentrated expansion into the Trans-Missouri West by capturing eight river valleys, which became the core of the Lakota domain. The Lakotas reduced the agricultural Pawnees, Omahas, Arikaras, Mandans, and Hidatsas effectively to vassals who had to provide corn, squash, and other necessities to Lakotas under duress. By the late eighteenth century, the Lakotas dominated the deep interior as a budding empire. That Indigenous empire was not a kind of empire that colonial powers sought to establish in North America. The Lakota empire was founded on kinship ties and the incorporation of enemies. That kind of maneuvering turned rivals into relatives and allies. The Lakota empire was a malleable and shape-shifting confederacy that dominated much of the Great Plains from the early 1800s to the 1870s. The Lakota empire could also be characterized as a kinetic empire that relied not on institutional prowess, but on mobility, suppleness, and flexibility. The U.S. Army struggled with that and, as a result, suffered one of its worst defeats in the Battle of the Little Big Horn in the summer of 1876.

During this same era is when the state of South Dakota literally took shape, a topic taken up in Tom Isern's chapter. Counterfactualists, Isern notes, love to second-guess the shape of South Dakota. The borders are, in the first place, uninteresting, delineating just another generally-rectangular state of the Great Plains. Moreover, they do not conform to salient landforms or vernacular geography; they seem arbitrary. The opinions of critics who judge the state's borders in terms of east vs. west have an able spokesperson in James D. McLaird, author of the much-read article "From Bib Overalls to Cowboy Boots: East River/West River Differences in South Dakota." McLaird adjudges the northern boundary of South Dakota "artificial" and wishes Dakota Territory had been divided east and west, rather than north and south. All such judgments are ahistorical, Isern argues. Investigated in context, the borders of South Dakota emerge as logical and sensible according to the knowledge and aspirations of the people of Dakota Territory. Moreover, such investigation goes to more fundamental questions: the definition of a state (as distinct from a region) and the chronicling of its history. Borders, and thus the physical shape of the state, resulted, first, from federal processes, and second, more and more as time passed, from the active agency of territorial citizens. Indeed, the last major segment of border to fall into place—the boundary between South Dakota and North Dakota—was, arguably, the one that was most grounded in popular desires and historical circumstances. In the end, however, the shape of South Dakota is not so much lines on a map but rather, as territorial governor William A. Howard declared in 1879, "the organized power of the good." To define the shape of South Dakota in such terms—"the people in a given territory and their institutions," as Howard said—is a worthy task for state historia.

Perhaps as fundamental to the early stages of South Dakota history as the shaping of the state's boundaries was the coming of the railroads. From the territorial period into the post-World War II era, railroads strongly impacted business and personal life in South Dakota. Although the state failed to benefit from a transcontinental carrier that served Sioux Falls and other urban centers except Aberdeen, it ultimately claimed more than 4,000 route miles. Just as population became concentrated east of the Missouri River, railroad mileage did as well. Eastern sections, however, would not be connected directly to the Black Hills until 1907 when the state's two dominant railroads, the Chicago & North Western and the Chicago, Milwaukee & St. Paul, built from the Missouri River to Rapid City. Lasting legacies of the South Dakota railroad experience involved more than providing connectedness with the outside world. Steel rails triggered a population explosion during the Great Dakota Boom between 1878 and 1887 and advanced commercial agriculture. The coming of the iron horse likewise fostered the creation of multiple communities. Railroads platted 138 of the 285 towns launched during these boom years. Until the coming of dependable motor vehicles and the triumph of the "Good Roads Movement," railroads monopolized most intercity passenger travel and freight shipments. Throughout the state the local depot served as the public gateway. The local station agent was the most knowledgeable about current international, national, and state happenings, and he (occasionally she) was a respected member of the community. By the mid-twentieth century and after, the "Railway Age" changed noticeably for South Dakotans. Diesel replaced steam, line abandonments increased, depots closed, and companies merged. What ultimately occurred was that one mega-carrier, Burlington Northern Santa Fe, reigned supreme, being an amalgamation between 1970 and 1995 of the Chicago, Burlington and Quincy, Great Northern, Santa Fe, and several other trunk roads. During this time the Milwaukee Road fell into bankruptcy and later withdrew from the state. This prompted

South Dakota lawmakers to acquire hundreds of miles of former Milwaukee trackage to ensure continued freight service for scores of railroad-dependent customers. Independent shortlines and larger regional railroads also appeared along with public ownership and line retrenchments. By the early 1960s passenger trains had disappeared, becoming victims of automobile, bus, and air competition, leaving little but a diminished web of freight railroads in the state.

Whether early South Dakota settlers arrived by rail or wagon or other means, they quickly realized they would have to contend with the weather. South Dakota sits in the mid-latitudes, and as such finds itself in the battleground between cold, dry arctic air and warm, moist tropical air. Where differing types of air masses collide, weather happens. Climate "normals," or averages of weather variables over at least a 30-year period, are only part of the climate equation. "Extremes" are also important, especially in "continental" climates in places such as South Dakota, where there are massive swings in summer high and winter low temperatures. South Dakota has the second largest difference between its record cold and record high temperatures: -58°F on February 17, 1936 (at McIntosh) and 120°F in the same year on July 5 (at Gann Valley) and again on July 15, 2006 (near Fort Pierre), a difference of 178°F. The state is on the northern edge of Tornado Alley: in the central part of North America, the collision of differing air masses, along with the flatness of the topography, help create the setting for tornadoes. Most occur May through August. Since records began being kept by the National Weather Service in 1950, tornadoes in South Dakota have killed 19 people, injured 475, and caused well over $250 million in property damage (through 2021). Air masses can easily approach and sweep over the barrier-free Great Plains from all directions. If the air masses do not take turns, and either arid or humid air masses begin to dominate the weather pattern, the region can easily move into an arid drought cycle (the Dust Bowl of the 1930s) or a moisture-rich, humid flood-producing cycle like the state experienced in 2019, its wettest year on record. And during the winter, the state's location along the track that many winter storms take each year means that the state is susceptible to storms that may dump deep amounts of snow and pack cold temperatures and high winds that create life-threateningly-low wind chill temperatures.

The importance of weather and topography are readily apparent in John Henris's chapter, which broadly examines the environmental transformation of the West River country of western South Dakota during the last decades of the nineteenth century. Confined to the Great Sioux Reservation after 1876, Lakota and Cheyenne families were forced to reimagine their traditional relationships with the land and its resources. At the same time, white ranchers settled lands north and east of the Black Hills mining districts where they encountered new, and often unforgiving, environmental constraints that differed markedly from their prior experiences back east. Stretching for more than 200 miles from the western bank of the Missouri River to the eastern face of the Black Hills, the rolling mixed-grass prairie of the West River country emerged as a center of both agroecological experimentation and negotiation with nature for both Native Americans and American ranchers during the last quarter of the nineteenth century. American ranchers responded to the ecological margins of the West River country by appropriating the best agricultural lands adjacent to the Black Hills, grazing public lands, and engineering nature to maximize crop yields and livestock carrying capacity. They constructed ditches to appropriate water runoff from the Black Hills and introduced hardy cultivars to increase winter fodder for livestock and to produce fruits and vegetables for neighboring mining communities. Lakota and Cheyenne farmers adopted Euro-American agricultural practices to their own needs and combined them with traditional communal practices to forge a secure subsistence on the more marginal lands of the Great Sioux Reservation. By 1900 Lakota and Cheyenne ranchers had created a great grass reserve in the West River country to provide forage, security, and self-autonomy while American ranchers adjacent to the Black Hills managed a highly profitable, but ecologically unstable, ranching economy which also placed intense pressure on diminishing open range. After 1900, the Native American worldview of autonomy and security came into conflict with American values of market production as white ranchers lobbied to open reservation grass reserves to their own livestock herds.

The experience of West River ranching brought questions of conservation to the fore. In his chapter, Frank Van Nuys addresses the policy work of South Dakota's early conservationists and, in particular, the advocacy of the state's most prominent early leader in conservation. No other political leader in South Dakota's history exemplifies accomplishments in conservation like the two-term governor and three-term United States Senator Peter Norbeck. His practical approach to conservation policy-making addressed traditional concerns with protecting natural resources for sustainable economic development, but increasingly embraced a growing appreciation for the recreational and scenic assets to be found in South Dakota's outdoors. Assisted by a network of conservationist allies, Norbeck pushed for years to depoliticize and professionalize the administration of game and fish policies, improve protection of wildlife in Custer State Park and other refuges, and try to convince fellow South Dakotans to create additional state parks. Resistance to the conservationists' agenda was robust, however, and many of Norbeck's goals took years to achieve. Opponents balked at projected costs and questioned the necessity of the types of recreational amenities for which the conservationists advocated. One of the more intriguing motivations driving skepticism about adding state parks during the 1920s centered on the work ethic of some farmers, who perceived expanded opportunities to enjoy the outdoors as dangerous and economically disastrous invitations to idleness in the midst of a severe agricultural depression. Debates over conservation policy in the 1920s and 1930s also reflected many of the typical political and regional fault lines often seen in South Dakota politics: Democrats versus Republicans; conservatives versus progressives; East River versus West River; farmers versus sportsmen and recreationists. By the end of the "Age of Norbeck" in the late 1930s, however, the state's conservationists had largely succeeded in shifting toward more recreational and scenic amenities as a crucial element of their policies and created a stronger and less politicized system of conservation management.

Politics is also the focus of Jeffrey Johnson's chapter. Instead of addressing the slow and incremental and modest reforms proposed by Norbeck, however, Johnson explores radicals in South Dakota's past. While conservative, "traditional" norms and sensibilities surround the conceptions of the state's political reality, Johnson also finds evidence to the contrary. His chapter examines the modern period, specifically from the Gilded Age into the late twentieth century and centers not only on expressly political moments but also broader activism from women and Native Americans. From the agrarian radicalism of the late nineteenth century to more contemporary Indigenous movements, there is evidence of a pattern of (broadly conceived) "radical" movements in South Dakota. Throughout the modern period, Johnson contends, agrarian discontent remained endemic, from the Alliance and Populist challenges of the 1870s-1890s to Farmer-Labor activism. Johnson's chapter pays particular attention to the rise and prominence of socialist politics around the turn of the twentieth century and to how the Socialist Party of America and its affiliates provided a viable and regular third-party challenge to the norms of two-party politics. It also examines how the Red Scare in the middle of the twentieth century and in the context of the Cold War provided another flashpoint for both the expression of radicalism and generated a strong anti-communist reaction.

Some of the agrarian activists that Johnson examines were German immigrants, who constituted the largest ethnic group in South Dakota from 1890 to 1930. With these immigrants came the need for a German-language press. In her chapter, Samantha Litty describes the history of that press, which came into existence decades later than German-language presses across the Midwest and survived in some cases even beyond World War II. While German-language newspapers were widespread in the Midwest by the 1850s, the first German-language paper in South Dakota dates to 1874, following German-speaking settlement of the region. Over the course of its decades-long run, the German-language press became an integral pillar of German-speaking communities across the state. The newspaper business forced many name changes and mergers among smaller papers, but the longest-running German-language newspaper in South Dakota, the *Dakota Freie Presse*, ran from 1874 to 1954. Litty looks in depth at language use in three categories of German-language press, those which were *majority German*, those which published German and English *parallel editions*, and those which were *majority English*, but used some German in their publication. Previously held ideas for the downfall of the German-language press, such as the impact of the Trading with the Enemy Act of 1917, which required translations of foreign-language print, newspaper, or publication regarding the war, are discussed. A case study of the *Süd-Dakota Nachrichten* takes a closer look at the trajectory of the second-longest running German-language paper in South Dakota, tracking mergers, name changes, and addresses to the German readership. Despite beginning later than the English-language press in South Dakota and in other areas of the Midwest, the German-language press in South Dakota showed its viability as it evolved and adapted to the needs of its readership to remain in existence for over eighty years, surpassing expectations of only serving as a transitionary aid to new immigrants.

The German immigrants to South Dakota brought a particular culinary tradition to the state, and in her chapter Sara Egge uses such traditions to explore a new arena of South Dakota history. In particular, Egge examines how cookbooks produced by South Dakota's home cooks contested the efforts of domestic scientists, the national food industry, and the federal government to standardize the American diet. Their collaborative work both upheld and defied twentieth-century gender norms. Food was at the center of women's domestic lives, which emphasized their roles in their homes, but it was also a source of power. While economic upheaval, agricultural consolidations, population decline, and, for the Lakota, assimilationist federal policies created periods of disruption and fractured bonds in small towns and rural neighborhoods, women reforged relationships around tables both big and small. Controlling how people ate together, what they consumed, and what that food meant sustained people in these communities and countered narratives of decline. Egge's chapter draws on the massive community cookbooks collection in the Special Collections and Archives Department at South Dakota State University. Boasting over five hundred cookbooks to date, the collection reflects the background of those white settlers who came to call South Dakota home. This collection reveals that while the work of white domestic scientists from the Northeast and new household technologies profoundly influenced South Dakota's culinary traditions over the course of the twentieth century, home cooks also resisted a complete takeover of their kitchens. Nutritional ratios featured sweets, fats, and carbohydrates, all ingredients that domestic scientists sought to limit in the American diet. Home cooks also shifted to store-bought items as grocery chains increasingly introduced them after World War II, but many featured recipes were still entirely from-scratch. Sections labeled "foreign" or "heritage" also grew substantially after mid-century, a testament to the powerful hold ethnic cookery had on South Dakota's foodways. Perhaps most striking about these cookbooks is how they acted as commemorative devices. Most produced in the 1970s, 1980s, and 1990s marked an anniversary—the founding of a church, school, hospital, or retirement home—and many contained sections of local history. Writing their own histories was powerful, an act of collective storytelling that emphasized women's roles in their respective communities. Egge's chapter reveals that these cookbooks were sources of collected memory and lasting reminders to their communities of their central roles in them. Lakota recipes were largely absent from twentieth-century community cookbooks, and when they were featured, they were full of substitutions for traditional ingredients in Lakota dishes. By the late-twentieth century, however, Lakota women like Spuka Sni Win collected recipes that showcased indigenous foodways. These cookbooks celebrated the resourcefulness of Lakota cooks as an act of resistance against the food commodity programs of the federal government.

Another neglected area of historical research but one that was crucial to everyday life in South Dakota is the role of sports. In his chapter, Paul Higbee explains how South Dakota towns developed simultaneously with major American sports, including baseball, basketball, and football, and later the state played key roles in fine-tuning and promoting spectator sports that included ski jumping and rodeo. Regardless of the sport, South Dakotans have taken special pleasure in demonstrating that small towns can defeat bigger places, be it Sioux Falls or an out-of-state opponent. Originally local success in athletics communicated that a newly established town claimed young, fit, and energized citizens, indicating a bright future. Further, sports in schools made a statement that a town was committed to raising athletic and responsible residents. By the 1920s, it had become obvious that towns hosting school tournaments, professional sports, and Olympic trials were tapping into a reliable revenue source. Even the most casual sports fans over the years understood that South Dakota regularly sent men and women to the highest levels of national and international competition, including Olympic gold medal runner Billy Mills, World Series-winning manager Sparky Anderson, charter Ladies Professional Golf Association (LPGA) members Alice and Marlene Bauer, world saddle bronc champion Casey Tibbs, National Football League (NFL) kicker Adam Vinatieri, and longtime National Basketball Association (NBA) stars Eric Piatkowski and Mike Miller. Less understood was the impact South Dakotans made in leading and financing American professional sports, including American Football League (AFL) commissioner and visionary Joe Foss, NFL Players Association president Ordell Braase, Miami Dolphins founder Joe Robbie, and women's sports pioneer Becky Hammon, an early Women's National Basketball Association (WNBA) standout and the first woman hired as a fulltime NBA coach. Meanwhile, back in South Dakota, sports were the lens through which citizens most clearly saw certain issues that transcended games, including growth of girls' school activities through Title IX, school consolidation in districts where enrollments declined, questions about whether Catholic schools belonged in state tournaments, and the issue of transgender athletes. Games and weighty discussions about those matters played out in uniquely South Dakota sports settings: tiny but noisy high school gyms, the big Corn Palace and warm-in-November DakotaDome, and the open-air Canton ski jump and Black Hills Roundup rodeo arena.

Another arena of sport is hunting and fishing, a common and deeply-rooted activity in South Dakota, as Lance Nixon explains in his chapter. South Dakota is frequently ranked as having some of the best destinations for upland game bird hunting in the United States, and it leads all other states in the percentage of its population that buy hunting licenses. It was known since prehistoric times as an ideal location to hunt and exploit abundant game such as bison, with archaeological finds suggesting kill sites such as the ridge near Ree Heights were used to harvest large numbers of animals and process some of the meat for trade. Trade in hides continued in the white settlement era, when observers such as the painter George Catlin began to fear for the extinction of the bison. A look at records in South Dakota history suggests several trends have affected game populations over the past two centuries, sometimes happening concurrently: harvesting and overharvesting of a seemingly abundant resource; expansion and then reduction of game populations such as greater prairie chickens when grain farming first provided new feed sources and then depleted grassland habitat; depletion of game populations such as elk and antelope due to over-hunting, and efforts to re-introduce or protect such species from hunting, sometimes over decades; a tendency to blame Native Americans, in particular, for the depletion or extirpation of game species in some areas; outright extinction of a subspecies of sheep called Audubon's bighorn sheep, which inhabited the Black Hills and surrounding areas; introductions of desirable new species such as the ring-necked pheasant, or reintroductions of native species such as wild turkeys; and ongoing concerns about dwindling habitat for game species such as the ring-necked pheasant, which need the right mix of grassland, row crops and small grains in order to thrive. Fishing opportunities have increased due to the Missouri River dams and state stocking efforts that have expanded the locations in which fish can be taken. The state's recognition of hunting and fishing as a valuable part of its culture and the need to protect habitat and hunting and fishing opportunities for future generations will be an ongoing topic of public discussion in South Dakota.

The final two chapters discuss a prominent event in the state's recent past and how South Dakota has been viewed on the big screen. In his chapter, Carson Walker considers the long-term implications of the activism of AIM, or the American Indian Movement. AIM originated a half-century ago to protect Native Americans from police abuse and provide them with jobs, housing, and education in cities like Minneapolis, where its headquarters remains. Yet many of AIM's most notorious events happened on sparsely populated South Dakota tribal lands. While attracting the sympathies and money of many non-Indian groups, churches, and individuals, it also drew the ire of the Federal Bureau of Investigation as well as some non-Indians and other native people. The latter did not support the violence that often accompanied demonstrations intended to focus attention on broken treaties, the plight of Native Americans, and their mistreatment. Perhaps AIM's most famous act of defiance happened in 1973, with the 71-day takeover of the Pine Ridge Indian Reservation village of Wounded Knee, chosen for its historical significance as the site of the last major conflict between the federal government and Indian tribes. With the 2022 death of AIM co-founder Clyde Bellecourt, most of AIM's main players are gone. Other leaders include his brother, Vernon Bellecourt, as well as Dennis Banks, Russell Means, Leonard Crow Dog, and John Trudell. AIM's most famous heroine, Anna Mae Pictou-Aquash, was shot to death in 1975 on Pine Ridge. The slaying went unsolved until AIM members John Graham and Arlo Looking Cloud were convicted of the killing that investigators said was ordered by AIM leaders, which they denied. Testimony at Looking Cloud's 2004 trial in Rapid City included a witness who connected the murder to one other famous AIM character, Leonard Peltier. In 1975 FBI Special Agents Jack Coler and

Ron Williams and AIM member Joe Stuntz were fatally shot during a shootout near Oglala. Peltier was the only suspect convicted and remains in federal prison. Besides maintaining support for him, AIM's focus now largely includes urging sports teams to abandon Native American mascots and protesting projects such as the Dakota Access Pipeline. But it lacks the well-known, charismatic leaders that defined its early days when it landed on the national stage.

Some of the events surrounding AIM-led protests have resulted in cinematic productions set in South Dakota. In his chapter, Jon Schaff addresses the wider universe of films in which South Dakota features prominently. While one does not think of South Dakota as a hotbed of filmmaking, Schaff explains how several films have either been shot in South Dakota or tell stories based in South Dakota. The dramatic geography of South Dakota, particularly in the Badlands and Black Hills, provides opportunity for filmmakers who wish to feature a rugged outdoor ambiance. Additionally, aspects of South Dakota history contain dramatic elements that storytellers have returned to on numerous occasions. This chapter considers South Dakota on film in two respects. The lives of Native peoples in general have often prompted filmmakers to tell South Dakota tales. Films such as *Dances with Wolves* (shot in South Dakota), *Thunderheart*, the HBO film version of *Bury My Heart at Wounded Knee*, and the South Dakota films of Academy Award winning director Chloé Zhao all center on Native American themes. These films tend to focus on the attraction of "white" civilization, the hardships of Native life, and the tension felt by various characters torn between two worlds. Secondly, there are stories that take place in South Dakota but do not include Native American life as a central plot point. Three of those movies are considered in this chapter: *The Revenant*, *The One and Only, Genuine, Original Family Band*, and *Tater Tot and Patton*. *The Revenant* is a fictionalized account of explorer Hugh Glass, who in 1823 was mauled by a bear in what is now Northwest South Dakota, crawling almost two-hundred miles to seek aid. The 1968 Disney film *The One and Only, Genuine, Original Family Band* is a musical comedy about the settling of South Dakota in its territorial years and the territory's drive toward statehood. The 2017 film *Tater Tot and Patton* was written and directed by a South Dakota native, Andrew Kightlinger. These non-Native-focused films place themselves in South Dakota to address stories of people remote from civilization, putting the focus on characters and, at times, the fight against nature. The chapter concludes with an examination of the one television show set substantially in South Dakota, HBO's *Deadwood.* The chapter argues that the origins of Deadwood as a mining camp allows series creator David Milch to explore the need for violence and the pursuit of justice in the founding of a new city. *Deadwood* takes a Machiavellian approach to the attempt by miners, entrepreneurs, and politicians to make a city out of nothing. In so doing, *Deadwood* represents as compelling storytelling as television has ever seen.

All of these angles on and explorations of South Dakota history John Miller would have loved. These chapters are sent into the world in John's honor and are designed to advance the cause he championed, the chronicling of South Dakota history, with the hope that they generate more Johns and more work on this state's neglected story. Even with great losses such as the death of John, the work of finding South Dakota's history must go on.

Notes

1 Jonathan Ellis, "John E. Miller, SDSU historian, Laura Ingalls Wilder expert, dies," *Argus Leader*, May 3, 2020.

2 Jon Lauck, "SD historian Miller passes into history," *Brookings Register*, May 7, 2020. See also Jon Lauck, "Mr. South Dakota history dies; let's keep his legacy alive," *Pierre Capital Journal*, May 5, 2021.

3 John E. Miller, *First We Imagine: 22 Creative South Dakotans Speak on the Subject of Creativity* (2014).

4 See Harry F. Thompson, *"Bright, Clear Sky Over a Plain So Wide": The Center for Western Studies, 1964-2020* (Sioux Falls: Center for Western Studies, 2021).

5 Jon K. Lauck, *From Warm Center to Ragged Edge: The Erosion of Midwestern Literary and Historical Regionalism, 1920-1965* (Iowa City: University of Iowa Press, 2017), 2, 23.

6 Jon K. Lauck, ed., *The Interior Borderlands: Regional Identity in the Midwest and Great Plains* (Sioux Falls: Center for Western Studies, 2019); Jon K.

Lauck, ed., *Heartland River: A Cultural and Environmental History of the Big Sioux River Valley* (Sioux Falls: Center for Western Studies, 2022).

[7] Krystyna Poray Goddu, "The 'Pioneer Girl' Project: The Long Road to Bringing Laura Ingalls Wilder's 1930 Autobiography into Print," *Publisher's Weekly*, August 21, 2014.

[8] John E. Miller, "Is South Dakota Experiencing a Literary Renaissance?" *South Dakota History* 45:3 (Fall 2015), 228-57.

[9] "Jones Named New State Historian," *Pierre Capital Journal*, November 19, 2020; Jody Heemstra, "Legislation Providing $12 Million to Upgrade Cultural Heritage Center in Pierre Passed and Signed," Dakota Radio Group News, March 11, 2022.

[10] Jessa Crispin, "Portals of Discovery," *Baffler* 62 (March 2022).

1

In the Heart of the Continent: Lakota Power in South Dakota and the Greater West

Pekka Hämäläinen
University of Oxford

The Lakota Indians, arguably the world's best-known Indigenous nation, were peripatetic buffalo hunters in the late seventeenth century. They had traveled across the eastern part of North America with their Dakota relatives and had sojourned at the Gulf of Mexico, searching for spiritual and material fulfillment. By around 1700, they lived at the margins of a bustling new world of Native Americans and European colonists that had emerged in the Eastern Woodlands. The Lakotas had no guns and no metal weapons and they carried little political clout, all of which spelled danger: the odds of survival were slim for people who lacked access to Europeans and their new technologies of killing. Other Native nations saw the Lakotas and Dakotas as enemies and turned the entire eastern front of the Očhéthi Sakówiŋ, the Sioux Indian Confederacy of Seven Council Fires, into a war zone.

That crisis set off what may be the most improbable expansion in American history. The Lakotas left their ancient homelands in the East and reinvented themselves as horse people in the vast continental grasslands in the west. They launched an expansion that would eventually bring them into South Dakota. This was the genesis of what could be called Lakota America, an expansive and constantly shapeshifting Indigenous regime that controlled human fates in the North American interior for generations. What enabled them to achieve such centrality was the horse, which had brought a military, political, and cultural revolution among the Indians in the North American West.[1]

Lakotas called the horse *šúñka wakȟáŋ*, or "sacred dog," the religious moniker capturing the enormity of the change that had suddenly befallen their world. The dog had been their only domesticated animal for several generations, but now there existed what seemed to be a bigger and far more powerful dog. The Lakotas, the westernmost of the Sioux nations, were stirred by the sudden increase of mobility and military power. They had operated for decades in the shadow of more powerful and better-connected Native powers to the east—the Wyandots, Sauteurs, Assiniboines, Crees, Iroquois, Omahas, Odawas, Ojibwes, and many others—who traded with the continent's most prominent European merchants, the French in the Great Lakes. The horse was about to change all that, catapulting the Lakotas into unexpected prominence and power.[2]

In 1680 the Pueblo Indians had rebelled against their self-styled Spanish overlords and banished them and their horses from their world. That spawned one of the most significant turning points in the history of the North American West. The liberated Spanish horses spread across the West and, in 1708, the Lakotas secured their first horses from the Omahas. Searching for more, the Lakotas turned to the west where untapped opportunities beckoned. Lakota winter counts, *waníyetu iyáwapi*, pictographic calendars, capture the magnitude of the sudden burst of ambition. The change was so momentous that Lakotas seemed to think that history itself had begun anew: many winter counts start with the arrival of horses in the early eighteenth century. The Lakotas were about to reverse the horse frontier to the west, changing the history of the continent irrevocably.[3]

From the Mississippi River Valley, eight smaller river valleys—the Des Moines, Little Sioux, Floyd, Big Sioux, Minnesota, James, Red River of the North, and Missouri—stretched westward and northward and virtually invited the Lakotas and their Cheyenne and Arapaho allies in, allowing them to expand their domain one valley at a time. Sicangus and Oglalas, the leading Lakota groups, fought the resident farmer-hunters—the Otoes, Poncas, and Iowas—whose earth-lodge towns dominated the Big Sioux valley, forcing them to abandon the region and retreat to the Missouri Valley, which became a refugee zone for multiple Native nations. The Lakotas and their allies had extended their dominance in what would become the easternmost part of South Dakota.[4]

In the early and mid-eighteenth century, the Lakotas secured guns from competing French and English traders: the French canoed into Native settlements in the deep interior, while the Hudson's Bay Company traders pushed west through the Ohio Country. The fur trade became big business, fueling fierce struggles over guns and horses. Besides sacred dogs, the West abounded with other magnificent things, most notably the bison herds which grew bigger and bigger to the west. The lands west of the Minnesota valley drew the Lakotas in, triggering the first of their self-reinventions: they became fully-fledged horse people who relied on their mounts for travel, transportation, hunting, trade, and warfare.[5]

The Lakotas pushed deeper into the West, seeking more horses and forage that sustained their growing horse herds. It was a risky undertaking. The odds were stacked against this nation that was about to plunge into the unknown, while detaching itself from the larger Sioux confederacy. During the 1780s, the Lakotas were also pulling *away* from the major continental trade corridors, entering a strange new world in the western plains that were already occupied. The Lakotas clashed with several prairie peoples who saw them as strangers and invaders. The rivalries became pitiless, lasting for generations. They were North America's longest wars. Although powerful horse people, the Lakotas found themselves in a debilitating political and commercial limbo. Surrounded by enemies and cut off from the colonial trade circuits that channeled guns and metal weapons into the interior, the Lakotas were exposed.[6]

But the Lakotas possessed two distinctive advantages in the escalating wars over the western grasslands. One was their palpable capacity to change. The Lakotas were guided by Iktómi, an ambiguous shapeshifting spider-trickster culture hero who embodied what may be the defining attribute of the Lakota people: their stunning ability to adapt and change and assume a new mindset. The Lakotas adjusted to the new conditions, whether political, environmental, or spiritual, and they forged a tight alliance with the Cheyennes and Arapahos and pushed west. The Lakotas' gamble paid off handsomely when their oyátes—bands or people—reached what they called the "muddy water," the mighty Missouri, and entered the largest and the lushest of the prairie river valleys in the mid-eighteenth century. Dozens of Native villages, squeezed there by Lakota pressure, dotted the valley's long middle section like unevenly strung pearls. It was the greatest concentration of humans and material wealth in the heart of the continent. As many as fifty thousand people may have lived in grand riverside villages that abounded with corn, squash, horses, and human energy. The Missouri exerted an irresistible pull on the Lakotas who desperately needed horses and carbohydrates for their rapidly growing population.[7]

But the Missouri villagers—the Arikaras, Mandans, and Hidatsas—were troubled by the Lakota newcomers who had large needs but little to offer. For them, the Missouri was home and sacred, a place where they had lived for countless generations. They were determined to keep the Lakotas out. Repulsed, the Lakotas relied on their increasingly palpable military might, but they absorbed more damage than they inflicted. The middle Missouri Valley Indians fought with state-of-the-art guns secured from British traders in Canada, killing Lakotas from the safety of their palisaded villages. The mid-seventeenth century emerges as a dark period in their winter counts: mounted, gun-wielding enemies storming their camps; women joining men in fighting enemies; soldiers defecating next to their lodges, bows in their hands, too afraid to venture out. "The Great mystery was crazy," states an Oglala winter count for 1770-71.[8]

But the Lakotas had one great advantage in the struggle over the Missouri: although they had pushed further west, they remained members of the Očhéthi Sakówiŋ, around which the continental commercial and diplomatic circles had started to converge. Alarmed by the virulent conflict called Pontiac's War in the Great Lakes region, British officials adopted the old French system of diplomacy, gifts, and trade. Guns started flowing into the West in unprecedented quantities, reaching the Dakota villages in the Mississippi Valley. Dakotas also welcomed traders and their guns from the south where St. Louis had emerged as the focal point of the interior trade. Now kinship as a political force became essential. What belonged to Dakotas belonged to Lakotas. Goods did not move automatically from east to west, but familial ideals of sharing obliged the Sioux people to take care of each other's needs.[9]

North America's two great technological frontiers had converged on the Lakotas, making them the first Native nation to fight on horseback with substantial firepower. In the early 1770s, the Oglalas and their Yanktonai kin attacked a Mandan village in the Upper Missouri, some two hundred miles north of the regular Oglala camping grounds. "They burnt the Mandans out" notes the pithy Oglala winter account. The sacking of that Mandan village was a decisive event that marked the beginning of a long Lakota ascendancy along the Missouri. Lakota horse soldiers raided almost all upper Missouri villages, which began falling with shocking rapidity. Already depleted by war and raids, the villagers suffered massive losses in 1781, when a smallpox epidemic raged up and down the Missouri Valley. The epidemic shocked Lakotas, but it nearly destroyed the villagers whose confined settlements become death-traps: the Arikaras may have lost more than 75 percent of their people and they abandoned all but seven of their thirty-two villages. Capitalizing on the catastrophe, the Lakotas attacked a Mandan village of fifty-eight lodges, killing everyone in it. The carnage disheartened the villagers and they fled far to the north. A two-hundred-mile expanse of the Missouri now lay vacant in front of the Lakotas. They pushed in. It was the single most important expansion in the history of the Očhéthi Šakówiŋ, the moment when the long struggle to secure horses, guns, and military power translated into unqualified and reassuring success. Before long, several Lakota villages stretched out along the Missouri and its western feeders. By the early 1800s the Lakotas had shifted shape for the second time, making the Missouri Valley the center of their world and reinventing themselves as river people.[10]

The Lakotas had carved out a vast riverine domain in a long and often brutal war, but they were not some blind conquering machine bent on subjugation. They shifted from violence and war to diplomacy and coexistence fluidly and swiftly. Now they set out to harness the Missouri's two great resources: the expanding upriver trade from St. Louis and the weakened but still wealthy Native villages. In the 1790s, the lower Missouri Valley had become saturated with Franco-Spanish traders who began to look upriver for untapped markets and fur domains. These commercial impulses converged with the geopolitical ambitions of Spanish officials in Louisiana who agonized over imperial challenges from the north: British traders had entrenched themselves among the Mandans, deflecting the upper Missouri fur trade towards Canada from its southbound flow. Desperate to secure the lucrative trade, Spanish officials began granting trade licenses to the far reaches of the Missouri. There, they calculated, the British could be contained, and there, they imagined, would be a water route to the Pacific Coast, the key to an everlasting Spanish empire in the heart of North America.[11]

It was not to be. The Franco-Spanish traders were about to crash into a Lakota barrier they did not know existed. In 1793 an enterprising trader Jacques d'Eglise embarked upriver, aiming for Mandan villages, only to be stopped three hundred miles shy of his destination by Lakotas who promptly confiscated most of his goods. D'Eglise's interception was more than thievery; it was policy. St. Louis traders were determined to push far upriver to maximize their client base and drive out their British rivals, whereas Lakotas were determined to prevent the traders from moving past their Missouri Valley settlements. They wanted to cut out their Native rivals and reserve the bulk of the critical goods—guns, powder, and lead—for themselves. It was a scene that would be repeated over and over again along the Missouri where Lakotas now ruled supreme, policing the river they now considered theirs. By 1800 Lakota dominance in the upper Missouri had become an accepted fact. The diminished Mandan villages still loomed large in Spanish plans, but what preoccupied the Spanish merchants most was how to move upriver without alienating the Lakotas. The Spaniards resigned to pay tolls for access. The Lakotas had turned one of North America's great commercial arteries into a tribute-yielding machine: they could reap massive profits by simply allowing people and goods to pass by.[12]

While exploiting the colonial river traffic, the Lakotas reduced the remaining Missouri villagers to virtual vassals. They blended raiding and extortion with diplomacy and trade into a flexible economy of violence that rendered the villagers weak, needy, and compliant. A French observer thought that the Lakotas had reduced the Arikaras to "a certain kind of serf who cultivates for them and who, as they say takes, for them, the place of women." The gendered metaphor announced Lakota power in the Upper Missouri Valley: the Arikaras would raise corn, squash, and other vegetables for the Lakotas and balance their meat and protein-heavy diet. To further boost their bargaining power, the Lakotas used naked force to create artificial demand for their exports. More mobile than the Arikaras, they isolated them from the bison and forced them to buy meat from them. As a result, huge amounts of precious corn poured into Lakota villages, allowing the Lakotas to enjoy one of the best diets on the continent. Three thousand Arikaras had become Lakotas' wards, their economies and their very lives remolded to accommodate the new masters of the Missouri whose authority now extended dozens of miles in the Upper Missouri.[13]

In the spring of 1803, the United States bought Louisiana from France, and in the fall of 1804, the Lewis and Clark Expedition crashed all but blindly into the expanding Lakota domain. It was not because of lack of preparation; it was rather a failure to see, learn, and adapt. Had the Americans approached Lakotas as traders and generous allies, things might have turned out differently. Instead, they came to the Lakotas as conquerors, determined to reduce them to wards of the President of the United States, a man Lakotas had never heard of. Making matters worse, the explorers came with vessels full of goods, but refused to share their wealth with Lakotas. The Lakotas not only sent these arrogant nothings on their way; they shadowed them upriver, asserting themselves in their wake and undoing their efforts to pull the Arikaras into their orbit. The Lakotas followed the Corps of Discovery all the way to their winter camp among the Mandans. Lewis and Clark had traversed the Missouri Valley in the aftermath of Lakota expansion and they found it difficult to accept. Clark's hurt seeps through in his compiled observations on the Missouri Indians. He reported that the Lakotas were "the vilest miscreants of the savage race and must ever remain the pirates of the Missouri." Rather than opportunistic pirates, however, the Lakotas were the protectors of a newly-established Indigenous hegemony. Lewis and Clark had been cut down to size by what could be called the Lakota Meridian, a long, integrated corridor of power in the heart of the continent. The explorers had muddled through the Lakota Meridian as also-rans.[14]

The Lakotas' treatment of the Corps of Discovery established a pattern. For several decades afterward, Lakota soldiers kept policing the Missouri Valley, sometimes plundering American boats that refused to share their goods and sometimes joining U.S. soldiers in punishing their errant subordinates. Placating the "Pirates of the Missouri" became the new normal, a necessary evil that had to be factored in as a built-in cost so that America's interior trade could reach its full potential. By the 1830s, the Lakota Meridian stretched from the Missouri's northern turn to the western one, and the Americans were firmly in the Lakota orbit. They built numerous trading posts for them and sold guns to them, delivered by steamboats. The Americans also vaccinated them against smallpox during the catastrophic smallpox outbreak in 1831-32, while denying vaccines to the Lakotas' Native rivals. The Americans openly admired the Lakotas' military prowess and even praised their looks and clothing.[15]

The Lakotas' long Missouri epoch was the most formative period in their history. It was there that they assumed their sacred form as the seven oyátes, splitting up and linking up along the Missouri.

Articulating a distinctive intermesh of the sublime and the practical is the Lakota way of being, Slow Buffalo, a prominent Lakota itȟaŋčhaŋ—leader—announced, "We are seven bands and from now on we will scatter over the world, so we will appoint one chief for each band . . . . The Mysterious One—Wakȟáŋ Tȟáŋka—has given us this place and now it is up to us to expand ourselves: we will name every person and everything." A blend of humility and confidence, Slow Buffalo's message captured how the Lakotas were about to embark on a new phase in their history.[16]

In the 1830s and 1840s, guided by Slow Buffalo's vision, the Lakotas made their second concerted push into the West, this time from the Missouri Valley, their home for more than half a century. It was a phase that centered to a remarkable degree on a single point in the West: Pahá Sápa—the Black Hills, "the heart of everything that is," the spiritual birthplace of the Lakota people. The Lakotas had frequented Pahá Sápa from their Missouri homelands since the late eighteenth century, drawn by its divine primacy, its moist, high-altitude microclimate and its massive herds of bison and wild horses. Now Lakotas responded to Pahá Sápa's ancient draw. Once again basic geography seemed to favor them. From the Missouri's west bank eight great tributaries—White, Bad, Cheyenne, Moreau, Grand, Cannonball, Heart, and Knife, all flushed with protective riparian forests that provided shelter against the elements as well as cottonwood bark, a vital winter forage for horses—pointed westward like fingers towards the life-affirming mountain range. Lakota control of Pahá Sápa became an end in itself.[17]

But the Lakotas were not secure yet. The western plains were occupied. People and their animals could not survive in the grasslands without secure access to river valleys. All farming, all trapping, and much of the hunting and gathering took place on their wooded banks and nearly all those riparian zones were already taken. This meant, once again, war, now against other horse nations: the Crows, Kiowas, Shoshones, Flatheads, Crees, and Assiniboines. Entrenched in the Black Hills, the Lakotas were surrounded by numerous enemies that matched them in equestrian warfare. They met the challenge in

A point of entrance into the spirit world for the Lakota, Mathǒ Pahá, or Bear Butte, rises 1,200 feet in a cone-like projection from the plains floor northeast of the Black Hills. *The Center for Western Studies.*

their customary way: they shifted shape. Building on their Missouri Valley power politics, they transformed into an imperial power that could coordinate decision-making on a national level and implement large-scale mobilizations. They created more centralized political institutions, moving power from local bands to tribal councils and to a select group of "praiseworthy men" who executed council decisions. On a national level, the Sun Dance became an annual event, reaffirming Lakotas' sense of themselves as single kindred. Such unifying reforms made possible an ambitious, coordinated, and yet flexible foreign policy. The Lakotas raided their nomadic rivals far to the north, west, and south, capturing horses and humans, and prevented their enemies from entering their hunting ranges. Closer by, their mobile war parties kept Pawnee, Otoe, Ponca, and Omaha farmers in what is now Nebraska under siege, raiding them for horses, corn, and captives. Within easy reach there were several American trading posts that provided guns, powder, lead, cloth, and other necessities, keeping the Lakota nation impregnable.

By the 1840s, at long last, the Lakotas controlled the western plains between the Missouri Valley and the Rocky Mountains, having turned the region into a massive extractive hinterland. The Lakotas—especially the Oglalas and the Sicangus, the most numerous of the Lakota oyátes—dominated the western grasslands and kept rivals out. Pahá Sápa became the western anchor of the Lakota domain, imbedding the Lakota nation into South Dakota's high plains and into present-day Wyoming. Wealthy, safe, and confident, the Lakotas expanded their commercial network. Lakota women processed tens of thousands of buffalo robes a year for American markets securing munitions, clothing, and luxuries for their communities, thus protecting the military might and the prestige of the Lakota nation. All seven Lakota oyátes lived by this ethos and kept people and power movable and channeled both wherever they were needed. This made them appear far more formidable than they actually were, allowing them to control an oversized portion of the continent with only thirteen thousand people. But thirteen thousand was enough to maintain the Lakota hegemony over a large domain between the Missouri River and the Black Hills. By comparison, their Dakota allies may have numbered thirty-eight thousand in the mid-seventeenth century, but their historical impact in the interior would remain more modest.[19]

Lakota ascendancy rested not on territorial control, but on a horse-powered capacity to connect and exploit key strategic nodes: river valleys, prime hunting grounds, corn-yielding Native villages, American trading posts, and Pahá Sápa. The Lakotas controlled resources without controlling people. Ranging widely but ruling lightly, they moved constantly through space seeking markets, tribute, plunder, pastures, and game: theirs was a malleable and constantly transmuting regime, a kinetic empire built on mobility and fluid power politics, rather than institutionalized control. It could be understood as an action-based regime, whose power rested on systematic repetition of specific foreign political acts: short and long-range raids, tribute-extraction, and diplomatic missions, which gave it a fickle on-and-off-again character. It could be all over the map one instant and nowhere to be seen the next. The Americans never saw it. By the mid-nineteenth century, the Americans and the Lakotas—two expanding powers—had managed to coexist peacefully for generations in the North American West, a region that would be later known as northwestern South Dakota.[20]

When California suddenly became the richest place on earth in 1848, in the aftermath of John Sutter's strike, the relationship between the Lakotas and U.S. officials became increasingly tense. The U.S. government invited Lakotas and other plains nations to talks at Fort Laramie to secure access to California gold. The Lakota itȟáŋčhaŋs arrived well prepared. Fully aware of their pivotal role as the masters of the western plains, they negotiated hard in exchange for rights-of-way along the Platte Valley. U.S. officials offered them a reservation north of the Platte, but the Lakotas demanded the central plains all the way south to the Arkansas Valley, much of it still a Pawnee domain. "We are a large band," Sicangu itȟáŋčhaŋ Clear Blue Earth, announced. "We claim half of all the country," he continued, "but, we don't care for that, because we can hunt everywhere." It was a concise description of the Lakota nation's way of using and claiming land: mobility, not treaties with colonial powers, defined the Lakota territory. Any agreed borders would have to be fluid.[21]

The Lakotas demanded the central plains by right of conquest. "These lands once belonged to the Kiowas and the Crows," Oglala itȟáŋčhaŋ Black Hawk explained, "but we whipped these nations out of them . . . in this we did," he explained, "what the white men do when they want the lands of the Indians." The put down worked. The U.S. officers had no response. Desperate to appease the most powerful Native nation in North America, they yielded. The 1851 Horse Creek Treaty obligated the U.S. government to provide the Lakotas with ten thousand dollars for fifty years, the length of the commitment revealing something about the American sense of weakness in the face of the increasingly confident Lakota nation. U.S. officials recognized Lakota title to nearly one hundred thousand square miles north of the North Platte, and in the west their domain extended all the way to the Powder River. Lakota leaders insisted that their domain would be defined by the needs of the hunt and by action on the ground, not some lines on a map. They made it clear that whenever necessary their expansion would continue. Terrified of losing access to the distant gold, U.S. officials simply caved. The Lakotas had affirmed their hegemony in the Great Plains and their right to expand their domain if necessary. Secure of their position—their alliance with the Cheyennes and Arapahos was still strong—the Lakotas allowed overland traffic along Oregon Trail to continue: the settlers, after all, were moving far away from the Lakota core area. The Lakotas were more concerned about the Crows, a formidable horse nation, and forged a peace with them. Indigenous affairs were still far more important to them than the relations with the United States.[22]

The Horse Creek Treaty could have offered a feasible framework for continuing coexistence in the western plains had not the ambitious and reckless Lieutenant John Grattan plunged the United States into a war with the Lakotas over a dead cow: in the summer of 1854, near Fort Laramie and the Oregon Trail, a Sicangu man killed a cow that belonged to a Mormon overlander. The U.S soldiers moved to punish the Sicangus, but the Lakotas killed Grattan and his twenty-nine men in a swift battle. The U.S. government felt compelled to punish the Lakotas. In came the experienced General William Harney who delivered what many policymakers wanted: revenge and a lesson. Harney promised to "whip" the Lakotas and launched a running fight that ended in a massacre that left at least eighty-six Lakotas—women and men—dead. After that, Lakotas kept the Americans at arm's length. Moderate leaders kept collecting treaty annuities at government agencies, concealing the fact that the vast majority of Lakotas were now what the Americans called militants.[23]

Bison herds were the foundation of the Lakota power and sovereignty and they were now their primary concern. The herds had started to fail under swelling overland traffic and droughts. Tightening their old alliance with the Cheyennes and Arapahos, the Lakotas set out to control the remaining viable hunting grounds that centered in the Powder River Country in the western high plains. The result was a decades-long war with the Crows, Shoshones, Flatheads, Utes,

Blackfeet, Assiniboines, Pawnees, and others. This buffalo imperialism may have stemmed from a sense of vulnerability, but it was transforming the Lakotas into a territorial giant. Their enormous territory—their empire—was an archipelago of rivers, highlands, and plains, and they needed every part of it intact, for each offered a specific source of food, refuge, and sacred power. Residing in faraway agencies, U.S. officials did not understand this, nor did they know how completely the Lakotas had marginalized other Native nations. The coexistence with the Lakotas had been a necessary compromise for the U.S. government, which was reluctant to wage war against the superbly mobile people who seemed to be all over the map. The costs were simply too steep.[24]

But then the American Civil War erupted, changing the geopolitical dynamics in the interior. The 1862 U.S.-Dakota War in Minnesota triggered a sprawling conflict with the Union Army whose generals now labeled all Sioux nations as enemies. Dakota soldiers killed between six and seven hundred white settlers, and thirty to forty thousand settlers fled to the east. For the Dakotas the war became a massacre that left five hundred of their people dead, many of them women and children, in the aftermath of the conflict. But still the Americans demanded retribution. As a result, thirty-eight Dakota soldiers were executed in the largest mass execution in North America. When the Civil War ended, the U.S. government quickly determined that there had to be two reconstructions: one to reform the Confederate South and the other to pacify the Indigenous West. From the U.S. perspective, the time of sovereign Native nations was over. More pointedly, the Lakota hegemony in the West should be demolished. The United States had emerged from the Civil War as an empire, and its officials now meant to govern, not negotiate, with Indians.[25]

That was the context for the Powder River War in 1865 and the so-called Fetterman Massacre in late 1866, the United States' worst defeat during its protracted Indian Wars. Lakota leaders had repeatedly warned the Americans that they would not allow any military forts in their lands, and when the army ignored the mandate and started building forts in the Powder River Country, the Lakota Empire snapped into action. Red Cloud, the charismatic Oglala war leader and *blotáhuŋka átaya*, the first among the equals, announced that killing Americans was now as valuable as killing Native enemies. Lakota soldiers eliminated the invading army swiftly and clinically, with Crazy Horse, a superior strategist, executing the critical military maneuvre and luring a group of U.S. soldiers into an ambush. Red Cloud held off signing a peace treaty until the U.S. Army dismantled its last fort in the Powder River Country, the sanctuary of the Lakota nation.[26]

Portrait of Oglala Lakota leader Red Cloud, by Jules Tavernier, c. 1847, for *Harper's Magazine*. Pastel and charcoal on paper. *The Center for Western Studies*.

The United States had lost a war, and the 1868 Treaty of Fort Laramie reflected that. In addition to the Great Sioux Reservation itself, Article 11 recognized Lakota hunting rights all the way south to the Republican Valley. Article 16 gave them a massive unceded territory that reached the Bighorn Mountain range, and it did not specify its northern limit, effectively leaving the door open for Lakotas to expand their reach all the way into Canada, which they promptly did. This newest version of the Lakota Empire was a colossal creation covering nearly four hundred thousand square miles. The empire received traders—both Canadian and American—from all directions, and it commanded a vast raiding domain that yielded masses of horses and captives. The empire also blocked railway construction and, by extension, the United States' westward expansion in its tracks. The U.S. Army Corps of Engineers, established in 1802, had mapped much of the continent, but mapping Indigenous power systems was simply beyond their grasp for a single reason: they still saw Indians as primitive people, incapable of large-scale strategizing and geopolitical maneuvring. The U.S. Army misread the situation with devastating consequences.[27]

Since the Treaty of Fort Laramie, many Lakotas had settled in government agencies. That did not mean that they had accepted the United States' authority over them. The Lakotas continued to pursue their mobile lifestyle, moving in and out from the agencies as they saw fit, trading with independent American merchants near the agencies and staging regular bison hunts in the open plains. U.S. agents thought that the Lakotas had split into militant "hostiles" and non-militant "friendlies" and to some degree that was the case. But the friendly-hostile dichotomy was a strategy that allowed the Lakotas to show two kinds of political stances—one accommodating and the other unyielding and defiant. The Lakota nation became all but illegible to Americans. Yet, at the same time, the U.S. Army was spending $144,000 a day to fight and subjugate Lakotas, Comanches, and countless other Native nations. Three Lakota oyátes, Sans Arcs, Two Kettles, and Minneconjous, thought that the U.S. president was "a white fool and a dog, without eyes or brains." To a remarkable degree, the Lakotas retained their sovereignty and independence. That had momentous repercussions: protected by the Lakotas, the North American West remained a resolutely Indigenous space. The core of that Indigenous domain was Pahá Sápa, which was becoming even more central for the Lakotas and their Cheyenne and Arapaho allies.[28]

That was unacceptable to Washington, D.C., the U.S. Army, and the westward pushing settlers. The U.S. government had to take the initiative. With railroad tracks inching westward, it seemed inevitable that Pahá Sápa would be the very center of the conflict between the Lakotas and the United States. In the spring of 1873, General Sheridan announced that the Northern Pacific was "a national enterprise and we are forced to protect the men during its survey and construction, through, probably, the most warlike nation of Indians on this continent, who will fight every foot of the line." The Lakotas were about to prove him right. They were already shifting from their first western domain between the Missouri Valley and the eastern Rocky Mountains into the greater West where the outcome of the continent's Indian wars would be determined.[29]

In 1874 Lieutenant Colonel George Armstrong Custer led the Black Hills Expedition into Pahá Sápa, aiming to build a new military fort to protect railway construction. The expedition found traces of gold, which triggered a rush. Pahá Sápa was soon teeming with illegal prospectors. One empire had invaded the vital center of the other, forcing a gross imbalance. The Lakotas and Americans had coexisted in the Northern Plains for decades, but from now on both found coexistence overwhelmingly difficult. Thousands of Lakotas already lived at U.S.-sponsored government agencies, pushed there by shrinking bison herds and drawn by government annuities. U.S. agents believed that they had managed to separate the hostiles from the friendlies, thereby shattering the solidarity of the Lakota people. It turned out to be wishful thinking. Lakota leaders sent runners to call in soldiers from all agencies, and the outwardly divided Lakota nation snapped into collective action. Custer and the Seventh Cavalry pushed into Pahá Sápa, forcing a war.[30]

The Hunkpapa oyáte sponsored a Sun Dance in the Rosebud Creek, and Sitting Bull ritually gave flesh to Wakȟáŋ Tȟáŋka, cutting his arm fifty times. He predicted a galvanizing victory. At the same time, the Lakotas and their Cheyenne and Arapaho allies moved up the Little Bighorn. As battles go, the Little Bighorn was face-to-face, fluid, fragmented, uncontrollable, and largely improvised, because the Lakotas and their allies willed it so. They were simply better at it, and knew it. Custer and his men reacted to Indian maneuvres rather than executing their own. It was Crazy Horse—not Custer—who executed a singular tactical maneuver, riding nearly a mile downstream with a band of horse soldiers, outflanking the enemy and reducing them to sitting ducks. The United States had suffered its worst defeat in the late nineteenth-century Indian Wars on the cusp of its centennial. A ferocious, flamboyant Indian killer had met his fate at the hands of Indians who eliminated him routinely. The Lakotas and their allies had won the war, but their victory would not be long-lasting. By 1876 most Indian wars were over and the U.S Army could concentrate on subjugating the Lakotas and confining them to reservations.[31]

Today, there are nine federally recognized Sioux reservations in South Dakota, which reflects the Lakotas and Dakotas' long and repeatedly successful wars and resistance against colonial powers, settlers, soldiers, oil companies, and government agencies over three centuries. The reservations face enormous economic, political, and social challenges, and yet they preserve Indigenous presence, sovereignty, self-determination, and territory. The Lakota fight for rights continues in courts, in media, and in activism. The controversy and the resistance over the Dakota Pipeline and the threat it posed to the Standing Rock Reservation reinforced their reputation as the globally essential Native nation.[32]

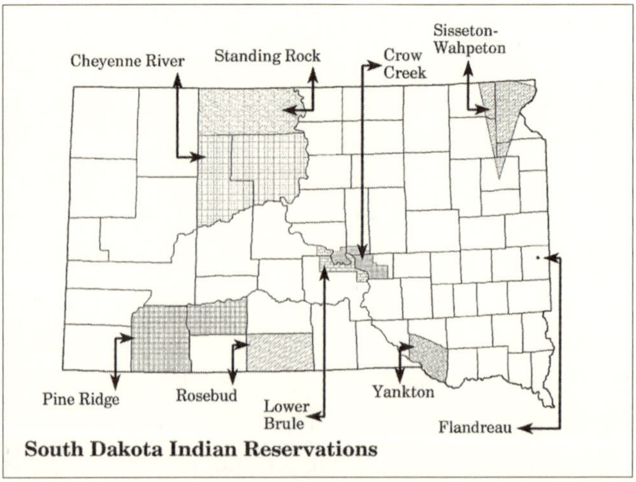

There are nine federally recognized Native American reservations in South Dakota, constituting approximately 4.7 million acres, or six percent of the land. *The Center for Western Studies.*

Notes

1 Vine Deloria, Jr., "Spirits and the South Dakota Land, in *A New South Dakota History*, 2d ed, ed. Harry F. Thompson (Sioux Falls: Center for Western Studies, 2009), 1-6; Richard White, *The Middle Ground: Indians, Empires, and Republics in the Great Lakes Region, 1650-1815* (New York: Cambridge University Press, 1991), 5-185; Nicolas Perrot, in *The Indian Tribes of the Upper Mississippi Valley and the Region of the Great Lakes*, ed. Emma H. Blair (Cleveland: Arthur H. Clark, 1911-12), vol. 1: 170; Pekka Hämäläinen, *Lakota America: A New History of Indigenous Power* (New Haven: Yale University Press, 2019), 22-28.

2 Hämäläinen, *Lakota America*, 28-35. For the Great Lakes, see White, *Middle Ground*; Michael Witgen, *The Infinity of Nations: How the Native New World Shaped Early North America* (Philadelphia: University of Pennsylvania Press 2012); Heidi Bohaker, "Nindoodemag: The Significance of Algonquian Kinship Networks in the Eastern Great Lakes Region,1600-1701," *William and Mary Quarterly* 63 (Jan. 2006), 23-52.

3 Hämäläinen, *Lakota America*, 55; Candance S. Greene and Russell Thornton, *The Year the Stars Fell: Lakota Winter Counts in the Smithsonian Institution* (University of Nebraska Press, 2007), 72 ("camped"). For the Great Lakes, see White; Witgen; Bohaker, 23-52.

4 Hämäläinen, *Lakota America, 56-59.*

5 For a comprehensive study of the bison ecology, see Andrew C. Isenberg, *The Destruction of the Bison: An Environmental History* (New York: Cambridge University Press, 2000).

6 For the prairie people, see David Wishart, *Unspeakable Sadness: The Dispossession of the Nebraska Indians* (Lincoln: University of Nebraska Press, 1994).

7 For Iktómi, see Martha Warren Beckwith, "Mythology of the Oglala Dakota," *Journal of American Folklore* 43 (Oct.-Dec.,1930), 339-442; James R. Walker, *Lakota Belief and Ritual*, ed. Raymond J. DeMallie and Elaine A. Jahner (Lincoln: University of Nebraska Press, 1980), 51, 53, 72, 101, 106-7, 112, 128-29; J. R. Walker, "The Sun Dance and Other Ceremonies of the Oglala Division of the Teton Dakota," *Anthropological Papers of the American Museum of Natural History* 16, Part 2 (New York: American Museum of Natural History, 1917), 90; Zitkala-Za, Old Indian Legends (1901; rprt. Lincoln: University of Nebraska Press, 1985), vi, 2-3.

8 Donald J. Lehmer, "Plains Village Tradition: Postcontact," *Handbook of North American Indians*, 13, Part 1: 247-48; Greene and Thornton, *Year the Stars Fell*, 94 ("The Great Mystery").

9 Hämäläinen, *Lakota America*, 92.

10 Greene and Thornton, 95 ("They burnt"); Hämäläinen, *Lakota America*, 97-100.

[11] For the explosively expanding fur trade, see Jay Gitlin, *Bourgeois Frontier: French Towns, French Traders, and American Expansion* (New Haven: Yale University Press, 2010), esp. 13-22; "Extract from the Journals of the Voyage of J-Bte Trudeau, in *A Fur Trader on the Upper Missouri: The Journal of and Description of Jean Babtiste Truteau, 1794-1796*, ed. Raymond J. DeMallie, Douglas Parks, and Robert Vézina; trans. Mildred Mott Wedel (Lincoln: University of Nebraska Press, 2017), esp. 177-79, 205.

[12] Hämäläinen, *Lakota America*, 103-17.

[13] Annie Heloise Able, ed., *Tabeau's Narrative of Loisel's Expedition to the Upper Missouri* (Norman: University of Oklahoma Press 1939), 130 ("a certain"); Hämäläinen, *Lakota America* 121-24.

[14] *Journals of the Lewis and Clark Expedition*, ed. Gary E. Moulton (Lincoln: University of Nebraska Press, 1983-2001), 3: 115-23, 418 ("the vilest," 418); Hämäläinen, *Lakota America*, 160-63.

[15] *"Ben Kindle's Winter Count," Becwith, 356-57; Able, 130-50;* Hämäläinen, *Lakota America*, 118-38.

[16] Hämäläinen, *Lakota America*, 125.

[17] Hämäläinen, *Lakota America*, 142-43, 66-69.

[18] Hämäläinen, *Lakota America*, 201-7.

[19] For Dakota numbers, see Gary Clayton Anderson, *Kinsmen of Another Kind: Dakota-White Relations in the Upper Mississippi Valley, 1650-1862* (1984; rpt. Lincoln: University of Nebraska Press, 1997), 16-19. For Lakota numbers, see Kinglsey M. Bray, "Teton Sioux: Population History, 1655-1881," *Nebraska History* 75 (1994), esp. 176.

[20] Hämäläinen, *Lakota America*, 234-47.

[21] *Missouri Republican*, Nov. 9, 1851 ("We are").

[22] *Missouri Republican*, Nov. 9, ("These lands"); "Treaty with the Sioux—Sisseton and Wahpeton Bands, 1851," "Treaty with the Sioux—Mdewakanton and Wahpakoota Bands, 1851," and "Treaty of Fort Laramie with the Sioux," Etc.,1851; Charles J. Kappler (Washington D.C., 1904), vol. 2: 588-96; Hämäläinen, *Lakota America*, 220-22.

[23] Paul N. Beck, *First Sioux War: The Grattan Fight and Blue Water Creek, 1854-1856* (Lanham, MD, University Press of America, 2004), 80 ("whip").

[24] Hämäläinen, *Lakota America*, 274-75.

[25] For the U.S.-Dakota War, see Anderson, *Kinsmen of Another Kind*; Gary Clayton Anderson, *Massacre in Minnesota: The Dakota War of 1862, the Most Violent Ethnic Conflict in American History* (Norman: University of Oklahoma Press, 2019).

[26] John H. Monnett, *Where a Hundred Soldiers Were Killed: The Struggle for the Powder River Country in 1866 and the Making of the Fetterman Myth* (Albuquerque: University of New Mexico Press, 2008); Kinsley M. Bray, *Crazy Horse*: *A Lakota Life* (Norman: University of Oklahoma Press, 2008), esp. 97-102.

27 "Treaty with the Sioux—Brulé, Oglala, Miniconjou, Yanktonai, Hunkpapa, Blackfeet, Cuthead, Two Kettle, Sans Arcs, and Santee, in Indian Affairs: Laws and Treaties," ed. and comp. Charles J. Kappler (Washington D.C., 1904), vol. 2: 998-1,000; Jeffrey Ostler, *The Plains Sioux and the U.S. Colonialism from Lewis and Clark to the Wounded Knee* (New York: Cambridge University Press, 2004), 48-51.

28 David E. Wilkins, *American Indian Sovereignty and the U.S. Supreme Court: The Masking of Justice* (Austin: University of Texas Press, 1997), 52; John A. Burbank to Ely S. Parker, Sept. 30, 1870, *Annual Report of the Commissioner of Indian Affairs for the Year 1870, U.S. Department of the Interior* (Washington, D.C., Government Printing Office, 1870), 208 ("a white fool"); Hämäläinen, *Lakota America*, 300-4.

29 D.S. Stanley, *Report of the Yellowstone Expedition of 1873* (Washington, D.C., Government Printing Office, 1874), 3 ("a national").

30 Catharine R. Franklin, "Black Hills and Bloodshed: The U.S. Army and the Invasion of the Lakota Land, *Montana: Magazine of Western History* 63 (Summer 2013).

31 Hämäläinen, *Lakota America*, 358-67.

32 Nick Estes, *Our History Is the Future: Standing Rock Versus the Dakota Access Pipeline, and the Long Tradition of Indigenous Resistance* (New York: Verso, 2019).

2

The Shape of South Dakota: State, Region, and Lines on a Map

Thomas D. Isern
North Dakota State University

Perhaps the best-read and most-heeded historical article in the history of South Dakota is the 1989 essay by James D. McLaird, "From Bib Overalls to Cowboy Boots: East River/West River Differences in South Dakota."[1] McLaird makes a forthright argument that the shape of South Dakota as we know it is all wrong, that the congressional authors of the Enabling Act of 1889, as well as the territorial authors of the Constitution of 1889, made an error of judgment. For they prescribed that the vast Dakota Territory should be "divided on the line of the seventh standard parallel" (the injunction in the enabling act) and that thus the northern border of South Dakota should run from the Minnesota border "west on the line of the seventh standard parallel . . . due west to its intersection with the twenty-seventh meridian of longitude west from Washington" (the stipulation in the constitution).[2] "The division of Dakota Territory in 1889 into North and South Dakota," McLaird declares, "was an artificial separation."[3]

McLaird is the most articulate exponent of the bad-border argument, but he is hardly the first or only commentator to make it. There have been other critics, too, who have second-guessed the shape of South Dakota, based on other arguments. All such contentions as to the illogical nature of the borders of South Dakota are to a good degree ahistorical, for investigated in context, the boundaries emerge as logical and sensible according to the knowledge and aspirations of the settler people of Dakota Territory. Moreover, such an investigation takes us to more fundamental questions that pull the props out from under all the critics. It causes us to consider the very definition of a state, as distinct from a region, and its purposes and potentials. It leads us to consider not only the nature of statehood but also the enterprise of state history—how we tell the story of South Dakota.

The fundamentals for determination of the borders and shape of both Dakota Territory and the state of South Dakota were matters of the United States territorial system—which is not to say they were matters of federal dictation. When the territorial historian Howard Roberts Lamar wrote his book on Dakota Territory, he began his chapter on U.S. territorial policy with the statement, "One of the supposedly unique accomplishments of the American federal system has been its solution of the age-old 'colonial problem' through the adoption of the Northwest Ordinance of 1787."[4] With the adverb "supposedly" Lamar did not mean to say the American territorial system failed to live up to its billing, but only that the United States was not the sole country to achieve enlightened colonial administration. Two generations of western historians before Lamar established that not only did the act of 1787 provide for development and democracy, it also established a democratic trajectory whereby over time, the statutory and practical balance in territorial governance shifted from simple appointive authority toward popular assertiveness.[5] This is why Lamar's subtitle describes Dakota not as a federal fiefdom but rather as "a study of frontier politics." Territorial processes, and frontier politics, generated jurisdictions and borders.

State-making emerged from the same processes and politics and was pertinent to the state of South Dakota before it existed, in that some of its boundaries were established borders with the preceding states of Iowa and Minnesota. "The American pioneer . . . characteristically did not always wait for what was legal and safe," writes the dean of American territorial historians, Earl S. Pomeroy. "The territory of self-government thus looked to statehood. . . . The West is both independent and dependent in spirit."[6] Iowa achieved statehood in 1846, Minnesota in 1858, thus chunking into place the shape of South Dakota's eastern border before Dakota was even a territory. The establishment of Dakota Territory in 1861, a benchmark in the political organization described by Lamar, made the new territory the next assertive player in the projection of sovereignty across the map.[7]

State borders, after all, do not necessarily derive from self-evident physical facts on the ground. Some borders or parts thereof indeed make use of physical features such as mountain ranges, or divides, or rivers. It is difficult to argue that such apparently natural designations rest on solid logic. Divides are difficult to discern, particularly for ordinary citizens on the ground, and complicated to mark; moreover, the only thing they physically divide is water. Human enterprises other than hydraulic disregard them. As for rivers, they, too, can be tricky, for rivers change their courses, but by and large they are convenient boundaries. Convenience and visibility are, however, about their only virtues as boundaries. Rivers possess inherent significance not as borders but as centers, centers of watersheds and often bioregions.

Thus when Stephen Sargent Visher, a geographer at Indiana University who had grown up in South Dakota, set about to describe the boundaries of the state of his youth and detail their origins in 1918, he allowed that the "influences" of "geographic, economic, political, and historical conditions" were determinative—and "geographic" factors might not be physical, but rather matters of human geography.[8] Visher made his general observations about the origins of borders not by theorizing but rather by studying the earlier, definitive-for-its-times work by Henry Gannett, *Boundaries of the United States and of the Several States and Territories with a Historical Sketch of the Territorial Changes*, published by the United States Geological Survey in 1885.[9] From Gannett and Visher, as well as from the writings and notes of South Dakota historian Doane Robinson and his son Will G. Robinson, we may abstract a chronological précis of how South Dakota shaped up.[10]

<table>
<tr><th colspan="3">Shaping Up: Jurisdictions and Borders of South Dakota
(Major changes only)</th></tr>
<tr><td>To 1803</td><td>Native lands</td><td>Indigenous sovereignty intact despite territorial assertions of France and Spain</td></tr>
<tr><td>1803-12</td><td>Louisiana Territory</td><td>Undemarcated lands within the American territory purchased from France</td></tr>
<tr><td rowspan="5">1812-58
Slicing and dicing territories</td><td>1812-24</td><td>Congress organizes previous Louisiana Territory north of new state of Louisiana into Missouri Territory, encompassing all of present South Dakota</td></tr>
<tr><td>1824-36</td><td>Present South Dakota east of the Missouri River becomes part of the new Territory of Michigan, carved out of Missouri Territory</td></tr>
<tr><td>1836-38</td><td>Present South Dakota east of the Missouri River becomes part of the new Territory of Wisconsin; west of the Missouri is Missouri Territory</td></tr>
<tr><td>1838-49</td><td>Present South Dakota east of the Missouri River becomes part of the new Territory of Iowa; west remains Missouri Territory</td></tr>
<tr><td>1849-58</td><td>Present South Dakota east of the Missouri River becomes part of the new Territory of Minnesota; west remains Missouri Territory, subsequently (1854) Nebraska Territory</td></tr>
<tr><td>1858-61</td><td>Interregnum</td><td>With Minnesota statehood, future Dakota Territory is unorganized territory referred to as "Land of the Dakotahs"</td></tr>
<tr><td rowspan="4">1861-89
Dakota Territory</td><td>1861</td><td>Territory encompassing all of present South Dakota and North Dakota, and extending west to the Continental Divide</td></tr>
<tr><td>1863</td><td>With creation of Idaho Territory, Congress sets 27° West as western boundary of Dakota Territory</td></tr>
<tr><td>1864</td><td>With creation of Montana Territory, Congress temporarily moves the southern segment of the western boundary of Dakota Territory back west to the Continental Divide</td></tr>
<tr><td>1868</td><td>With creation of Wyoming Territory, the western boundary of Dakota Territory reverts to 27° W — the "permanent reduction" — thus fixing the border at its present place</td></tr>
<tr><td>1889-</td><td>Statehood</td><td>Dakota Territory divided at 46° N to form states of South Dakota and North Dakota — thus substantially completing the shape of the state of South Dakota</td></tr>
</table>

Certain observations as to the future shape of South Dakota are evident from this précis. First, prior to the organization of Dakota Territory in 1861, Congress made the decisions as to borders pertaining to the area of future South Dakota without consideration of any internal needs or desires. EuroAmerican settlement was sparse, and Native preferences were not germane. Second, the eastern border fell into place by default, as Congress defined the western border of Iowa Territory. Third, the logic influencing the definition of the eastern border was driven by the conception of the state-making process by Congress. As Visher observes, Congress pursued a process intended to "give average-sized states" rather than searching for defining landmarks or consulting local interests. "In 1848 there was great objection in Congress to the making of states of large size."[11] Third, the Missouri River was employed as a territorial boundary for convenience during the existence of the territories of Michigan, Wisconsin, Iowa, and Minnesota. Once attention turned to the creation of a territory, and a future state or states, on the plains west of Iowa and Minnesota, the Missouri River was emplaced as the center of the emerging Dakota Territory.

The first segment of the modern South Dakota border to take shape, then, was the southern segment of the eastern border, which was the Big Sioux River. The congressional designation of this border long predated Dakota Territory and had to do with the issues of Iowa statehood, which was consummated in 1845. The border's location flowed from the geometry of state-making in the Midwest. There was sentiment in Congress for the multiplication of small free states, but on the ground in Iowa Territory, framers were thinking more expansively—westward to the Missouri River. In fact, already in 1839 territorial governor Robert Lucas had outlined a package of expansive proposed boundaries for a future state of Iowa that became known as "the Lucas boundaries" and designated the Missouri River as the western border. Constitution-makers in Iowa liked the way Lucas (who was one of them) thought. Congress thought otherwise and sought some point from which to jog north from the Missouri and make Iowa a suitably-sized rough rectangle. Well to the north, the Red River seemed a likely axis on which to split jurisdictions. From the Missouri, the Big Sioux River pointed upstream toward that axis. So Congress made it the western border of Iowa—and thus the future eastern border of Dakota Territory and South Dakota.[12]

The Big Sioux River acts as a natural border with Iowa on the southeast corner of South Dakota. *The Center for Western Studies.*

The logic of the balance of the eastern border, the northern part, begins far to the north, at the intersection of the Red River with the Canadian border, 49° N latitude. With its north-south alignment, the Red invites invocation as a convenient boundary, complicated only by the issues of determining the head of the Red and crossing over in a credible way thence to the Big Sioux. As the act creating Dakota Territory says:

> Commencing at a point in the main channel of the Red River of the North, where the forty-ninth degree of north latitude crosses the same; thence up the main channel of the same, and along the boundary of the

> State of Minnesota [the middle of the Red] to Big Stone Lake [source of the Red]. . . .[13]

From which point a short stretch of the meridian directly led to the Big Sioux, hooking up with the Iowa line. Once Dakota was admitted as a territory in 1861, there were no questions to resolve about its eastern line except for quibbles owing to the wayward behavior of river courses.

Much the same can be said of the southern border: it was largely decided by Congress without consideration of interests in Dakota. The Missouri River, making its big bend, was the convenient line to make a border in 1861 when Dakota Territory was created north of Nebraska Territory (except for a little diversion to the south between the Missouri and the Niobrara, which aberration would be corrected by Congress in 1882). West from the big bend, the border followed the line of 43° N latitude. Again, except for the odd minor adjustment owing to riverbed shift, there was nothing to dispute about the southern border.[14]

It was easy to make arbitrary decisions spanning territory uninhabited by significant numbers of EuroAmericans to dispute the details. This was more graphically illustrated yet by the manipulation of the western border of Dakota Territory (and future South Dakota) in adjustment of beautifully straight lines to accommodate the organization of other territories. Dakota Territory achieved its shape as the territory would appear just prior to statehood via stroke-of-the-pen decisions mainly motivated by the rise of mining interests in the Rocky Mountains. Originally boasting the Great Divide as its western border, Dakota Territory lost its west with the creation of Idaho Territory in 1863. Congress set 27° W of Washington, D.C., as the new western border of Dakota Territory for no good reason other than it was the eastern border of Idaho Territory. Then, as gold discoveries demanded organization of Montana Territory, its borders left a hole in the area of future Wyoming without governance, so the area was reattached to Dakota, thus briefly re-extending Dakota to the divide. This did not last long, for with the creation of Wyoming Territory, the western border of Dakota reverted to 27° W. Whether aesthetically interesting on the map or not, rectangles were efficient vehicles for defining sovereignty.[15]

After this, the story gets more complicated, because citizens, assertive and obstreperous territorial citizens of the sort described by historians Lamar and Pomeroy, also politically savvy citizens of the sort admired by South Dakota historian Herbert S. Schell, even republican citizens of the sort lauded by revisionist Jon K. Lauck, arrived on the scene and commenced asserting themselves.[16] The external borders of Dakota Territory were in place, but within them, there was plenty of room to maneuver. Eventually people responding to circumstances and pursuing aspirations would spin from two states one territory and emplace the most contentious border of them all—the one dividing Dakota Territory into the two states of South Dakota and North Dakota.[17]

In 1861 the new Territory of Dakota had little EuroAmerican population in place. Territorial governor William Jayne, on arrival in Dakota, commenced essential tasks immediately, beginning with a census—which was oddly constructed. The handwritten compilation of returns attested to the presence of 696 persons, including a "half-breed" element of but 37. This seems absurd, inasmuch as a constituent return from the Red River district—the district along the Red, in the northern half of the territory, populated mainly by Métis—counted 524 "mixed" persons. The new administration was ignoring the existence of the northern population, indicating that from the beginning, race and distance were dividing south and north.[18] Governor Jayne set a trajectory for deeming the northern citizenry invisible, and governing from the south, that eventually would bear bitter fruit. The trajectory runs through to historical treatments of the era. In Herbert Schell's formative bulletin on territorial Dakota, the historian manages to work through the formation of the territory and its early settlement without the word "Pembina" (Métis center of the north) ever appearing in his narrative.[19]

A little-known and vaguely-reported incident in 1862 epitomizes this estrangement. According to one source, a proposal known as the General Half Breed Bill came under legislative consideration. It would extend full citizenship rights to all mixed-bloods in the territory who could read or speak English. Governor Jayne opposed it, the receiver of the land office, Jesse Wherry, favored it, and the two of them "engaged in a fistic encounter" in a Yankton hotel over the matter including "hair pulling, choking, striking, blood spitting and pugilistic exercises . . . performed with grit and relish."[20] Another source only says the governor engaged in "logrolling" in the street over the issue, but that may have been veiled language.[21] Either source makes the point.

The presumption seems to have been that it was the EuroAmerican citizens of the southern half of the country who were making the territory and making history, although they started slowly.[22] During the mid-1850s settlement had crept up the Missouri River and to the Big Sioux on the Iowa side, with Sioux City founded in 1855. A treaty with the Yankton Sioux in 1858 gave settlers access to the country between the Missouri and the Big Sioux, then in the unorganized lands, and so settlement crossed into future Dakota Territory. This was one finger reaching in, but at the time, a more potent digit was military, pointing the way directly up the Missouri deep into future Dakota Territory. The William S. Harney Expedition of 1855 brought about the purchase of Fort Pierre, the post of Pierre Chouteau and Company, where Harney brought his 1,200 troops. Thus the army had begun the occupation of the upper Missouri. While holding onto Fort Pierre, Harney in 1856 chose a more desirable location for a more substantial post, Fort Randall, establishing what Schell terms "a symbol of order on the northern plains" five years before the arrival of Governor Jayne. The two fingers crossed, historically. John B. S. Todd marched with Harney, took part in the establishment of Fort Randall, left the army, took part in the Yankton treaty negotiations, joined a trading firm—and next turned up in Sioux City, with business partners promoting settlement—while still serving as sutler for Fort Randall.[23]

Still in the period of the interregnum, 1858-61, a rivalry developed between two interest groups intent on settlement of future Dakota Territory. One comprised settlers and speculators along the

Missouri River, an area referred to as the Missouri slope, including Yankton (called by Schell "the mother town of the Dakotas").[24] The other comprised settlers and speculators on the Big Sioux River, with Sioux Falls emerging as their most salient settlement. Members there of the Dakota Land Company tried to send a purported representative to Congress in 1859 (despite residence in no organized territory of the United States) and were rebuffed. This stirred the folks on the Missouri, to which vicinity Todd had gravitated, who convened meetings in Yankton and Vermillion and sent to Washington their own petition for organization (not bothering to include their rivals at Sioux Falls). Also rebuffed, they redoubled their agitation in the territory, engaged in various types of electoral and promotional fraud, held another big meeting in Yankton—and this time, in 1861, put over the territorial organization. Thus there was no great momentum for civil settlement during the infancy of the territory. Since the activists were ignoring the northern communities, their vision for the great Dakota Territory was blue sky.[25]

During the early 1860s, although politics flourished, agricultural settlement in southeastern Dakota Territory stagnated, for obvious reasons: the Civil War, with its massive diversion and destruction of material and human resources, and closer to home, the U.S.-Dakota War. The Dakota conflict that broke out in Minnesota in 1862 was not contained therein. Settlers in Dakota Territory were terrified and agitated by the conflict. Even as they joined in the western Indian war, raising the companies of the Dakota Cavalry that were the origin of the South Dakota Army National Guard, they seemed unaware that the prosecution of the war was, in terms of potential settlement and development, outflanking them. As Major General Alfred H. Sully, operating under the command and within the Department of the Missouri, led invasions of the Dakota-Lakota makoche in 1863, 1864, and 1865, then went on to establish military posts (beginning with Fort Rice, near the future site of Bismarck) in the northern half of the territory, he accomplished several things in terms of geopolitics. First, he centered activity on the Missouri River, upon which he relied for transport and supply, and in the valley of which he founded or projected military posts that would take possession of the land. Second, Sully embraced, explicitly, with the support of his superior, Major General John Pope, the conquest of the northern half of the territory, looking toward settlement to follow the war. Third, Sully softened up Teton resistance in the region, arguably making it untenable for the Hunkpapa and their allies and making railroad construction more feasible. All these things would serve eventually to strengthen the northern hand in territorial affairs.[26]

During and following the war, the settlements in the southeast became intensely interested in developments far to the north and west, hinging on gold strikes in the northern Rockies (the same developments that would reshape the western borders of Dakota Territory). First, there were the strikes beginning on Clearwater Creek and on Salmon River in Idaho Territory, attracting miners from points east of the plains. They spread out and found new diggings in what would soon be organized as Montana, investing Bannock City, Alder Gulch, Virginia City, Helena, and a multitude of other rich sites people in Yankton never had heard of before, but now were intensely interested in. Paying little attention to attempts of Minnesota interests to open routes direct to the diggings across the north half of their territory (another initiative aided by Sully and his forces), southeastern Dakotans figured the Missouri River (as the first steamboat had reached Fort Benton, head of navigation on the Missouri, in 1859) would be the favored route to gold country, and they would be the outfitters of the enterprise. They enjoyed seeing the steamers ply to and fro on the river, and observing the mackinaw boats of miners coming home laden with treasure, but they wanted more. So they lobbied Congress to build roads through their territory to the mining settlements. Congress responded in 1865 by providing support for three roads, all of them crossing the southern half of the territory. One of them included a federally funded bridge across the Big Sioux River. Unfortunately for the territorians, federal support ceased on account of fear of exacerbating Indian relations around the Black Hills and in the Powder River country, and then

Red Cloud's war of resistance against transportation to the mines doomed the wagon-road initiative.[27]

During the late 1860s several factors coalesced that would hold import for the future shape of the territory-becoming-states. The first of these was the establishment of the Great Sioux Nation covering essentially all the western half (west of the Missouri) of the southern half of Dakota Territory. During the years 1865-66 territorial governor (and thereby ex officio superintendent of Indian affairs in the territory) Newton Edmunds sought to achieve peace on the Northern Plains through negotiated treaties with the Teton and Yanktonai peoples. These treaties included abandonment of wagon roads across their lands. His efforts were superseded when Congress and the federal government stepped in to negotiate the more comprehensive Treaty of Fort Laramie in 1868. The new treaty did not require tribes to go on reservation immediately, but it pointed the way to that eventuality, while setting aside the Great Sioux Nation as the area in which they would be located. This was an evident loss for promoters of settlement in the southern half of the territory, barring them from the west—while it did not pose any similar bar to western expansion in the northern half of the territory. Southeastern Dakota Territory protested, but the scheme was logical. By this time the Union Pacific Railroad had built across Nebraska, so there was no immediate national need for a railroad to cross southern Dakota Territory. In his classic description of the Great Sioux Nation, historian Robert M. Utley writes, "The seven tribes of the Teton Sioux held the reservation in common, but they were individually assigned to one of six separate agencies." Scattered agencies, the Indians not required to go on the associated reservations—in the southeast, this seemed like a waste of time and territory and a barrier to aspirations.[28]

Moreover, they began to pine for one particular piece of real estate within the Great Sioux Nation, one precious to the tribes: the Black Hills. Possibly the agitation for wagon roads in the early 1860s was as much about the approach to the Black Hills as it was the passage to the Rockies. As early as 1861 parties in Yankton had formed a Black Hills Exploring and Mining Association and petitioned Congress for support. The interest was not only in possible mineral production but also in the dark stands of pine that bedecked the hills—lumber that could feed construction of farms and communities across the territory.[29]

For by 1868 the pace of agricultural settlement, sluggish for so long, had quickened. Agricultural settlement, much of it by immigrants, infilled the Big Sioux River country, with that district poised to be a hearth for extension across the territory. The arrival in 1868 of the Sioux City and Pacific Railway in Sioux City promised to energize settlement further. It raised hopes the southern half of the territory might yet benefit from the Pacific Railway bill. The territorial legislature incorporated the Missouri and Niobrara Valley Railroad Company to extend track west, hoping to get Congress to make it a northern branch of the Union Pacific and provide land grants. The politics of the deal fell apart, however, as even the people of the territory opposed bonding the railroad. Meanwhile, the southerners had to watch while preparations moved along to construct the Northern Pacific Railroad across the northern territory with the full support of the Pacific Railway Act. Planning ahead, the federal government opened a land office in Bismarck in 1870. Still, the great majority of land entries were happening in the southern territory.[30]

The Panic of 1873, as well as the grasshopper plagues of the mid-1870s, quashed development across the territory. Construction of the Northern Pacific stalled out at Bismarck, and land-taking to the south nearly ceased, although speculative town-making continued. The very depressed state of conditions made news of the discovery of gold in the Black Hills in 1874 "electrifying," writes Schell. "For the older settlements of Dakota Territory the economic developments of the gold rush were particularly opportune, counterbalancing in large measure the adverse conditions."[31] Charles Collins, the Irish-American newspaper editor in Sioux City, was the foremost cheerleader for Black Hills development. As Black Hills historian Watson Parker observes:

> The gold of the Black Hills might have lain for another generation in the fastness of the mountains if the hopes and ambitions of the people of Iowa and eastern Dakota had not urged forward the movements which revealed and publicized its presence. These pioneers, disappointed in their fortunes, sought, as frontiersmen have always sought, to enlarge their prospects by expanding their borders.[32]

Without doubt, the partisans of southeastern Dakota wanted the Black Hills in their future. They had agitated for them, had dispatched explorers and compiled reports, since 1861.[33]

The discovery of gold set into motion the train of events—Custer's reconnaissance of the Black Hills, the resumption of construction of the Northern Pacific Railroad, the outbreak of the Great Sioux War of 1876, the Black Hills cession of 1876, the confinement of tribes on reservations, the miner's rush to the hills, the transition to hard-rock corporate mining—that revitalized Dakota Territory, north and south, once again.[34] Development in the north followed the Northern Pacific, but in the south also, railroad activity stirred in the 1870s, owing mainly to decisions by the Chicago & North Western Railway and the Chicago, Milwaukee & St. Paul Railway to build boldly across Dakota. The Chicago & North Western, coming west from Tracy, Minnesota, was expected to cross the Missouri River somewhere—but where? That question was answered after railway agents secretly bought out landholders on the east bank of the river, opposite Fort Pierre, and founded the city of Pierre, where its first train arrived on 4 November 1880. Meanwhile the Milwaukee, coming west from Canton, reached Chamberlain at about the same time. Neither railroad crossed the river. Both, however, concerned themselves with filling in the railroad landscape, building additional east-west lines spaced reasonably apart, then extending connecting lines north and south herringbone style to compete with one another.[35]

Railroads were the impetus for that historical phenomenon known as the Great Dakota Boom, 1878-1887, but the pattern of their building prompts the question: Was it one boom, or was it two?[36] Railroads, including their north-south connectors, locked communities into east-west alignments like beads on strings. Given the previous history of Dakota Territory, whereby north and south developed separately and even at times antagonistically, it seems crucial that at the very time, in the 1870s, when statehood movements coalesced, railroad developments entrenched east-west transportation and east-west thinking. This is the context for some of our most popular stories about territorial chicanery, having to do with agitation for statehood during the 1870s and 1880s and the maneuvering that led to splitting the territory along an east-west line—finalizing the shape of South Dakota. Circumstances aligned, certainly, but assertive people acted.

To begin with, there was a particularistic revolt in the Black Hills. As Governor John L. Pennington proceeded with appointments in newly-created counties, some voices in the hills renounced governance by the "cow counties" back east. The discontents were mainly men who had come from other mining regions, rather than from eastern Dakota, and they were, disproportionately, Democrats. In July 1876 they sent a petition to Congress for separation from Dakota and constitution of a Lincoln Territory in the hills. The following year local forces in neighboring territories threw in with the cause, proposing to combine with the Black Hills into the new territory. At this point the delegate from Dakota Territory, Jefferson P. Kidder, produced a bill to divide Dakota Territory on the 46th Parallel into northern and southern territories. As if the waters were not muddied enough, politicians from Bismarck brought in a bill to split the territory on the 100th Meridian, thus producing a west Dakota and an east Dakota. Bismarck expected to become capital of the western part. All these proposals failed, and so the Black Hills had to reconcile to life in Dakota Territory as it was, although the people there retained a large sense of their own importance and grievances.[37]

Political stability did not ensue. Instead, the peak years of the Dakota Boom became climactic years for political intrigue. Political authority seemed to settle into Yankton, but that power begat countervailing force, emanating from the Big Sioux country, connecting up with Black Hills discontent, and animated by the personage of Richard F. Pettigrew, who thrived in the fluid situation of counties and alliances forming and reforming. Pettigrew was something like an irresistible force. His erstwhile antagonist, Governor Nehemiah G. Ordway, was not merely an immovable object—he was a nimble rock. Pettigrew tried to get Ordway removed, whereupon Ordway in 1883 sought to defeat Pettigrew as delegate. Pettigrew responded by playing the northern card: he withdrew in favor of John Raymond, of Fargo, thus forging an alliance of middle and northern territorial politicians. There followed legislative provision for essentially a shadow territory—possibly a state—in the north, with establishment of a penitentiary, a mental hospital, a university, an agricultural college, and three normal schools. At this point, it seems in retrospect, the die was cast; the territory, at some opportune point, would split north from south.[38]

In the meantime, factions in the south, with northern allies, commenced intrigue to move the capital from Yankton, and Yankton no longer could stave them off. Northern figures were integrally involved; in 1883 Councilman John Walsh of Grand Forks brought in a bill to make Huron the capital. It failed, but the legislature did pass a bill creating a capital commission—with northern counties providing key support. Ordway was in the mix, about to assume unexpected postures, and Alexander McKenzie, the Northern Pacific lobbyist from Bismarck, was active. On April 3, 1883, the members of the capital commission boarded a special train from Sioux Falls to Yankton, arriving early morning to accomplish a quick organization for business. As the so-called "capital on wheels" they then wheeled and dealt their way through various suitor cities. Most were in the southern half of the territory, but their partisans could not agree among themselves, and so on the thirteenth ballot, Bismarck emerged victorious—a dark horse, or so, at least, it appeared to the world at large.[39] Ordway was popularly blamed for selling out Yankton. Statehood was still years away, but the capital-relocation fight probably made it impossible for north and south to remain bedfellows. The territory was cloven. Northern representatives were fairly pleased with themselves and the situation, but southern ones redoubled their efforts to achieve separate statehood.[40]

There was another, more eminently upright force at work for division, which was a campaign launched some years earlier by William H. H. Beadle, Superintendent of Public Instruction. He was a true believer; he felt he had a mission to save school lands, designated for support of the common schools, from being appropriated by grafters and sold without proper return to the school fund. Beginning in 1879, he commenced a campaign to obtain statehood for the south, leave the north as a territory, and require a minimum bid for any lands sold. A popular convention in June 1882 embodied Beadle's ideas and sent them to Congress, and Republicans there favored them, but failed to act before Democrats won control of the House of Representatives. Ordway vetoed a bill for a constitutional convention to force the issue. His old enemies thereupon united with the friends of Beadle and in June 1883 called for a constitutional convention, irrespective of the governor's veto. The convention met, attended to Beadle's interests, and sent a document out to the voters, who approved it. Northern interests were angered, southern partisans went to Washington, but found themselves opposed there by Ordway's people. Their constitution failed acceptance by a divided Congress.[41]

The situation turned more ironic yet. The governor who replaced Ordway in June 1884, Gilbert A. Pierce, got sworn in at Yankton, then promptly departed for Bismarck to govern the territory. The legislature answered by calling another constitutional convention—this one for only the southern counties. Its delegates specified the border between the new state of Dakota and the northern remnant territory should be not exactly the 46th Parallel, but rather the 7th Standard Parallel, which is to say, a parallel adjusted for curvature, thus avoiding potential difficulties with county line readjustment along the border. Otherwise the 1885 constitution was substantially the same as that of 1883. In November 1885 the voters approved it, designating Huron the capital.[42]

Additional reversals followed. National electoral victories for the Democrats, who opposed division and favored admission of a single state of Dakota, swung some activists and voters in the territory toward that position. Louis K. Church, a new governor arriving in February 1887, thought their way, although most in the south still seemed to favor division. So they declared at a public meeting in Aberdeen in December 1887. In the elections of 1888 Republicans were triumphant, setting up president-elect Benjamin Harrison to take office with a Republican Congress alongside him. The lame-duck Congress preempted his expected actions by passing an Omnibus Bill, which outgoing President Grover Cleveland signed on February 22, 1889, creating four new states: Montana, Washington, North Dakota, and South Dakota. Certainly, members of Congress had their own reasons, including specifically partisan ones, for acting as they did in 1889, but the substance of their action in regard to splitting Dakota territory and making two states from it flowed from the sentiments and struggles of the people of Dakota. At long last the shape of South Dakota was complete.[43]

In a physical sense, lines on a map and on the ground, yes—but this whole investigation sheds new light on a still-ongoing discussion having to do with the shape of South Dakota, the virtues and faults of its borders as constituted, and matters of citizen identity. The discussion, however civilly and articulately it may once have been framed by Professor McLaird, suffers from some confusion as to definitions of place, region, and state. It is worth sorting out, because borders, and the shape of a state, are things that matter. The border dividing South Dakota from North Dakota mattered enough to merit federal expenditure for its marking with impressive quartzite boundary posts; those posts themselves were of sufficient weight to draw the attention of historian Gordon L. Iseminger, resulting in the regional classic, *The Quartzite Border: Surveying and Marking the North Dakota-South Dakota Boundary, 1891-1892*.[44] Moreover, if the sociological journalist John Gunther is to be believed, the quartzite border is anything but artificial. "Nothing is more remarkable in the United States than the difference between the Dakotas," he writes. "What is more, the two Dakotas, though companions for 330 miles, have practically no contact with one another."[45]

There remains, however, the historical and popular chestnut: should Dakota have been divided on an east-west axis into North Dakota and South Dakota, or might it have been better if it were divided on a north-south axis into West Dakota and East Dakota. Historically, we see that the latter alternative was a non-starter. It was once proposed by a party who might have been speaking only for himself, and it went nowhere. We see that contention over divisions and borders never was about abstract considerations of place-identity, but rather about aspirations, struggles, and yes, sometimes, animosities on the ground. Nevertheless we continue to talk as though the physical shape of South Dakota is some kind of identity question—that people who are alike should be grouped together and separated from people who are unlike.

This term, "West River," which prompts the obverse, "East River"—does it have lineage we should revere? The first documented usage of "West River" occurs in the *Huron Daily Plainsman* of April 24, 1890. A writer was litigating the state capital location fight, seeking the capital for Fort Pierre, on the west bank, and attempting to rally citizens west of the river to Fort Pierre's cause. So the origin of the term lay in a practical political ploy, not a cerebral conception of identity. For a generation thereafter rhetorical deployment of "West River" was rare, and such deployment was practical or descriptive. "West River" is not a rallying cry of long standing.[46]

McLaird mentions a western separatist campaign ostensibly mounted by one H. W. Fields, manager of the Roswell Farmer's Company, in 1914. Fields wrote letters to the editor advocating splitting the state down the middle on the Missouri River. "I have found no one to whom it was presented that was not only in favor but anxious that a move be made in that direction," Fields is quoted as saying.[47] He argues on uncertain basis that the split might improve western farmers' chances for credit on reasonable terms, but mostly he sounds as though he just thinks like should be grouped with like, tribally. Notably, Roswell is in east-central South Dakota, so what is this chap's beef, exactly? It is hard to tell, but it is worth noting that another of his letters-to-the-editor, a lengthy one, was concerned with his objections to his wife's receipt of a traffic ticket in Mitchell.[48]

There is quite a bit of literary bulk to the East River-West River distinction, including allusions by Walter Campbell a.k.a. Stanley Vestal (*The Missouri*, 1941), John Steinbeck (*Travels with Charley*, 1952), and John Milton (*South Dakota: A Bicentennial History*, 1977). Campbell, although a master of literary nonfiction, is a southern plainsman from Oklahoma. Steinbeck makes his famous remark about how the road map should fold on the Missouri River immediately after recounting a conversation with his poodle dog. Milton, although a thoroughgoing literary scholar, often seems confused as to whether he is attempting to define South Dakota, the Dakotas, or the Great Plains. Not that those definitions might not overlap, but perhaps they are worth parsing.

An examination of an interesting work by Joel Garreau, *The Nine Nations of North America*, helps to clarify thought.[49] The journalist Garreau sets out to help others understand the cultural diversity of the country. He names and draws lines around nine cultural regions, describing them in terms of attributes that define them and inviting us to "consider the way North America really works." Political lines are, to borrow McLaird's term, artificial. This is the real America. South Dakota, incidentally, Garreau splits between "the Breadbasket" and "the Empty Quarter." Laying aside whether those terms are offensive to anyone, they are not meant as prescriptive for the organization of political sovereignty, but rather as aides to cultural understanding. Garreau gives us a view of what the world might look like if re-ordered by cultural perceptions.

South Dakota may be parcel to an Empty Quarter, to a Breadbasket, to the Great Plains, to the Midwest, to Flyover Country, or to the Heartland. These, however, are all regional terms, and South Dakota, in our federal, constitutional system, is not, never has been, a region. It is, always has been, a state, a political jurisdiction and agent. It is worth considering that in the course of world history, attempts to make states conform to cultural or regional identities often have led to grief, if not outright tragedy. It is, after all, a commonplace that the ties which bind Americans are, at their best, adherence to certain political ideals, not membership in a particular culture.

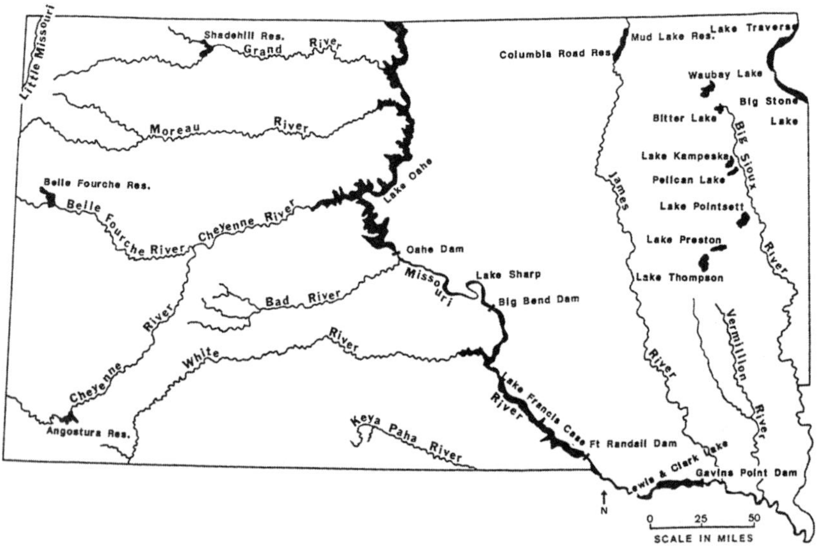

***Map 9.* Major Rivers and Lakes of South Dakota.**

Major Rivers and Lakes of South Dakota, from Edward P. Hogan and Erin H. Fouberg, *The Geography of South Dakota*, 3d ed. (Sioux Falls: Center for Western Studies, 2001). *The Center for Western Studies.*

The story of the shape of South Dakota turns out to be about not only physical borders—lines on a map—but also the state's *shape* in a more fundamental sense. It has to do with the very definition of a state and how it is to be treated historically. These are questions approached in recent years by Jon Lauck in *Prairie Republic* and subsequent works produced under his initiative. The first modern South Dakota historian to wrestle and define this question was the great Herbert S. Schell of the University of South Dakota, author of the landmark work of 1961, *History of South Dakota*. Previously Schell had written a school text, *South Dakota: Its Beginnings and*

Growth, and a solid monograph, *Dakota Territory during the Eighteen Sixties*.[50] In the textbook Schell refers to South Dakota's past as a "colorful drama" full of challenges, an inspirational narrative of "the vigor and resoluteness with which the early settlers of South Dakota attacked the overwhelming difficulties that blocked their way."[51] Politics and statecraft figure only in the middle reaches of the text. In the territorial monograph Schell seems more comfortable with the genre, and his focus is political affairs. Indeed, the author describes politics as "an exception" deserving focused and extended treatment.[52]

Such remarks indicate a trajectory for the *History of South Dakota*. Although Schell promises "a full-scale history," it is clear that politics and statecraft are his preoccupation. His narrative comprises the territorial struggle to supplant dependency with autonomy; the political economy of farm protest; the rise and efflorescence of progressivism; as well as the impact of the Great Depression and the New Deal which combatted it. In the introduction to *A New South Dakota History*, Herbert T. Hoover reflects on Schell's state history and characterizes it as "Paxsonian"—that is, work under the influence of Schell's Wisconsin mentor, the Western historian Frederick Logan Paxson. Paxson, says Hoover, advised his students "that the charge of a professional historian was mainly to deal with political and economic subjects."[53] Such sentiments were in line with founding principles for advanced study of History in America. Herbert Baxter Adams includes in his 1887 bulletin on History in American colleges and universities a line drawing of the Johns Hopkins University seminar room. Prominent on the wall is the legend, a quotation from the historian Edward Augustus Freeman: "History is past politics and politics present history."[54]

None of this is to suggest that politics are the end-all, or that they transpire in some vacuum chamber secure against environmental, economic, social, and intellectual forces. It is to suggest that in both the designation of physical boundaries for a political entity—such as the state of South Dakota—and in the writing of the history of such an entity, that sphere of human affairs which used to be called "political economy" is rather fundamental. It also is to suggest—getting back to the rationale for this essay—that there is nothing wrong with drawing boundaries as a political process. Whether the participants are grasping opportunists à la Lamar, or upstanding republicans as described by Lauck, such a process may be the best basis for establishing a state.

Historians often pride themselves on their ability to transcend boundaries, to hold the larger, cosmopolitan view. Certainly it is best to be aware of context and forces ranging from the local to the global. It is also important, however, to respect boundaries and do constructive things within them. The world historian William McNeill reminds us of our obligation as historians to be aware of the stories we tell and to use our powers for good, for narrative defines identity.[55] The great historian of nation-making Benedict Anderson defines "imagined community" as the quality essential to making a state.[56] For South Dakota to function and thrive as a state, it needs enlightened historians who are willing to work within its boundaries, take the state seriously, and tell its stories, like Herb Schell.

In 1879 William A. Howard, in his message to the legislative assembly, contemplated the prospect and the gravity of statehood. "What, then," he asked, "is a state? . . . A free government is simply the organized power of the good, consolidated and wielded to restrain the bad, and to protect the weak from the encroachments of the strong; or, in other words, to establish justice and secure the blessings of liberty to all the people. . . . A State is the people in a given territory and their institutions."[57] Borders define the physical extent of sovereignty. The people define the shape of the state, and in doing so, emerge as worthy subjects for historians.

Notes

1 James D. McLaird, "From Bib Overalls to Cowboy Boots: East River/West River Differences in South Dakota," *South Dakota History* 19:4 (Winter 1989): 117-42. The beloved South Dakota historian McLaird taught at Dakota Wesleyan University, Mitchell, for thirty-seven years—thus lecturing daily to students in the East River even while his research interests and scholarly publications focused on the West River. See, among many

reverent notices of his death in 2017, the one of September 5 in the *Mitchell Republic*, https://www.mitchellrepublic.com/obituaries/james-mclaird.

2 Enabling Act, 22 February 1889, as per *Laws Passed at the Second Session of the Legislature of the State of South Dakota* (Pierre: Free Press, 1891), iii; Constitution of the State of South Dakota, as per *Laws Passed at the First Session of the Legislature of the State of South Dakota* (Pierre: State Bindery, 1890), iii. The seventh standard parallel is essentially 45°56'07" North Latitude.

3 McLaird, "From Bib Overalls to Cowboy Boots," 456.

4 *Dakota Territory, 1861-1889: A Study of Frontier Politics* (New Haven: Yale University Press, 1956), 1.

5 Ray A. Billington, "The Historians of the Northwest Ordinance," *Journal of the Illinois State Historical Society* 40:4 (1947): 397–413; Frederick L. Paxson, *History of the American Frontier, 1763-1893* (Boston: Houghton Mifflin, 1924); Earl S. Pomeroy, *The Territories and the United States, 1861-1890* (Philadelphia: University of Pennsylvania Press, 1947); Howard Roberts Lamar, *The Far Southwest, 1846-1912: A Territorial History* (New Haven: Yale University Press, 1966).

6 Pomeroy, *The Territories and the United States*, 95, 99.

7 Chapter 1 of Lamar's *Dakota Territory*, 28-66, is "Background to Political Organization, 1855-61."

8 Stephen Sargent Visher, "The Boundaries of South Dakota," *South Dakota Historical Collections* 9 (1918): 330-95. Biographical information on Visher can be gleaned from his obituary in the *Bloomington Daily Herald Telephone*, October 1867, accessed via Family Search, https://ancestors.familysearch.org/en/2Z3B-7GF/stephen-sargent-visher-1887-1967.

9 United States Geological Survey Bulletin 13. For another view and context of the making of states and borders, see Brandon Stanley Plew and Samuel Otterstrom, "Statecraft on the Eve of the Civil War: Influences on New Territories and States in the 36th U.S. Congress," *Historical Geography* 42 (2014): 361-85.

10 "Outside Boundary of South Dakota," note card, Vertical File, "Boundaries, South Dakota (and others)," South Dakota State Archives, Pierre; Will G. Robinson, 'South Dakota Boundaries," *South Dakota Historical Collections* 32 (1964): 232-59 (which subsumes the essay by Donald D. Parker, "Surveying the South Dakota-Minnesota Boundary Line," 236-45).

11 Visher, "Boundaries of South Dakota," 10.

12 Visher, "Boundaries of South Dakota," 380-82; Todd E. Pettys, *The Iowa State Constitution* (2d ed., New York: Oxford University Press, 2011), 15; Robinson, "South Dakota Boundaries," 232-33.

13 Henry Gannett, *Boundaries of the United States and of the Several States and Territories*, Bulletin 171 (Washington, DC: GPO, 1900), 4.

[14] Gannett, *Boundaries of the United States and of the Several States and Territories*, 4; Visher, "Boundaries of South Dakota," 383; Robinson, "South Dakota Boundaries," 233-35, 248-50.

[15] Gannett, *Boundaries of the United States and of the Several States and Territories*, 4; Visher, "Boundaries of South Dakota," 382-83.

[16] Jon K. Lauck, *Prairie Republic: The Political Culture of Dakota Territory, 1879-1889* (Norman: University of Oklahoma Press, 2010).

[17] This essay relies on Harry F. Thompson, ed., *A New South Dakota History*, 2d ed. (Sioux Falls: Center for Western Studies, 2009), Chapter 7, "Territorial Politics and Politicians," by Herbert T. Hoover, 95-116, for its framework of territorial development, while disagreeing with that work's suggestion that East River/West River terms and cleavages had currency in territorial times.

[18] Report of the Secretary of Dakota Territory, November 23, 1861, General Records of the Department of State, 1763-2002: Territorial Papers, 1789-1873: Dakota, 1861-1873, Record Group 59, National Archives, https://catalog.archives.gov/id/221206286.

[19] Herbert S. Schell, *Dakota Territory During the Eighteen Sixties* (Vermillion: Report No. 3, Governmental Research Bureau, University of South Dakota, 1954).

[20] Moses K. Armstrong, *The Early Empire Builders of the West* (St. Paul: E. W. Porter, 1901), 74.

[21] *Sioux City Register*, May 17, 1862.

[22] The most solid survey of settlement here treated is in Thompson, *A New South Dakota History*, Chapter 8, "Yankee and European Settlement," by Gary D. Olson, 117-42, along with Chapter 10, "Cities and Towns," by Gary D. Olson, 157-81.

[23] Schell, *Dakota Territory During the Eighteen Sixties*, 4-17; Lamar, *Dakota Territory*, 36-38.

[24] For the most current work on settlement of the Big Sioux country, see Jeff Bremer's chapter, "The Big Sioux Valley Frontier, 1851-1889," in Jon K. Lauck, ed., *Heartland River: A Cultural and Environmental History of the Big Sioux River Valley* (Sioux Falls: Center for Western Studies, 2022), 171-97.

[25] Schell, *Dakota Territory During the Eighteen Sixties*, 10-18; Lamar, *Dakota Territory*, 38-66.

[26] This assessment of the geopolitical effect of the Dakota War draws upon standard works such as Paul N. Beck, *Columns of Vengeance: Soldiers, Sioux, and the Punitive Expeditions, 1863-1863* (Norman: University of Oklahoma Press, 2013, and *Doreen Chaky, Terrible Justice: Sioux Chiefs and U.S. Soldiers on the Upper Missouri, 1854-1868* (Norman: Arthur H. Clark, 2012), but more so on the reinterpretations presented in three reports prepared for the Battlefield Protection Program of the National Park Service by Thomas D. Isern, Richard Rothaus, Dakota Goodhouse, and Aaron Barth: *Fort Abercrombie Battlefield Survey, Richland County, North Dakota,*

2017; *Battles and Forts of the Dakota War*, 2018; and *Killdeer Mountain Battlefield Survey*, 2018, copies deposited with the Institute for Regional Studies, NDSU Archives, North Dakota State University, Fargo. See also Chapter 7, "The War Years," in William E. Lass, *Navigating the Missouri: Steamboating on Nature's Highway, 1819-1935* (Norman: Arthur H. Clark Co., 2008), 193-228.

27 Schell, *Dakota Territory During the Eighteen Sixties*, 36-42; Alton B. Oviatt, "Steamboat Traffic on the Upper Missouri River, 1859-1869," *Pacific Northwest Quarterly* 40:2 (1949): 93; Lass, *Navigating the Missouri*. 207-35.

28 Schell, *History of South Dakota*, 86-92; Robert M. Utley, *The Last Days of the Sioux Nation* (New Haven: Yale University Press, 1963), 20.

29 Schell, *Dakota Territory During the Eighteen Sixties*, 41-42; Watson Parker, *Gold in the Black Hills* (Lincoln: University of Nebraska Press, 1966), 193-97; Lamar, *Dakota Territory*, 148-76. See also Chapter 15, "Black Hills in Transition," in Thompson, *A New South Dakota History*, by David A. Wolff, 288-309.

30 Schell, *Dakota Territory During the Eighteen Sixties*, 28, 26-27, 44-46; Schell, *History of South Dakota*, 110-15; Lamar, *Dakota Territory*, 127-38.

31 Schell, *History of South Dakota*, 125.

32 Parker, *Gold in the Black Hills*, 19.

33 Parker, *Gold in the Black Hills*, 19-37.

34 See Parker, *Gold in the Black Hills*, Chapter 8, 123-40, and Utley, *Last Days of the Sioux Nation*, Chapter 3, "The New Life," 18-39, for the two sides of these events. See also Lamar, *Dakota Territory*, 148-76.

35 Schell, *History of South Dakota*, 160-68; Lamar, *Dakota Territory*, 178.

36 "The Great Dakota Boom" is the subject of Schell's *History of South Dakota*, Chapter 12, 158-74. Chapter 7 of Elwyn B. Robinson's *History of North Dakota* (Lincoln: University of Nebraska Press, 1966), 133-55, has the same title. Classic historians of both South Dakota and North Dakota use the term habitually, but they apply it almost exclusively to their own states.

37 Schell, *History of South Dakota*, 194-97; Lamar, *Dakota Territory*.

38 Schell, *History of South Dakota*, 203-09; Lamar, *Dakota Territory*, 177-203.

39 Perhaps significantly, the first known newspaper usage of "capital on wheels" emanated from the *Bismarck Tribune*, May 18, 1883.

40 Schell, *History of South Dakota*, 208-11; Lamar, *Dakota Territory*, 203-07.

41 Schell, *History of South Dakota*, 211-13; Lamar, *Dakota Territory*, 198-207.

42 Schell, *History of South Dakota*, 214-16; Lamar, *Dakota Territory*, 208-43.

43 Schell, *History of South Dakota*, 216-19; Lamar, *Dakota Territory*, 244-73.

44 Gordon L. Iseminger, *The Quartzite Border: Surveying and Marking the North Dakota-South Dakota Border* (Sioux Falls: Center for Western Studies, 1988). For documentation of the genesis of *The Quartzite Border*, see Correspondence, Gordon L. Iseminger and John J. Gerken, Commissioner, Department of School and Public Lands, 1979-80, Vertical

File, "Boundaries, South Dakota (and others)," South Dakota State Archives, Pierre.

45 John Gunter, *Inside U. S. A.* (New York: Harper & Bros, 1947), 237.

46 See, for instance, *Sioux Falls Argus-Leader,* October 7, 1898, *Pierre Weekly Free Press*, March 26, 1914, *Sioux Falls Argus-Leader,* April 29, 1914, and *Lead Daily Call*, March 12, 1916.

47 McLaird, "From Bib Overalls to Cowboy Boots," 473. McLaird gets the story from Paula Nelson, *After the West Was Won: Homesteaders and Town-Builders in Western South Dakota, 1900-1917* (Iowa City: University of Iowa Press, 1986), 150.

48 *Mitchell Capital*, September 6, 1917.

49 Joel Garreau, *The Nine Nations of North America* (New York: Avon Books, 1981).

50 Herbert Samuel Schell, *South Dakota: Its Beginnings and Growth* (New York: American Book Company, 1955); Schell, *Dakota Territory during the Eighteen Sixties*.

51 Schell, *Beginnings and Growth*, vii.

52 Schell, *Dakota Territory*, v.

53 Thompson, *A New South Dakota History*, ix. For a sound explanation of Paxson's philosophy of history by one of his disciples, see Earl Pomeroy, "Frederic L. Paxson and His Approach to History," *Mississippi Valley Historical Review* 39:4 (March 1953): 673-92.

54 Herbert B. Adams, *The Study of History in American Colleges and Universities*, US Bureau of Education Circular of Information No. 2 (Washington: Government Printing Office, 1887).

55 William H. McNeill, *Mythistory and Other Essays* (Chicago: University of Chicago Press, 1986).

56 Benedict R. Anderson, *Imagined Communities: Reflections on the Origin and Spread of Nationalism* (London: Verso, 1983).

57 *Message of His Excellency William A. Howard to the Legislative Assembly, Dakota Territory* (Yankton: Daily Press & Dakotan, 1879), South Dakota State Archives, Pierre.

3

THE SOUTH DAKOTA RAILROAD EXPERIENCE

H. Roger Grant
Clemson University

Every region possesses a unique railroad past. South Dakota stands out as being different from other states on the Great Plains and arguably from much of the nation. What is most obvious is that the Mount Rushmore State lacked a heavily patronized transcontinental rail line, having only a modest, late-date arrival. Not until construction workers employed by the Chicago, Milwaukee & Puget Sound Railway, a Chicago, Milwaukee & St. Paul Railway (Milwaukee) subsidiary, hammered down the last spikes near Garrison, Montana, on May 14, 1909, did a route to the Pacific operate through a corner of the state. This 2,212 mile artery linked Chicago with Tacoma and Seattle, Washington. Of the approximately 300 miles in South Dakota, Aberdeen, Milbank, and Mobridge became its principal stops. West of Mobridge (named for the Missouri River railroad bridge opened in 1906) tracks hugged the North Dakota border and served Lemmon and a few other scattered stations. East of Mobridge this "transcon," except for Aberdeen and Milbank, benefited only a handful of small communities.[1]

The transcontinental railroads, which sliced through the northern and central plains states, received tens of thousands of acres of federal land. The Great Northern Railway (GN) is somewhat of an anomaly. Builder James J. Hill acquired public lands, but they came indirectly through his acquisition of the St. Paul & Pacific Railroad.

South Dakota, then part of Dakota Territory, lost out on this largess. Yet territorial lawmakers had repeatedly petitioned Washington for such aid, and hope blossomed forth with the projected Dakota & Northwestern Railroad. In 1870 a bill, which granted the company the standard ten alternate sections of land on each side of the wagon road from the Big Sioux River to Yankton and then up the valley of the James River to the Canadian border, passed in the U.S. Senate but died in the House of Representatives. Technically, there was a land grant in what became South Dakota. When the Winona & St. Peter (Chicago & North Western property) built west from New Ulm, Minnesota, it gained about 2.4 million acres as far west as Lake Kampeska, but at the time that piece of Dakota was in Minnesota Territory. After 1871 Congress rejected additional requests for grants, largely because of the scandals associated with the building of the first transcontinental railroad, and the belief that the private sector could finance railroad construction.[2]

About 1940 a Chicago & North Western passenger train speeds through Brookings. The agent prepares to hand up train orders "on the fly." *Courtesy H. Roger Grant.*

What also stands out about South Dakota railroad history is what occurred in the Black Hills during the gold mining boom of the 1870s and 1880s. Initially the immediate area lacked direct railroad access. Although the Union Pacific (UP), the only long-distance carrier in the region, was far from the "color," its Cheyenne, Wyoming, and Sidney, Nebraska, stations served as popular railheads. For the final leg of their journey to the "Hills," argonauts and others needed to take cramped and rough-riding stagecoaches that operated over miserable wagon roads from connecting rail links at Cheyenne, Sidney, and Yankton or perhaps from the Missouri River steamboat landing at Fort Pierre. Some rode horseback or walked. Freight moved slowly by teams of oxen, mules, and horses. The solution: railroads. Although by 1887 the Fremont, Elkhorn & Missouri Valley Railway (FE&MV), controlled by the North Western, provided a speedier, more dependable and comfortable way to reach the Hills, narrow-gauge (36-inch width) roads for some time dominated local transportation. In the early 1880s the Homestake Mining Company opened the Black Hills & Fort Pierre Railroad (BH&FtP). Although this slim-gauged road had big plans, its mileage remained limited to the Lead area. Eventually, the Chicago, Burlington & Quincy Railroad (Burlington), which had installed a branch between Edgemont and Deadwood with several small extensions from its Alliance, Nebraska, to Billings, Montana, line, took control and added a third-rail to accommodate standard-gauge rolling stock. In the latter part of the 1880s the Deadwood Central made its debut. Its promoters had big plans, wanting to build a nearly 350-mile radial network to serve gold mining operations and coal deposits in neighboring Wyoming Territory. Yet the road, later electrified, operated fewer than twenty miles. The BH&FtP also entered the orbit of the Burlington. Then in 1901 these two appendages became a single narrow-gauge network within the Burlington system. The Black Hills region could boast of the only slim-width rail cluster on the Great Plains.[3]

The first railroad project in what became South Dakota took place in the southeastern corner. This was hardly surprising since Yankton served as the initial seat of government for Dakota Territory.

In 1862 lawmakers incorporated the Missouri & Niobrara Valley Railroad (M&NV). The expectation was that its rails would run from the Big Sioux River, where it would connect with a future trans-Iowa railroad, to Elk Point, Vermillion, and Yankton. The road would proceed to the Niobrara Valley "in order to reach, by the shortest and most practicable route, the South pass of the Rocky Mountains." At some point the railroad would connect with the aborning Union Pacific. Big ambitions, indeed. The M&NV proposal, however, turned to dross when the federal government decided that Sioux City and not Yankton should be where rails linked with Chicago.

During the latter part of the nineteenth century, several narrow-gauge lines appeared in the Black Hills region. The trackage between Deadwood and Lead, constructed in the early 1890s by the Fremont, Elkhorn & Missouri Valley Railway, came under control of the Chicago & North Western Railway in 1903. In 1924 passenger service ended, and about this time, a photographer captured the abandoned cars. Rails were removed in 1928. *Courtesy H. Roger Grant.*

Dakotans were not about to give up on obtaining the iron horse. Railroad fever gripped its growing post-Civil War population. "The whistle of the locomotive would be the sweetest music a resident of the broad prairies of Dakota could hear, and the mere rumor that a party of railroad surveyors had been seen in a locality, was enough to fill every settler with joy, and cause visions of townsite and county seat speculators to color with all the beauteous hues of the rainbow his dreams at night." Public roads were at best primitive, and faster, all-weather land transport was critical for development and prosperity. In 1867 another "paper" proposal appeared, and it was the Minnesota & Missouri Railroad. The hope was to connect a trans-Minnesota carrier with Yankton. The inability to win a federal land grant again meant failure. That same year the Dakota & Northwestern Railroad was chartered, and it, too, never became an up-and-running project.[4]

The next historically significant railroad proposal fulfilled the desire of residents of southeastern Dakota to join the expanding web of Midwestern rails. This would be the Dakota Southern Railway. It was launched officially in early 1871, being spearheaded by Yankton businessmen, political leaders, and territorial officials. The presumptions were that it would build-up the community at the expense of rival Sioux City, which had become a boomtown with the arrival of the Sioux City & Pacific (North Western) in 1868. And a railroad would help to attract a stream of settlers to the surrounding area. Farmers required reasonably close access to rail transportation if they had any expectation of becoming more than semi-subsistence producers.[5]

For a modest carrier the Dakota Southern claimed a complex history. Its backers planned to connect with an Illinois Central subsidiary in Le Mars, Iowa, rather than Sioux City. The Dakota Southern charter, however, permitted it to enter the emerging Sioux City gateway. Although the charter itself was of dubious legality, the company forged ahead. Before construction could commence, voters of Yankton County overwhelmingly approved a $200,000, twenty-year bond issue with an 8 percent interest rate. Additional but less substantial assistance later came from several places along the projected route. Actual work began in June 1872, but because of higher than expected construction costs the company abandoned Le Mars for Sioux City. On January 22, 1873, a red-letter day occurred when the *Judge Brookings*, the first locomotive in the future state, steamed into the Yankton County capital over this hastily constructed sixty-one-mile road. Its independent status ended in 1881 when the Milwaukee took control. At that time, the affiliated Sioux City & Pembina, which linked Jefferson (Davis Junction) with Sioux Falls, was also included. Unfortunately, bond payments became a contentious and expensive burden for Yankton taxpayers. Not until 1913 were the last bonds retired.[6]

Once the financial impact of the Panic of 1873 had ended, Dakota rapidly entered the Railway Age. What took place until the Panic of 1893, which badly disrupted construction projects, was a rail network that blanketed much of the country east of the Missouri River. By the late 1880s approximately 2,200 miles of lines served what became South Dakota. The dominant carriers were the Milwaukee and North Western and included its quasi-independent Chicago, St. Paul, Minneapolis & Omaha Railroad (Omaha) unit. These two prosperous and conservatively managed Granger Roads were strong competitors, and both were in an expansive mood. (By the mid-1920s the Milwaukee operated 1,802 miles and the North Western 1,305 miles, controlling collectively seventy-three percent of the state's railroad network.) Other railroads contributed to the surge in mileage: Burlington; Burlington, Cedar Rapids & Northern (part of the Chicago, Rock Island & Pacific after 1902); Great Northern; Illinois Central; and Minneapolis & St. Louis.[7]

Railroad building and the Great Dakota Boom, which extended from 1878 to 1887, went hand-in-hand. "Boom was in the atmosphere," observed future state historian Doane Robinson in 1904, "and that hope which has ever characterized the true Dakotan–hope that no untoward circumstances could blight–everywhere carried the people into new enterprises for development and growth." Although the lines of the Milwaukee and North Western became interlaced, the former covered large portions of southeastern South Dakota by the time of statehood in 1889. Mitchell served as its operational hub. Milwaukee arteries extended from Iowa through Canton and Mitchell to Chamberlain; across southern Minnesota through Madison and Woonsocket; and from the Twin Cities through Aberdeen to near the

Missouri River. Its line from Sioux City through Mitchell to north of Aberdeen closely paralleled the Oakes, North Dakota, branch of the North Western. The North Western was more heavily concentrated in the central section with Huron being its center for operations. Early in the twentieth century the North Western absorbed the FE&MV that connected Deadwood and Rapid City to northwestern Nebraska and points east.[8]

The Milwaukee and North Western each transported thousands of settlers to lands east of the Missouri River. The North Western probably had somewhat greater impact in terms of promotion, development, and over-all quality of service. For decades the company not immodestly (or incorrectly) employed the "Best of Everything" tag line. It was according to historian Herbert Schell, "a leading highway into the Territory."[9]

The North Western used its Dakota Central Railroad subsidiary to extend westward from Minnesota and direct connections with the Twin Cities, Milwaukee, and Chicago. (Resembling other trans-Chicago carriers, it incorporated or took control of separate companies. If one of these entities failed financially, its negative impact on the parent corporation would be lessened.) In 1879 and 1880 the Dakota Central pushed west from Tracy, Minnesota, and built to the future state capital of Pierre, a route that led to creation of multiple towns, including Brookings, Arlington, De Smet, Iroquois, Huron, St. Lawrence, Miller, Highmore, and Blunt.[10]

The North Western enthusiastically promoted its "Minnesota and Central Dakota Line." One piece of company-circulated advertising, "All About Hand County Central Dakota," highlighted farming and business opportunities. A lengthy text written in December 1882 by J. B. and J. T. Cogan, co-editors of the *Bramhill Free Press*, said in part: "In addition to the superior advantages in climate, soil, water, and varied resources bestowed upon this vast principality by a generous Providence, there are numerous other inducements, resulting from the achievements of man, which must commend themselves to the favorable consideration of every one seeking a new home, a new business location or a new field of labor." In their glowing, if not highly exaggerated commentary, the Cogans did not ignore the North Western. "Daily trains, equipped with all the accessories usual to the fast mail and express service, give us perfect and rapid communication with all sections of the country. All this is nicely supplemented by a reasonable freight tariff, which makes it possible to live in this new country (where everything has to be bought for the first season at least) almost, if not quite, as cheaply as in the most favored section of the states." They added: "Fares for land seekers and immigrants are reduced to a mere nothing."[11]

The timing of the Great Dakota Boom created a positive environment for railroad expansion into the region. Farming opportunities were good during much of the 1880s, including favorable climactic conditions, no insect invasions, and relatively strong demands for wheat, livestock, and other agricultural products. Furthermore, cheap farm lands to the east, especially in Illinois and Iowa, were rapidly disappearing. In the minds of newcomers, farmers and businessmen, Dakota was the "Last Best West." With railroad connections much needed supplies such as coal, lumber, and the like could be readily received and at rates much lower than those charged by operators of overland freight wagons.

Part of the population surge involved town creation, and railroads played the key role. The path of lines directly correlated with settlement patterns. "During the Great Dakota Boom the railroad companies platted 138 of the 285 towns platted in South Dakota," concluded historian James Hamburg. Usually a company-owned townsite firm, for example the North Western's Western Town Lot Company, selected the site and sold (perhaps at public auction) commercial and residential parcels. The advantages to this approach were varied. At an affordable price the railroad affiliate could select the location, being appropriately spaced for train control and farmers' needs of traveling to town and returning in one day (team-haul principle), and having a practical street layout. Often the latter meant a T-format. The main street began at the railroad, creating an arrangement in which the tracks formed the bar of a T-configuration. "T-towns" had their principal road stopping directly at or near the depot and retail and professional businesses appeared along that street. On the opposite side of the tracks the placement of grain elevators ("elevator row"), lumber yards, creameries, and other facilities reduced wagon traffic on the main thoroughfare. A townsite affiliate gave investors, often railroad officials, attractive returns.[12]

The process of town creation could be messy if not chaotic. Take Woonsocket in Sanborn County. This junction town on the Milwaukee, platted by its Milwaukee Land Company in 1883, was situated west of Madison and north of Mitchell. "The first sale of town lots had taken place just the day before," recalled a contemporary observer. "The town was full of home seekers, carpenters and prospective merchants. One or two of the saloons were already in operation. We could hear men yelling and shooting through the night. Saloons, livery stables, and stores were full of men, sleeping, at breakfast time the restaurants were a perfect jam." There was more. "Milwaukee Junction, the town which had been platted where they thought the railroad junction was to be, moved enmasse [sic] before the town of Woonsocket was platted. By looking at the lumber piles one could tell where the street would eventually be." The town exploded, and within a year it had about 800 residents and sixty business places. Locals called the place "Boom-strucket."[13]

As the go-go years neared to a close due to falling wheat prices and drought, several other trunk roads appeared. Their collective destination was Sioux Falls, with more than 10,000 residents in 1890 and the largest city in the new state. Railroad service had begun in 1878 when the Omaha built from Worthington, Minnesota, and a connection with its main stem between the Twin Cities, Sioux City, and Omaha gateways. Five years later the Burlington, Cedar Rapids & Northern entered Watertown from Ellsworth, Minnesota, and in 1886 it installed a forty-two-mile line that extended from Ellsworth to Sioux Falls. The following year the Illinois Central came to the Minnehaha County capital with a ninety-six-mile extension from Cherokee, Iowa, and in 1888 the 146-mile Willmar & Sioux Falls (Willmar, Minnesota to Sioux Falls), controlled by Hill's St. Paul, Minnesota & Manitoba Railway (soon the Great Northern), appeared. That same year the GN opened a 136-mile line from Breckenridge, Minnesota, to Aberdeen. Two years later it constructed the 162 miles from Benson, Minnesota, through Watertown to Huron. Then in 1893 the GN expanded from Sioux Falls to Yankton, a distance of sixty-three miles. James J. Hill's extensive penetration of the area did not please either the North Western or Milwaukee.[14]

Although drought and depression caused the Great Dakota Boom to collapse, renewed railroad construction and town-building occurred when moisture levels increased and prosperity returned by the dawn of the twentieth century. Major line extensions came with contraction of Indian reservation lands and their opening to Euro-American settlement in large sections of the West River country. "The Red Devils have been placed where they properly belong," opined a North Western official, "and white civilization can come to thousands of acres."[15]

When the North Western entered Dakota Territory, it had planned to push beyond the Missouri River to the Black Hills. The inability to build across Indian country and little interest by potential settlers in this region made Pierre the stopping point. Understandably, the West River country featured a rough topography, having less rainfall and soil fertility than lands to the east. The Milwaukee had considered building further west, but it, too, had quit at the Missouri River; Chamberlain became the endpoint.

It would be the North Western that first arrived in the West River country (excluding its earlier FE&MV presence in the Black Hills). In 1902 its soon-to-be absorbed FE&MV satellite installed sixty-nine miles of track from Verdigre, Nebraska, to Bonesteel in the Rosebud reservation district. This line would be extended: Bonesteel to Dallas, thirty miles in 1907; Dallas to Colome, ten miles in 1910; Colome to Winner, eleven miles in 1911, and finally Winner to Wood, thirty-five miles in 1929. The latter construction turned out to be a poor business decision.[16]

In 1904 the North Western and Milwaukee each decided to build to Rapid City. The race was on in what became two of the last major construction projects in the state. The North Western won with its

Pierre, Rapid City & North Western affiliate (*P*retty *R*ough *C*ountry & *N*o *W*ater). On August 7, 1907, its first train steamed into Rapid City; three months later the Milwaukee arrived. The North Western had a decided advantage; its line extended 167 miles from the river while the Milwaukee needed to build 220 miles. Both roads sparked new or expanded communities. These included Midland, Philip, Wall, and Cottonwood on the North Western and Presho, Murdo, Kadoka, and Interior on the Milwaukee. At last Rapid City area residents and businesses gained better access to the eastern part of the state and to the Twin Cities, Milwaukee, and Chicago.[17]

Another major "twilight era" construction in South Dakota involved the expansion of the "West End" of the Minneapolis & St. Louis (M&StL). Already the company had a presence in the state; it linked the Twin Cities with Watertown. A year after the North Western and Milwaukee committed to their Rapid City lines, the M&StL formed the Minnesota, Dakota & Pacific Railway to head westward. Within a year 114 miles of trackage extended to Conde, Aberdeen, and Leola. In 1907 the company installed another 115 miles between Conde and Le Beau on the "Big Muddy." Although the M&StL contemplated bridging the river, allowing direct entry into the Cheyenne Indian Reservation that the government in 1909 opened partially to settlement, it remained on the east bank. Beginning in 1910 and 1911 the Milwaukee, which served this trans-Missouri region with approximately 170 miles of branch lines from near Mobridge to Isabel and to Faith, effectively blocked M&StL expansion. It captured nearly all of the grain and livestock traffic.[18]

Not to be overlooked was a sizeable, independent shortline, South Dakota Central Railway. It sought to forge a north-south Dakota trunk route. Opened in 1905 and backed by Iowa industrialist Frederic Maytag, this road built a 103-mile line between Sioux Falls and Watertown. The company failed financially, and a 1916 reorganization created the Watertown & Sioux Falls Railway. Then in 1922 the property became a leased GN property, providing that railroad with a second entrance into Sioux Falls.[19]

After a fitful start another shortline emerged about the time trains operated on the South Dakota Central. This railroad was not in the eastern section but in the Black Hills. It was the Missouri River & Northwestern Railroad, a thirty-two-mile road that linked the Burlington's Deadwood line near Mystic with Rapid City and served mining operations along Rapid Creek. In 1909 the company failed but reorganized as the Rapid City, Black Hills & Western Railroad (RCBH&W). Amazingly, this "Rapid Canyon Line" lasted until the 1940s.[20]

Nearly a decade after the South Dakota Central and the RCBH&W appeared, the Fairmount & Veblen Railway (F&V) opened in 1913 between Fairmount, North Dakota, and Veblen, South Dakota, and a year later built to Grenville. In 1915 the Minneapolis, St. Paul & Sault Ste. Marie Railroad (Soo Line) acquired this eighty-seven-mile road. What is exceptional about the "Dakota Hills Route" is that it was one of the few railroads in the nation that was a bonafide bootstrap "farmers' railroad." It was promoted and built by local backers, mostly farmers, who contributed their labor and materials to forge an avenue for their agricultural products and other commerce.[21]

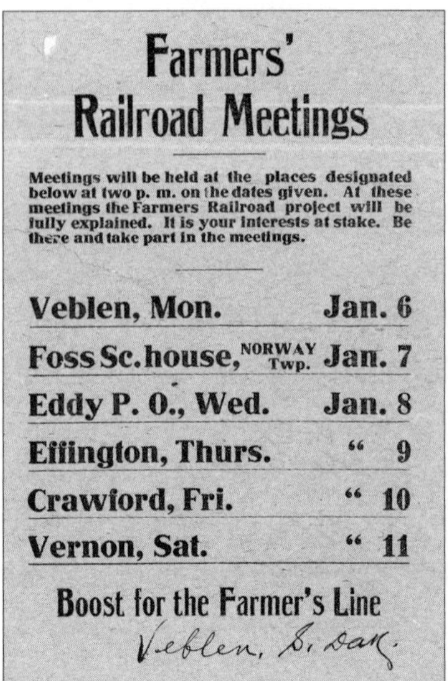

Few states can claim to have had a "true" farmers' railroad. This utopian concept of how to establish railroad service involved classic self-help. Farmers and town and village residents contributed their labors and materials (and money, if possible) to bring the "steam car civilization" to their communities. In South Dakota this grass-roots agitation led to creation of the Fairmount & Veblen Railway, connecting Fairmount, North Dakota, with Veblen and Grenville, South Dakota. The completed road opened between 1913 and 1914, but soon thereafter entered the orbit of the Soo Line Railroad. *Courtesy H. Roger Grant.*

Although the formative years of the Fairmount & Veblen are unusual, the Mound City & Eastern Railway (MC&E) is bizarre. About the time of World War I Minneapolis real-estate promoter Julius Rosholt, who had railroad experience as F&V president and founder of Rosholt in Roberts County in 1913, had his eyes on the railroad situation in the poorly served Campbell County area. To his dismay no trunk road showed interest in adding trackage. Finally, in 1927 Rosholt responded, undertaking his own construction. He planned to build a railroad from a M&StL connection in Leola toward Mound City. Rosholt died a year later, and only eighteen miles opened to the new townsite of Long Lake. MC&E's motive power: "a curious gasoline engine contraption capable of dragging five or six [freight] cars." The company struggled with intermittent service, but it survived the drought and depression of the 1930s. However, the road shut down in 1940.[22]

By the time the Mound City & Eastern emerged, automobiles, buses, and trucks, which operated over an ever-improving network of public roads, made additional railroad mileage, with a few modest exceptions, a thing of the past. Of note the Milwaukee in 1945 relocated sixteen miles of its Pacific stem between Aberdeen and Mobridge. In the mid-1930s, when line abandonments were rare, South Dakota claimed nearly 4,200 route miles of railroad. Still this constituted only a fraction of the national total of approximately 240,000 miles.[23]

It would be wrong to suggest that during the Railway Age South Dakotans always had positive feelings toward the industry. Where a carrier enjoyed a local monopoly, complaints centered on matters of rates, freight car availability, and over-all service. Anti-railroad feelings became especially pronounced during the late 1880s and 1890s as the Farmers' Alliance and then the People's Party gained strength. National ownership became the objective. Although the state had had a railroad commission since the territorial period, it failed to satisfy the needs of the public. Following the Populist victory in 1896, the legislature passed a maximum freight and passenger rate act and increased valuations on railroad property. An aggressive railroad lobby, consisting largely of representatives from the Milwaukee and North Western, challenged these laws, and in 1901 the State Supreme Court ruled them unconstitutional. Fortunately, the public already had won a degree of protection when in 1887 Congress passed the Interstate Commerce Act that created the Interstate Commerce Commission (ICC). During the Progressive Era meaningful state legislation in 1907 and 1909 produced intra-state rate controls, and this time the State Supreme Court viewed them as constitutional. Moreover, lawmakers in Washington strengthened the ICC with the Hepburn Act (1906) and the Mann-Elkins Act (1910). The rise of stiff modal competition in the 1920s, however, lessened public antagonism toward carriers, but complaints never disappeared.[24]

In the heyday of rail usage, the depot became the gateway to the nation and a center of community life throughout South Dakota. In most places the agent served as the face of the railroad. He (occasionally she) became well known to residents and farmers by planning travel itineraries, selling tickets, and handling carload and less-than-carload (LCL) freight, express shipments, and U.S. mail. As the master of the telegraph, which included commercial messages, the agent knew the latest national and state news as well as railroad happenings.[25]

Reflecting depots on the Great Plains and throughout much of the West, South Dakota railroads embraced standard building designs except for their largest stations. Early on the combination layout (waiting room, central office, freight and baggage section) became the norm. Scores of these depots also contained living quarters. Both represented practical and cost-effective solutions for how to serve the ubiquitous small stations. "It became a simple task for us to use the standard combination passenger and freight station with living rooms for agent on the second floor for the more important sites or the Standard No. 3 depots without living quarters at other station locations," commented the structures engineer after the North Western's Rapid City line opened. The former likely appeared in larger, busier communities and the latter in more isolated locations that were designed mostly for train control. Although the

Milwaukee installed multiple two-story depots in the state, it had single-story ones with apartment space. The Garden City depot on its Bristol-Madison branch was such a structure. It contained a single bedroom while two-story ones always had two.[26]

Agents and patrons generally appreciated depots with living quarters. Agents likely discovered an acute shortage of rental housing in smaller communities. Buying or building a house was unrealistic; they expected to move to busier stations as they advanced on the seniority list. Usually they lived rent free and did not pay for coal, kerosene, and related supplies. Likely less relished was the reality that agents were essentially on duty twenty-four hours a day. That was convenient for those who had an emergency telegram to send or LCL freight or express to retrieve, and companies would have employees available to assist with operational problems.[27]

First class, high-speed passenger trains were largely unavailable to South Dakotans. After all, the state had only the Milwaukee transcontinental route and its premier train the *Olympian*. For five decades it made scheduled stops in Milbank, Aberdeen, and Mobridge. Sioux Falls, though, had respectable service to Chicago, but none of the trains were "ballast scorchers." Still, they usually offered Pullmans, dining cars, and perhaps parlor cars. In the post-World War I era the Illinois Central operated the *Hawkeye Limited*; the Milwaukee offered the *Sioux* and later the *Arrow*. A major improvement came in 1940 with introduction of the *Midwest Hiawatha*, a streamliner that used the route of the *Arrow*. The Burlington, which sliced through the southwestern corner of the state, dispatched similar equipment on its runs between Denver and Billings, Montana, via Alliance, Nebraska. For decades the North Western provided sleeping cars on its *Minnesota and Black Hills Express* between Chicago and Rapid City, and it added a cafe-parlor outside the state. Finally, the company had something much better to offer travelers: the *Dakota 400*, an air-conditioned streamliner, entered service in 1950 between Chicago and Huron. "It is surprising what the establishment of a first class train by a railway will do to public thinking about that railway," editorialized the *Daily Plainsman*. "Before the Chicago and North Western Railway established the 'Dakota 400' the [South Dakota] public's opinion of the North Western line was nothing to brag about. It ranged from 'lousy,' 'antiquated,' to an absolute zero. But today the story is different." Yet the operational life of this Huron streamliner was short-lived.[28]

Local passenger and mixed trains (combination freight and passenger cars) long dominated. They made scheduled or flag stops at every station along a line. Some improvements, but not in speed, began in the 1910s with the introduction of gas-electric (later diesel-electric) motor cars, and over time they appeared statewide. This equipment meant the end to smoke and cinders, the most detested aspects of steam-powered trains. After World War II, the diesel revolution came to the state, and steamers on passenger runs were the first to disappear.[29]

Special passenger trains regularly appeared. They might carry circus performers, soldiers, or excursionists. And their appearance at the station became a community event. For decades major carriers handled "homeseeker" trains; after all, it was in their interests to encourage settlers to locate along their lines. Most extra movements occurred during the summer. The M&StL offers but one example. "[The company] early recognized the recreational potential of Lake Kampeska and as soon as its rails reached four miles west of Watertown, A. B. Cutts (general passenger agent) began to boom Yahota as a new summer resort town on the 'best lake in South Dakota,'" noted railroad historian Don Hofsommer. "During the summer months the M&StL ran three shuttle trains each Sunday between the Watertown depot and the Outlet: fare, twenty-five cents."[30]

After World War I passenger traffic, except during World War II, declined steadily. Over a thirty-year period the drop off had been dramatic, plummeting ninety percent between 1919 and 1949. By the 1950s the remaining trains were limited almost exclusively to several main arteries; branch line service had virtually disappeared. The Interstate Commerce Commission and Public Utilities Commission repeatedly allowed discontinuances, but some communities joined by railroad labor fought to retain the remaining trains.

One of the most fascinating human-interest stories to come from South Dakota involved the "Little Fellow." During the late 1880s, a Chicago & North Western crewman, "Big Bill" Chambers, while working on a ballast train on the Watertown-Redfield line, met a boy whose family lived in a company bunk car. The never-identified lad subsequently died of smallpox and would be buried at trackside a short distance from Elrod in Clark County. Beginning on Decoration Day 1889, and for the next forty years, Chambers brought flowers to the grave. And the tradition continued. In 1946 his son-in-law stands in this photograph at the site with crew members of the westbound motor train. *Courtesy H. Roger Grant.*

Companies argued that the public had alternatives, automobiles and buses. Patron support, for example, flourished for Sioux Falls-based Jack Rabbit Lines, whose buses served the most heavily populated parts of the state. In the early 1960s rail passenger service finally ended. In 1960 the M&StL ran its last motor train between Watertown and Minneapolis, and the following year the Milwaukee abandoned its transcontinental *Olympian* (after 1946 the *Olympian Hiawatha*). A remnant, though, operated briefly between the Twin Cities and Aberdeen.[31]

Freight service remained. Yet the frequency of branch line traffic dropped considerably. By mid-century it often meant tri-weekly runs, but additional movements occurred during the annual grain rush. These trains poked along over weed-choked rails at speeds of fifteen to twenty miles per hour or less. Trucks and good roads were the culprits. In time railroads centralized their grain collection, ending service to closely spaced line elevators. This sea change helped to trigger extensive line abandonments.

In the late 1950s South Dakota gained national attention due to a bitter fight between Order of Railroad Telegraphers (ORT) and the North Western. The railroad, whose financial condition had become shaky, sought to end "featherbedding," i.e. "unused, unneeded and unproductive" work among small-town agent-operators. Initially the company focused on the sixty-nine one-person stations in the state where the duties of agents required no more than two hours of daily service. Some agents worked an average of only fifteen minutes a day. Management sought to establish a statewide "central agency set up," thus eliminating these redundant employees. Times had changed. When the state's railroads were built, explained a company official, "they served a farm economy geared to horse-drawn transportation. Today passenger and LCL traffic have [sic] virtually disappeared from one-man stations, but station forces have not been adjusted to modern requirements." The ORT disagreed. Intent on membership protection, it demanded that *no* job held by a member be abolished without its approval. Negotiations dragged on, but in August 1962 the union struck the North Western. Binding arbitration followed. The company ultimately got most of what it wanted; scores of agents received severance payments or reassignments, and some took retirement. Numerous depots were permanently shuttered, and that process continued.[32]

South Dakotans saw other important changes. In the 1960s "merger madness" began to dramatically alter the industry. In 1960 the North Western acquired the M&StL, and a decade later the Burlington, GN, and Northern Pacific united to form the Burlington Northern Railroad (BN). That company, though, had a limited corporate life, merging with the Atchison, Topeka & Santa Fe Railway in 1995 to create Burlington Northern Santa Fe Railway (BNSF).

Also in 1995 the UP bought the North Western (since 1972 the employee-owned Chicago & North Western Transportation Company). In 1977 the Milwaukee entered bankruptcy and nine years later its greatly reduced network entered the orbit of the Soo Line. These consolidations along with altered traffic patterns accelerated line shrinkages. Mileage in operation dropped: 3,916 in 1960, 3,721 in 1970, 3,017 in 1980, 1,182 in 1990, and 1,012 in 2000. Although by 2020 approximately 800 miles of out-of-service lines have been restored, increasing the total mileage to 1,822.[33]

Not long after the Milwaukee ended operations on February 29, 1980, between Miles City, Montana, and the Pacific Northwest, fear spread about the fate of its mileage in South Dakota. The response, led by Governor William Janklow, occurred in November. A special session of the legislature authorized purchase of up to 1,254 miles of threatened trackage. The state subsequently acquired 835 miles of Milwaukee lines and then leased them to the BN together with 303 miles of "local option lines." A temporary sales tax (except on food) of one percent provided the funding. In the process the South Dakota State Railroad Authority emerged. Although critics believed that public ownership smacked of "socialism," it might be better described as "lemon socialism," acquiring threatened trackage to maintain a needed service, especially for shipments of grain, fertilizer, lumber, and other bulk commodities. [34]

Since 1980 the South Dakota railroad experience has been fluid and complex. A variety of shortline railroads have appeared and disappeared. By the mid-1990s four carriers operated on former Milwaukee trackage: D&I Railroad, Dakota Rail, Dakota Southern, and Twin Cities & Western, and one on the former North Western, the Dakota, Minnesota & Eastern (DM&E). By 2022, a significant change had taken place during the intervening years, and it involved the DM&E. Launched in 1986 this "regional" carrier stretched from Rapid City to Winona, Minnesota, with branches to Aberdeen, Oneida, and Watertown, but in 2007 the Canadian Pacific (CP) acquired ownership. Seven years later CP sold the trackage west of Tracy, Minnesota, to the newly organized Rapid City, Pierre & Eastern (RCP&E), a unit of shortline and regional railroad conglomerate Genesee & Wyoming. Recently, too, the 190 miles of the former Milwaukee line from Mitchell to Kadoka and previously operated by Dakota Southern became the Ringneck & Western (R&W), a subsidiary of Watco, another shortline operator. Unlike the Dakota Southern, the R&W expects to operate beyond Kadoka to Rapid City, creating a 285-mile route from Mitchell and ending the out-of-service portion of the Milwaukee's one-time Black Hills line. *Trains* editor Jim Wrinn considers the RCP&E representative of the spirit of contemporary shortline and regional railroads: "Entrepreneurial, enterprising, innovative, and tightly connected to the communities they serve."[35]

Nowhere can the dramatic changes in the state railroad map be seen better than in Sioux Falls. Once sporting five trunk railroads, it presently has only a single trunk road and two shortlines. In 1972 the Rock Island retired its Sioux Falls line, and eight years later the Illinois Central left the city. BNSF currently operates the former GN together with portions of what were once the South Dakota Central and the Milwaukee between Sioux Falls and Madison. The D&I appeared in 1982 on ex-Milwaukee trackage between Sioux City and Dell Rapids, and five years later the Ellis & Eastern began operations on ex-North Western trackage between Brandon and Ellis. In 2017 it expanded to Org in Nobles County, Minnesota.[36]

Revival of any intercity passenger service is highly unlikely. After all, hundreds of miles of the Milwaukee's former transcontinental route no longer exist or have been acquired by trunk and shortline carriers. South Dakotans today may lack an understanding of their state's railroad past. In April 2021 the *Sioux Falls Argus Leader* commented on the impossibilities for Amtrak trains to serve the state: "As a result, many were left with residual anger, sadness for the lack of alternative transportation options." That's a disappointment, but not having convenient access to long-distance, first-class trains has historically haunted residents. Instead the state benefitted from several thousand miles of secondary and branch lines, and virtually all of this trackage was needed when built. If South Dakotans wish to ride on flanged wheels, they have two options: heritage rail carriers Black Hills Central Railroad in Hill City and Prairie Village, Herman & Milwaukee Railroad near Madison. Both are reminders of the state's rich and changing railroad history.[37]

Notes

1 August Derleth, *The Milwaukee Road: Its First Hundred Years* (New York: Creative Age Press, 1948), 178-95.

2 Augustus J. Veenendaal, Jr., *The Saint Paul & Pacific Railroad: An Empire in the Making* (DeKalb: Northern Illinois University Press. 1999), 24, 26; Kenneth Merle Hammer, "Dakota Railroads," (Ph.D. diss. South Dakota State University, 1966), 28; Robert S. Henry, "The Railroad Land Grant Legend in American History Texts," *Mississippi Valley Historical Review* 32 (September 1945):194.

3 See Mildred Fielder, *Railroads of the Black Hills* (Seattle, WA: Superior Publishing Co, 1964); Howard Roberts Lamar, *Dakota Territory, 1861-1889* (New Haven, CT: Yale University Press, 1956), 150.

4 *First Annual Report of the Board of Railroad Commissioners of the Territory of Dakota* (Fargo: Dakota: The Argus Company, 1886), 8.

5 Herbert S. Schell, "The Dakota Southern, A Frontier Railway Venture of Dakota Territory," *South Dakota Historical Review* 2 (October 1936):110; Lamar, *Dakota Territory, 1861-1889*, 143.

6 Doane Robinson, *History of South Dakota*, (Chicago: B. F. Brown & Company, 1904), Vol 1, 246-247; Schell, "The Dakota Southern," 99; *First Annual Report of the Board of Railroad Commissioners*, 24; Herbert S. Schell, *History of South Dakota* (Lincoln: University of Nebraska Press, 1961, 3d ed. rev.), 113-15.

7 James F. Hamburg, "Railroads and the Settlement of South Dakota During the Great Dakota Boom, 1878-1887," *South Dakota History* 5 (Spring 1975):168-71; Doane Robinson, *Doane Robinson's Encyclopedia of South Dakota* (Pierre: Privately Published, 1925), 603-05; Mark Hufstetler and Michael Bedeau, *South Dakota Railroads: An Historic Context* (Pierre: South Dakota State Historic Preservation Office, 1998), 7.

8 Robinson, *History of South Dakota*, vol. 1, 299.

9 H. Roger Grant, *The North Western: A History of the Chicago & North Western Railway System* (DeKalb: Northern Illinois University Press, 1996), 101-25; H. Roger Grant, "Experiencing the 'Best of Everything': Passenger Service on the Chicago & North Western Railway," *Railroad History* 169 (Autumn 1993):35-53; Schell, *History of South Dakota*, 161.

10 Grant, *The North Western*, 59.

11 "All About Hand County Central Dakota," (Chicago: C. N. Trivess, Printer, ca. 1883), broadside in possession of the author.

[12] Hamburg, "Railroads and the Settlement of South Dakota During the Great Dakota Boom," 173-74; John C. Hudson, "The Plains Country Town," in Brian W. Blouet and Frederick C. Luebke, eds., *The Great Plains Environment and Culture* (Lincoln: University of Nebraska Press, 1979), 103-05; John C. Hudson, "Towns of the Western Railroads," *Great Plains Quarterly* 2 (1982): 41-54.

[13] Hammer, "Dakota Railroads," 129.

[14] Ralph W. Hidy, Muriel E. Hidy and Roy V. Scott, with Don L. Hofsommer, *The Great Northern Railway: A History* (Boston, MA: Harvard Business School, 1988), 62-63.

[15] Unidentified newspaper clipping, July 4, 1904, in author's possession.

[16] Robert J. Casey and W. A. S. Douglas, *Pioneer Railroad: The Story of the Chicago and North Western System* (New York: Whittlesey House, 1948), 315-16. For a picture-postcard review of railroads in South Dakota during this general time period see Mike Weise and Tom Hayes, *Images of Rail: South Dakota Railroads* (Charleston, SC: Arcadia Publications, 2004).

[17] Casey and Douglas, *Pioneer Railroad*, 236.

[18] Don L Hofsommer, *The Tootin' Louie: A History of the Minneapolis & St. Louis Railway* (Minneapolis: University of Minnesota Press, 2005), 88-100; Derleth, *The Milwaukee Road*, 296.

[19] Hidy, et al., *The Great Northern Railway*, 110; *Poor's Manual of Railroads* (New York: Poor's Publishing Company, 1922), 515, 534.

[20] *Poor's Manual of Railroads,* 1922, 1786; Fielder, *Railroads of the Black Hills*, 144-67.

[21] John A. Gjevre, *Saga of the Soo: West from Shoreham* (Moorhead, MN: Guevre Books, 1990, 2d ed.), 120-124; Fairmount & Veblen Railway public timetable, March 1915.

[22] Hofsommer, *The Tootin' Louie*, 201-202.

[23] Jim Scribbins, *The Hiawatha Story* (Milwaukee: Kalmbach, 1970), 159. South Dakota experienced an early line abandonment. In 1911 the nineteen-mile Forest City & Gettysburg Railroad, which opened in 1890 between the two communities in its corporate name, folded. Its raison d'etre was to transport government supplies from a connection with the North Western at Gettysburg to the Cheyenne River Indian Agency via a ferry across the Missouri River at Forest City. After 1907 the penetration of the Milwaukee into the region ruined its financial health.

[24] See *Second, Third* and *Fourth Annual Reports of the Board of Railroad Commissioners of the Territory of Dakota* (Grand Forks and Bismarck, DT, 1885-1888); *Dakota Ruralist* (Aberdeen, SD), May 19, 1892; Schell, *History of South Dakota*, 225, 232, 237, 259, 261-62.

[25] H. Roger Grant, *Railroads and the American People* (Bloomington: Indiana University Press, 2012), 110-21. For the autobiography of a South Dakota agent, see H. A. Stimson, *Depot Days* (Boynton, FL: Star Publishing Company, 1972), 1-91.

[26] Quoted in letter to author from William Armstrong, Structures Engineer, Chicago & North Western Transportation Company, December 14, 1976; Charles W. Bohi and H. Roger Grant, "Country Railroad Stations of the Milwaukee and the Chicago & North Western in South Dakota, *South Dakota History* 9 (Winter 1978):1-23.

[27] See H. Roger Grant, *Living in the Depot: The Two-Story Railroad Station* (Iowa City: University of Iowa Press, 1993).

[28] *Daily Plainsman* (Huron, SD), August 24, 1950.

[29] H. Roger Grant, *Transportation and the American People* (Bloomington: Indiana University Press, 2019), 108-09; Donald Duke and Edmund Keilty, *RDC: The Budd Rail Diesel Car* (San Marino, CA: Golden West Books, 1990), 25-33.

[30] Don L. Hofsommer, "The Watertown Express and the 'Hog and Human' Passenger Service in South Dakota," *South Dakota History* 3 (Spring 1973):139.

[31] Hofsommer, *Tootin' Louie*, 289; Scribbins, *The Hiawatha Story*, 187.

[32] Grant, *The North Western*, 197-200.

[33] William D. Middleton, George M. Smerk, and Roberta L. Diehl, eds., *Encyclopedia of North American Railroads* (Bloomington: Indiana University Press, 2007), 84-85. Railroad mileage statistics for South Dakota compiled from *Railroad Facts* and other publications of the Association of American Railroads, Washington, DC.

[34] Rick W. Mills, *Railroading in the Land of Infinite Varity: A History of South Dakota Railroads* (Hermosa, SD: Battle Creek Publishing Company, 1990), 167.

[35] Jim Wrinn, "You've Come a Long Way, Short Lines: An Appreciation in South Dakota for the State of the Industry," *Trains* 81 (April 2021):33.

[36] Dennis C. Opferman and R. Milton Clark, "Sioux Falls and the Rock Island," *Railroad History* 224 (Spring-Summer 2021):82-83.

[37] *Argus Leader* (Sioux Falls, SD), April 2, 2021; "Ride this Train!" *Trains* 81 (May 2021):17.

4

The Extremes of South Dakota's Weather[1]

Christopher R. Laingen
Eastern Illinois University

Introduction

Weather and climate affect and shape an area's physical landscapes, as well as its anthropogenic landscapes of culture, settlement, economy, and land use.[2] South Dakota sits nearly at the geographic center of the North American landmass–in fact, the geographic center of the fifty United States is located just north of Belle Fourche on a nondescript piece of rangeland. As such, the state is in the crosshairs of continually converging air masses that have and continue to create a smorgasbord of unique weather characteristics and events. Annual temperature swings of more than 120 degrees are commonplace throughout the state, as are severe weather events and multi-year droughts or deluges that can wreak havoc upon the state's (mostly) rural and urban landscapes.

Many of the state's most populous cities (57% of the state's population is urban) are found along rivers that have experienced major flooding caused by short-term precipitation events (1972 Rapid City Flood) or the longer-term melting of winter snow coupled with spring rains that raise the waters of the Missouri, James, Big Sioux, and others. Tornadoes, spawned from the violent mixing of cool, dry air and hot, humid air–on average, 26 per year–and other severe thunderstorm-related weather events, also periodically affect South Dakotans, their property, and their communities.

In April 2022 the Sioux Falls National Weather Service office posted a Tweet about a recent three-day stretch of weather advisories, watches, and warnings that wonderfully introduces this chapter: "DYK [did you know]: Since Friday the Dakotas have experienced…Tornado Warnings, Blizzard Warnings, Severe T-Storm Warnings, Flood Warnings, High Wind Warnings, Red Flag Warnings, Wind Advisories, Flood Advisories, Winter Weather Advisories, Tornado Watch, Severe T-storm Watch, Fire Weather Watch."[3]

The Driving Forces of South Dakota's Weather Extremes

Weather and climate in South Dakota are a function of the state's geographic location. Atmospheric properties related to temperature and moisture classify specific types of air masses. Air masses that form over oceans have moisture characteristics referred to as "maritime" (moist) because of the higher amount of water vapor that has evaporated from the ocean surface into the air above; those that form over land have "continental" (dry) characteristics because the amount of evaporated moisture is less. Temperature characteristics also relate to where those air masses formed. "Arctic" (cold) air masses originate nearest to the poles; "polar" (cool) air masses form a bit further south; and "tropical" (warm) air masses form near the tropics.

On the North American Great Plains, these air masses do battle with one another. Maritime tropical (moist, warm) and continental tropical (dry, warm) air masses move northward from the sub-tropics while continental polar (dry, cool), continental arctic (dry, cold), and maritime polar (moist, cool) move south. When air masses of differing temperature and moisture characteristics collide, a release of energy and the formation of a "weather event" is likely to occur. Warm air likes to rise, and cold air likes to sink. This is due to the density and activity-level of the air molecules in a given volume of air. Even though we tend to think that humid air is "thicker" (and heavier) than dry air, it is lighter;[4] warm air also has the capacity to "hold" more moisture than colder air. This is what causes us to feel the oppressive humidity on a 95°F July afternoon and not on a 20°F December day. When it comes to "weather," heat and moisture are the ingredients–the gunpowder–that simply need a trigger to be pulled.

Cold, dry (continental polar) air from Canada hugs the flat topography of the Northern Plains, acting like a bulldozer as it plows its way south. The leading edge of this air mass is known as a cold front. We often see these on the nightly weather report as blue lines with triangles. As winter turns into spring, the invisible divide between the colder air of the north and the warmer air of the south–referred to as the Polar Jet Stream[5]–begins migrating northward, passing over South Dakota, as the sun angle at higher latitudes increases with the changing of the seasons. This increasing solar radiation warms the northern hemisphere (including South Dakota), bringing it out of winter. As moist, warm (maritime tropical) air begins moving north, originating from the Southeast and Gulf of Mexico, the battle begins.

As cold (dense) Canadian air moves south, the less-dense, warmer, and more humid maritime tropical air mass in front of it is abruptly forced upward–the only direction the air can go–along the leading edge of the advancing cold front. This upward forcing initiates a rapid cooling of the warm and humid tropical air. As air rises away from the surface–the source of the lower atmosphere's heat energy–the temperature of the air begins to drop. As it does so, the air's capacity to hold its humidity (water vapor) decreases until the air cools and reaches its dew point temperature (or saturation point). This is the temperature at which the invisible water vapor gas begins to condense into liquid water. As the uplift continues, so does the condensation process, and the tiny water droplets begin to coalesce with one another and form larger water droplets that eventually become what we see as clouds. If enough heat and moisture are available, uplift and condensation will continue, and the cloud will grow larger and larger in size. As the cloud is forming, if enough lift and water vapor are present, the water droplets continue to form and grow until they become large and heavy enough to overcome gravity and atmospheric winds, eventually falling to the ground as precipitation.

The difference between this process creating a simple cloud, a benign spring rain event, or a supercell thunderstorm that produces hail or a tornado, is largely a function of the amount of available energy (heat and moisture) ahead of the cold front and the temperature and moisture differences between the two air masses.

Normals versus Extremes

South Dakota is a state that straddles the Midwest and Great Plains.[6] It gradually rises in elevation from east to west. The lowest elevation, 968 feet, is on the state's eastern border with Minnesota at Big Stone Lake; the highest is 7,244 feet at the summit of Black Elk Peak in the Black Hills. In between, while there are unique landscape features, especially in the "east river" part of the state (e.g., Coteau des Prairies, the James River Valley, the Missouri Coteau, the Missouri River itself), the western, short-grass-prairie portion rises gradually to the west.

The importance of geographic variables such as latitude and elevation are important criteria to consider. Interior, in the southwestern part of South Dakota, has the highest average annual temperature of anywhere in the state: 50.4°F. In contrast, Deerfield has the lowest average annual temperature: 36.4°F. However, these two communities are only about 100 miles from one another and for all intents and purposes at the same latitude. The difference here is elevation: Interior is located at 2,382 feet above sea level and Deerfield is at 6,100.

Normals

The state's geographic location also helps explain its general temperature and precipitation "normals." The state's average temperatures decrease from south to north, with the exception of the Black Hills (cooler because of their higher elevation). This is explained by the simple fact that the southern part of the state receives sun energy at a greater angle than locations further north. Regarding state climate averages, here is a brief sampling: July average temperatures range from more than 75°F in the south-central part of the state to less than 64°F in the Black Hills. January has averages of more than 24°F in the southwest to less than 12°F in the northeast.

The state's precipitation pattern is one of decreased wetness from southeast to northwest, again except for the Black Hills receiving increased precipitation because of their elevation. This "drier in the west" trend occurs because the eastern part of the state receives much of its moisture from warm, moist air masses that move northward from the Gulf of Mexico. That moisture is typically not available for most of the central and western portions of the state due to the prevailing "westerly" winds that move most of the state's weather systems west-to-east.

South Dakota's centralized location on the North American landmass helps explain its climate. Land masses heat up and cool down more rapidly than large bodies of water. To illustrate this, take a blow torch in each hand. Turn both of them on and begin heating up the surface of a brick (representing land) and the surface of a pot of water (representing an ocean). Hold the flames on each for five minutes, and then shut them off. Which one would you like to touch with your finger?

If you chose the water, you are correct (and smart). The torch, representing solar radiation, increases the surface temperature of the brick much more quickly than the surface of the water in the pot. This is because the heat in the brick is absorbed and trapped mostly at the surface, whereas the water absorbs and distributes the heat throughout the entire vertical profile of the pot. Land and water surfaces on the Earth work in much the same way.

However, the same processes are at work when the flame (or the sun) is shut off. Because the heat in the brick was stored near its surface, it escapes very quickly, whereas the heat in the pot of water–because it was absorbed and dispersed throughout the pot's entire vertical profile–leaves much more slowly. Therefore, we can deduce that land, especially large areas of land (like the middle of the North American landmass), heats up and cools off very quickly when exposed to increasingly direct sources of heat energy; hence, South Dakota's "continental" climate of hot summers and cold winters. Because the averaging-out of hot summers and frigid winters can statistically mute reality, one cannot overlook the importance of climate extremes.

Extremes

As with most climate "normals," they fail to showcase the breadth and depth of South Dakota's climate "extremes." Take for instance South Dakota's average annual temperature. Statewide, the warmest average temperature on record was 50.2°F in 1931; the coldest was 41.8°F in 1917. Yes, you did the math correctly: the difference between the hottest and coldest years on record is only 8.4°F. This distorts the reality of South Dakota's weather and climate.

Here we can begin to dig into the extremes: of the six Great Plains states, South Dakota has the second largest difference between its record cold and record high temperatures: -58°F on February 17, 1936 (at McIntosh) and 120°F in the same year on July 5 (at Gann Valley) and again on July 15, 2006 (near Fort Pierre)–a difference of 178°F. This massive temperature range is surpassed in only one other state: North Dakota (181°F). Compare this with Honolulu, Hawaii's maritime tropical situation: a record low temperature of 52°F and record high of 95°F. This measly range of 43°F (compared to 178°F) showcases the difference between maritime and continental temperature extremes.

Statewide, the warmest summer (77.6°F) and coldest winter (8.6°F) on record occurred in 1936. The warmest month on record was 84.3°F in July 1936, with Pierre, that year and month, claiming the record for the warmest month of any specific location at 87.7°F, while the coldest month on record was -3.6°F in February 1936, with Pollack, again that year and month, claiming the record for the coldest month of any specific location at -11.0°F. In short, 1936 was a rough year to be living in the state of South Dakota.

Average temperatures have risen approximately 2°F in South Dakota throughout the twentieth century, although the increases have a specific temporal trend: warming has occurred in certain parts of the year and times of the day. Looking at average monthly temperatures from 1991 to 2020 compared to the entire twentieth century for the east-central region of the state, November through March temperatures have increased by 1.3, 2.6, 3.0, 2.0, and 1.6°F, respectively. Average temperatures from April through August, except for June, have all decreased, albeit by less than 0.25°F. However, when looking at the average *maximum* monthly temperature (how hot it gets each day of a month, on average), every month from April to October decreases, this time anywhere from 1°F to 2°F, while November through March again warms by the same 1°F to 2°F range.

Switching to average *minimum* monthly temperature (or how cold, on average, it gets each night), every month's average increased, with December and January now experiencing 3.5°F and 4.0°F warmer monthly lows, respectively, with the remaining months of the year being warmer by 1.5°F on average. It is not that summertime high temperatures are increasing (they are actually decreasing), but rather the typically cooler seasons of the year (late fall, winter, and early spring) and cooler times of the day are gradually warming.

Tornadoes

South Dakota is not an awfully windy state, though some regions and specific locations may be more prone to windier conditions than others. A sampling of wind data from 15 weather stations across the state–from Lemmon to Leola, Rosebud to Redfield, and places in-between–reveals the average wind speed in 2021 was 8.2 mph, with maximum sustained winds averaging 39 mph and gusts averaging 57 mph.[7] No month or season was immune from these conditions, but the wind events that South Dakotans are most familiar with are tornadoes.

The National Weather Service defines a tornado as ". . . a violently rotating column of air extending from the base of a thunderstorm down to the ground . . . capable of completely destroying well-made structures, uprooting trees, and hurling objects through the air like deadly missiles."[8] They are most common in the Central Plains and the southeastern U.S., though they have been reported in all 50 states.

Tornadoes are ranked using the Enhanced Fujita (EF) Scale. This scale replaced the Fujita (F) Scale in 2007, which had been introduced in 1971 by Dr. T. Theodore Fujita. This scale categorizes tornadoes using a damage assessment after a tornado has passed. The kind of damage certain wind speeds can inflict on buildings, automobiles, trees, and other structures can be studied in controlled, laboratory settings. When inspectors survey damage after a tornado has passed, the tornado's EF ranking can be retrospectively estimated.[9]

Most tornadoes are relatively weak. Those rated EF-0 and EF-1 account for 80% of all tornadoes in the U.S., yet they account for only 4% of tornado-related fatalities, whereas only 1% of tornadoes are of the monstrous EF-4 or EF-5 variety, but those account for 64% of all tornado-related fatalities. There appears to be an increase in the number of total tornadoes that have occurred nationally since 1950, but no such trend exists with EF-3 or stronger storms. The increase in weaker tornadoes is likely due to enhanced public awareness and better detection and reporting methods in recent decades, as well as people who "storm-chase" and capture smaller tornadoes in sparsely populated areas that would have otherwise gone unreported.

Tornado Ingredients

The ingredients necessary for severe thunderstorms that have the potential to spawn tornadoes do not occur everywhere. While tornadoes have occurred on every continent (except Antarctica), most of them occur in North America–specifically in the Great Plains, Midwest, and Southeast regions of the United States in an area known as Tornado Alley.

South Dakota is in the mid-latitude region of the globe, meaning that it resides in an area where, during the spring and summer months, prevailing global circulation systems drive warm, moist air north from the Southeastern U.S. where it collides with colder, drier air moving south from Canada. For severe weather such as thunderstorms and tornadoes to occur, these two opposing air masses must meet.

As spring transitions into summer, that dividing line between these opposing air masses–the Jet Stream–moves north and begins to undulate over the Northern Plains: for a few days the Jet Stream will reside further north, giving the state access to warmer and more humid air that originated from further south. At the same time, colder, drier air north of the Jet Stream, originating from northern Canada, is plowing its way south. This colder, drier air is heavier and denser, so as it makes its way south and east across the Plains, it hugs the part of the atmosphere nearest to the surface. As the leading edge of this air mass encounters the warmer, more humid air, it abruptly forces it up.

This "forcing" triggers two important events that add fuel to the atmospheric fire that can ultimately lead to severe weather: 1) the rapid cooling of the uplifted warm air and 2) the condensing of invisible (gaseous) water vapor into the liquid water droplets that become clouds and precipitation. Condensation, a process that occurs all around us on most days and is responsible for the formation of clouds, also releases heat into the atmosphere. This heat adds additional uplift that causes even more condensation, and the process keeps occurring until the temperature of the air masses equalize or there is no more moisture to condense. The warmer and moister the air is and the quicker it is forced up, the greater the release of energy.

Therefore, severe weather typically happens on days when the temperature is hot and humidity high. The *greater the difference* between two air masses with respect to temperature and humidity, the greater the potential release of energy might be, and the greater likelihood of the formation of cumulonimbus clouds (aka "thunderheads") that spawn severe thunderstorms that may contain large hail, damaging winds, and possibly tornadoes. South Dakota's central location on the North American landmass, where cold, dry air from Canada meets warm, moist air from the U.S. South, is key to their formation.

Tornado Timing

From 1950 to 2020, there have been 1,833 tornadoes in South Dakota.[10] As late spring and early summer arrive in South Dakota, the potential for severe weather increases as the energy required to fuel such storms–heat and moisture–are found in larger quantities. Forty percent of all tornadoes have occurred in the month of June, and 93% have touched down from May through August. Fewer tornadoes occur in the cooler months of the year. Since 1950 South Dakota has had zero tornadoes from November through February.

Tornadoes are not only found in greater abundance during the warmer months of the year, but within those months tornadoes usually occur during or just after the warmest times of the day. It might seem counterintuitive, but the Earth's atmosphere is not warmed by the sun's rays passing through it. Most warming occurs when the Earth's surface releases long-wave infrared (heat) radiation back into the atmosphere, initially warming air molecules in direct contact with the surface. Adjacent air molecules are then warmed, and the transfer of heat from molecule to molecule begins and continues upward. This is partially why the atmosphere cools with an increase in altitude: as you go up, you move further away from the heat source.

We can dig into this further by explaining the Earth's daily energy budget. Again, one might think that the warmest part of a day would be when the Sun's rays are at their most direct/intense angle, a time of day referred to as solar noon. In South Dakota, because it is north of the Tropic of Cancer, the Sun will never shine directly, at a 90-degree angle, above one's head; at Brookings, on the Summer Solstice, the Sun's rays will be 69 degrees above the southern horizon. On a typical day, it is coldest just after sunrise, *after* the Earth's surface has released as much of the previous day's heat energy as it could have back into the atmosphere, but *before* it begins absorbing that day's incoming energy. As the sun rises and its energy reaches the Earth, the surface begins absorbing it. This absorption continues throughout the day. However, because of the lag-time between when the Earth absorbs the thermal energy and when it is transferred back into the atmosphere to warm it, the warmest part of the day occurs typically in the mid- to late-afternoon hours. It is because of this lag-time in heating that most severe weather events coincide with the late-afternoon hours of the day.Of the 1,833 tornadoes that occurred between 1950 and 2020, the greatest percentage of them (16%) occurred between 6:00 pm and 7:00 pm, just *after* the warmest part of the day. That increases to 51% between 3:00 pm and 7:00 pm, and to nearly 75% when all tornadoes that began between 3:00 pm and 9:00 pm are counted. These storms can linger into the late-evening hours, but typically when the sun sets and the atmosphere loses its fuel source, severe weather dissipates. Indeed, between 3:00 am and 10:00 am only 39 tornadoes, 2.1% of the total, were recorded during the entire 70-year period, with most of them being very weak EF-0 or EF-1 tornadoes.

Historic South Dakota Tornadoes

Situated on the northern edge of Tornado Alley, South Dakota has experienced its fair share of devastating tornadoes. Since records began being kept by the National Weather Service in 1950, tornadoes in South Dakota have killed 19 people, injured 475, and caused well over $250 million in property damage (through 2021).[11]

South Dakota's strongest tornado occurred on May 6, 1965, in eastern Tripp County. It occurred as part of a large tornado outbreak associated with a storm that moved out of Colorado and into Nebraska and South Dakota. Thirty tornadoes touched down that day, including the only F-5 tornado in state history, with estimated wind speeds of over 200 mph. The tornado's path, though not an F-5 during its entire lifespan, was 30-miles in length and at times a mile wide. Fortunately, because its path traversed a very rural part of the state, only one injury was reported. And in true "crazy South Dakota weather" fashion, as tornadoes were whipping through the south-central part of the state, on the cold side of the storm, locations in and around the Black Hills experienced a late-May heavy-snowfall event: 36 inches fell in Lead, 25 inches at Hill City, 18 inches at Pactola Reservoir, and 10 inches at Belle Fourche.[13]

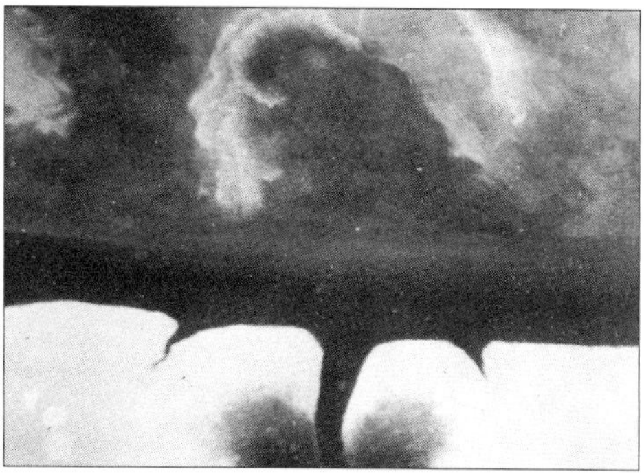

Figure 4:1. South Dakota is notable in tornado history. In 1884, F. N. Robinson took the second known photograph of a tornado–one that occurred just west of Howard, in Miner County, in what was then Dakota Territory on August 28, 1884.[12] *Courtesy Christopher R. Laingen.*

The deadliest tornado in South Dakota, though it occurred before the National Weather Service officially began tracking such data, occurred on June 17, 1944, where at least six F-2 to (potentially) F-5 tornadoes moved through the northeastern counties of Brown, Codington, Day, Faulk, Grant, and Roberts. According to Red Cross records, these storms killed 13 and injured 560 people; the single-largest tornado killed 8 and injured 43. That tornado began just after 5:00 pm about five miles south of Summit and ended shortly after it crossed Big Stone Lake and entered Minnesota. It traveled nearly 30 miles and was estimated to be almost a mile wide. "Farm devastation southwest and south of Wilmont, Minnesota, was as complete as it could be with some farms reportedly left without even debris on the property."[14]

The second-deadliest tornado in state history occurred around 8:38 pm on May 30, 1998, in McCook County–the Spencer tornado–one of eight associated with the early-evening outbreak. The Spencer tornado was rated an F-4, but radar-sampled winds of 260 mph were measured. The tornado traveled 14 miles and the base of the tornado reached its maximum, measuring a half-mile wide, just as the storm hit Spencer. Most of the town's homes, buildings, and other structures were leveled with debris scattered over a large area, including a paper receipt that was discovered 80 miles east in Chandler, Minnesota. Six people lost their lives and 150 were injured in the state's most destructive tornado on record, with damage estimates topping $18 million.[15]

On June 24, 2003, according to the National Weather Service, 67 tornadoes touched down in eastern South Dakota within an eight-hour period; this day became known as "Tornado Tuesday."[16] At the time, this tied a record for the most tornadoes occurring in a single state on a single day (this was surpassed five years later in Kansas when 73 tornadoes touched down). June 24 was part of a larger, three-and-a-half-day outbreak that produced a staggering 125 tornadoes– a record for South Dakota for the month of June. The best-known tornado, an F-4 with winds over 200 mph, destroyed the small town of Manchester in Kingsbury County. Though no one was killed and only four were injured, every structure was damaged heavily or destroyed completely, and the town was eventually abandoned. This storm is also significant because instrumentation laid out in the path of the tornado measured the greatest drop in atmospheric pressure ever recorded: 100 millibars over only 12-seconds.[17]

Droughts and Flooding

Like temperature, South Dakota's geographic setting creates an environment where natural extremes in precipitation are also common. Applied climate scientist Ken Dewey, in his book "Great Plains Weather," explains why South Dakota experiences both severe drought and prolonged rainfall: "Air masses can easily approach and sweep over the barrier-free Great Plains from all directions. If the air masses don't take turns, and either arid or humid air masses begin to dominate the weather pattern, the region can easily move into an arid drought cycle or a moisture-rich, humid flood-producing cycle. It is not surprising, then, that the annual precipitation on the Great Plains has an extreme variability, unlike anywhere else in the U.S."[18]

As with temperature, precipitation normals and extremes are important to differentiate. During the twentieth century, the northwest (and driest) part of South Dakota averaged 15.7 inches of precipitation annually; the wettest part of the state, the southeast, received 23.5 inches. Those 8 inches are important in an agricultural state where every inch of precipitation counts, but 8 inches turns out to be a small difference in precipitation variability–even for a single location. Aberdeen provides a notable example of the extreme variability in precipitation that locations across the state may experience in any given year. In 1976 Aberdeen, in the northeast part of the state, received only 7.72 inches of precipitation. Eighty years earlier, in 1896, 42.12 inches of precipitation fell on the Hub City–a difference of 546%.[19]

Drought and the Great Plains go hand in hand. The most well-known drought was the 1930s Dust Bowl–a drought that wreaked havoc across the Great Plains, including South Dakota. South Dakota's summer of 1936 was 4.5 inches of precipitation below normal, with only 3.5 inches falling in June, July, and August. Additionally, summer temperatures averaged 76.5°F, 6.8°F above the long-term average. More recently, during a widespread, national drought that began in 2012, the state received only 2.86 inches of rainfall from July through September, the driest on record for those three months. The speed at which the drought began and the severity it reached led some to refer to the 2012 event as a "flash drought."[20]

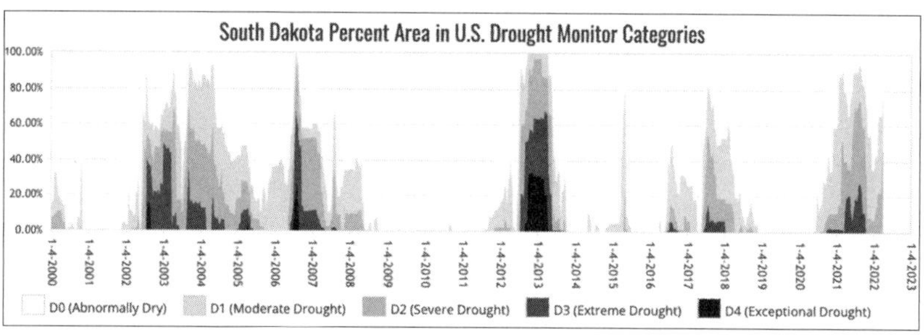

Figure 4:2. Percent of South Dakota area in each U.S. Drought Monitor category, 2000 to present. Source: https://droughtmonitor.unl.edu/. *Courtesy Christopher R. Laingen.*

Conversely, South Dakota can also experience times of excess precipitation that can lead to widespread flooding hazards, especially considering that several large rivers run through the state. The frequency of large-scale, heavy rain events has also increased. Over the past three decades, the state has averaged 14% more one-inch rainfall events as compared to the long-term average. Related to this increase, South Dakota's daily rainfall record occurred at Groton, 20 miles east of Aberdeen, on May 6, 2007, when 8.74 inches fell, and seven years later the record was nearly broken when 8.43 inches were measured at Canton.

Also contributing to the potential for flooding, as well as adding moisture to the agricultural soils of the state, is spring snowmelt. Runoff from a record Northern Plains and eastern Rockies' snowpack in 2011 caused devastating flooding along the Missouri River. Because snowmelt flooding is a longer-duration event than a typical rain-flood event, the duration of the impacts of the Missouri River flood was felt, in some locations, for months. At Pierre, the river was above flood stage from May 24 to September 7.

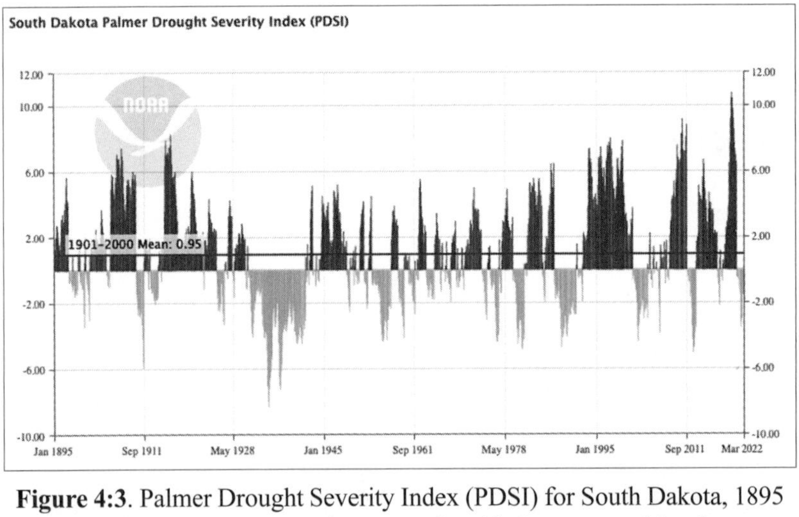

Figure 4:3. Palmer Drought Severity Index (PDSI) for South Dakota, 1895 to 2021. Above zero = wetter than normal and below zero = drier than normal. *Source: https://www.ncdc.noaa.gov/cag/. Courtesy Christopher R. Laingen.*

The ebb and flow and extreme variability of drought and flood cycles in South Dakota are difficult to predict, and in fact no predictable regularity in this cycle has been found. Dewey suggests it was once thought that a 22-year drought cycle existed, but any scientifically grounded proof of that has yet to be found.[21] Some droughts are intense but short in duration, while others have lasted multiple years to more than a decade.

2019: South Dakota's Wettest Year on Record

> SIOUX FALLS, S.D. — "An unprecedented wet year in South Dakota came through in the year-end facts and figures, according to the National Weather Service, with numerous communities breaking precipitation records in a year deemed the state's wettest in 125 years"[22]

Mitchell broke a single-year record (in 2019) for precipitation with 36.5 inches, three-tenths of an inch more than what fell in 1993. Mitchell also had its wettest September on record with 7.63 inches of rain, as well as 117 days with at least one-hundredth of an inch–its average number being only 87. The city accumulated a two-year (2018-19) rainfall total of 58.5 inches, which is more than 15 inches above normal; this was only 5 inches less than the record two-year total set in 1908-09.

Howard experienced more than 7 additional inches of precipitation than normal (43.23 inches in total) and Forestburg received 40.48 inches, breaking its 104-year-record of 36.41. Madison broke its annual record by the largest margin–more than 8 inches–when it received 44.58 inches and, like Mitchell, dealt with flooding in mid-September. Canton and Sioux Falls, among other cities, set precipitation records in 2018 only to break them in 2019, with Sioux Falls receiving 39.17 inches in 2018 and 39.54 inches in 2019. These two years broke the record for any two-year period by over 26 inches. The record precipitation year of 2019 was indeed statewide–from

Rapid City (a record 31.73 inches) to Sisseton, Watertown, Mobridge, and Pierre–all with at least 10 inches more than normal.

The record rainfall totals of 2019 had an impact, not surprisingly, on the state's agricultural landscape. The U.S. Department of Agriculture reported that across the country more than 19 million acres of cropland were fallowed as farmers found their fields too wet to plant, and by the time they dried too late to produce a viable crop.[23] This was 17.5 million more unplanted acres than in 2018, and the most since the data began being reported in 2007. South Dakota made up 3.9 million acres (21%) of that total–the most of any state. Hutchinson County farmers were unable to plant 47% of their cropland, the most of any South Dakota county.[24]

Black Hills Flood of 1972

The deadliest flood in South Dakota history, and one of the worst floods in American history, took place on the night of June 9, 1972. Already strong thunderstorms that had developed over the Black Hills stalled to the west of Rapid City during the late-afternoon hours. As runoff from the estimated 10-inch rainfall event accumulated in Deer Creek, Victoria Creek, Prairie Creek, and countless other small tributaries, Rapid Creek grew to over 300-times its normal volume west of Rapid City. Eventually, the Canyon Lake Dam, clogged by debris, failed, causing severe flash flooding around midnight, and continuing on into the early morning hours of June 10.[25]

Stream gauge data above Canyon Lake showed water levels rose twelve feet in just two hours, with peak flow on Rapid Creek measured at 50,600 cubic feet per second–ten times the amount of the next largest flood on record. All told, 238 people were killed in Rapid City, with another 8-13 (reports vary) killed in Keystone, west of Rapid City along Grizzly Bear Creek and Battle Creek. Three thousand more were injured, 1,300 homes were destroyed, along with 5,000 automobiles which, along with other property/infrastructure damage, totaled $160 million (in 1972 dollars). In its aftermath, the floodplain of Rapid Creek was re-developed into a "greenway"–mostly open, green-space (parks) where development is limited. In

1997 a flood warning system was implemented by the U.S. Geological Survey in cooperation with the Rapid City-Pennington County Emergency Management and the National Weather Service.[26]

Hail

Hail forms inside of updrafts within thunderstorms where a portion of the cloud is below freezing. While hail does not contribute any meaningful amount of moisture to the ground in the same way as rain or snow does, hail events can have significant impacts such as causing damage to homes, cars, livestock, wildlife, and even people.[27]

Hail forms when raindrops within a thunderstorm are carried upwards by intense winds where they freeze into small pieces of ice. Hailstones grow by collecting additional layers of ice when they collide with liquid water droplets that freeze onto their surface. Hail falls to the surface when the winds (updrafts) within the storm can no longer support its weight, either because the hailstone grows large enough in size or the updrafts weaken.

Nebraska, Colorado, and Wyoming experience the most hailstorms in the U.S. This region of the country has been referred to as "hail alley," and areas within this region average 7 to 9 hail days per year. Southern and southwestern South Dakota lie along this region's northern edge.

Hail in the Black Hills tends to be a much more common occurrence than elsewhere in the state due to the Hills' higher elevation. Summertime thunderstorms in mountainous areas are common because of orographic lifting (air moving over elevated areas, which causes it to cool and condense, leading to the potential formation of clouds and "weather") as well as the heating of an already elevated topography. So, because of the almost "clock-work" formation of afternoon thunderstorms, the presence of hail–albeit small and of the (usually) non-damaging variety–is more pronounced. Further, because the Hills are elevated, the atmosphere is cooler, so any hail that forms in a thunderstorm is less likely to melt into rain before hitting the ground.

Across the rest of the state, hail is much less common, though when it does occur it can, on occasion, grow quite large and do considerable damage to cars, homes, buildings, crops, and livestock. In June 2015, just north of the Black Hills, a severe thunderstorm produced hail the size of softballs and winds around 100 mph. The hailstones killed livestock and damaged irrigation equipment around the community of Nisland, about fifteen miles east of Belle Fourche.[28]

Like tornadoes, hailstones that are small tend to fall more frequently but do little to no damage, whereas large, damaging hailstones fall far less frequently. Further, most of the state's land area is rural, so the chances of a major hail event occurring over a town/city are small; most of the monetary damage that hail does in any given year tends to be done in rural areas.

In late June 2018 a severe thunderstorm with damaging hail "slashed and destroyed crops and even killed birds and deer across 100 to 150 square miles mostly in Sully and Hughes counties early Wednesday." The storm's path was five miles wide and stretched some 50 miles from north of Pierre to Fort Thompson: "'It was devastating,'" Jerry Sperry told the *Capital Journal*. He farms northeast of Pierre and looked incredulous himself as he surveyed damage Wednesday afternoon. "'I lost half my crop. Some guys lost 14,000, 15,000 acres. There are dead fawns around,'" Sperry said. "'In one field, a blackbird looked like it had been dashed against the rock where its crumpled body lay on the edge of an ex-wheat field. A half-mile from a dead pheasant cock, a hen cowered in the ditch, along a barbed-wire fence, apparently in distress, unable or unwilling to move, even with a camera only a couple feet away.'"[29]

Hail can also cause damage to urban or other developed areas. Houses can have roofs destroyed or broken windows, and automobile dealerships cringe at the thought of hail, but on July 13, 1997, a unique type of damage occurred to an incredibly unique South Dakota institution. The U.S. Geological Survey's EROS Data Center, located about seven miles east-southeast of Baltic, received extensive damage from a severe thunderstorm that moved through Minnehaha County in the late afternoon hours. Just before 4:30 pm, baseball-to-softball-size hail smashed windows in the main EROS building, caused extensive roof damage, and dented government vehicles. Also damaged were the facility's large satellite-tracking dishes, as well as the complete destruction of the center's 504-panel solar array.[30]

South Dakota does hold one particularly important distinction when it comes to hail: the largest hailstone ever recovered and measured in U.S. history fell near Vivian on July 23, 2010.[31] That day, a strong supercell thunderstorm moved across Stanley, Jones, and Lyman counties. The hailstone was found by Vivian resident Les Scott shortly after the severe thunderstorm passed. He immediately placed the hailstone, and a few others, in his freezer, but a power outage caused by the storm allowed time for the hailstone to melt slightly, thus reducing its size. When measured by the National Oceanic and Atmospheric Administration (NOAA) weather forecast office out of Aberdeen, the hailstone measured 8.0 inches in diameter, 18.62 inches in circumference, and weighed 1 pound, 15 ounces. These measurements made it larger than previous record-holders that fell in Coffeyville, Kansas, in 1970 and Aurora, Nebraska in 2003.[32]

Snowfall and Blizzards

South Dakota's neighbor to the east, Minnesota, often claims to have only two seasons: winter and road construction. Winter is an important, often memorable, and sometimes dangerous season for South Dakotans, too. Winter weather conditions, just like droughts and floods, can be highly variable from year to year. The state's location along the track that many winter storms travel makes it susceptible to storms that may dump deep amounts of snow and pack cold temperatures and high winds that create life-threateningly-low temperatures. However, slight deviations north or south of the usual storm track means that winter storms can also miss the state, or portions of it, altogether and instead deposit their snow and blustery conditions in North Dakota or Nebraska.

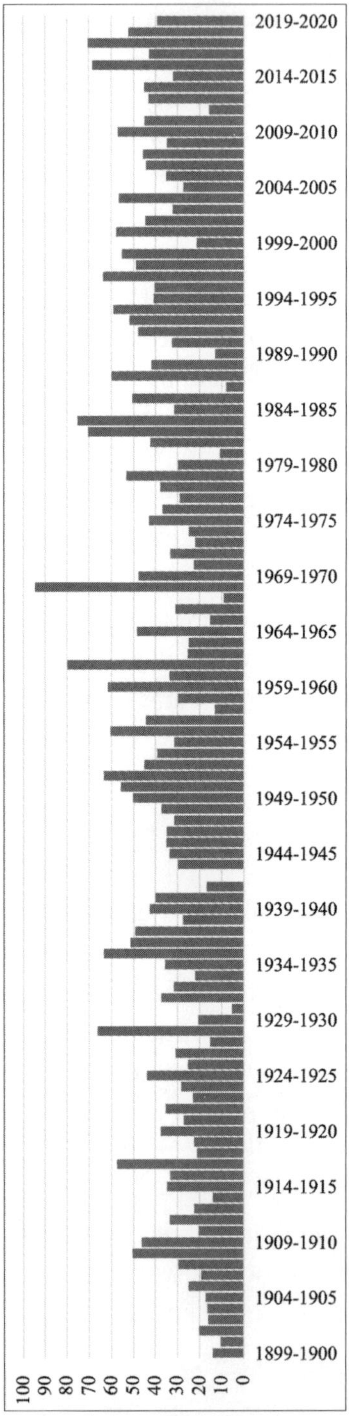

Figure 4:4. Inches of annual snowfall reported at Sioux Falls Regional Airport, 1900-2020. Note: no data were available for the winter of 1942-43. *Source: Midwestern Regional Climate Center's cli-MATE data query tool, https://mrcc.purdue.edu/CLIMATE/. Courtesy Christopher R. Laingen.*

Winter snowfall amounts vary widely spatially and temporally, but the probability of somewhere in the state being hit by a blizzard in any given year is 50%.[33] The Sioux Falls Regional Airport has a nearly continuous record of snowfall amounts from the late 1800s to the present. Other locations across the state do as well but focusing on one reporting station helps make the point that winter snowfall levels can fluctuate greatly. Four winter seasons in the historical record saw less than ten inches of snow: 1894-95, 1930-31, 1967-68, and 1986-87. Five winter seasons have had more than seventy: 1961-62, 1968-69, 1982-83, 1983-84, and 2017-18. Notice that, as with floods and droughts, there are no discernible patterns to years that receive either low or high amounts of snowfall. In fact, in back-to-back seasons, Sioux Falls experienced the third smallest snowfall amount on record (9.1 inches in 1967-68) followed immediately by the largest on record (94.7 inches in 1968-69).

Sioux Falls' greatest 24-hour snowfall (26.0 inches), single storm total (32.2 inches), and greatest monthly total all occurred in February 1962. Seasonally, its earliest measurable snow fell on September 25, 1939 (a trace amount fell as early as September 9, 2020) and its latest measurable snowfall occurred on May 18, 1968 (a trace amount fell in the month of June in 1998).[34]

As mentioned above, blizzards are also common.[35] An early season blizzard raged across western South Dakota in early October of 2013, with 70 mph winds and more than 20 inches of accumulated snow.[36] Lead reported 55 inches over a 3-day stretch, 42 inches of which fell on October 4 alone. Rapid City experienced 23.1 inches, the second heaviest amount in the city's recorded history. Still on their summer ranges, western South Dakota livestock herds were devasted by the early event, with an estimated 45,000 killed and some individual herds in the worst hit areas experiencing a 90% fatality rate. Many have since referred to this event as the "Cattlemen's Blizzard."[37]

Two other historic blizzards occurred in January 1949 and March 1966. In 1949 an otherwise normal winter turned deadly on January 2.[38] Twenty-to-thirty-foot-tall drifts were sculpted on the West

River prairies as 20 inches of snow and 70 mph winds shut down the western half of the state for multiple days. Four hundred travelers were stranded in Wall; railroad lines were blocked nearly everywhere between the Missouri River and the Black Hills. Livestock losses were great, too. Drifts suffocated cattle when they attempted to shelter in areas out of the wind: "Cattle were also cut off from feed, prompting South Dakota's U.S. Representative Francis Case to arrange for the U.S. Air Force out of Rapid City to drop hay on endangered animals in South Dakota and Nebraska. The project was called "Operation Haylift" and saw the USAF, the Farmer's Home Administration (FHA) and the Pennington County Extension working together to coordinate with ranchers. A system of signals was developed so the C-47 pilots knew how much hay to drop at each location. The ranchers drew large "fox-and-geese" symbols in the snow. A circle with an additional spoke meant they needed feed for over one hundred cattle."[39]

The March 2-4, 1966, blizzard was also remembered as one of the worst in state history. What began as a spring-like morning quickly turned into one of heavy snow, high winds, and blizzard conditions, much the same as those experienced in January 1949. Bowdle reported 39 inches of snow, with many West River locations experiencing two straight days of whiteout conditions. This was an especially dangerous storm as many people were scattered across the state for the state high school basketball tournament. Livestock were again decimated with an estimated 100,000 sheep and cattle lost, valued at over $20 million.[40]

Maybe the most tragic blizzard to have ever affected the state of South Dakota, still only a territory at the time, was the January 12, 1888 "Children's Blizzard." Also known as the "Schoolhouse" or "Schoolchildren's" Blizzard, this storm became legendary because it struck suddenly during what began as a mild, sunny day. When the storm began, children were sent home across the featureless prairies by teachers–many of them new to the prairies of the Midwest and unaware of the ferocity of such storms–only to have them lost in the blinding snow and -40°F windchill.[41] The same fate befell others away from their homes, including rescuers who ventured out into the storm in search of their children or farmers attempting to save their livestock. Many bodies were not found until the snow melted the following spring; some were never found. Total death estimates range from 250 to 500; an official number was never settled upon, but at least 170 of the fatalities occurred in South Dakota.[42]

World's Fastest and Greatest Temperature Change

The final extreme weather event to be discussed–and one of the strangest–took place in the Black Hills on January 23, 1943. As mentioned earlier, the atmosphere usually cools as you move further away from the surface. But in certain conditions an "inversion" can form, where when one goes up in elevation the temperature warms. This is more common in mountain regions where cold, dense air sinks and collects in the lower-elevation valleys. This is just what occurred in 1943.[43]

Warm air was moving in from the west on the morning of the 23. Temperatures were above freezing in the early morning hours in the higher elevations of the Black Hills, while temperatures further east in the foothills were still well below zero. As the morning progressed, the front dividing the frigid and warm air advanced and retreated across the region multiple times. In Spearfish, the most extreme change occurred during only a two-minute period when temperatures rose from -4°F to +45°F. This increase of 49°F in only two minutes set the (still standing) world record for the greatest temperature change in the shortest amount of time. Though the record was set, the fluctuations continued. By 9:00 am the temperature in Spearfish had risen to 54°F, only to drop once more to -4°F less than a half-hour later.

In Lead, plate-glass windows cracked, and at one point in the day when the temperature was 52°F, in nearby Deadwood–only two miles away but 600 feet lower in elevation–the temperature was -16°F. As motorists moved into and out of these warm and cold pockets of air, many experienced their windshields immediately, and dangerously, frosting over as they drove.[44]

South Dakota's Weather and Climate Future

Thanks to advancements in the technologies that drive severe weather warning and alert systems, South Dakota residents are today much safer from the state's sometimes severe, life-threatening weather events. The earliest weather alerts were sent by telegraph and eventually by telephone before the adoption of technologies such as radar after World War II. Today's most advanced system is known as NEXRAD (next generation radar). South Dakota has three NEXRAD sites: Aberdeen, Rapid City, and Sioux Falls. These three installations provide nearly complete coverage of the state, with gaps filled in by stations in Bismarck and North Platte. Gaps are also often filled with local and regional television stations that have their own (non-NEXRAD) radar installations that help keep their viewers safe and informed.

Looking ahead, the future of weather (and ultimately climate) in South Dakota–like everywhere else–is subject to change. Average annual temperature in South Dakota has increased nearly 2°F during the twentieth century, a warming trend that is expected to continue. But this doesn't mean that summertime temperatures will become increasingly unbearable. Thus far most of the warming has, and will likely continue, to be observed during the cooler months of the year and cooler times of the day. With a warmer atmosphere, its ability to hold more moisture increases, which is expected to lead to annual precipitation increases, again with the largest increases occurring during the spring and winter. The number of heavy precipitation events that occur throughout the state, as well as increased winter snowfall amounts, are also expected to increase by 10-20%, which could cause increased flooding. Conversely, South Dakota will also remain vulnerable to episodic droughts as warmer temperatures speed up evapotranspiration rates that quicken the loss of any available soil moisture.[45]

South Dakota is one of the greatest places to find oneself with regard to the ability to experience a majority of the planet's overall weather arsenal–minus hurricanes–from one year to the next: floods, droughts, hail, thunderstorms, tornadoes, strong winds, dust storms, blizzards, heavy snows, and extreme hot and cold temperatures. It is this variety in weather which has and will continue to shape South Dakota's history.

Notes

1 All data in this chapter, unless otherwise referenced, were obtained from National Oceanic and Atmospheric Administration (NOAA) or National Weather Service (NWS) sources, including NOAA's National Centers for Environmental information Climate at a Glance website (https://www.ncdc.noaa.gov/cag/) and various sub-pages of https://www.weather.gov.

2 "Weather" refers to specific events or short-term, happening-right-now atmospheric conditions. "Climate" refers to the accumulation and averaging of weather statistics, temperature for example, over *at least* a 30-year period.

3 NWS Sioux Falls (@NWSSiouxFalls), "DYK: Since Friday the Dakotas have experienced…," Twitter post, April 24, 2022, https://twitter.com/NWSSiouxFalls/status/1518280242787356672?cxt=HHwWgMCszcX1gZIqAAAA.

4 Jack Williams, "Why Dry Air is Heavier Than Humid Air," *The Washington Post*, August 5, 2013, https://www.washingtonpost.com/news/capital-weather-gang/wp/2013/08/05/why-dry-air-is-heavier-than-humid-air/.

5 "The Jet Stream," National Weather Service, accessed April 13, 2022, https://www.weather.gov/jetstream/jet.

6 Jon K. Lauck, ed., *The Interior Borderlands: Regional Identity in the Midwest and Great Plains* (Sioux Falls: Center for Western Studies, 2019), 327.

7 "Archives, Local Data," Mesonet at SDState, accessed April 22, 2022, https://climate.sdstate.edu/archive/.

8 "Tornado Safety," National Weather Service, accessed April 13, 2022, https://www.weather.gov/safety/tornado.

9 EF-Scale rankings and associated wind speeds are as follows: EF-0 = 65-85mph (gale); EF-1 = 86-110 mph (moderate); EF-2 = 111-135 mph (significant); EF-3 = 136-165 mph (severe); EF-4 = 166-200 mph (devastating); EF-5 = >200mph (incredible).

10 "Storm Events Database," National Oceanic and Atmospheric Administration, National Centers for Environmental Information, accessed April 13, 2022, https://www.ncdc.noaa.gov/stormevents/choosedates.jsp?statefips=46%2CSOUTH+DAKOTA.

11 Undoubtedly, countless other undocumented tornadoes occurred in South Dakota prior to 1950 which killed, injured, and destroyed property. While those that occurred in more recent decades prior to 1950, such as the outbreak of June 17, 1944, had accounts that were written down about their path, damage, fatalities, and injuries, no exhaustive, accurate list of South Dakota tornadoes exists. Official severe weather statistics kept by

the National Oceanic and Atmospheric Administration can be found here: https://www.ncdc.noaa.gov/stormevents/.

[12] John T. Snow, "Early Tornado Photographs," *Bulletin of the American Meteorological Society* 65:4 (April 1984): 360-63, https://doi.org/10.1175/1520-0477(1984)065<0360:ETP>2.0.CO;2.

[13] "May 8, 1965 Tripp County F5 Tornado," National Weather Service, accessed April 13, 2022, https://www.weather.gov/unr/1965-05-08.

[14] "This Day in Weather History: June 17th," National Weather Service, accessed April 13, 2022, https://www.weather.gov/abr/This_Day_in_Weather_History_Jun_17.

[15] Michael Klinski, "Spencer Tornado: Twenty Years Ago, Six People Died During Storm," *Argus Leader* (Sioux Falls), May 30, 2018, https://www.argusleader.com/story/news/crime/2018/05/30/spencer-south-dakota-tornado-twenty-years-ago-six-people-died-during-storm/655233002/. Additional information can be found here: https://www.weather.gov/images/fsd/events/spencer1998/Slide1.PNG

[16] "24 June 2003 Tornado Outbreak," National Weather Service, accessed April 13, 2022, https://www.weather.gov/fsd/20030624-tornadooutbreak.

[17] "Record Pressure Drop Recorded with Manchester Tornado–24 June 2003," National Weather Service, accessed April 13, 2022, https://www.weather.gov/fsd/20030624-tornadosamaras.

[18] Kenneth F. Dewey, *Great Plains Weather* (Lincoln: University of Nebraska Press, 2019), 76.

[19] Dewey, 77.

[20] Dewey, 77.

[21] Dewey, 77-78.

[22] Marcus Traxler, "South Dakota Communities Rack Up Record Precipitation Totals in 2019," *Aberdeen News*, January 2, 2020, https://www.aberdeennews.com/story/news/2020/01/02/south-dakota-communities-rack-up-record-precipitation-totals-in-2019/43643893/.

[23] "Report: Farmers Prevented from Planting Crops on More than 19 Million Acres," Farm Service Agency, U.S. Department of Agriculture, accessed April 13, 2022, https://www.fsa.usda.gov/news-room/news-releases/2019/report-farmers-prevented-from-planting-crops-on-more-than-19-million-acres#:~:text=19%20Million%20Acres-,Report%3A%20Farmers%20Prevented%20from%20Planting%20Crops%20on%20More%20than%2019,Department%20of%20Agriculture%20(USDA).

[24] Beth Burger and Doug Caruso, "Nearly 4 Million Acres Unplanted in South Dakota Because of Excess Rain," *Aberdeen News*, August 14, 2019, http://www.aberdeennews.com/news/nearly-4-million-acres-unplanted-in-south-dakota-because-of-excess-rain/article_776e3119-f4b8-587d-80c2-f45b112b779c.html?utm_medium=social&utm_source=email&utm_campaign=user-share.

[25] "Flooding in South Dakota," National Weather Service, accessed April 13, 2022, https://www.weather.gov/safety/flood-states-sd.

[26] "The 1972 Black Hills-Rapid City Flood," U.S. Geological Survey, Dakota Water Science Center, accessed April 13, 2022, https://www.usgs.gov/centers/dakota-water/science/1972-black-hills-rapid-city-flood?qt-science_center_objects=0#qt-science_center_objects.

[27] "Severe Weather 101: Hail Basics," National Oceanic and Atmospheric Administration, National Severe Storms Laboratory, accessed April 13, 2022, https://www.nssl.noaa.gov/education/svrwx101/hail/.

[28] "June 19, 2015 Tornado, Softball Hail, and 100 MPH Winds," National Weather Service, accessed April 13, 2022, https://www.weather.gov/unr/2015-06-19.

[29] Stephen Lee, "Hail, Wind, Rain Ruin Crops, Kill Wildlife in Wide Swath Across Sully, Hughes Counties, *Capital Journal* (Pierre), June 27, 2018, https://www.capjournal.com/news/hail-wind-rain-ruin-crops-kill-wildlife-in-wide-swath-across-sully-hughes-counties/article_81c755c2-7a80-11e8-87b8-cf89491fb6e6.html?utm_medium=social&utm_source=email&utm_campaign=user-share.

[30] "The EROS Hail Storm–July 13, 1997," National Weather Service, accessed April 13, 2022, https://www.weather.gov/fsd/19970713-hail-eros.

[31] A.G. Sulzberger, "Storm Upon Storm for South Dakota," *The New York Times*, November 20, 2010, https://www.nytimes.com/2010/11/21/us/21weather.html.

[32] "Record Setting Hail Event in Vivian, South Dakota on July 23, 2010," National Weather Service, accessed April 13, 2022, https://www.weather.gov/abr/vivianhailstone.

[33] "South Dakota, State Climate Summaries 2022."

[34] "Snowfall Records for Sioux Falls, SD," National Weather Service, accessed April 13, 2022, https://www.weather.gov/fsd/FSDsnowrec.

[35] Blizzards are defined by the National Weather Service as sustained winds or gusts of 35 mph or greater with considerable falling and/or blowing snow causing visibility to drop to <1/4 mile.

[36] "South Dakota, State Climate Summaries 2022."

[37] "October 3-5, 2013 Historic Blizzard," National Weather Service, accessed April 13, 2022, https://www.weather.gov/unr/2013-10-03_05.

[38] David W. Mills, *Operation Snowbound: Life Behind the Blizzards of 1949* (Fargo: North Dakota State University Press, 2018).

[39] "South Dakota Blizzards of 1949 and 1966," South Dakota Public Broadcasting, accessed April 13, 2022, https://www.sdpb.org/blogs/arts-and-culture/south-dakota-blizzards-of-1949-and-1966/.

[40] "South Dakota Blizzards of 1949 and 1966."

[41] Eric F. Grelson, "Blizzard Stories," in *Encyclopedia of the Great Plains*, ed. David J. Wishart (Lincoln: University of Nebraska Press, 2004), 291-92.

[42] David Laskin, *The Children's Blizzard* (New York: HarperCollins, 2004), 252.

[43] "Spearfish's World Record Temperature Change–1943," South Dakota Public Broadcasting, accessed April 13, 2022, https://www.sdpb.org/blogs/images-of-the-past/spearfishs-world-record-temperature-change-1943/.

[44] "The Black Hills Remarkable Temperature Change of January 22, 1943," National Weather Service, accessed April 13, 2022, https://www.weather.gov/unr/1943-01-22.

[45] "South Dakota, State Climate Summaries 2022."

5

"PLENTY OF GRASS WATER AND WOOD": INDIANS, RANCHERS, AND THE NATURE OF THE WEST RIVER COUNTRY, 1876-1916

John Henris
University of Arkansas-Monticello

On 5 March 1903 Chief Lip reminded William Jones, Commissioner of Indian Affairs, that his people had "plenty of grass water and wood" and that "those who lived at the Bad Lands to raise cattle, sheep, and horses should have the land in common."[1] Chief Lip's Sicangu band had settled the Pass Creek District near Eagle Nest Butte on the Pine Ridge Reservation during the 1880s, and in the spring of 1903, they faced increasing pressure from American ranchers across the nearby White River to open their lands to white cattle grazing. After 1876 the destruction of the Lakota Empire and nascent American settlement transformed the nature and environment of western South Dakota. Lakota families adapted new farming and ranching practices within the cultural traditions and ecological margins of the Great Sioux Reservation. American ranchers pushed hard, and sometimes recklessly, against the ecological constraints of the Black Hills and adjacent lands to maximize commercial agricultural production and profit. Lakota families and American settlers often embraced differing worldviews of the nature of the country between the Missouri River and the Black Hills that were sometimes in conflict with one another.

One hundred and thirty years earlier, the seven bands of the Lakota acquired guns and horses from Euro-Americans, pushed across the Missouri River and established footholds in the riparian bottoms of the Cheyenne River, Bad River, and White River watersheds. By the mid-nineteenth century the Pahá Sápa, or Black Hills, and surrounding short grass prairie and bottomlands comprised the heart of the Lakota Empire on the northern Great Plains.[2] Especially important were the Cheyenne River and its tributaries which wrapped around the Black Hills like the roots of a cottonwood tree draining the interior, and the White River, which drained both the Badlands and the Pine Ridge escarpment to the southeast. When winter came, Lakota bands dispersed with their pony herds into timbered bottoms that provided shelter and firewood. Tall and mid-grass on the bottoms greened in spring providing early nourishment to power pony herds impoverished by the long winter months. The land also provided sustenance for Lakota families as they gathered berries, herbs, roots, and hunted small game. Short grasses on the vast steppe prairies that matured in June and July fueled both bison and pony herds, driving the Lakota people into several heady months of activity; the Sun Dance, bison hunts, and the raiding of old enemies such as the Pawnee and the Crow would all take place before the return of cold weather drew the Lakota into the bottoms to renew the cycle.[3] The nature of the Black Hills became more central to the Lakota people as they encountered U.S. settlers, traders, and military personal during the 1850s and 1860s.

The Black Hills uplift, an outlier of the same geological forces that created the Rocky Mountains to the west, was better watered and timbered, and home to more diverse flora and fauna than the surrounding short grass steppe. In drought years, the Black Hills provided the Lakota with a biological reserve; an island of water, grass, timber, and game when such resources became scarce on the high short grass prairies. As bison populations diminished during the 1860s and 1870s, the Lakota began to imagine the Black Hills as a food pack; an ecological enclave of timber, water, grass, and small game that might allow them to maintain traditional ways after the bison could no longer support them. The discovery of gold in the Black Hills in 1874, however, culminated in the military con-

Lakota leader on horseback in full ceremonial regalia.
The Center for Western Studies.

quest of the Lakota people a few years later.[4] The loss of the Black Hills and confinement to the short-grass steppe of the Great Sioux Reservation in 1877, as crippling as it was to Lakota sovereignty, did not necessarily lead to the abandonment of traditional hunting and gathering strategies. Bison hunting continued until the last herds were extirpated in 1883, while riparian bottomlands of the Great Sioux Reservation continued to provide protection from winter, timber for fuel, berries, roots, small game, and early spring grass for a few remaining Indian ponies. More significantly, the Lakota people continued to compete with American settlers for antelope, deer, and other natural resources in a vast swath of country west of the Great Sioux reservation and north of the Belle Fourche River, including the Slim Buttes and Cave Hills, well into the 1890s.[5]

When the Great Sioux War ended in 1877, the U.S. government determined not just to take the Black Hills but also reengineer traditional Lakota relationships with nature by turning the Lakota into farmers and ranchers. Indian agents sought to dismantle the mobile Indian camps and encourage individual families to take up scattered settlements along the river bottoms where they could raise cattle and work the soil. In 1881 Agent Valentine McGillycuddy wrote that the Oglala were "scattering out" on the Pine Ridge Agency and settling "the creek bottoms for a distance of forty miles."[6] The end of Lakota sovereignty compelled the Lakota people to use the natural resources of the bottoms in new ways. Taking home-lots and planting gardens fixed Lakota families to the land and compelled them to think of the bottoms in terms of timber, cultivation, and grasses for winter forage. Riparian woodland groves, a traditional source of firewood, were now expected to provide additional timber for permanent dwellings, barns, outbuildings, corrals, and fence posts. Bottom meadows of invaluable mixed grasses where Indian ponies and bison once grazed, now needed to be managed and cut for hay to provide winter feed; prairie sod needed to be broken for garden plots and small till fields to produce corn, English grains, and garden vegetables.[7]

As the Lakota constructed permanent homes in river bottoms, established cattle herds, and fenced garden lots, they altered their relationship with the limited timber resources of cottonwood, green ash, oak, elm, cedar, and yellow pine, of the Great Sioux Reservation in unexpected ways. On the Standing Rock Agency cottonwood logs were used for home construction.[8] While on the Cheyenne River Agency logs from extensive cedar breaks proved much more durable for cabins, those cedar groves were quickly exhausted.[9] Lakota cut green ash, oak, and cottonwood for firewood and fence posts, and gathered driftwood from sand bars and deadfall as well. Oglala and Sicangu of the Pine Ridge and Rosebud Agencies were more fortunate still, in that they had access to stands of yellow pine south of the White River along the aptly named Pine Ridge escarpment. Indian agents provided the Oglala and Sicangu with access to portable sawmills from which they harvested logs to produce pine shingles, roofing timber, and floorboards.[10] Timber depletion by wildfire in bottomland groves across the Great Sioux Reservation was somewhat offset by Lakota livestock practices; there was a reduction in fire damage to trees along bottoms where Indian herds tended to graze which kept down combustible grass during the hot dry summer months.[11] Agent McGillycuddy thought that the transition from lodges to log homes conserved bottomland timber. "Another and not insignificant benefit resulting from the use of stoves," wrote McGillycuddy, "is the protection of trees in the valleys, consisting of ash, cottonwood, box elder, and hackberry, as an open fire in a lodge precludes to a great extent the use of pine on account of smoke."[12] McGillycuddy explained that the addition of cooking stoves to log dwellings allowed Indians to conserve bottomland timber by burning pine instead, "the proper fuel of the country."[13]

During the 1880s Lakota families who had constructed permanent homes in river bottoms embraced the new seasonal cadences of tilling the soil, growing crops, and cutting and storing hay. Lakota farmers discovered that Indian ponies were too diminutive to break prairie sod, and agency officials stepped in to provide teams of oxen, or to preemptively till the one-to-five-acre plots strategically placed along river bottoms to encourage Indian agricultural settlement.[14] Some Lakota farmers held back cattle from their beef rations and broke the steers in to create their own plow teams.[15] By the early 1880s the bottomlands of the Great Sioux Reservation were awash in gardens, and less often small till fields, consisting of pumpkins, melons, potatoes, corn, and wheat with sturdy fences to keep out roving livestock. Indian agents noticed, however, that many Lakota families tended to work small patches in larger fenced fields communally; and they preferred to abandon their fields each year and break new ground rather than cultivate or weed existing land.[16] These agricultural strategies were likely introduced by the Lakota to save labor and allow for travel and hunting during the summer months, and to conserve timber and wire for fencing.

Soils on the Great Sioux Reservation were generally fertile, especially in the bottoms; the limiting environmental factors to successful Lakota cultivation were rainfall and the growing season. Corn and wheat could not be considered reliable, as spring often arrived late on the steppe prairie while drought, heat waves, incessant wind, and autumnal frost often prematurely ended the growing season before the harvest matured. In 1882, for example, Agent William Swan reported that a "succession of storms" followed by drought and "intensively hot winds have destroyed all kinds of vegetation" on the Cheyenne River Agency.[17] Precipitation varied across the Great Sioux Reservation averaging from sixteen to twenty inches; enough reliably to grow corn and grains; however, rainfall was erratic, varying significantly from year to year, and often rain did not fall during the five-month growing season from May to September when it was most needed by Lakota farmers. Most Indian agents on the Great Sioux Reservation had only to experience a few growing seasons to become convinced that ranching was the future of the Lakota people, and that extensive agriculture must be abandoned for small garden lots. Agent McGillycuddy stated frankly in 1882 that the Pine Ridge Agency was not to be regarded as "a practical agricultural region for Indians," except perhaps for "raising kitchen vegetables," and seven years later in 1889 he similarly confided that the district should be regarded as "pre-eminently a grazing country."[18]

The Great Sioux Reservation was more adapted to ranching than agriculture; however, excessive summer heat, frigid winters, and erratic rainfall stymied Lakota efforts to raise beef cattle. During the 1880s Indian Agents annually distributed cattle, sometimes as compensation for Indian pony herds taken by the federal government in 1876, to Lakota families for the purpose of starting family herds.[19] Lakota ranchers further increased their nascent herds by augmenting them with cattle from their beef rations; and by the early mid-1880s, some Lakota ranchers were participating with white neighbors in the annual Black Hills Roundup on the open range between the White and Cheyenne Rivers and selling two and three-year-old steers to neighboring white settlers and commercial buyers.[20] Summer drought diminished the carrying capacity of the short grass prairie, while blowing winter snows covered short grasses utilized for winter grazing. Agent Swan reported that "grass is very thin and scarce this season," on the Cheyenne Agency in 1884, and Agent James McLaughlin recounted that the winter of 1891 set in by November 10 and that a foot of snow blanketed parts of the Standing Rock Agency making it difficult for cattle to find winter feed "except on the hill tops from which the snow has blown off."[21] Hay meadows might be burned over one year and ruined by excessive rainfall the next as Oglala ranchers on the Pine Ridge Agency were only too aware. Agent McGillycuddy, for example, recounted in 1888 that the "haying season" was very rainy causing much of the crop to be spoiled and the work to be done again, while the following summer in 1889 the grass crop was "greatly injured" during the first weeks of June on account of "hot south winds."[22]

On the steppe prairie of the West River country, climate and short grasses converged in the proper combination to create an excellent winter grazing pasture. Short grasses, even those un-grazed during the summer, could not be cut for hay; but, in the absence of significant precipitation during the autumn months, the grass naturally cured on the range and retained nutritional value nearly comparable to meadow grass cut and cured during haying season. Indian cattle could graze on this naturally cured range through the winter months, but only provided that the hard winters of the northern Great Plains were mild enough so that heavy snow did not cover these short grasses or inhibit the movement of livestock in and out of the bottomlands which provided shelter from heavy weather.[23] Because of the potential for hard winters on the Great Sioux Reservation, Indian agents believed that cutting and gathering hay each summer from native bottoms grasses was singularly important to the Lakota's success as ranchers. Agent Swan reported that Cheyenne River Indians gathered 1,800 tons of hay in 1884 and increased their yield to 2,500 tons in 1885.[24] In 1889 Agent McGillycuddy lauded Pine Ridge Oglala for increasing their hay production from 4,482 to 6,525 tons year over year; and Agent McLaughlin confided in 1893 that Lakota families on the Standing Rock Reservation "secured a supply of hay last summer and most of them therefore being very well prepared to feed their cattle should the winter turn severe."[25]

During the 1880s and 1890s Indian agents and Lakota ranchers worked in tandem to create cattle herds that would thrive within the environmental margins of native hay and winter grazing which defined the West River country. In addition to compensation for ponies, Indian agents provided cattle as part of annual annuities during the 1880s.[26] Lakota ranchers added to their growing herds by integrating livestock meant as beef rations; as a result of the natural increase in their herds, they were sending a few animals to market by the early 1880s. Growing the size of nascent Lakota herds was important to the success of Lakota ranchers during the 1880s; but not so much as the timing of the introduction of cattle onto the ranges of the Great Sioux Reservation, or the geographic lineage of the stock. Agent McLaughlin, for example, believed that cattle needed to be introduced onto the ranges of the Standing Rock Reservation by summer, and that cattle needed to come from northern Nebraska or the Dakotas to thrive in the region. Summer introduction of livestock allowed time for animals to gain strength and acclimate before the onset of winter; cattle from the Dakotas or northern Nebraska were more likely than stock from Minnesota, or other eastern states, to have already been introduced to winter range grazing, which increased the probability that the animals would survive a difficult winter.[27] By 1890 Lakota ranchers appeared to have mastered the environmental margins of the short grass steppe where they created a stable livestock ecology.

During the 1890s Lakota families discovered the ecological limits of cattle husbandry when the condition and productivity of their native bottomland hayfields began to sharply decline. In 1893 Agent McLaughlin wrote that "grass of suitable length" for cutting and curing for hay could only be gathered "in narrow strips in bottom lands bordering the water courses and ravines leading into them." McLaughlin lamented that "the mowing of these bottoms every successive season also exhausts the meadows in from five to ten years so that the grass runs out and weeds grow up in its place."[28] In response to charges by outside interests that "hundreds of tons of hay every year" was going unused by Lakota families in 1893, Agent McLaughlin reiterated that continuous haying in the bottoms exhausted root systems of beneficial native grasses causing them to give way to weeds, and asserted that "there is not one half the amount of grass suitable for hay on the reservation along the Missouri River bottoms that there was ten years ago."[29] Lakota families faced a stark choice: they could push past the ecological margins of their bottomland hayfields, embracing the open range mentality of maximum resource exploitation and capital gain, or they could manage their cattle herds within the agroecological confines of the West River country.

When confronted with declining natural hayfields and the specter of overgrazed short grass pastures, most Lakota resisted exploitation at the cost of personal economic gain by continuing to embrace communal strategies which strengthened traditional kinship networks and proved to be agroecologically sustainable at the same time. Lakota families continued to limit the size of their herds and fenced off both bottoms meadow and steppe pasture for winter grazing. In 1897 for example, David Griffiths, field agent for the Division of Agrostology in South Dakota, noted while traveling up the Moreau River Valley on the Cheyenne Reservation, that "the Indians have only a few cattle, and it appeared they were taking great pains to keep the feed along the Moreau River for winter use."[30] Griffiths observed that "the Indians make almost no preparation for winter feeding, except to save, as much as possible, the feed around their winter quarters" and that "as they have but a small bunch of cattle, they are able to keep close watch on them."[31] When cattle interests purchased "one hundred and twenty four head of steers" from the Oglala on the Pine Ridge Reservation in 1900, they came from 41 brands each contributing from one to five head, and the district farmer for the Medicine Root District reported just nine families with herds in excess of 100 head.[32] By 1900 Lakota bands had limited their herd sizes, looked to their winter feed, and created a vast untapped grass reserve across the reservations. When drought struck the Pine Ridge Reservation during the summer of 1900, this grass reserve provided Agent John Brennan and Oglala stock raisers with the flexibility to move cattle from the drought-stricken pasture of the western reservation to unaffected range on the east side. Brennan grasped that this reserve provided the Oglala with both autonomy and insurance from the environmental extremes of the district and responded by rejecting all requests from outsiders for permits to graze the so-called empty quarters of the Pine Ridge Reservation.[33]

When American prospectors arrived in the Black Hills in 1876, a few chose to till the soil instead. Isolated mining camps two hundred miles from railheads in Sidney, Nebraska, or Cheyenne, Wyoming, required provisions for men, and fodder for draft animals. The northeastern face of the Black Hills, particularly between the Rapid Creek and Spearfish valleys, was a transition zone between short grass steppe and yellow pine forest often clothed in luxuriant mixed grasses and stands of oak or boxelder; water flowed from spring-fed streams, and precipitation fell in greater abundance than on the short grass prairies stretching away 140 miles east to the Missouri River. Before summer turned to autumn, prospective ranchers cut natural hay on the Centennial Prairie and along Rapid Creek, grazed cattle on False Bottom Creek, and planted oats in the Whitewood Valley.[34] Ranchers extracted capital from cultivated plants and livestock, on lands that only a few years earlier, the Lakota had traditionally used for the seasonal provisioning of timber, wild game, berries, herbs, roots, and native grasses. The Black Hills and adjacent prairie were transformed into ranching country between 1876 and 1916; ranchers took advantage of the microclimate of the Black Hills to push the agroecological margins of the region creating a world of mixed dry farming, intensive irrigated cultivation, orchards, market gardens, and commercial stock grazing.[35]

Between 1876 and 1906 Black Hills ranchers developed a system of mixed cattle grazing and dryland farming, producing wheat, corn, oats, rye, barley, timothy, and alfalfa. The microclimate of the Black Hills, which moderated temperature extremes and provided additional moisture and protection from prairie winds, allowed some ranchers to cultivate wheat and corn in commercial quantities for extra-local markets. Ranchers in the valleys immediately east of the Black Hills gained advantage from the more abundant precipitation and protection from winter winds the isolated mountain chain provided. The relatively mild climate in the shadow of the Black Hills made it possible to grow higher yield winter wheat, cast down upon fields in abundance in late autumn; however, most growers preferred the safety of less prolifically yielding "hard spring" varieties which were planted early to prevent the possibility of winterkill.[36] Ranches near Whitewood, in the northeastern Black Hills, yielded 3,500-4,000 bushels of wheat while Henry Frawley, a rancher on the Centennial Prairie, harvested wheat in yields that rivaled growers east of the Missouri River.[37] Black Hills growers valued corn and wheat that could easily be turned into a fodder crop for livestock. When the summer months were too dry, the growing season too short, or drought made hay and other fodder crops for wintering livestock scarce, corn would provide "stover," earless stocks used for feed; when grass was scarce, wheat, if it became clear that it would not ripen, could be cut as hay for winter feeding to cattle and sheep.[38]

Sheep herding on John Peterson's ranch near Deadman Creek, Pennington County. *The Center for Western Studies.*

Ranchers raised dryland crops, oats, rye, barley, timothy, and alfalfa, almost exclusively as winter feed for cattle and sheep, especially on ranches away from the well-watered northeast face of the Black Hills. Native grasses provided most winter forage when cut and cured, but Henry Frawley and other ranchers improved native hayfields by seeding "tame grasses" such as timothy and alfalfa.[39] One cutting might be expected from wild hay or alfalfa on rain impoverished steppe meadows; however, it was not uncommon to gather two crops of native hay and timothy nearer the Black Hills. Introduced into the Black Hills by Deadwood Lawman and Redwater rancher Seth Bullock in 1881, alfalfa proved especially valuable for winter feed.[40] Under irrigation, the deep tap rooted legume produced three cuttings each season; while on dry semi-arid prairie lands, it could be counted on to reliably produce at least one cutting no matter how dry or backward the season.[41] Still, dryland farming beyond the shadow of the Black Hills was always precarious, as one observer noted in 1903 that "many who in earlier days, attempted to farm without being able to irrigate have abandoned it and use unirrigated land wholly for grazing purposes."[42]

Ranchers recognized that the additional precipitation which fell on the Black Hills and tumbled down mountain streams could be channeled into ditches to irrigate crops such as timothy, alfalfa, oats, garden vegetables, and fruits. Irrigation shielded crops from failure during dry years and often significantly increased yields compared to dryland fields during years of adequate precipitation. In 1876 settlers from the Montana Territory began dividing the valley and constructing irrigation ditches along Spearfish Creek.[43] Soon 5,000 acres were under irrigation, and valley ranchers constructed similar ditches along the east flowing streams of the Black Hills from Spearfish south to Cascade Creek near Hot Springs. The forty-mile-long Redwater Canal which had the capacity to irrigate nearly 9,000 acres in Lawrence and Butte County, was constructed by corporate interests. In 1890 C. L. Wood of Rapid City recounted that he had experienced three summers of extreme drought since moving to the Black Hills in 1878, and that in the irrigated valleys along the eastern fringe of the mountains "crops were as good during this dry season as at any other time."[44] By the 1890s ranchers irrigated 25,000-35,000 acres along the east face of the Black Hills providing insurance against drought, winter fodder for cattle, and high value crops such as apples, small fruits, and garden vegetables for neighboring mining towns.[45]

Black Hills ranchers devoted a significant amount of their irrigated acreage to the production of fodder crops for livestock. In 1902 for example, Spearfish irrigators reported they were able to make three cuttings each season of alfalfa, and two of timothy and clover, extracting from three to four tons an acre.[46] H. M. Gregg of Spearfish reported in 1887 that garden crops including "potatoes, cabbage, turnips, beans, peas, melons, squashes, cucumbers, and tomatoes, grow in great quantity and of superior quality."[47] The yield potential of the irrigated districts of the Black Hills often came at the cost of additional labor and, increasingly after 1900, the specter of water scarcity. Each spring, for example, ranchers formed committees to organize the laborious task of repairing headgates and flumes, cleaning out and cutting back brush and other growth from irrigation ditches, and keeping watch over fish-screens which often clogged with debris, inhibiting water flow.[48] In 1909 the Hawthorne Ditch in Rapid City held water "barely sufficient" to cover its 1,028 irrigated acres, while the last twelve miles of the Redwater Canal had already been abandoned in 1904 on account of insufficient water supply.[49] Still, Black Hills ranchers constructed a hydraulic machine allowing them to push past the environmental margins of the district; this facilitated the production of prodigious quantities of winter fodder for livestock and market crops for Deadwood, Lead, and other mining towns each growing season.[50]

When prospectors arrived in the Black Hills in 1876, they found the district awash in wild fruits such as strawberries, raspberries, currents, and wild plums. During the 1880s and 1890s, a few settlers in the valleys began experimenting with orchards and small fruits knowing that such produce would command top prices in the mining districts.[51] Even in the shadow of the benign micro-climate of the Black Hills, fruit culture was at its northern limit in the eastern valleys in terms of precipitation, growing season, and threat of winterkill. Practical experimentation demonstrated that pears, plums, peaches, and grapes could not be reliably grown in the Black Hills;

many traditional eastern varieties of apples and raspberries similarly failed. During the 1890s and early 1900s, however, Fayette Cook, John Robertson, and others tested apple and small fruit varieties under local conditions to develop a fruit list for the Black Hills.[52] In the Black Hills, most growers, with the notable exception of John Robertson, believed irrigation was necessary for reliable commercial production of fruits. Hot Springs, Rapid City, and Belle Fourche all produced apples and small fruits in commercial quantities; however, Spearfish emerged as the leading apple district in the Black Hills by 1909.[53] In a good year Spearfish ranchers produced thousands of boxes of Wealthy and McIntosh Red apples from their irrigated orchards, which commanded high prices in the neighboring mining towns of Lead and Deadwood.[54]

For a time, a few ranchers in the Black Hills managed to make the annual production of apples and small fruits a commercial success; however, they encountered mounting agroecological crises as orchards matured after 1900. Hailstorms, common during the summer months in the Black Hills, damaged orchards and small fruits alike, while the protection of the neighboring mountains was often not enough to stave off winterkill of orchard trees and raspberry canes. Orchards and small fruits were much more labor intensive and costlier to replace than annual crops such as hay, oats, wheat, corn, and rye. Red raspberry growers such as Fayette Cook and John Robertson were never able to find an eastern variety or hybrid where the canes did not have to be buried, at great expense in time and labor, during the winter months. Irrigated apple producers tended to overwater their orchards, making them more susceptible to diseases such as canker.[55] Black Hills ranchers, for a time, extracted significant capital from horticultural endeavors, though their efforts probably peaked during the first decade of the twentieth century.

Commercial ranching fueled environmental change. Livestock grazing transformed the grassland ecology of the Black Hills and adjacent prairie lands even after the hard winter of 1886-1887 culminated with the destruction of tens of thousands of cattle on the over-stocked open range.[56] Where short grass prairie transitioned to mixed grasses along the Black Hills, or in the Cave Hills or Slim Buttes, even modest overgrazing would see the destruction of tall grasses, and short grass associations would become dominate.[57] On the southeastern fringe of the Black Hills near Hot Springs, where annual average rainfall dropped to just sixteen inches and overgrazing was endemic, prairie grasses would be replaced by sage and cactus.[58] On the steppe prairie east and north of the Black Hills, overgrazing exhausted more nutritious grasses; James Todd observed in 1895, that the "Fort Pierre area seems to have been overfed and weeds are taking the place of native grass."[59] David Griffiths wrote that remaining open range was overgrazed and "as a result, the grasses and better forage plants are eaten or trampled into the ground before the end of the season."[60] "What wonder that the grasses are dying out on the open range," lamented Griffiths while traveling the country around Belle Fourche in 1898.[61]

Ranchers adopted several strategies to increase herd size and stave off the exhaustion of pasturelands in and around the Black Hills. Common approaches for taking grazing pressure off privately held pasturelands during the summer months included sending cattle away by arranging for them to graze on the open range, paying to keep them in grass on other private ranches, or applying for a permit to let them range on the high limestone plateau of the Black Hills Forest Reserve.[62] The Driskill family, prominent ranchers from Spearfish, held grazing permits for the Black Hills National Forest and regularly shipped cattle in autumn from Elmore in Spearfish Canyon after 1908.[63] Henry Frawley, for example, reduced grazing pressure on his Centennial Prairie pastures by arranging with John Baird in 1899 to take Frawley's cattle to graze in the "Cave Hill Country" one hundred miles north of the Black Hills; Frawley made a similar arrangement with Wilbur Newland to take his cattle to pasture on "North Indian Creek, Butte County" in 1904. Frawley paid Baird $1.25 a head to graze his cattle between June and November 1899; while, five years later, he paid Newland $1.50 a head to pasture his cattle between June and November on the assurance that his stock "be kept on good grass and supplied with good water."[64]

As ranchers settled the open range north of the Black Hills, the need to develop timber and water resources in the semi-arid and mostly treeless short grass prairie, or gain access to the "rich soil and luxuriant grass" of the Short Pine Hills and Slim Buttes, became particularly acute.[65] Excellent pasture on the steppe prairie and buttes between the Lakota reservations and the Black Hills were often inaccessible during the 1890s on account of insufficient water for livestock during the summer; the region was too dry for ranchers with allotments to produce sufficient hay to carry their animals through autumn and winter. In 1901 Butte County residents petitioned legislators for new land policies that would encourage small scale irrigation "remote from running streams" for the purpose of constructing "dams, dikes, and ditches."[66] In the Cave Hills, *The Weekly Pioneer-Times* reported, "on the west side of the hill" the Davis brothers had a 180-acre pond which they "use to irrigate meadows" and John Hoskins' dam "irrigates a fine garden and orchard and several acres of alfalfa."[67] After 1900 ranchers constructed thousands of stock ponds to make these ranges more accessible for summer pasturage.[68]

Sheridan Lake, a 375-acre reservoir, is located on Spring Creek, Pennington County. The town of Sheridan, originally called Golden City, was an early mining camp, and is now submerged under the lake. *The Center for Western Studies.*

The buttes, bluffs, breaks, and bad lands of the region north of the Belle Fourche River had in the 1870s been clothed in stands of yellow pine, red cedar, green ash, and cottonwood.[69] By 1900, however, woodcutters with portable mills had stripped merchantable yellow pine from the Cave Hills and Slim Buttes, while cedar breaks and hardwood bottoms groves were consumed for fence posts or firewood, and area ranchers burned low grade lignite coal strip-mined from shallow pits to offset pressure on remaining timber stands.[70] Boosters encouraged tree planting and the setting of shelterbelts to provide fuel and protection, buffering homes, outbuildings, and cultivated fields from winter snows and prairie winds. Settlers planted rows of drought tolerant cottonwood; some used Norway poplars, jack pine, or golden willow, while others recommended native Black Hills evergreens, yellow pine, and "Black Hills Spruce" on the account that they were acclimated, required fewer protective rows than deciduous species, and had proven drought resistance.[71] H. L. Jeffries, a rancher west of the Missouri River, called for ranchers to seed new deciduous woodlots by planting ash and cottonwood on the region's growing number of stock dams, where the young trees would be able to tap into moisture and seepage from these earthen dams.[72]

Remaining open range east and north of the Black Hills, however, continued to decline in productivity, and in 1897 David Griffiths observed that the grass "on the Indian reservation is much superior" to that under the direction of white ranchers to the west "being that it is not pastured so closely."[73] Desperate for good pasture, even small ranchers along the Cheyenne and White Rivers east of Hot Springs began to press for access to reservation grasslands after 1900; these constituted the only grass reserves still largely untouched by grazing pressure. In September of 1900, J. E. Reddick, of Hermosa, hoped to gain access to some part of the neighboring Pine Ridge Reservation to the east to winter over his livestock.[74] In January of 1901 Francis Pouch, a rancher from Folsom, east of Hermosa, inquired about leasing a small section of land in the Indian Creek basin. The land was within the Pine Ridge Reservation, but the country was so rough that the reservation fence did not enclose this land and passed instead to the south of the head of the basin. John Brennan, Pine Ridge Indian agent, approved of the permit arguing that "it is right on the edge of the Bad Lands, and a more desolate or God-forsaken piece of country would be hard to find."[75] As the quality of open range north and east of the Black Hills declined after 1900, pressure increased to compel the Lakota to lease unallotted lands to outsiders for grazing livestock.[76]

After 1900 the world the Lakota weaved together of bottomlands home-lots, gardens, small grains plots, timber, meadow, and pasture tied to a vast steppe common short grass reserve began to unravel. White ranchers wielded increasing political pressure to open the vast grass commons of the former Great Sioux Reservation to outside grazing, while mixed-blood Lakota families petitioned to increase cattle herds, lease allotments to outside grazing, and sell hay off the reservation. The isolated nature of the Black Hills initially shielded orchards from common diseases. However, apple rust from neighboring infected cedar trees was not uncommon, and the fire blight, likely introduced into the district by contaminated nursery stock, burned through Spearfish orchards not many years later. In the Spearfish Valley, the powerful Homestake Mining Company faced the threat of legal action from valley ranchers over water rights in 1899, which foreshadowed an age of greater water rights conflict during the first quarter of the twentieth century. A few years later, the opening of Indian lands to settlement by white farmers further threatened Lakota autonomy and only hastened the demise of the open range for white ranchers. By 1916 one era of settlement-induced environmental change had ended, and the decades which followed would bring new agroecological challenges for both Lakota families and white ranchers in western South Dakota.[77]

Notes

[1] Chief Lip to Commissioner of Indian Affairs, March 5, 1903, Bureau of Indian Affairs, Special Case Files, 1893–1905, microfilm edition, MF 5043, South Dakota Historical Society, Pierre, SD.

[2] Richard White, "The Winning of the West: The Expansion of the Western Sioux in the Eighteenth and Nineteenth Centuries," *The Journal of American History* 65:2 (September 1978): 321–24; Pekka Hämäläinen, "The Rise and Fall of Plains Indian Horse Culture," *The Journal of American History* 90:3 (December 2003): 859–62.

[3] Pekka Hämäläinen, *Lakota America: A New History of Indigenous Power* (New Haven: Yale University Press, 2019), 171–74; Jeffrey Ostler, *The Lakotas and the Black Hills: The Struggle for Sacred Ground* (New York: Penguin Books, rpt ed., 2011), 13–20.

[4] Ostler, *The Lakotas*, 75; Hämäläinen, *Lakota America*, 191–92, 234–36.

[5] R. M. Allen to Daniel M. Browning, April 30, 1894, James McLaughlin Papers, microfilm edition, MF 1427, South Dakota Historical Society, Pierre, SD; Jeffrey Ostler, "'The Last Buffalo Hunt' and Beyond: Plains Sioux Economic Strategies in the Early Reservation Period," *Great Plains Quarterly* 21:2 (Spring 2001): 119. Lee R. Boyer, "Conflict Over Hunting Rights: Lightening Creek, 1903," *South Dakota History* 23:4 (Winter 1993): 301.

[6] US Office of Indian Affairs, *Annual Report of the Commissioner of Indian Affairs, for the Year 1881* (Washington, DC, 1881), 46; See also *US Office of Indian Affairs, Annual Report of the Commissioner of Indian Affairs, for the Year 1884* (Washington, DC, 1884), 37, 43.

[7] Ostler, "Last Buffalo Hunt," 120.

[8] James McLaughlin to Commissioner of Indian Affairs, August 21, 1890, McLaughlin Papers, MF 1425.

[9] F.C. Campbell to Commissioner of Indian Affairs, July 20, 1914, Cheyenne River Agency, Records, 1884–1948, microfilm edition, MF 5397, South Dakota State Historical Society, Pierre, SD.

[10] US Office of Indian Affairs, *Annual Report of the Commissioner of Indian Affairs, for the Year 1879* (Washington, DC, 1879), 41; *Annual Report Indian Affairs, 1884*, 46; US Office of Indian Affairs, *Annual Report of the Commissioner of Indian Affairs, for the Year 1889* (Washington, DC, 1889), 160.

[11] US Department of Agriculture, Division of Agrostology, *A Report Upon the Grasses and Forage Plants and Forage Conditions of the Eastern Rocky Mountain Region*, by Thomas Williams, Bulletin No. 12 (Washington, DC, 1898), 21.

[12] *Annual Report Indian Affairs, 1881*, 46.

[13] *Annual Report Indian Affairs, 1881*, 46

[14] *Annual Report Indian Affairs, 1879*, 21.

[15] *Annual Report Indian Affairs, 1884*, 37.

[16] *Annual Report Indian Affairs*, 1884, 43; US Office of Indian Affairs, *Annual Report of the Commissioner of Indian Affairs, for the Year 1887* (Washington, DC, 1887), 44. For weeds and Indian agriculture among the Hidatsa in the upper Missouri Valley see Mark Fiege, "The Weedy

West: Mobile Nature, Boundaries, and Common Space in the Montana Landscape," *Western Historical Quarterly* 36:1 (Spring 2005): 28.

[17] US Office of Indian Affairs, *Annual Report of the Commissioner of Indian Affairs, for the Year 1882* (Washington, DC, 1882), 19.

[18] *Annual Report Indian Affairs*, 1882, 37; *Annual Report Indian Affairs, 1889*, 156.

[19] Jeffrey Means, '"Indians SHALL DO THINGS in Common,': Oglala Lakota Identity and Cattle-Raising on the Pine Ridge Reservation," *Montana: The Magazine of Western History* 61:3 (Autumn 2011): 4–5.

[20] *Annual Report Indian Affairs, 1884*, 37; Means, "Indians SHALL DO THINGS," 10.

[21] *Annual Report Indian Affairs, 1884*, 20; James McLaughlin to Commissioner of Indian Affairs, January 28, 1892, McLaughlin Papers, MF 1427.

[22] US Office of Indian Affairs, *Annual Report of the Commissioner of Indian Affairs, for the Year 1888* (Washington, DC, 1888), 51; *Annual Report Indian Affairs, 1889*, 156.

[23] James McLaughlin to Commissioner of Indian Affairs, January 28, 1892, McLaughlin Papers, MF 1427.

[24] *Annual Report Indian Affairs, 1884*, 20; US Office of Indian Affairs, *Annual Report of the Commissioner of Indian Affairs, for the Year 1885* (Washington, DC, 1885), 17.

[25] *Annual Report Indian Affairs, 1889*, 156; James McLaughlin to Commissioner of Indian affairs, January 5, 1893, McLaughlin Papers, MF 1427.

[26] Means, "Indians SHALL DO THINGS," 9–10.

[27] James McLaughlin to Commissioner of Indian Affairs, January 28, 1892, McLaughlin Papers, MF 1427.

[28] James McLaughlin to Commissioner of Indian Affairs, January 28, 1892, McLaughlin Papers, MF 1427.

[29] James McLaughlin to Commissioner of Indian Affairs, June 28, 1893, McLaughlin Papers, MF 1427.

[30] Williams, *Report Upon the Grasses*, 21.

[31] Williams, *Report Upon the Grasses*, 21–22.

[32] White Clay District Records of Cattle, September 10, 1900, Pine Ridge Agency, Records, Series 16: Monthly Reports of District Farmers and Related Lists, 1888-1903, microfilm edition, MF 5209, South Dakota State Historical Society, Pierre, SD; Medicine Root District Records of Cattle, December 8, 1900, Pine Ridge Agency, Records, Series 16, MF 5209.

[33] John Brennan to Commissioner of Indian Affairs, December 3, 1900, BIA Special Case Files, MF 5043. For Native Americans and cattle ranching on the northern Great Plains see also Peter Iverson, *When Indians Became Cowboys: Native Peoples and Cattle Ranching in the American West,* rev. ed. (Norman: University of Oklahoma Press), 52–85.

[34] George Baldwin, ed., *The Black Hills Illustrated: A Terse Description of Conditions Past and Present of America's Greatest Mineral Belt* (Deadwood: Black Hills Mining Men's Assoc., 1904), 55–59.

[35] Bob Lee, "Ranching: East to West," in *A New South Dakota History*, 2d ed., ed. Harry F. Thompson (Sioux Falls: Center for Western Studies, 2009), 262–65. For dry farming see, Mary Hargreaves, *Dry Farming in the Northern Great Plains, 1900-1925* (Cambridge: Harvard University Press), 1957. For discussion of environment and the ability of settlers to adapt see, Jon K. Lauck, "Introduction–Finding the Center Line: In Search of the Great Plains/Midwest Borderlands," in *The Interior Borderlands: Regional Identity in the Midwest and Great Plains*, ed. Jon K. Lauck (Sioux Falls: Center for Western Studies, 2019), xxxviii–xxxix.

[36] Baldwin, *Black Hills Illustrated*, 71, 73; US Department of Agriculture, *Grains for Western North and South Dakota*, by F. Ray Babcock, John Martin, and Ralph Smith, Farmers' Bulletin 878 (Washington, DC, 1917), 2.

[37] Baldwin, *Black Hills Illustrated*, 73; Frawley Ranch Invoice, D.J. Toomey, July 22, 1914, series 1, box 2, folder 21, Frawley Family Collection, Homestake Adams Research and Cultural Center, Deadwood, SD.

[38] US Department of Agriculture, *Dry Farming in Western South Dakota*, by O.R. Mathews, Farmers' Bulletin 1163 (Washington, DC, 1920), 8–9, 16. For ranching on the northern Great Plains see, Stanley Vestal, *Short Grass Country*, (New York: Duell, Sloan & Pearce, 1941); Bob Lee and Dick Williams, *Last Grass Frontier: The South Dakota Stock Grower Heritage* (Sturgis, SD: Black Hills Publishers, Inc., 1964).

[39] "Hay in 240 Acre Field," September 20, 1914, series 1, box 2, folder 21, Frawley Family Collection. In September of 1914, for example, Henry Frawley cut 87.80 tons of alfalfa and 34 tons of timothy in one 240-acre field on the Centennial Prairie, south of Spearfish, South Dakota.

[40] Seth Bullock quoted in South Dakota Agricultural Experiment Station, *Comparative Yields of Hay, From Several Varieties and Strains of Alfalfa, at Brookings, Highmore, Cottonwood, and Eureka*, by Albert Hume and Manley Champlin, Bulletin No. 163 (Huron: Bowen Publishing Company, 1916), 319.

[41] Mathews, *Dry Farming*, 10.

[42] US Department of Agriculture, "Irrigation in the Black Hills," by A.B. Crane, in *Report of Irrigation Investigations for 1902*, ed. Elwood Mead, Bulletin 133 (Washington, DC, 1903), 177.

[43] Crane, "Irrigation," 166; Baldwin, *Black Hills Illustrated*, 75; David Wolff, "Black Hills in Transition," in *A New South Dakota History*, 302.

[44] C.L. Wood, "Statement of C.L. Wood, of Rapid City, Pennington County," in Report of the Special Committee of the United States Senate on the Irrigation and Reclamation of Arid Lands, vol. 1, The Northwest, 51st Cong. 1st sess. 1890, S. Rep. 928, 64–65.

[45] US Department of Agriculture, *Irrigation in South Dakota*, by Samuel H. Lea, Bulletin 210 (Washington, DC, 1909), 24.

[46] Lea, *Irrigation in South Dakota*, 25; Crane, "Irrigation," 171. George Baldwin claimed Spearfish irrigators produced three cuttings of timothy and four of alfalfa. See Baldwin, *Black Hills Illustrated*, 75.

[47] H.M. Gregg, "Dakota," in Irrigation in The United States, by Richard Hinton, 49th Cong. 2d sess. 1887, S. Mis. Doc. 15, 114.

[48] Samuel Sandusky, Cook Evans Case Transcript, vol. 2, 8-9, box 6, folder 15, Homestake Vested Water Rights Collection, Homestake Adams Research and Cultural Center, Deadwood, SD; Henry Davenport, Cook Evans Case Transcript, vol. 6, 294–95, box 7, folder 9, Homestake Vested Water Rights Collection.

[49] Lea, *Irrigation in South Dakota*, 34, 51.

[50] Fayette Cook, Cook Evans Case Transcript, vol. 1, 42–44, box 6, folder 13, Homestake Vested Water Rights Collection.

[51] V.S. Johnson, "Commercial Fruit Growing in the Black Hills," in *Fifth Annual Report of the South Dakota State Horticultural Society,* ed. N.E. Hansen (Pierre: Hipple Printing Co., 1908), 124–27.

[52] "Culture of Small Fruits," *Queen City Mail* (Spearfish), April 8, 1896; George Trimmer, "Fruit Culture and Gardening in the Black Hills," in *Early Records of the South Dakota State Horticultural Society, 1884-1904* (Sioux Falls: The Society, 1936), 163–64; John Robertson, "Horticulture in Fall River County," *The Black Hills Engineer* 16:1 (January 1928), 49–50.

[53] Baldwin, *Black Hills Illustrated*, 59.

[54] John Henris, "Spearfish: The Environmental Margins of a Northern Great Plains Apple District," *Agricultural History* 94:2 (Spring 2020): 205–7, 212.

[55] John Robertson, et al., "South Dakota Reports," in *Sixth Annual Report of the South Dakota State Horticultural Society,* ed. N.E. Hansen (Sioux Falls: Mark D. Scott, 1909), 205–16; Henris, "Great Plains Apple District," 216–23.

[56] Nathan Sanderson, "We were all Trespassers: George Edward Lemmon, Anglo-American Cattle Ranching, and the Great Sioux Reservation," *Agricultural History* 85:1 (Winter 2011): 66–67; Bob Lee, "Ranching: East to West," in Thompson, 269–70.

[57] Arthur McIntosh, "Botanical Features Northern Black Hills," *The Black Hills Engineer* 18:1 (January 1930), 86; Herman Hayward, "Studies of Plants in the Black Hills of South Dakota," *Botanical Gazette* 85:4 (June 1928), 389; Frieda Knobloch, *The Culture of Wilderness: Agriculture as Colonization in the American West* (Chapel Hill: University of North Carolina Press, 1996), 102–7.

[58] Hayward, "Studies of Plants," 389.

[59] James A. Todd, "A Reconnaissance into Northwestern South Dakota," in South Dakota Geological Survey, *The First and Second Biennial Reports on*

The Geology of South Dakota, With Accompanying Papers, 1893-6, Bulletin 2, (Vermillion: Dakota Republican, 1898), 67.

[60] Williams, *Report Upon the Grasses*, 50. Weeds were also dispersed in seed, along roads and railroads, livestock, and irrigation water. Fiege, "Weedy West," 29, 31.

[61] Williams, *Report Upon the Grasses*, 50.

[62] John Freeman, *Black Hills Forestry: A History* (Boulder: University Press of Colorado, 2015), 42.

[63] "Spearfish News (Special Correspondence)," *Deadwood Pioneer-Times*, October 15, 1930; "Spearfish News," *The Weekly Pioneer-Times* (Deadwood), October 6, 1932.

[64] "Memorandum of Agreement," Henry Frawley and John T. Baird, May 6, 1899, series 1, box 2, folder 22, Frawley Family Collection; "Articles of Agreement" Henry Frawley and Wilbur F. Newland, May 18, 1903, series 1, box, 2, folder 22, Frawley Family Collection.

[65] Todd, "Reconnaissance Northwestern South Dakota," 46.

[66] "Butte County Citizens Would Reclaim Arid Lands with Dams," *The Weekly Pioneer-Times* (Deadwood), July 18, 1901.

[67] "Butte Citizens Reclaim Lands," *The Weekly Pioneer-Times* (Deadwood), July 18, 1901.

[68] South Dakota Geological Survey, *The Geography of South Dakota: A Study in Regional Geography,* by Stephen Visher, Bulletin 8 (Pierre: State Publishing Co., 1918), 118.

[69] Todd, "Reconnaissance Northwestern South Dakota," 46; South Dakota Geological Survey, *Report on the Biology of Harding County, Northwestern South Dakota*, by Stephen Visher, Bulletin 6 (Pierre: State Publishing Co., 1914), 12.

[70] "Attempts Being Made to Develop the Deposits," *Argus-Leader* (Sioux Falls), September 18, 1906; "Lignite Coal in Harding County," *The Weekly Pioneer-Times* (Deadwood, SD), December 1, 1910; South Dakota State Planning Board, *South Dakota Coal: A Preliminary Report of the Mineral Resources Committee*, (Brookings: Central Office, 1936), 4, 11–12.

[71] Rudolph Jaeger, "Directors Report for Dewey County," in *Eleventh Annual Report of the South Dakota State Horticultural Society,* ed. N.E. Hansen (Aberdeen: News Printing Co., 1914), 4; A. Norby, "Evergreens for Shelter and Ornament," in *First Annual Report of the South Dakota State Historical Society,* ed. N.E. Hansen, (Aberdeen: News Printing Co., 1904), 84–85; South Dakota Agricultural Experiment Station, *Evergreens in South Dakota*, N.E. Hansen, Bulletin 254 (Brookings, 1930), 25–27.

[72] H.L. Jeffries and George Whiting, "Discussion on President Krueger's Address," in *Ninth Annual Report of South Dakota State Horticultural Society,* ed. N.E. Hansen (Pierre: Hipple Printing Co., 1912), 68.

[73] Williams, *Report Upon the Grasses*, 21.

[74] R. F. Pettigrew to Commissioner of Indian Affairs, September 21, 1900, BIA Special Case Files, MF 5043.

[75] John Brennan to Commissioner of Indian Affairs, January 10, 1901, BIA Special Case Files, MF 5043.

[76] Sanderson, "We were all Trespassers," 62–63.

[77] Sanderson, "We were all Trespassers," 68–69; Means, "Indians SHALL DO THINGS," 10–11; Henris, "Great Plains Apple District," 216–20; Paula Nelson, *After the West was Won: Homesteaders and Town-Builders in Western South Dakota*, 1900-1917 (Iowa City: University of Iowa Press, 1986), 14–19.

6

The Politics of Nature: "Conserving, Protecting, and Improving" Wildlife and Parks during the "Age of Norbeck"

Frank Van Nuys

South Dakota School of Mines and Technology

Prior to 1940, South Dakota's politics and policy making were often linked to conservation. South Dakotans spent much of their time living and working out-of-doors, so the appeal of a conservationist ethos was a "natural" orientation. It was a conservationist impulse, for the most part, strongly tied to support for agricultural and industrial growth, a pragmatic or utilitarian strain typically associated with Theodore Roosevelt in the early twentieth century.[1] Progressive conservationists in the Roosevelt mold maintained that responsible stewardship of the nation's resources would ensure their beneficial use for generations. Irrigation, dam building, timber cutting, mining, and other economic development processes were seen as necessary and positive catalysts to maintaining the nation's capitalist system. Wise and efficient scientific management of natural resources would ensure sustainability and guarantee Americans could enjoy abundance indefinitely.[2]

The one political leader in South Dakota consistently referenced in relation to these features of "Rooseveltian" conservationism was Peter Norbeck. From his entry into public life upon election to the state legislature in 1908 until his death in 1936, no other figure worked harder to advance conservation priorities. In this context, these decades could be christened the "Age of Norbeck" and he offers a template for providing some coherence to uncovering the major threads of conservationist politics in South Dakota. One particularly significant element of Norbeck's contributions lies in the growing emphasis placed on activities without overt attachments to traditional economic development. With the rapid advances of America's industrial economy and burgeoning middle classes in the first decades of the century, conservationists increasingly added recreational and scenic opportunities provided by fishing, hunting, and automobile-based tourism to their agenda.[3]

Conservationist and politician Peter Norbeck holding the reins of a burro, being ridden by Clyde James, at the State Game Lodge, in Custer State Park, in 1927. *Courtesy South Dakota State Historical Society—State Archives.*

As an examination of the material in Norbeck's voluminous papers and state documents shows, other South Dakotans worked just as tirelessly on conservation issues. Inside and outside of the political system, allies furthered the conservation goals with which Norbeck identified, particularly in depoliticizing and professionalizing the administration of game and fish policies, advancing the protection of wildlife in refuges such as Custer State Park, and advocating for creating additional parks and recreation areas. Others pushed back, reflecting diverse perspectives on how best to achieve similar objectives, how much to spend on recreational conservation, or simply skepticism about the value of state parks or other outdoors amenities to the citizenry. Moreover, before, during, and after the "Age of Norbeck," agriculture typically stood out as the economic imperative in most desperate need of lawmakers' focus. As seen during a debate over creating a state park system in 1929, some of the state's farmers and their political representatives were loath to have attention shift away from their existential concerns and settle on recreation opportunities that looked like invitations to idleness. Divisions over these types of conservation questions would also expose the partisan fault lines, intra-party tensions, and regional jealousies that impacted South Dakota politics generally. Ultimately, however, South Dakota conservationists succeeded in shifting toward more recreational and scenic amenities as a core element of their policies and creating, strengthening, and depoliticizing the administrative structure of conservation management in the Game, Fish and Parks system.

The South Dakota in which Peter Norbeck and his fellow conservationists came of political age rested on an economic foundation of providing resources for capitalist markets, and no category of resources held more significance than that produced on farms and ranches. Agricultural policy making at all levels in the late nineteenth and early twentieth centuries was a high-stakes enterprise, as South Dakota's agricultural system underwrote the state's overall economic progress, and its people would exult in the booms and suffer the economic and ecological consequences of the not infrequent busts. In a similar fashion, residents in and around the Black Hills rode the waves of the mining and timber industries dominated by the powerful Homestake Mining Company and subjected to a halting and frequently confusing blend of local, industry, and federal practices and regulations.[4]

South Dakota's "first conservation and development congress," convened in Pierre in late June 1910, represented a milestone in the early decades of South Dakota's agricultural and natural resource conservation policies.[5] Such events grew out of Theodore Roosevelt's hosting of a 1908 meeting of governors for a national conservation conference in Washington, D.C. A National Conservation Commission, headed by Roosevelt's ally Gifford Pinchot, inventoried the nation's natural resources and sought to forge a comprehensive resource management approach. Over the next several years a multitude of state, regional, and national conferences and commissions addressed the complexities of managing natural resources in responsible ways.[6] At Pinchot's request, South Dakota Progressive Republican Governor Coe I. Crawford named a standing State Commission on State Conservation in August 1908.[7]

Elected governor in 1906, Crawford, a railroad attorney from Huron, reflected a rising tide of enthusiasm for Roosevelt and progressive reform among a growing segment of the Republican electorate in the state. Local Roosevelt Clubs and a statewide Roosevelt League had been established in 1905, and the faction's successes in the 1906 election contributed to the 1907 legislative session's achievements on progressive reform measures.[8] On the conservation agenda, an effort to pass a comprehensive game management law failed, primarily due to opposition by "farmer members of the house" who feared trespassing upon their properties by cavalier hunters. More narrow bills protecting wild birds and placing an emergency ban on "killing, hunting, trapping, [and] pursuing" pheasants before January 1, 1915, did become law.[9] In between legislative sessions, Crawford appointed the State Conservation Commission and then won his party's nomination and the legislature's selection as a U.S. Senator. The 1909 legislative session successfully overcame continuing farmer opposition in the house to codify a state game code, which set resident and non-resident hunting license fees and allowed for appointment of the first State Game Warden.[10]

Neither pheasants nor the recently revamped game laws preoccupied the hundreds of registered delegates who began streaming into Pierre on June 29, 1910, for the inaugural Conservation and Development Congress. Chaired by the Conservation Commission, this affair was primarily about agricultural economics, with nods toward the mining and timber concerns of West River attendees. Governor Robert S. Vessey's welcoming remarks extolled the state's unmatched natural resources and potential for continual development but also cautioned against careless destruction. "Great and increasing inroads are daily being made on our resources by our constantly growing industries and our steadily increasing population," Vessey noted, "and he is indeed myopic who cannot see that the enormous demands of our modern complex system of living will rapidly deplete the same unless carefully conserved."[11] Although the two-day agenda dealt with a broad array of topics, including a slate of home economics papers by "several of the most talented women in the state," the bulk of the program dealt with "agricultural conservation."[12]

Irrigation and dry farming garnered a significant amount of attention, but still simmering tensions over Black Hills resources provided the backdrop to the chief drama to be played out at the Conservation Congress. Elements hostile to what they perceived as overbearing federal domination over Western lands by Eastern politicians and bureaucrats in league with corporations hoped to sway the proceedings. "The delegations from west of the river," reported the *Aberdeen Daily News*, "will push resolutions asking that the general [federal] government turn over to the state the control of the coal, timber and water of the state under such restrictions as they [the state] may desire and that the arid lands of the state be turned over to state control."[13] The Congress in the end passed a series of mundane resolutions, beginning with a pledge to make itself a permanent body. An endorsement of the "aim and purpose" of a dry farming congress scheduled a few weeks later in Rapid City denoted backing for that variety of agricultural conservation. In addition, there was a paean to conserving and developing "coal, minerals and timberland, and water power." Wildlife management did not appear in the resolutions and, outside of a recommendation for improving the state's highways, neither recreation nor tourism merited any mention.[14]

Only the first of what state leaders hoped would be many more such meetings, the Conservation Congress in 1910 reflected the aspirations of leading figures in conservation policy making at that moment. Ultimately, however, neither the Conservation Commission nor the Conservation and Development Congresses endured over the long term.[15] While South Dakota Republicans did commit rhetorically to advancing the economic development version of conservation that predominated in 1910[16] and conservation policies would continue to address "coal, minerals and timberland, and water power," deepening concerns about vanishing wildlife and the need to preserve some areas for human recreation would predominate in South Dakota conservation politics for years to come. Peter Norbeck would assume prominence as the most thoroughly committed conservation leader in South Dakota and strongly influence progress on constructing the essential structure of the state's conservation administration in these areas.

Rising at about the same time as the State Conservation Commission and its Congresses, but destined not to disappear so quickly, Peter Norbeck would become synonymous with conservation battles, and a few significant successes, at both the state and national levels. Following hardscrabble beginnings on the family farm near Vermillion, Norbeck's development of an artesian well drilling business led to financial stability. After establishing himself, his family, and business in Redfield, Norbeck turned to politics, winning election to the state senate as a Progressive Republican in 1908. He supported Theodore Roosevelt's progressive insurgency in 1912 while securing his own election to a third term in the state senate. After one term as lieutenant governor, Norbeck parlayed his popularity among farmers, voters of Scandinavian extraction, and fellow progressives into election as governor in 1916 and 1918. From there it was on to Washington, where he served in the U.S. Senate from 1921 until his death in December 1936.[17]

It is unclear what sparked Norbeck's passion for conservation, but, according to his biographer, Gilbert C. Fite, it was clearly there.[18] A feature article on Norbeck published in *American Forest* magazine in 1932 centered his devotion to conservation in his Scandinavian background and rural upbringing. "I couldn't help it; it was in my blood," Norbeck explained. "My father's folks were Swedes. They were mountain people. You might have called some of them hill-billies. But they were lovers of nature. I grew up hearing the beauties of nature freely discussed and having them pointed out to me. My mother came from one of the most beautiful sections of Norway and the love of beauty and of nature was born in her and in her people."[19] A nature-loving family heritage and a working life of farming and well-drilling hardly separated Norbeck from other South Dakotans of his generation. As integral as he turned out to be in advancing conservation policy for the state, Norbeck was certainly not alone. He had a multitude of allies from every corner of South Dakota, among them newspaper editors, such as John A. Stanley of the *Lead Call*, legislators like State Senator John R. Boland of Rapid City, State Game Warden Oscar H. Johnson, local conservationists such as Dr. H. E. Fankhauser from Woonsocket, and leaders and members of the State Division of the Isaac Walton League.

The establishment and development of Custer State Park, widely acknowledged as the conservation lodestar of Norbeck's career, reflected his combination of pragmatism and "in-my-blood" love for nature. It began, at least as an idea, in 1905, when he undertook the first automobile trip to the Black Hills.[20] Concerned with the depletion of native wildlife, Norbeck conceived of a state-owned game park in the southern Hills[21] and first proposed using state game fund monies to "make a collection of our native wild game, such as antelope, deer, mountain sheep and even buffalo" while a state senator in 1912.[22] In the 1913 legislative session, a game preserve bill sailed through the senate, with a lone Democratic senator casting the one no vote on behalf of farmers, and then passed in the house.[23] Intertwined with the game preserve bill in 1913, a restructuring of the state's administration of game and fish laws created a State Game and Fish Commission consisting of the Governor, Attorney General, and State Game Warden and replaced all county game wardens with three deputy state game wardens and up to five seasonal deputies to assist during hunting seasons.[24]

An early automobile excursion into the Black Hills on the Needles Highway. *The Center for Western Studies.*

As policy, the game preserve and Game and Fish Commission laws demonstrated a couple of important priorities for Norbeck and fellow conservationists. Centralizing state authority over game laws with the Commission, for one, fit well progressive conservationists' desire for efficiency and accountability.[25] Growing appreciation of an increasingly mobile, middle-class public intent on a variety of recreational opportunities likely impressed itself upon them as intently as just protecting game animals for hunters. "The game feature will be the most important attraction in the Park," he wrote to State Game Warden Harry S. Hedrick in July 1914. "In fact, [it] will to tourist[s] and observers be as important a feature as the Park itself." The new state preserve, they hoped, would draw mostly Midwesterners not only to the Black Hills but to ancillary sites of interest around the state and region.[26]

Pushback from area ranchers and some East River opponents who complained of the costs plagued supporters of the preserve during the first several years of its existence.[27] As governor, however, Norbeck's ability to protect the game preserve and transform it into a permanent state park, further improve management of the state's wildlife, and advance other conservation policies received a significant boost. In his 1917 inaugural message to the legislature, Norbeck sang the praises of the game preserve as "a place of beauty and . . . an inspiring sight to see our native wild game grazing quietly along the wayside" and as an eternal "source of profit" from timber sales. His legislative priorities on the conservation front during that session, however, focused on two other areas, protection of game birds and waterpower development.[28]

Re-elected in 1918 after guiding the state through the emergency brought on by American entry into World War I, Norbeck determined to solidify the state's still tenuous and contentious hold on the game preserve. "It is not in fact a State Park," he explained in his message at the opening of the 1919 session, "being school land subject to sale at any time; and unless some action is taken it may within a few years pass into private hands." The legislature, according to the governor, had to act quickly "to create a permanent State Park, a place of scenic grandeur, an ideal recreation spot, and a home for the preservation of the fast disappearing wild animal life of the state." In addition, he recommended a permanent park board to handle oversight and reassured legislators about the costs going forward. "The taking over of this land would not really be an expense to the state; the people of the state own it now; they would own it afterwards."[29] Unanimously adopted in the senate and plowing through minimal opposition in the house, the Custer State Park bill created a board, comprised of the governor and two others appointed by him, with power to hire a forester and assistants to manage the park. The law provided for acquisition of title to school lands in Custer County located within the game preserve and to re-designate them as parts of the park. It also empowered the Board to acquire other state-owned or private property within or adjacent to the park boundary line.[30]

Norbeck's successful machinations to establish Custer State Park with a powerful board capped a remarkable set of achievements in conservation policy making. As a legislator and then as South Dakota's chief executive, the well driller from Redfield had guided and overseen consequential developments in advancing statewide conservation interests, particularly for wildlife protection and management. Over the remainder of his second term as governor, he worked successfully to incorporate Sylvan Lake, the Needles, and the Harney Peak (now Black Elk Peak) area as part of Custer State Park, another 30,000 acres previously under federal control. This addition, designated the Custer State Park Game Sanctuary, operated under auspices of the Norbeck-chaired board, although the federal government still possessed title and managed timber and fire suppression. A proud Norbeck boasted to fellow park board member John A. Stanley that South Dakota now possessed the "largest State Park of any state in the Union, but what is much more important, it is one of the scenic wonders of [America] and second to no region except, possibly, two or three of the large national parks."[31] Solidly wedded to the state park as a crown jewel of the state's attractions, Norbeck personally took part in laying out locations for park roads, such as the Needles highway, tramping around on foot with the state engineer.[32]

Located in Custer State Park, in the Black Hills, Sylvan Lake is a popular tourist attraction. Covering 17 acres, the lake was created in 1881 when Theodore Reder built a dam across Sunday Gulch Creek. *The Center for Western Studies.*

The jump to the U.S. Senate launched Norbeck into national prominence on conservation issues, as his "intense devotion to the cause" and lack of interest of most other senators meant that conservationists relied on him to introduce important measures.[33] Because U.S. Senate sessions often did not begin until as late as December, Norbeck spent considerable amounts of time in South Dakota, even visiting Pierre while the legislature was at work between January and March.[34] A selective examination within his copious correspondence files reveals how deeply invested he remained in conservation policy at the state level. Having just left the governor's office and only weeks prior to beginning work in Washington, Norbeck was still writing Custer State Park bills for legislators to introduce. "Pardon me for giving so much advice," he wrote W. A. Guilfoyle, a house member from Edgemont in February 1921, "but I have for ten years been looking after these Park measures personally, and I have often encountered unexpected difficulties."[35] His immediate post-gubernatorial involvement in state affairs included letters to legislators about budgeting and park expansion, attempts to procure moose and mountain sheep, and an increasingly nettlesome problem of extracting holdout settlers still residing within the park. "I had been in hopes that the present legislature could make arrangements for purchasing the [remaining] privately-owned lands in the Park (as well as taking over the remaining acreage now held by the School and Land Department)," he informed another house member, "but when the Budget Board adopted the policy of retrenchment, it became necessary to pare on everything."[36] Norbeck badgered Governor William H. McMaster about the settlers as well, asserting in one letter that "Our Park will never be a success until we can get the settlers out of there." Stanley, Norbeck's right-hand man on park matters, devoted a considerable amount of his time to negotiating sales with some of the old-timers who often wanted more than the park board considered a reasonable price.[37]

Time-consuming efforts on land purchases took place, for the most part, behind the scenes. Adjustments to policies relating to game and fish and Custer State Park occurred in full view of the public and provided plenty of grist for partisan and intra-partisan battles throughout the 1920s. Neither of Norbeck's fellow Republican successors as governor, McMaster and Carl Gunderson, shared his passion for conservation matters, and his tense political relationship with Gunderson mirrored the widening progressive-conservative split in the state Republican party. A particularly irksome example arose during the 1926 gubernatorial election, when the incumbent gave speeches exploiting the state's east-west divide to question the overall value of the state park. "He [Gunderson] tried to raise a sectional issue by saying that a large part of the money spent in the Black Hills State Park came from East of the Missouri River," Norbeck pointed out to *Watertown Public Opinion* editor George B. Elliott, "in the belief that the larger number of taxpayers East of the river will sustain him." Norbeck coached Elliott and other friendly editors to counter the governor's attacks "along the line that the Custer State Park is a State Park, that unfortunately the mountains lie in the Western part of the State instead of the central part, –but that nevertheless they are in South Dakota." Whether or not voters on either side of the state factored the park and how it was financed into their decisions, Norbeck chortled that "When Gunderson reads this in a few of the papers he will not be so cock sure of himself."[38]

Intra-party tensions, financial disasters, a declining farm sector, and the deepening unpopularity of the prickly Gunderson contributed to the election of South Dakota's first Democratic governor, William J. Bulow, in 1926.[39] In a fascinating letter from Norbeck to Bulow in late November 1926, the senator brought the governor-elect up to speed on a variety of conservation matters, including game conditions in Custer State Park and an antelope preserve established in Harding County. Especially concerning to Norbeck, both the Game and Fish Department and the Game and Fish Commission had been eliminated as part of an administrative reorganization enacted by the legislature in 1925. The duties formerly carried out by the State Game Warden and the Commission were now handled by the director of the Division of Game and Fish within the Department of Agriculture–in this case former State Game Warden Oscar H. Johnson.[40] Norbeck described Secretary of Agriculture B. F. Myers, to whom Johnson reported, as a "man of little judgment" who had harmed the game preserves by hiring incompetent cronies, selling off livestock herds, and making extravagant purchases. "I am wondering if it might not be advisable to amend the Reorganization Act by re-establishing the old Game and Fish Commission, —a Commission that never cost a dollar of expense to the taxpayers," he suggested to Bulow.[41]

Norbeck's maneuverings related to game, fish, and park policy ultimately folded themselves into some extraordinary political drama in 1927. His wishes regarding a new Game and Fish Commission also entailed vesting the same with spending authority, reversing the 1925 reorganization's requirement that game and fish funds revert to the state's general fund, subject to legislative appropriation. "It is utterly impractical to have a Legislature apportion such a fund," Norbeck argued to Bulow; "it leads to trading and log-rolling. It is impossible in a sixty-day session to plan a constructive policy for a two-year period; it becomes a fight between different localities and different interests."[42] Norbeck informed the governor-elect that he had asked Attorney General Buell F. Jones to draft a bill, reflecting the wishes of the state's leading conservation organization, the Izaak Walton League, to place game and fish funds "at the disposal of the Game and Fish Department." Although members of both parties in 1927 essentially agreed on removing the legislature from appropriating the funds, comity broke down on Norbeck's and the Izaak Walton League's funding proposal. Bulow and Democrats wanted the state secretary of agriculture to control the funds whereas Republicans sought to give a reconstituted Game and Fish Commission that authority.[43] In early February the house passed a bill giving the Commission power over funds, but prospects in the senate were dubious. Republicans sat one vote short of the necessary two-thirds majority to pass appropriations bills and override a veto Bulow promised would be forthcoming.[44] Efforts to amend the bill to lure at least one Democratic senator into the fold and soften the governor's insistence on keeping revenues under the secretary of agriculture's control proved fruitless.[45]

When the senate failed to pass the measure after "[fifty] days of argument," attention turned to House Bill 44, an alternative introduced by a Joint Committee on Fish and Game early in the session but held in abeyance until the other bill "went into the grave."[46] As the final days of the 1927 session devolved into increasingly testy partisan bickering, H.B. 44 traveled a tortuous path through a succession of floor debates and futile attempts to amend the measure and achieve a breakthrough. The major problems remained the same: control of game and fish funds and whom to place on a new commission. Democrats balked at allowing a Republican-majority commission, with Bulow outnumbered by any two Republican constitutional officers, possessing absolute control of funding. A late attempt to amend the bill, offered in the house by Democrat A. O. Steensland, from Lake Andes, proposed re-constituting the commission as a six-member, non-partisan body. While an intriguing idea, the amendment found no purchase among the chamber's Republicans and failed. Ultimately, the house passed H.B 44 on another party-line vote, only to have it fall short once again in the senate.[47]

The stalemate over game and fish funds and administration represented part of a larger dilemma in 1927. A budget-conscious Democratic governor confronting a Republican-dominated legislature, Bulow stood firm in holding the line on state spending. His veto of the session's appropriations bill was overridden in the house but sustained in the senate due to that body's failure to achieve the two-thirds majority required to override.[48] The situation led to creation of a special court to hear a case brought by the Republicans against Bulow, arguing that the governor had no veto power over appropriations bills. Three Republican and two Democratic lawyers were chosen for the panel, which decided in favor of the governor, prompting the calling of a special session in June 1927.[49]

"We had no difficulty in getting together on a new appropriation bill," Bulow recollected about the special session, which coincided with the beginning of President Calvin Coolidge's summer-long retreat at the State Game Lodge in Custer State Park.[50] While Coolidge conducted business from Rapid City High School and caught hatchery-bred trout in Black Hills streams, legislators (with Norbeck's quiet assistance from the sidelines) finally attended to reviving the Game and Fish Commission. In the end, Representative Steensland's abortive effort to amend H.B. 44 during the regular session became the basis for successfully establishing a six-member bipartisan commission. Although opposed to "creation of a so-called non-political commission for the purpose of taking over the activities of the Game and Fish Department," Bulow did not issue a veto and the bill became law without his approval.[51] Under the new law, the commission had to be composed of three Republicans and three Democrats, with no more than two members from any of the then three U.S. House districts and no fewer than one from each of those districts engaged in farming. Administrative and funding authority, moreover, was stripped from the Department of Agriculture and restored to a stand-alone Department of Game and Fish. For Custer State Park, the legislators created the post of park superintendent, expanded the park board's management authority, and guaranteed an annual share of Game and Fish license revenues for the board and appropriated funds to purchase more private holdings within the park.[52]

State Game Lodge, in Custer State Park. The original lodge was destroyed by fire shortly after it opened in 1921 but was rebuilt in 1922. *The Center for Western Studies.*

The 1927 Custer State Park legislation also authorized the park board–basically Norbeck and John Stanley–to study and report to the next regular session on a "state wide plan for a State Park system embracing the different scenic and recreational areas in different sections of the state."[53] In addition, the 1927 legislature's regular session also established a Park Survey Committee to gather information on the most promising sites for new state parks. The resolution establishing this committee, introduced by Representative Emil J. Waltner, from Hurley, in Turner County, lamented that the "inroads of civilization are rapidly destroying the wild life, wild flowers and wooded regions, and obliterating the places of historic interest and scenic beauty." Waltner also alerted his colleagues to the "great progress" being made by neighboring states, namely Iowa, Minnesota, Nebraska, and North Dakota, "in the matter of establishing State Parks and carrying out a program of conservation."[54] These seemingly innocuous moves to investigate prospects for creating more parks and thereby satisfy more South Dakotans rather predictably engendered a new round of complicated politicking.

Norbeck, as always, did all in his power to generate momentum for expanding the state park idea, engaging in constant correspondence with lawmakers, editors, businessmen, and other supporters. While pulling as many strings as possible to move the parks plan forward, Norbeck always went to great lengths to shield his engagement, insisting "that I can work more effectively by being in the background."[55] Worried about diminishing natural recreational and scenic areas being lost to privatization and commercial development, he inquired about possible candidates for addition to a state park system. "I have in mind especially that the southeastern corner of the State, where the heavy population reside, are entitled to first consideration," he wrote to one correspondent in November 1928.[56] A letter to Al J. Adams, editor of the *Sisseton Courier*, demonstrated Norbeck's behind-the-scenes work to drum up public support as well for the northeastern corner. "At present I am trying to arrange for some booster articles for each of the areas I have in mind," he explained, and asked if Adams could write some material for newspapers in Aberdeen and Watertown as well as his own.[57]

Augmenting the argument for protecting lakes and wooded areas from degradation, the rapidly developing automobile tourist trade emerged as one of the favored rationales for expanding the state park system. Oscar W. Coursey, a revered author and educator from Mitchell, attempted to generate a surge of enthusiasm with an editorial first printed in the *Sioux Falls Argus Leader* several weeks before the 1929 legislative session began. "Good roads and the auto make this a part of our national life. We must catch step with it," Coursey urged. "These [state parks], with the Badlands which congress plans to convert into a national park, will put us on the map. Let's go!"[58] Norbeck, given his experiences in slowly building support for Custer State Park, appreciated both the tourist angle and the amount of time likely required to convince many of his fellow South Dakotans to create a park system. "I am painfully aware of the fact that the people do not share my enthusiasm for Parks, and I plugged along for a dozen years on the Black Hills Park before I was able to convert the Black Hills people to the idea," he confessed. "In fact, they never became converted until the tourists came along and spent their money with them. I am wondering whether it will be more difficult or easier to stir up some interest in the eastern section of the State, where parks are so far more important to the population than the Black Hills, where 'a Park is found in [every] section.'"[59] Expensive as establishing additional parks promised to be, supporters repeatedly pointed out that much and possibly most of the financial burden would ultimately fall on out-of-state visitors attracted by the growing number of "recreation spots" who would "swell the gasoline tax totals sufficient to offset the original investment."[60]

Preparing for the 1929 session of the legislature, Norbeck and his allies anticipated that financing more parks would preoccupy opponents and even many sympathetic legislators would be reticent. Dr. H. E. Fankhauser, a dentist from Woonsocket, informed the Senator that "[t]he only objections we would encounter here would be from a class of farmers who have been stressing the economy question" and sportsmen convinced that the game fund will be raided to pay for new parks.[61] First on the agenda for park system backers, however, was to simply present a framework, make suggestions, and fuss over costs later. On February 11, the house and senate received Norbeck and Stanley's park board report. "While the western part of our State offers a large number of possibilities for additional State Parks," they advised, "we are of the opinion that our present great need lies in the eastern half of the State." Oakwood Lakes, eight miles north of Volga in Brookings County, was the first suggestion, followed by a collection of northeastern lakes in Marshall County, the Ruskin Park district just south of Forestburg, in Sanborn County, and Armadale Island, situated between Redfield and Aberdeen near the Spink and Brown County lines. Big Stone Lake, north of Milbank, in Grant County, was briefly mentioned as another possibility.[62]

Missteps and delays would sink the admittedly slim prospects for parks expansion in 1929. Representative Waltner's Park Survey Committee's report was delayed until a mere three days before the deadline to introduce committee bills. A "hastily" drafted park system bill, S.B. 219, incorporating elements of both Norbeck's and Waltner's reports, did not get introduced until the final day possible. Among its provisions, the bill proposed five new parks: Oakwood Lakes; Lake Region; Ruskin; Armadale Island; and Big Stone Lake. The ability to locally petition for "minor state parks" made its way into the bill as well.[63] After passing the senate by a 36-7 margin, the parks bill slammed into a wall in the other chamber.[64] With Norbeck looking on from the visitor's gallery on March 6, his allies "called attention to the state's income from the tourist trade, and championed the park measure as a means of developing the state's scenic resources." Those speaking against the bill decried it as a "blank check" and "one of the biggest jokes ever perpetrated on the farmers of this state."[65] One of the opponents, R. R. Buikema, from Ipswich, in Edmunds County, bore in from a particularly unique angle. "He said that the trouble is farmers spend too much time now in chasing around the country," reported the *Pierre Capital-Journal*. "That in driving across the country you can tell by the looks of fields whether a man is staying home and taking care of business, or is chasing around the country to recreation places. The fields which show neglect and will be a short crop are the ones where the farmer is not attending to his business." Whether Buikema's argument that more state parks would tempt too many farmers to abandon their fields to go fishing or frolic along a lakeshore made an impression, the parks bill fizzled out in the house on a 48-49 vote.[66]

In a post-mortem several days after S.B. 219's failure in the house, Norbeck told Robert D. Jones, head of the South Dakota Division of the Izaak Walton League, that "it became apparent ten days ago that it would be impossible to muster a two-thirds vote involving expenditure for any parks."[67] He complained, as some cautious supporters had earlier warned, that the parks bill had asked for too much too soon.[68] The legislation "lost out because the program was too large and too involved and we failed to get any additional votes on account of the enlargement."[69] Particularly aggravating was the addition of Big Stone Lake to the list of prospective parks when neither of Grant County's two representatives backed the legislation. The Izaak Walton League's Jones, a resident of Milbank, relayed to Norbeck his disappointment in the no votes of these members, "neither of [whom] have any interest in outdoor life, and they see no value in parks, lakes and streams."[70]

Norbeck admitted to parks ally Clifford Wilson, a state senator from Hot Springs, to being hesitant about even a four-park program, but the addition of a fifth and an amendment by Waltner that "provided for an unlimited number" scared off some members.[71] Yet progress had been made and even members who had voted against them could be converted. "We can hardly expect a man who has handled a plow all his life to enthuse over a state park," Norbeck admitted to the Izaak Walton League's Jones. The Farmers Union leaders' "formidable opposition" had effectively guaranteed defeat in the midst of a seemingly perpetual agricultural depression. "They had to be against something and this was a convenient object. At that I think they reflected the views of their members who have been hard hit the last ten years."[72] More encouraging was the solid backing of Black Hills and West River representatives. "All of the Hills house members voted for the bill," a *Rapid City Journal* editorial noted, "and all but six of those from the big prairie empire between here and the Missouri river. . . . The proposal was killed by East River members themselves, and they're the people to work on next time."[73] Another commentary in the *Aberdeen News* argued that people need "recreation and sport . . . and it should be remembered with gratitude by the farming sections that the Black Hills representatives without exception backed up their bill. It remained for the people whom it would directly benefit to turn it down."[74] Though frustrated at the outcome in the 1929 session, Norbeck and the state parks supporters harbored no regrets and presumed that support in the "farming sections" and the two-thirds votes in both houses would emerge in time.[75]

Insofar as consolidating administrative authority for game and fish management, solidifying the popularity and viability of Custer State Park, and beginning to massage public opinion on creating additional state parks, the state's conservationists had made great strides up to this point. The next several years, however, would test the mettle of South Dakota's residents, regardless of occupation, party, or section. A political culture attached to an ethos of individualism and wariness of centralized national power would endure the realities of economic disaster and become increasingly reliant on federal programs, among which would be some of the most extraordinarily important conservation measures in the nation's history. Simultaneously, state lawmakers and officials would build upon the accomplishments of Norbeck and his allies in solidifying the conservation of the state's recreational and scenic amenities.

As in many other areas of public affairs, politics in South Dakota during the Great Depression became increasingly intertwined with federal initiatives, especially with the advent of the New Deal in 1933. The state's agricultural and banking sectors, both of which had struggled throughout the 1920s, collapsed in the wake of the stock market crash.[76] Republican governor Warren E. Green's "lack of imagination and unwillingness to experiment" in the face of multiple crises ensured his defeat in 1932 at the hands of Democrat Tom Berry, a rancher and former legislator from Belvidere as well as a former member of the Custer State Park Board.[77] With the exception of Norbeck, reelected that year to his third term in the U.S. Senate, Democrats swept all major offices and took control of the legislature. Like Bulow, Berry was a conservative Democrat, "committed to traditional Jeffersonian principles of small and frugal government at the state level."[78] While not overly enthusiastic about every aspect of President Franklin D. Roosevelt's New Deal, Berry appreciated the influx of federal money into his suffering state. Governor Berry, Senator Norbeck, the state's now two congressmen, and farmers' organizations all expressed approval of the popular Civilian Conservation Corps, with the agricultural lobby continually pressing the Roosevelt administration and the congressional delegation for more soil conservation camps. Newspaper opinion was likewise generally supportive of the CCC and particularly enthusiastic about the infusion of federal funds.[79]

At the state level, many aspects of South Dakota's conservation policy–game and fish management, Custer State Park oversight, and efforts to create a state park system–that had concerned Norbeck, his allies, and his foes during the 1920s followed a bumpy path toward resolution during the 1930s. "My first interest is in the Custer State Park; second in the Badlands, and third, in the Park possibilities in the Eastern part of the State," Norbeck wrote Tom Berry. "They are all necessary–they are all important. We will get farther by working together."[80] Working with Republican governor Warren Green on conservation priorities dear to Norbeck's heart, however, was challenging. The hoped-for depoliticization of the Game and Fish Commission, for one, proved to be trickier than proponents had presumed. In July 1931, Norbeck reported to his brother Enoch on a meeting with Green, during which the Senator wanted to discuss several items, among them appointments to the commission. Green wanted to appoint Republicans Dr. Fankhauser from Woonsocket and "the Professor from Madison," Karl Mundt, plus possibly "[Chester K.] Snyder of Watertown, who has fought me for ten years." The governor was also "having great difficulty in finding three members who live on farms and three members who are Democrats," Norbeck told his brother.[81]

Norbeck found Green more troublesome on appointments to the Custer State Park Board and the position of park superintendent. For the three-man board, comprised before the 1930 election of Norbeck, Stanley, and Berry, Green was willing to re-appoint Norbeck and Stanley, but not the Democrat Berry, despite an earlier promise to Norbeck to keep the present bi-partisan board intact.[82] Berry spared Green by resigning, but when rumors circulated that the governor was waffling on Norbeck, alarms sounded. The *Rapid City Journal*, in an editorial entitled "He Is Needed," echoed Norbeck's own arguments about instability brought on by continually changing the administration of the park and composition of the board. "Norbeck ought to be kept on the Board as long as he lives," the *Journal* prophetically declared.[83] Green also wanted to hire a different superintendent for the park, although the power to do so was technically not his, but the board's. A flustered Norbeck complained to former congressman Eben W. Martin about how all of the governors that succeeded his tenure, McMaster, Gunderson, Bulow, and now, probably, Green, had gone around the board to force whomever they wanted in as superintendent.[84] A *Lead Call* editorial, likely the handiwork of John A. Stanley, expressed concern about the rumored dismissal of superintendent Charley Robertson, a Democrat appointed by Bulow. The position should not be partisan and the "place should never become a political foot-ball."[85] Green made his desired changes to the board and park management, anyway, as did Berry after the 1932 election. In declining health, Norbeck's waning influence was on display as the new, Berry-appointed superintendent Ray Milliken challenged his interference. The state Democrats' temporary dominance and growing federal authority with CCC programs and the National Park Service's expanding footprint in West River diminished his influence even further.[86]

Norbeck's ambitions for a state park system produced another bill in the 1931 legislative session, which went down to an even more ignominious defeat in the house after easily passing in the senate.[87] No additional attempts to establish more parks legislatively occurred during the 1930s, although the 1935 session did create a five-member non-partisan State Park Board with power to acquire and administer lands as additional "park areas."[88] Four years later, cost-cutting conservative Republican governor Harlan J. Bushfield recommended abolishing the two park boards and consolidating them with the Game and Fish Commission as a Conservation Commission. Instead, legislators abolished the State Park Board, transferred its duties to the Custer State Park Board and renamed it the South Dakota Park Board.[89] In a move that would have likely appalled Norbeck, who had died more than two years earlier, the same session acted on another Bushfield budget cutting recommendation to transfer Custer State Park to the National Park Service, should Congress ever authorize doing so. Amazingly, legislators passed the park transfer measure, introduced late in the session–unanimously in the senate and against only eight no votes in the House.[90] Realizing his mistake after an extensive visit to the park, Bushfield asked the 1941 session to repeal the law. "I know our Park now and I come to you with an admission of error for that recommendation," he told the legislators. "We must not permit such a transfer. The Park is our most priceless possession and must be kept forever as South Dakota's exclusive property."[91] Finally, in 1945, the State Park Board and the Game and Fish Commission were replaced by a new Department of Game, Fish and Parks and an eight-member Game, Fish and Parks Commission. The revised Commission could have no more than four members from the same political party, no fewer than four engaged in farming, and was empowered to create new state parks. Permanently liberated from legislative impediments, the Department and Commission established the first new state parks that year at Hartford Beach on Big Stone Lake, in Roberts County, and Oakwood Lakes, in Brookings County.[92]

To commemorate a half-century of South Dakota statehood in 1939, a Sioux Falls publisher produced a volume of essays and pictures entitled, straightforwardly enough, *South Dakota: Fifty Years of Progress*. Herbert Schell wrote on the state's history, Badger Clark on its literature, Gutzon Borglum on Mount Rushmore, and other luminaries covered mining, religion, education, women's contributions, the assimilation of Native Americans, farming, and media, among other topics. Karl Mundt, recently elected to represent the state's First District in Congress, added a useful essay on "Our Conservation Policies." In this piece, Mundt, himself a former member of the State Game and Fish Commission, lauded South Dakota's record of progressive conservation legislation and acknowledged many of the state's conservation leaders, including State Game Wardens Harry Hedrick and Oscar Johnson, the Woonsocket dentist H. E. Fankhauser, and members of the Izaak Walton League. Surprisingly absent from Mundt's list of conservation heroes was Peter Norbeck, and he only made passing mention of the 1913 creation of "Custer State Game Park."[93]

Mundt praised Orman Dam, near Belle Fourche, and the "feasibility of irrigation," the growing number of artificial lakes to provide "pure drinking water" and recreation, shelterbelts, and modern sewage treatment facilities "to preserve an unpolluted chain of rivers for future generations." He listed soil conservation methods–"Contour plowing, strip farming, listing, and planting of erosion-preventing shrubs and grasses"–which he claimed were "rapidly curtailing wind-erosion in the State" and bringing the horrific dust storms to an end. "Blessed by Mother Nature with a wealth of natural resources," Mundt proclaimed, "South Dakota stands second to no other State in the Union today in its program for conserving, protecting, and improving the great outdoor assets which make it a hospitable and happy place in which to live, and a magnet for tourists from throughout America." Abundant opportunities for fishing and hunting offered testaments to the "practices of wise conservation" implemented "[a]lmost from the very beginning" by far-sighted South Dakotans.[94]

Mundt's hyperbolic claim about being "second to no other State" fit well the self-congratulatory tone of the celebratory publication for which he wrote. In addition, a major point of emphasis in his article was the depoliticization of conservation policy making in South Dakota, proudly extolling the "now nationally famous and nationally envied six-man, bipartisan game and fish commission."[95] Draining politics away from policy sounded too good to be true, though, and even the designed bipartisan structure of the commission could not permanently remove the fits and starts, occasional pitched battles between competing interests, and unintended consequences typical of policy making. Political squabbles about conservation in South Dakota before 1940, particularly the constant back and forth on game and fish management and the lengthy period between creation of Custer State Park and additional pleasure grounds, tended to reflect a number of standard fault lines: Democrats vs. Republicans; conservatives vs. progressives; East River vs. West River; farmers vs. sportsmen and recreationists.

Despite Mundt's likely inadvertent omission from his acknowledgments in 1939, there is no way around Peter Norbeck as the central personality linked to conservation in South Dakota's first half-century of statehood. Still, conservation politics in the state during these formative decades was certainly about more than one man and demonstrated a surprising level of unpredictability and fluidity. In the end, the achievements of the Norbeck-era conservationists have endured and evolved. Farmers, their lobbying groups, and political representatives no longer express disapproval for taking some time off to relax by a lake or take a hike. Hunting and fishing, while declining in popularity in aggregate terms nationally, remain relatively popular and lucrative in South Dakota. The state park system now boasts thirteen parks, most of them east of the Missouri River, plus dozens of recreation and nature areas as well as a historic trail in the Black Hills. Millions of visitors from around the globe clamber all over the Hills, spill out into the Badlands, and beyond, fulfilling in large measure the early conservationists' anticipation for exploiting the state's scenic and recreational resources.

Notes

1 Though not entirely absent among South Dakota's conservationist leaders, the preservationist idea attached to John Muir and often cited as the philosophy guiding management of national parks played a less significant role in the state's conservation politics and development of policy. See Roderick Frazier Nash, ed., *American Environmentalism: Readings in Conservation History*, 3d ed. (New York: McGraw-Hill, Inc., 1990), 69-112; Nash, *Wilderness and the American Mind*, 5th ed. (New Haven: Yale University Press, 2014); Steven Fox, *John Muir and His Legacy: The American Conservation Movement* (Boston: Little, Brown, 1981); Donald Worster, *Nature's Economy: A History of Ecological Ideas* (New York: Cambridge University Press, 1985); Douglas Brinkley, *The Wilderness Warrior: Theodore Roosevelt and the Crusade for America* (New York: Harper Perennial, 2009).

2 See Samuel P. Hays, *Conservation and the Gospel of Efficiency: The Progressive Conservation Movement, 1890-1920* (Cambridge: Harvard University Press, 1959).

3 See John F. Reiger, *American Sportsmen and the Origins of Conservation* (New York: Winchester, 1975); Jen Corrine Brown, *Trout Culture: How Fly Fishing Forever Changed the Rocky Mountain West* (Seattle: University of Washington Press, 2015); Hal K. Rothman, *Devil's Bargains: Tourism in the Twentieth-Century American West* (Lawrence: University Press of Kansas, 1998); David M. Wrobel and Patrick T. Long, eds., *Seeing & Being Seen: Tourism in the American West* (Lawrence: University Press of Kansas, 2001).

4 For background on agricultural challenges, see Lynwood E. Oyos, "Farming: Dependency and Depopulation," in Harry F. Thompson, ed., *A New South Dakota History*, 2d ed. (Sioux Falls, SD: Center For Western Studies, 2009), 225-54; Gilbert C. Fite, *The Farmers' Frontier, 1865-1900* (New York: Holt, Rinehart and Winston, 1966), 94-112; Harold Edward Briggs, "The Great Dakota Boom, 1879-1886," *North Dakota Historical Quarterly* 4 (January 1930): 78-108; Herbert S. Schell, "Widening Horizons at the Turn of the Century: The Last Dakota Land Boom." *South Dakota History* 12 (Summer/Fall 1982): 93-117. For timber policies in the Black Hills, see Richmond L. Clow, "Timber Users, Timber Savers: Homestake Mining Company and the First Regulated Timber Harvest," *South Dakota History* 22 (Fall 1992): 213-37; John F. Freeman, *Black Hills Forestry: A History* (Boulder: University Press of Colorado, 2015); Martha E. Geores, *Common Ground: The Struggle for Ownership of the Black Hills National Forest* (Lanham, MD: Rowman & Littlefield Publishers, 1996); David A. Wolff, "Black Hills in Transition," in Thompson, *A New South Dakota History*, 307-9. For broader context on the Homestake and impacts on its workforce and nearby

communities, see Joseph H. Cash, *Working the Homestake* (Ames, IA: Iowa State University Press, 1973).

5 "First South Dakota Conservation Congress Opens in Pierre," *Minneapolis Journal*, June 29, 1910, photocopied newspaper clipping in Conservation Congress, 1910 (Pierre, SD) vertical file, South Dakota State Archives, Pierre.

6 Hays, *Conservation and the Gospel of Efficiency*, 127-41. Governor Coe I. Crawford led South Dakota's four-man delegation to the Washington, D.C. meeting. *Proceedings of a Conference of Governors in the White House, Washington, D.C., May 13-15, 1908* (Washington: Government Printing Office, 1909), xxiv. http://www.riversimulator.org/Resources/Sustain/ConferenceOfTheGovenorsOfTheUnitedStates1908.pdf

7 *Message of Governor Coe I. Crawford to the South Dakota Legislature, Eleventh Regular Session, 1909* (Pierre: State Publishing Co., 1909), 38-39. The members were U.S. Senator Robert J. Gamble, Chairman, U.S. Representative Eben W. Martin, State Land Commissioner O. C. Dokken, State Engineer Samuel H. Lea, and Doane Robinson as Secretary. "Preliminary Report of the State Conservation Commission of South Dakota, 1908," in *South Dakota Legislative Manual, 1909* (Pierre: State Publishing Company, 1909), 466.

8 Herbert S. Schell, *History of South Dakota*, 4th ed., Revised (Pierre: South Dakota State Historical Society Press, 2004), 261. Among the most significant progressive reforms passed at the 1907 session were laws providing for direct primaries, registration of lobbyists, a ban on corporate contributions to political candidates, maximum railroad passenger rates, establishment of a pure food and drug commission, and raising tax assessments on corporate property. John E. Miller, "Politics Since Statehood," in Thompson, *A New South Dakota History*, 201. See also Calvin Perry Armin, "Coe I. Crawford and the Progressive Movement in South Dakota," *South Dakota Department of History Report and Historical Collections*, vol. XXXII (Pierre: South Dakota State Historical Society, 1964), 72-131.

9 *Pierre Capital Journal*, February 12, 1907; *Session Laws of the State of South Dakota, Tenth Session, 1907,* (Aberdeen: News Printing Co., 1907), 337-40. Although containing rather broad generalizations, historian John F. Reiger's statement captures some of the essential tensions between farmers and sportsmen. "Farmers and ranchers usually made poor nature lovers, seeing wildlife primarily as competitors or sources of profit. Sportsmen, on the other hand, regarded most animals and birds with nonutilitarian motives." Reiger, *American Sportsmen and the Origins of Conservation*, 91. See too Daniel Justin Herman, *Hunting and the American Imagination* (Washington and London: Smithsonian Institution Press, 2001), 262-69.

10 *Session Laws of the State of South Dakota, Eleventh Session, 1909*, (Pierre: Hipple Printing Co., 1909), 369-77. Before the 1909 law, game and fish

regulations were handled by county wardens, a system described in a 1959 Game, Fish and Parks history as "ridden by local politics, splendid opportunities for graft, and a vast ignorance of game and fish management." Don Hipschman, "Department History, 1909-1959," in Department of Game, Fish and Parks, *Annual Report, 1958-1959*, 32, Dept. of Game, Fish, & Parks, Division of Administration. Agency History Files, 1909-1986. Box 5494 A. South Dakota State Archives, Pierre.

[11] "First South Dakota Conservation Congress Opens in Pierre."

[12] "Pierre Congress Big Help to State," *Minneapolis Journal*, June 29, 1910; "Conservation is Topic at Meet at Pierre," *Aberdeen Daily News*, June 29, 1910, photocopied newspaper clippings in Conservation Congress (Pierre, 1910) vertical file.

[13] "Conservation is Topic at Meet at Pierre." One of the dissenters, a Colonel James A. George, asserted that "many people" in the Black Hills were "disgusted with [federal] government control and the management of forests and natural waterpowers in that region." Moreover, the "policy of conservation, as promulgated by Roosevelt and Pinchot, had redounded to the benefit of corporations," leaving "struggling settlers" burdened by high prices for timber. According to a Minneapolis newspaper relaying pro-conservation reports from South Dakota Historical Society secretary Doane Robinson, Colonel George and former Judge A. J. Ploughman of Deadwood "both have talked anti-conservation, to the amusement and entertainment of throngs gathered in hotel lobbies." "Pierre Congress Big Help to State."

[14] "Resolutions," *Pierre Capital Journal*, July 1, 1910, photocopied newspaper clipping in Conservation Congress (Pierre, 1910) vertical file.

[15] A second Conservation Congress met in Pierre, January 23-28, 1911, with separate Good Roads and Dry Farming Congresses meeting concurrently. In January 1912, the third meeting, referred to in the *Rapid City Journal* as the "state conservation, good roads, and dry farming congress," took place in Sioux Falls. A Dry Farming and Conservation Congress met in Pierre in February 1913 and the last such meeting described as a "Conservation Congress" occurred in Sioux Falls in March 1914. At that particular gathering, listed topics did include parks, forests, and nature as well as the usual agricultural concerns. *Rapid City Journal*, January 19, 1911, January 12, 1912, February 2, 1913, February 28, 1914.

[16] Within a week of the Pierre Congress, the Republican party included the following plank in their platform: "We believe that all our natural resources should be carefully conserved and developed for the general good and that all public officials–state and national–whether holding by election or under appointment whose powers extend to the control of natural resources should be chosen for their peculiar fitness and for their known record and opinions touching the conservation and development of such resources." *South Dakota Legislative Manual, 1915* (Pierre: State Publishing Company, 1915), 460.

[17] Gilbert Courtland Fite, *Peter Norbeck: Prairie Statesman* (Pierre: South Dakota State Historical Society Press, 2005).

[18] Fite, *Peter Nobeck*, 74. Norbeck's personal papers do not shed much light on how well versed he was in the extensive conservation literature of the time. To what extent he paid attention to the work of leading biologists, ecologists, and other scientists in the Midwest and elsewhere is likewise unknown. For a broader discussion of conservation writing in the Midwest, see Christian Knoeller, *Reimagining Environmental History: Ecological Memory in the Wake of Landscape Change* (Reno and Las Vegas: University of Nevada Press, 2017).

[19] Laura Thornborough, "Conservation Leaders in Congress," reprint from *American Forests*, clipping in Conservation, 1928-1932 folder, Box 73a, Peter Norbeck Papers, Richardson Collection, University of South Dakota Archives and Special Collections, Vermillion (hereafter cited as Norbeck Papers).

[20] Sam Hurst, *Rattlesnake Under His Hat: The Life and Times of Earl Brocklesby* (Rapid City, SD: Vantage Point Historical Services, Inc., 2016), 16-25.

[21] Fite, *Peter Norbeck*, 25; Freeman, *Black Hills Forestry*, 89.

[22] Peter Norbeck to Mr. Bancroft, State Game Warden, August 28, 1912, State Park File, Box 99, Norbeck Papers; Fite, *Peter Norbeck*, 74; Freeman, *Black Hills Forestry*, 91-92; Suzanne Julin, *A Marvelous Hundred Square Miles: Black Hills Tourism, 1880-1941* (Pierre: South Dakota State Historical Society Press, 2009), 24-27.

[23] *Sioux Falls Argus-Leader*, March 1, 1913. *South Dakota Legislative Manual, 1913* (Pierre: State Publishing Co., 1913), 668; *Journal of the Senate, Thirteenth Legislative Session, 1913* (Pierre, 1913), 1239-1240, 1709; *Session Laws of the State of South Dakota, Thirteenth Session, 1913* (Sioux Falls: Brown & Saenger, 1913), 308-9.

[24] Peter Norbeck to H. S. Hedrick, Chamberlain, So. Dak., March 10, 1913, State Park File, Box 99, Norbeck Papers; *Session Laws, 1913,* 306-8; "The New Game Law," *Pierre Capital-Leader,* February 20, 1913.

[25] See Louis S. Warren, *The Hunter's Game: Poachers and Conservationists in Twentieth-Century America* (New Haven: Yale University Press, 1997).

[26] Peter Norbeck to H. S. Hedrick, July 16, 1914, State Park File folder, Box 99, Norbeck Papers. See Freeman, *Black Hills Forestry*, 89-105; Julin, *A Marvelous Hundred Square Miles*, 24-31.

[27] Fite, *Peter Norbeck*, 75.

[28] *Inaugural Address of Governor Peter Norbeck to the Fifteenth Legislative Session of the State of South Dakota, 1917* (Pierre, 1917), 21-22, 36. *Session Laws of the State of South Dakota, Special Session, 1916 and Fifteenth Session, 1917* (Pierre: Hipple Printing Co., 1917), 215, 404-6; Fite, *Peter Norbeck*, 55.

[29] *Inaugural Address of Governor Peter Norbeck to the Sixteenth Session of the State of South Dakota, 1919* (Pierre, 1919), 22-23.

[30] *Journal of the Senate, Sixteenth Session, 1919* (Pierre: Hipple Printing Co., 1919), 596; *Journal of the House, Sixteenth Session, 1919* (Pierre: Hipple Printing Co., 1919), 857; *Session Laws of the State of South Dakota, Special Session and Sixteenth Session, 1919* (Pierre: Hipple Printing Co., 1919), 151-2. The new park board began with members serving staggered terms, with all subsequently appointed to serve six-year terms; Board members received reimbursement for expenses but no salary. Besides Norbeck, the first Custer State Park Board's members were Norbeck's brother Enoch to represent "East River" and Lead newspaperman John A. Stanley, who "became Norbeck's main contact and the direct overseer of much of the development in the park during its first eight years." Park management was a complex interweaving of several different agencies: the Department of Game and Fish for the game preserve; School and Public Lands for timber and grazing lands; a state forester employed by School and Public Lands and a gamekeeper employed by Game and Fish; the South Dakota Highway Commission had jurisdiction over park roads. Julin, *A Marvelous Hundred Square Miles*, 42-44.

[31] Peter Norbeck to John A. Stanley, March 17, 1921, Custer State Park, 1921-1931 folder, Box 97, Norbeck Papers.

[32] Fite. *Peter Norbeck*, 76; Freeman, *Black Hills Forestry*, 92-96. Harry Gandy, a Democratic U.S. Congressman from Rapid City, negotiated with the Forest Service and authored a bill authorizing Custer State Game Park Sanctuary within Harney National Forest, officially established on October 9, 1920. The addition did not include the privately owned Sylvan Lake and hotel, but a special session of the legislature in June 1920 appropriated "fifty thousand dollars to purchase the 330 acres comprising Sylvan Lake and its environs." *Laws Passed at the Special Session of the Sixteenth Legislature of the State of South Dakota* (Pierre: State Publishing Company, 1921), 28.

[33] Fite, *Peter Norbeck*, 143. His work on shepherding the Migratory Bird Act, signed into law in 1929, stood out as a major accomplishment. Election to the Senate removed him temporarily from direct oversight of Custer State Park, but he still guided affairs through constant communication with John Stanley. Appointed to the board by Governor William H. McMaster in 1923, Norbeck stayed on until his death in 1936. Ibid., 144-148; Julin, *A Marvelous Hundred Square Miles*, 48.

[34] For example, after a brief special session in March 1921, the 67th Congress met relatively continually between April 1921 and March 1923. Following the 1922 mid-term elections, however, the 68th Congress did not convene its first session until December 3, 1923. Even after the presidential election year of 1924, the 69th Congress did not meet in regular session until December 1925. Following ratification of the 20th Amendment in 1933, the now familiar opening of regular congressional sessions on the January 3 following each election began with the 74th Congress in 1935. https://www.senate.gov/legislative/DatesofSessionsofCongress.htm.

[35] Peter Norbeck to W.A. Guilfoyle, February 4, 1921, Custer State Park folder, Box 97, Norbeck Papers.

[36] Peter Norbeck to E. O. Frescoln, Winner, SD, March 7, 1921, Custer State Park folder, Box 95, Norbeck Papers.

[37] Peter Norbeck to Hon. W. H. McMaster, February 28, 1921, Custer State Park folder, Box 95; see also Norbeck to McMaster, February 4, 1921; Norbeck to John Stanley, February 23, 1921. For more context on opposition to the park by homesteaders and ranchers within its boundaries, see Jessie Y. Sundstrom, *Pioneers and Custer State Park: A History of Custer State Park and Northcentral Custer County* (Custer: Jessie Y. Sundstrom, 1994), 82-85.

[38] Peter Norbeck to George B. Elliott, Editor, *Public Opinion*, Watertown, September 21, 1926, Custer State Park, 1921-1931 folder, Box 97, Norbeck Papers. Norbeck's stance on Gunderson's attempt at reelection in 1926 was neutral, but many of Norbeck's progressive Republican friends actively worked to help elect Democrat William J. Bulow. Fite, *Peter Norbeck*, 84, 122.

[39] Bulow, an attorney from Beresford, had been drubbed by Gunderson in the 1924 election, but prevailed by a 13,000-vote margin two years later. His coattails, however, were non-existent, as Republicans maintained their grip on all other elective state offices and majorities in both houses in the legislature. As Bulow put it in his unpublished autobiography, "I learned that it was not the people who voted for somebody, but rather it was the people who voted against somebody who win elections." Tonnis H. Venhuizen, editor and annotator, "'Three Score Years and Ten': Selections from the Autobiography of William J. Bulow, Sr.," *South Dakota History* 51 (Spring 2021): 30; Miller, "Politics Since Statehood," in Thompson, *A New South Dakota History*, 205.

[40] An efficiency report authorized by the legislature in 1921 had recommended what amounted to an overhaul of the state's executive branch, but the 1923 session failed to follow up. Governor Gunderson pressed lawmakers to act on the report in his 1925 inaugural address. The ensuing reorganization and consolidation bill, signed into law by Gunderson in March 1925, included the reconstituted Division of Game and Fish. *Inaugural Address of Governor Carl Gunderson to the Nineteenth Legislative Session, State of South Dakota, 1925* (Pierre: Hipple Printing Company, 1925), 6-7, 17; *Session Laws of the State of South Dakota, Nineteenth Session, 1925* (Pierre: Hipple Printing Co., 1925); 130; State of South Dakota, *Annual Report of the Department of Agriculture, 1925-1926* (Pierre: State Publishing Company, 1926), 4.

[41] Peter Norbeck to Hon. W. J. Bulow, November 24, 1926, Custer State Park, 1921-1931 folder, Box 97, Norbeck Papers.

[42] Ibid.

[43] Ibid.; "Game and Fish Fund is Subject of Battle Lines," *Pierre Capital-Journal*, February 7, 1927. Under the provisions of the 1927 session's

House Bill 75, the new Game and Fish Commission would be composed of the Governor, Attorney General, and State Treasurer.

[44] "Game and Fish Fund is Subject of Battle Lines; "House Passes Game and Fish Measure," *Pierre Capital-Journal*, February 8, 1927; *Proceedings of the House of Representatives, Twentieth Legislative Session, 1927* (Pierre: State Publishing Co., 1927), 443-4. The House vote in favor of H.B. 75 was a largely party-line 71-29.

[45] "Game Fund Bill Thorn in Side of Republicans," *Pierre Capital-Journal*, February 16, 1927.

[46] "G.O.P. Loses Fight For State Game Fund," *Pierre Capital-Journal,* February 22, 1927*; Proceedings of the Senate, Twentieth Legislative Session, 1927 (*Pierre: State Publishing Co., 1927*),* 656-57.

[47] "House Passes On Game and Fish Measure: Members Present Game-Fish Measure With Amendments," *Pierre Capital-Journal*, March 2, 1927; "Three Problems Face Senators As Closing Draws In," *Pierre Capital-Journal*, March 4, 1927; *South Dakota Legislative Manual, 1927* (Pierre: State Publishing Co., 1927), 281; *Proceedings of the House, 1927*, 927-32; *Proceedings of the Senate, 1927*, 980.

[48] Venhuizen, "'Three Score Years and Ten,'" 33; "Governor Vetoes General Money Bill," *Pierre Capital-Journal*, February 28, 1927.

[49] Venhuizen, "'Three Score Years and Ten,'" 33-35.

[50] Venhuizen, "'Three Score Years and Ten,'" 39-50; Julin, *A Marvelous Hundred Square Miles*, 70-101; Seth Tupper, *Calvin Coolidge in the Black Hills* (Charleston, SC: The History Press, 2017).

[51] In his remarks to the lawmakers at the outset of the special session, Bulow elaborated: "I am opposed to the creation of any new commissions. . . . The creation of a separate commission would entail duplication [of] expenditures and would be no more free from political influences than the present system. . . . Make the proper appropriation and then if you cannot agree as to who is to handle the funds let them be handled in accord with prior legislative direction until such a time when a legislature may agree upon a change, or until the people themselves by an initiated measure vote a change." *Message of Governor William J. Bulow to the Twentieth Legislature, Special Session, 1927* (Pierre: Hipple Printing Company, 1927), 3; *Session Laws of the State of South Dakota, Twenty-First Legislative Session, 1929* (Pierre: State Publishing Co., 1929), 37.

[52] *The Laws Passed at the Special Session of the Twentieth Legislature of the State of South Dakota* (Pierre, 1927), Special Legislative Report folder, Box 98, Norbeck Papers; *Session Laws, 1929*, 29-32, 34-37; Julin, *A Marvelous Hundred Square Miles*, 74-79.

[53] *Session Laws, 1929*, 32; *Proceedings of the Senate, Twenty-First Legislative Session, 1929* (Pierre: Hipple Printing Company, 1929), 238.

[54] *Proceedings of the House, Twenty-First Legislative Session, 1929* (Pierre: Hipple Printing Company, 1929), 437. The members of the committee were

Waltner, appointed by the Department of Game and Fish.; Louis N. Crill, secretary of agriculture, appointed by Governor Bulow; Lawrence K. Fox, the state historian, appointed by provision in Waltner's resolution.

[55] Peter Norbeck to Al J. Adams, Editor, *Sisseton Courier*, February 26, 1929, State Park Possibilities Correspondence, Misc. folder, Box 100, Norbeck Papers.

[56] Peter Norbeck to C. M. Day, November 19, 1928, State Park Possibilities Correspondence, Misc. folder, Box 100, Norbeck Papers.

[57] Peter Norbeck to Al J. Adams, December 3, 1928, State Park Possibilities Correspondence, Misc. folder, Box 100, Norbeck Papers. Adams did write a booster editorial for the *Sisseton Courier*, Dec. 19, 1928, State Park Possibilities Newspaper Clippings folder, Box 117, Norbeck Papers.

[58] "Urges State Park System Be Expanded," *Sisseton Courier*, December 6, 1928, State Park Possibilities Newspaper Clippings folder, Box 117, Norbeck Papers. Oscar William Coursey served in the Philippines during the Spanish-American War and became a major in the South Dakota National Guard. Regarded as "a notable figure in the educational affairs of South Dakota," Coursey wrote historical essays, taught, and worked in school administration in Mitchell. Doane Robinson, *South Dakota: Sui Generis. Stressing the Unique and Dramatic in South Dakota History. South Dakota Biography By a Separate Staff of Special Writers* (Chicago and New York: The American Historical Society, Inc., 1930), vol. II, 499-500.

[59] Norbeck to C. M. Day, November 19, 1928.

[60] *Aberdeen News* reprint in *Sioux Falls Argus Leader*, December 1, 1928, State Park Possibilities Newspaper Clippings folder, Box 117, Norbeck Papers.

[61] H. E. Fankhauser to Peter Norbeck, November 26, 1928, State Park Possibilities Correspondence, Misc. folder, Box 100, Norbeck Papers.

[62] *Proceedings of the Senate, 1929*, 239-241.

[63] Clifford A. Wilson to Peter Norbeck, April 15, 1929 and E. J. Waltner to Peter Norbeck, March 4, 1929, State Park Possibilities Correspondence, Misc. folder, Box 100, Norbeck Papers; "Declare Park Board Would Be Feasible: Committee Reports on Survey; Would Create State Parks," *Aberdeen News*, February 20, 1929.

[64] *Proceedings of the Senate, 1929*, 645-646. "But when every effort is being made to stem the rising tide of taxation, the suggestion that even a small sum be added here and there runs into rather frigid temperatures in the legislative atmosphere. Because of this, the legislature may not approve the proposed beginning of a state park system at this time. However, much valuable ground has been covered, and sooner or later this public enterprise will be authorized. Its advantages are too obvious." *Watertown Public Opinion*, February 23, 1929.

[65] "State Park Bill Fails In House: Measure Is Lost 49-48 Following Half Hour Parliamentary Snarl," *Mitchell Republic*, March 6, 1929.

[66] *Pierre Capital Journal*, March 6, 1929; *Proceedings of the House, 1929*, 894.

[67] Peter Norbeck to Robert D. Jones, March 10, 1929, State Park Possibilities Correspondence, Misc. folder, Box 100, Norbeck Papers.

[68] See *Sioux Falls Argus Leader*, December 22, 1928 and *Watertown Public Opinion*, December 21, 1928, State Park Possibilities Newspaper Clippings folder, Box 117, Norbeck Papers.

[69] Peter Norbeck to Robert D. Jones, March 14, 1929, State Park Possibilities Correspondence, Misc. folder, Box 100, Norbeck Papers.

[70] Robert D. Jones to Peter Norbeck, March 12, 1929, State Park Possibilities Correspondence, Misc. folder, Box 100, Norbeck Papers. The two Grant Country representatives in question were Carl Gerhardt, a Republican and a former minister from Big Stone City, serving his first year in the legislature and Adolph Weide, also a Republican from Revillo, involved with farm machinery and blacksmithing and banking. *South Dakota Legislative Manual, 1929* (Pierre, SD: State Publishing Co., 1929), 486-87. Milbank's newspaper had this to say about the two legislators: "No doubt Messrs. Gerhardt and Weide had reasons they considered sufficient to warrant them in voting as they did, but we can't imagine what they were." *Milbank Review*, reprinted in *Sioux Falls Argus Leader*, March 17, 1929, State Park Possibilities Newspaper Clippings folder, Box 117, Norbeck Papers. "It is rather discouraging when representatives from counties which would be directly benefited by such a measure, such as Grant County, vote against the proposition. However, due to matters which were entirely beyond the control of Senator Boland or myself, the bills were introduced in the senate much later than they should have been. With a proper amount of educational work during the next two years, I believe the bill for the establishment of statewide system of parks will pass at the next legislative session." Clifford A. Wilson to Peter Norbeck, March 26, 1929, State Park Possibilities Correspondence, Misc. folder, Box 100, Norbeck Papers.

[71] "I never could understand why a fifth park was added if the people representing that section in the Legislature were opposed to the program. I am afraid that fifth park lost some votes elsewhere and it certainly gained none in Grant County." Peter Norbeck to Clifford A. Wilson, April 1, 1929, State Park Possibilities Correspondence, Misc. folder, Box 100, Norbeck Papers.

[72] Norbeck to Jones, March 14, 1929.

[73] *Rapid City Journal*, reprinted in *Lead Call*, November 12, 1929, State Park Possibilities Newspaper Clippings folder, Box 117, Norbeck Papers.

[74] *Aberdeen News*, reprinted in *Rapid City Journal*, March 13, 1929, State Park Possibilities Newspaper Clippings folder, Box 117, Norbeck Papers.

[75] "I have no regret over the defeat of the bill. I think it was better to have it defeated than to have it win by a scratch. What we need is a two-thirds vote in each house; until we can get that we are not going to have any more parks." Peter Norbeck to Ronald D. Jones, April 22, 1929, State Park Possibilities Correspondence, Misc. folder, Box 100, Norbeck Papers.

[76] Beginning in 1920, commodity and land prices began a steady collapse and many of South Dakota's banks failed well before the stock market crash in October 1929. Debt-burdened farmers and ranchers continued throughout the decade with over-production and cultivation of sub-marginal lands, leaving many facing an apocalyptic reckoning–in both financial and ecological terms–prior to the beginning of the Great Depression. A drastic increase in the amount of land reverting back to counties occurred because of tax delinquency during the 1920s, a situation that worsened between 1931 and 1935. "This tax pressure served to encourage exploitation of the soil through repeated planting of the leading cash crop," pointed out one study conducted after World War II. Added pressure came from too many cattle and sheep grazing a shrinking amount of range during the drought years. Roger John Thomas, "A History of Soil Conservation in South Dakota through 1942" (M.S. thesis, University of South Dakota, 1949)," 7-8.

[77] Miller, "Politics Since Statehood," in Thompson, *A New South Dakota History*, 206. Paul S. Higbee, *South Dakota's Cowboy Governor Tom Berry: Leadership During the Depression* (Charleston, SC: The History Press, 2017), 27-40. Bulow won election to the U.S. Senate in 1930, was reelected in 1936, and defeated for reelection in 1942.

[78] Miller, "Politics Since Statehood," in Thompson, *A New South Dakota History*, 207. Higbee, *South Dakota's Cowboy Governor Tom Berry*, 41-52. Berry advocated budget cutting and more regressive tax policies than progressive Republicans and farm organizations. His conservative Democratic faction, according to a study in the early 1970s, was more interested in winning elections and doling out patronage than reform. Paul A. O'Rourke, "South Dakota Politics during the New Deal Years," *South Dakota History* 1 (Summer 1971): 237.

[79] Kenneth E. Hendrickson, Jr., "The Civilian Conservation Corps in South Dakota," *South Dakota History* 11 (Winter 1980): 2-4, 13.

[80] Peter Norbeck to Tom Berry, December 10, 1930, Tom Berry folder, Correspondence Files, Box 66, Norbeck Papers.

[81] Peter Norbeck to Enoch Norbeck, July 9, 1931, Custer State Park, 1921-1931 folder, Box 97, Norbeck Papers. Snyder, formerly an attorney, was a hotel proprietor in Watertown. He had also served in the Philippines during the Spanish-American War, rose to the rank of colonel in the South Dakota National Guard, and served in local offices in Watertown and Codington County. Robinson, *South Dakota: Sui Generis*, Vol III., 121-22.

[82] Norbeck to Enoch Norbeck, July 9, 1931.

[83] Julin, *A Marvelous Hundred Square Miles*, 110; "He Is Needed," *Rapid City Journal*, reprint in *Lead Call*, September 15, 1931, clipping in Custer State Park Board folder, Box 96, Norbeck Papers.

[84] Peter Norbeck to E. W. Martin, August 31, 1931, Custer State Park, 1921-1931 folder, Box 97, Norbeck Papers.

[85] *Lead Call*, reprint in *Pierre Capital-Journal*, October 15, 1931, clipping in Custer State Park Board folder, Box 96, Norbeck Papers.

[86] Julin, *A Marvelous Hundred Square Miles*, 108-09, 113-33.

[87] *Proceedings of the House of Representatives, Twenty-Second Legislative Session, 1931* (Pierre: State Publishing Co., 1931), 1107; *Proceedings of the Senate, Twenty-Second Legislative Session, 1931* (Pierre: State Publishing Co., 1931), 566.

[88] Custer State Park was exempted and remained under the jurisdiction of the Custer State Park Board. *Session Laws of the State of South Dakota, Twenty-Fourth Legislative Session, 1935* (Pierre: Hipple Printing Company, 1935), 306-07; *Proceedings of the House of Representatives, Twenty-Fourth Legislative Session, 1935* (Pierre: State Publishing Co., 1935), 513; *Proceedings of the Senate, Twenty-Fourth Legislative Session, 1935* (Pierre: State Publishing Co., 1935), 655.

[89] *Proceedings of the House of Representatives, Twenty-Sixth Legislative Session, 1939* (Pierre: State Publishing Co., 1939), 21-22, 407; *Proceedings of the Senate, Twenty-Sixth Legislative Session, 1939* (Pierre: State Publishing Co., 1939), 145, 147.

[90] *Session Laws of the State of South Dakota, Twenty-Sixth Legislative Session, 1939* (Pierre: Hipple Printing Company,), 298-299. *Proceedings of the Senate, 1939*, 562, 650; *Proceedings of the House, 1939*, 684, 688, 690, 741, 867.

[91] Both chambers passed the repeal measure unanimously. *Proceedings of the Senate, Twenty-Seventh Legislative Session, 1941* (Pierre: State Pub. Co., 1941), 10-11, 128; *Proceedings of the House, Twenty-Seventh Legislative Session, 1941* (Pierre: State Pub. Co., 1941), 264; *Session Laws of the State of South Dakota, Twenty-Seventh Session, 1941* (Pierre: Hipple Printing Company, 1941), 323.

[92] Hipschman, "Department History, 1909-1959," 59; *Session Laws of the State of South Dakota, Twenty-Ninth Session, 1945* (Pierre, SD: Hipple Printing Company, 1945), 94-96.

[93] Karl E. Mundt, "Our Conservation Policies," in *South Dakota: Fifty Years of Progress* (Sioux Falls, SD: S.D. Golden Anniversary Book Co., 1939), 37-38. Biographies of both Norbeck and Mundt describe no instances of personal or political tensions between the two. The absence of Norbeck in Mundt's essay may be a simple oversight, perhaps due to Norbeck's death a few years earlier.

[94] Ibid., 35, 37-38.

[95] Ibid., 36.

7

"Raise a Little Hell": The South Dakota Radical Tradition

Jeffrey A. Johnson
Providence College

In September 2020, the Trump Administration designated three American cities, New York, Seattle, and Portland, as "anarchist jurisdictions."[1] An unusual moment from the President (and later the Justice Department) on the whole, it also harkened back to the days of the 1886 Haymarket Riot in Chicago where authentic anarchists were involved in bomb throwing and ultimately deaths as part of the broader Gilded Age battle between labor and capital.

Chicago and the coasts, however accurate in the modern sense, do possess the reputation for radicalism in the American narrative. Yet if we think of the most "radical" American places, in the historical and contemporary sense, the Midwest and more specifically South Dakota might not be a part of our collective thinking. Historically its politics have been broadly more conservative and have reflected more agrarian and traditional interests and values. Indeed, its own trajectory has mirrored more, to borrow from the famed Progressive historian V. L. Parrington, "Main Currents" in American thought. While the country is not without its conflicts, as Parrington and his colleagues maintained when reflecting on the American experience, "illiberal" ideas remain outside of the mainstream.[2] Again, in the country's heartland, South Dakota, at first glance, is likely not the first state to come to mind as a particularly "radical" locale.

Digging a bit more below the surface, however, and if we think more critically about South Dakota's history in the long twentieth century, there is evidence to suggest a more apparent radical tradition. As historian William Pratt noted almost three decades ago, radicalism on the Northern Plains has an "extended history." Indeed, with a particularly robust agrarian brand of radicalism, extending from the Gilded Age through the Progressive Era, South Dakota is part of an often overlooked though significant unexpected ardor, political and otherwise. And that pattern of radical political alternatives–mostly from the left–extended well into the twentieth century as movements outside of agrarian politics saw militancy and radicalism, broadly conceived, extend to other rights for equality and justice.[3] While we might consider more carefully the full extent, for farmers, workers, women, and Natives, South Dakota boasts its own radical tradition.

Much of this radical custom, and particularly during the rise of "modern America," saw its impetus in the late-nineteenth century. Certainly, holding companies and trusts squeezed out competition (a phenomenon noted economist and social critic Thorstein Veblen dubbed "capitalistic sabotage"). As the wealth gap widened nationally during the age of the "Robber Barons," class difference grew increasingly apparent. And, for their part, the marginalized took notice. Finding only a frustratingly scant political voice for labor and farmers in the Democratic and Republican parties, the sidelined began to seek new political alternatives in the Gilded Age. Indeed, third party politics and those with sometimes radical agendas, took hold in much of the Midwest and a number of agrarian communities, and South Dakota was no exception. Unquestionably, the state might be considered one of the epicenters for agrarian discontent.

Born out of the earlier social cooperatives like the Grange movement, farmers joined clubs and the Farmers' Alliances beginning in 1877 as part of this agrarian protest that typified the reaction to eastern financiers and corporate control. Only three years later the Alliance boasted four million members. The Dakota Territory Alliance, chartered in 1881, boomed, and held their first annual meeting in Jamestown the next year. During the election of 1890, Alliances and their allies successfully elected 38 pro-alliance candidates to Congress and would hold control of the Nebraska legislature as well as the balance of power in Minnesota and South Dakota.[4]

In the American heartland and elsewhere, the Panic of 1893 emerged as a decisive event in the 1890s, and perhaps beyond the decade. A massive sell off of Philadelphia & Reading Railroad stock exposed the fragility of over speculation, and ultimately led to millions unemployed, a depleted treasury, and closer to the Midwest–spiraling agricultural prices, particularly for wheat. This financial crisis helped spur a key–and often radical–protest movement: the ultimate rise of the People's (or Populist) Party.

The rise of the Alliance and its pushback against the new industrial order represented a swelling agrarian radicalism and provided the institutional foundation for third party representation. After all, by the 1890s and accelerated by the hardship of the Panic, South Dakota farmers felt at the mercy of grain elevator and railroad transport costs. Speaking to those concerns, the Populists outlined their explicitly political goals at their famed Omaha, Nebraska, convention. There they proposed limiting monopolistic privilege and expanding direct democracy, such as a call for the direct election of U.S. senators and the political right of Americans for initiative and referendum. Populists seemed to speak–for decades–for the nation's farmers and rural areas, where even by 1910 a farmer's annual income was approximately $652. They also offered solutions to a sluggish post-Panic economy, the Populist call for "free silver" and the coinage of silver (at a 16:1 ratio to gold, called bimetallism) to stimulate currency and spending. They nominated, along with the Democrats (the famous moment of political "fusion"), William Jennings Bryan for President. The young Nebraskan squared off against William McKinley in the 1896 election, a contest Clarence Darrow called "the greatest battle of modern times."[5]

There were a number of central (and radical) figures in the broader Alliance/Populist story, but none as significant as South Dakota's Henry L. Loucks, who had worked at the center of the territory and state's agrarian reform movement, dating to the Alliance's founding in the state. At the 1894 Farmers' Alliance convention in Topeka, he laid out the causes of the Panic of 1893: Financial conditions were "appalling," the president said, and Wall Street financiers had "hood wink[ed] the people" into believing this was a normal economic hiccup. His 19-page speech typified a recurring call for monetary reform, direct democracy, agrarian rights, and economic and social fairness. "Until equal rights to all and special privileges to none shall be fact," he announced, continuing that the nation would never live up to what "our fore-father hoped . . . a beacon light to the oppressed of all nations of the world." He made a career of politics from the left and typified both the ideological protest at hand and also how those politics could be increasingly radicalized. On the one hand he liked to stir up a bit of trouble. "Before departing for my reward," he once wrote, "I want to raise a little Hell for the men who are doing their best to make a Hell on earth, and I am at least going to make some trouble for them." Yet he also represented this important Populist challenge, helping to articulate its aims, and his work remained in line with the varied political ideologies of South Dakota rural radicalism.[6]

"I want to raise a little Hell for the men who are doing their best to make a Hell on earth," wrote Henry L. Loucks, a leading proponent of early twentieth-century rural radicalism in South Dakota. *Courtesy South Dakota State Historical Society—State Archives.*

The purity of the radicalism of Loucks and South Dakota Populists can be debated, of course. Historian Chris Maier has argued that Great Plains Populism emerged somewhere in the ideological middle of previous interpretations from scholars like John Hicks and later Richard Hofstadter. For Maier, Populism was a "grassroots effort" of Midwesterners "in hopes of improving their rural communities." Much of this Populist agenda, however, later picked up by early twentieth-century Progressives, can be interpreted as fairly radical. We might ask *how* they proposed improving their communities and the ideas inherent in the Omaha platform–specifically the language against monopolistic power and the populist emphasis on class. Populists openly called for the government ownership of railroads, for example, and this, coupled with their classist anti-monopolistic privilege rhetoric, resulted in a fairly radical stance.[7]

Active in the Alliance and later as a candidate for U.S. Senate and governor, H. L. Loucks emerged as a key figure in that very 1892 Omaha Convention, serving as chairman of the meeting. And Loucks's enthusiastic leadership worked; in the 1890s South Dakota Populists elected a governor, senator, and congressmen, in addition to adoption of initiative and referendum legislation. His own political leanings exemplified these radical leanings, all within the contexts of disparate wealth, explicitly targeting the architects of monopolistic capitalism that squeezed out competition. "The trouble is not with the production of wealth," he explained, "but with its unjust distribution through special privileges." He, like his South Dakota colleagues, denounced railroad power, the failures of the Sherman Anti-Trust Act, and Loucks even penned a tome titled *The Great Conspiracy of the House of Morgan and How to Defeat It*.[8]

The discussion of the production of wealth from Loucks and his Populist allies, of course, alludes to the language of Marxism. And, in South Dakota as elsewhere, a burgeoning socialist movement did accompany the menagerie of reforms. Those movements often intersected, and it was not uncommon for someone in the state concerned with the new industrial order and matters of equity to move between causes and party affiliations. Loucks himself, for example, worked in the Farmers' Alliance, as a Populist, and later as a Progressive (with, at times, socialist leanings). That fluidity could prove problematic for the less radically inclined. The Omaha Platform's calls for a nationalizing of banking, currency, transport, and land use, after all, demonstrated both this link and radicalism. And in their 1908 call for the national convention in St. Louis, Populists (who among the National Committee were organizers like Deadwood's Freeman Knowles), made their intentions clear. The call explicitly invited delegates to "the great *radical* convention. . . and promised a *radical* mass meeting." In some Populist circles, like one of its organs, the *National Watchman,* the Alliance worried about that intersection and claimed that it was time for "populists and the socialists to part company." Activists seemed to understand the connection between a progressive Populism and a more radical socialism, and the Omaha Platform revealed this link. Believing this association underway, Senator James Kyle tellingly resigned as a member of the board of directors of the Populist *Aberdeen Star* "because of its radical position."[9]

Populism, however radical in its ideology and allegiances, spurred a number of ultimately Progressive reforms, particularly legislation aimed at direct democracy. It is worth mentioning that as the U.S. Constitution had allowed state legislatures the ability to elect U.S. senators, grift and greed corrupted the integrity of those appointments. And on the front lines of changing that were agrarian reformers like Loucks, but also his colleague Fr. Robert Haire. Fr. Haire arrived in Dakota Territory in 1880, was active in the Knights of Labor and the Farmers' Alliance, and worked on behalf of fairness for labor, politics, and women (specifically on the matter of suffrage). His clerical duties in northeast South Dakota were tightly linked with his political causes and Populist activism. Haire wrote that the initiative and referendum would place legislative power back to the "organic electorate" instead of "secret skullduggery." Given the long constitutional history of the idea of direct democracy (particularly if we are mindful of the Hamiltonian idea of the wider populace as the "great beast") was surely radical. Yet Fr. Haire and agrarian reformers like him brought this progressive reform to South Dakota, ultimately the first state to adopt the initiative and referendum in 1898. Fr. Haire's politics proved problematic for his vocation, however. He eventually left the priesthood amid criticism from church leadership.[10]

For the region's most left-leaning citizens and certainly some Populists, the new Socialist Party of America (SPA), established in 1901 in Indianapolis at the famed "Unity Convention," offered an outlet for activism against these radicalizing conditions. American socialists came in many different stripes, with some coming from the Socialist Labor Party (SLP) tradition of dogmatic Marxists and others embracing a less revolutionary and more tempered approach that centered on winning local elections. Certainly, the Midwest's Socialists, particularly the most moderate, focused their attention on municipal campaigns and grass roots activism. "Step by step we must conquer the political power," explained Girard, Kansas' *Appeal to Reason*, "municipal, state and national, until we have control of the machinery of government and when that day comes it will be the last of capitalism."[11]

In the early days of the South Dakota socialist party politics, and in keeping with national trends, electoral success remained scant. In 1902, for example, the state party ran John C. Crawford for governor, and he gained only approximately 3% of the vote. Chicago's *International Socialist Review*, which published in most issues a "News and Notes" section tracking activism around the country, did comment on the state's growing socialist presence and an increase from only 1,500 votes in 1900: "As is always the case with Socialist movements," it wrote, "an increased vote is the signal for increased activity in organization." By the next year its editors remained optimistic that the state party would soon be able to articulate a number of "immediate demands" into legislative proposals and petitions. The appointment of Comrade J. W. Bennett, of Iowa, as the key organizer in North and South Dakota in 1903 certainly would have raised expectations. With the party understanding that only five percent of petitioners in the state would trigger a statewide vote on demands, socialist items could be "enacted into law over the heads of old-party politicians, full credit accruing to the Socialist party initiating the desired legislation." In a familiar pattern for grass roots socialist organizing in these early years, that prediction was perhaps premature.[12]

South Dakota's Socialist Party came into its own in coming election cycles, however, and raised their visibility. Deadwood's Freeman Knowles, a Civil War veteran and former one-term South Dakota congressman (as a member, perhaps not surprisingly, of the Populist Party), twice ran for governor under the SPA banner in 1904 and 1906. Despite not winning the governor's race, Knowles remained active not just as an attorney and activist. On one occasion he addressed a group in Sioux Falls for a talk titled "the Social Paradox," and later sold the speech as a pamphlet. He also published newspapers in Nebraska and the Black Hills like his weekly *The Lantern*, all with the appearance of a "quiet mannered, inoffensive looking little man." Yet his activism could prove divisive, and some of his editorials were incendiary enough that the authorities took note. During 1907 and 1908 he faced an indictment from the federal grand jury for their messaging, and the U.S. government would not carry it in the mail. Knowles ultimately served 21 days in the Pennington County Jail, a sentence that perhaps signaled the antiradicalism to come.[13]

The profile for South Dakota's socialists seemed highest around 1906 and the Knowles era, and particularly in certain strongholds. For example, in that year socialists tallied the highest percentages in the northern part of the state (Brown County) and the northwest (Butte, Meade, and Lawrence Counties). In addition, two South Dakota socialists ran for congress in both 1904 and 1906. And, as was the pattern in the early twentieth century, socialists were considered a legitimate and open third party alternative. Anecdotally, H. F. Homstron wrote from Avon that he intended to travel to Oregon and penned a public letter to newspaper readers out West. Calling himself "a full fledged socialist," he announced that he currently considered a move to Oregon or somewhere on the coast, but sought information about business ventures in the state. He wrote publicly of some pragmatic economic concerns that sounded less like a dogmatic Marxist and more like a common-sense businessman. As someone in the "general merchandise" business in South Dakota, he hoped for "a better climate for balance in my life" as he scouted business prospects. He then published a series of questions about real estate, crop production, material prices, and more. He finished his open letter with "yours for the coming revolution, H. F. Homstron." Perhaps indicative of this recognizable socialism, Homston's travels certainly indicated a front-facing radicalism.[14]

Indeed, the Knowles era of socialist electoral success, with governor's races as a barometer, was never eclipsed. When John C. Knapp ran for governor, for example, he mustered only about 2.2% of the vote. And when Indiana's Eugene Debs–the consummate face of American socialism–enjoyed his greatest electoral success in 1912, earning about 6% of the vote in his campaign for president, South Dakota socialists failed to keep pace, with Samuel Lovett gaining about 3% of the vote for governor. And while elections are not the only barometer of radicalism, the early pervasiveness of South Dakota's third parties on the left, however successful electorally, provide some evidence of prevalence.

Notable South Dakota politicians increasingly aligned themselves with the left. Former U.S. Senator and longtime Republican Richard Pettigrew saw his politics grow more radical. In his writing and thinking he expressed an interest in Socialism and Communism and wrote two books that received praise from Soviet leaders Vladimir Lenin and Leon Trotsky. Indeed, his sympathies remained radical. "The remedy is not to correct abuses, but to revolutionize the whole system," he wrote. "The remedy is not rural credit or reform of any sort, but absolute revolution if we would rescue the American people from being plundered of the products of their toil." He remained keenly interested in countering the two-party stronghold and wrote to famed Populist H. L. Loucks, "I am going to join the Socialists, or, vote the Socialist ticket. I think it might be possible to build up a Socialist party so that it would have the balance of power between the two old parties." For his part, H. L. Loucks was not entirely dismissive of socialism, either, and similarly corresponded with the famed Chicago socialist publisher Charles Kerr, the editor of the *International Socialist Review*. Considering the broad ideas of socialism and economic fairness, Loucks wrote to Kerr that "I am very sure that our aim is the same although our method of reaching it may be somewhat different." Loucks even encouraged Pettigrew to help him establish a socialist paper. "Now as to the plan of propaganda," he said, I am more than ever convinced that we must have a medium . . . . But instead of one Daily at Sioux Falls, why not two or three?"[15]

The comparatively early flourishing of South Dakota socialism and populism may be best explained by understanding the late-nineteenth century agrarian radicalism so central to South Dakota political life that much of the country failed to experience with such pronouncement. While this occurrence stands outside of familiar electoral patterns for the left, the demise of South Dakota socialism mirrored national trends and, for perhaps the same ideological reasons as its rise, help explain its hasty exit. Indeed, the South Dakota experience appears in line with WWI-era repression of radical dissent and politics. For example, the socialist candidate for South Dakota governor in 1918 received only 741 votes (about 0.8%), while previous candidates during this period often gleaned around 3%. This was the last significant socialist appearance on the ballot for governor.The precipitous decline no doubt accompanied the events surrounding World War I. American socialists, as socialists did worldwide, objected to the conflict. After all, they claimed, all wars are capitalist wars and the working class would do the bulk of the fighting. In response, the government targeted radicals to halt anti-war politicizing, notably the Espionage Act (1917), the Trading with the Enemy Act (1917), and the Sedition Act (1918) combined to create the Red Scare climate. Accusations of "disloyalty" grew commonplace, as did crackdowns on activism generally and publications specifically. One particular government tactic was to restrict "disloyal" speech as disseminated through the U.S. Mail. Organs like the *International Socialist Review*, for example, ceased publication in 1918. And those in the Midwest, with that tradition of Populism, carried with them broader sensibilities that might have been counter to leftist anti-militarism and anti-interventionism. During the Populist era, as written into the Omaha platform and central to William Jennings Bryan's worldview, was a smattering of isolationism and at times anti-imperialism. While not as vehemently antiwar as socialists, certainly the Populist ethos was a domestic centric ideology, as historian Catherine Stock has explained.[16]

While the WWI era saw a crackdown on leftist politics, by this time the wider reform-minded Progressive Era was in full swing, as radicals and reformers worked endlessly on matters of justice and fairness. Rights for women emerged as another cause that proved radical to traditional American leanings, and activists in South Dakota accompanied the charge. During the period since the Civil War and into the early twentieth century, women still did not enjoy fundamental rights such as the ability to sign contracts, hold property and, of course, vote or hold office. Reformers such as Susan B. Anthony and Carrie Chapman Catt and organizations like the National Women Suffrage Association had worked tirelessly for decades to change gender roles in the United States, working for equality and suffrage.

In support of the Suffragist cause, South Dakota women organized parades throughout the state. *Courtesy South Dakota State Historical Society—State Archives.*

In South Dakota, with statehood a reality by late 1889, suffragists remained optimistic that greater fairness with the vote would come soon. A shrewd strategist, Catt had consistently stressed incremental work on local levels, an approach she called "the winning plan," and she believed this approach would culminate with national suffrage legislation. And by 1910, nine western states allowed women the vote. Yet South Dakota stood outside of this trend, in part because of silence on suffrage from the religious communities, specifically Lutherans, Catholics, and Methodists. As Catt observed, "our strongest friends everywhere else, are not so here."

This stymieing of the movement sometimes demanded more radical strategies. Elizabeth Cady Stanton, for example, penned *The Woman's Bible* in 1895 to dissect the argument that female submissiveness was rooted in scripture. One similarly radical activist in South Dakota was suffragist Matilda Joslyn Gage, of Aberdeen, who worked in South Dakota and on the national stage. Gage took on religious organizations in a number of ways, but most explicitly with the 1890 formation of the Woman's Liberal Union, which maintained that those Christian churches remained the true nemesis of women. She further articulated this in an 1893 text titled *Woman, Church, and State.* The National American Woman Suffrage Association, fearing the radicalism of these authors, distanced itself from them.[17]

In the context of radicalism, those opposed to suffrage (specifically, male voters in 1890 resoundingly voted nearly 2:1 against the measure) were quick to label the movement as militant and threatening. Presbyterian minister P. D. Stephenson, for example, asserted "This 'women's movement' is a revolution, radical in nature and influence, completely uprooting and destroying all the ideas, convictions, customs heretofore cherished by the Christian world." For critics like Stephenson, the notion of suffrage remained radical for a number of reasons. Opponents like him believed women possessed delicate natural characteristics and any infusion of male characteristics would be unnatural. Moreover, women who focused on suffrage or remained sympathetic to female celibacy as a protest abandoned their roles as wives and mothers and led the world to "moral suicide." These counter-protests may have limited the suffrage movement, but women in South Dakota eventually earned the right to vote in 1918, only one year before the federal amendment.[18]

Despite a seemingly moribund Populist movement in South Dakota, its tradition of agrarian radicalism persisted. Certainly, part of the longer history of the People's/Populist Party, the Nonpartisan League and the Farmer-Labor Party grew in prominence after World War I, as farmers in South Dakota battled a cycle of economic downturns and lowered farm prices in the late-nineteenth and early twentieth century. By the 1920s that discontent continued. With the 1923 establishment of the United Farmers League in Fargo, a new and more radical alternative to the earlier Nonpartisan League and Farmer-Labor Party had appeared. Indeed, the most "militant" constituents from those organizations found a home in the UFL and while small in number, the chapter north of Aberdeen in Frederick attracted organizers like Ella "Ma" Bloor and George Maki (both Communist Party operatives) and Charles Taylor of Plentywood, Montana (where he edited the *Producers News*), a self-described "Socialist in some terms." By the Depression Era, South Dakota (and farmers in both Dakotas) were further radicalized by the dire economic conditions.

Harvest hands in Mitchell, South Dakota, being marched to a northbound freight train after being searched for weapons, July 30, 1916. *The Center for Western Studies.*

Not surprisingly, many of those working on or with the Farmers' Holiday Association and/or Farmers Union had their political roots in previous agrarian protest movements. For example, the treasurer of the Holiday movement, Emil Loriks of Oldham, had served earlier in the Nonpartisan League. Similarly, Clarence Sharp of Bristol, who by the 1930s served as secretary of the state's Communist Party, was the son of a Populist, had sold socialist papers in the early years of the twentieth century, and had worked on behalf of the Nonpartisan League. This longer legacy of rural radicalism meant that a generation of organizers by the 1930s had a long history in the movement.

South Dakota's farm holiday–instituted in the summer of 1932–represented a radical spirit as well. Farmers from South Dakota (along with those in neighboring Iowa, Nebraska, Minnesota, and North Dakota) called for a farm strike. They blocked roads and demanded the "cost of production" as they battled dipping prices and impending foreclosures. A radical moment, certainly, as the means of production saw a challenge and a broad strike came. Still, historian John Miller argued that compared to the farm holiday in other states, South Dakota's moment was tempered and lacked the radicalism elsewhere. For Miller, and considering geographic, historic, and political factors, this brief moment of agrarian radicalism was softened. "In a basically conservative state," he wrote, "the Farm Holiday followed a moderate course."[19]

Indeed, by 1932, the state had seen what historian Allan Mathews called, in disagreement with Miller, "rapid growth in farm radicalism," and the UFL stood at the center of that continued activism. When they convened for their 1933 Farmers Relief Conference in Pierre, a number of other farmer organization members decided to not join them, feeling it too radical. After all, Mathews reminded us, communists dominated the speaker lineup and some of the meeting demands included those in line with Marxist agenda items, including condemnation of "imperialist wars." The next year the UFL executive council in Minneapolis even critiqued the South Dakota UFL membership for their leftist leanings. Dubbing them a "left wing organization," the council felt that the South Dakota leadership hoped only to emphasize class struggle "toward the final aim of establishing a workers and farmers government." There is little doubt that the South Dakota UFL not only had support from the Communist Party, but also some of its organizers spoke openly of a coming socialist revolution. Sisseton's David Gilbertson recalled that during the hard times of the 1930s, individuals passed out communist literature on Main Street. In addition, it was believed there was enough support for the Nonpartisan League across the border in North Dakota that some in northern Roberts County discussed secession from South Dakota.

Not surprisingly, pushback against these radical agrarian activists, the number of which is difficult to quantify, still reliably occurred. In Sisseton rumors circulated that government Bureau of Investigation agents around town were asking questions of suspected communists. According to David Gilbertson:

> There was another story up there where these folks were having a meeting in a pasture, so Legion members went to the local hardware store, got 10 gallons of red barn paint, went up in an old open cockpit biplane and dumped the paint on them while they were holding a meeting from the air–sending them a message.

Similarly, several UFL leaders were arrested and jailed in the summer of 1934 for "riotous assembly" after the attorney general secured an injunction again. In response the United Farmers League published a pamphlet titled FASCISM COMES TO SOUTH DAKOTA! Ultimately found not guilty, the governmental pushback against this type of leftwing activity in the northeast part of the state was firm. Moreover, the reputation for radicalism perhaps hindered the movement, one that was ultimately small, but nevertheless important. While the accounts of radical activism and response may involve some folklore, the radical past in the northern part of the state was hardly an entire fabrication.[20]

Undeniably, this pattern of radicalism and antiradicalism had unfolded for years. Even before McCarthyism formally emerged in 1950, when a Wisconsin senator told a group of Republican women in West Virginia that he had a list of "disloyal" Americans in government, anticommunism had come to South Dakota. As historian John Miller recounted in a piece titled "McCarthyism Before McCarthy," the 1938 election cycle demonstrated a familiar pattern of rhetorical challenges that questioned the loyalty of political opponents. In the congressional race that year, Madison's Karl Mundt, who had not held public office but enjoyed name recognition for previous races, ran against Democrat Emil Loriks. Loriks, an Arlington farmer, had been active in the Non-Partisan League and South Dakota Farmers Union. Throughout the campaign, Loriks' "un-Americanism" was questioned, and the *Sioux Falls Argus-Leader*, on the heels of those attacks, wrote that the paper "does not believe that Loriks is a Communist. It does maintain, however, that his radical approach to public problems is assisting the [labor organization] CIO and, in turn, the Communist party." The paper remained consequential in the public debate during the election cycle and, ultimately, helped sway the election. In another editorial, the paper declared "radicalism is a major issue in the South Dakota campaign and let no one forget it. . . . They are stirring class hatred. . . . Bear in mind that the Democratic candidates have received the endorsement of the Communists and other subversives." As a Congressman, Karl Mundt spent the next 34 years in Washington representing South Dakota, perhaps unsurprisingly given that campaign, as an ardent anti-communist.[21]

The worst fears of McCarthy devotees came to fruition later in the century. South Dakota State Department contract employee Kendall Myers and his wife Gwendolyn spied for the Cuban government for decades, all from South Dakota. He employed his security clearance for almost 30 years to collect classified information, and during that time she would help ensure Cuban go-betweens received it. His career as an adjunct professor in international studies and her work as a world affairs aide for Senator James Abourezk saw them increasingly radicalized. Ultimately, the FBI discovered that their activities included "dispatches to Havana over short-wave radio, dropped packages to handlers in shopping carts at local grocery stores, traveled across Latin America to meet with Cuban agents and used false documents to travel to Havana for an evening with Mr. Castro." They worked from Pierre but longed for the opportunity to one day sail to Cuba, a place they called "home." He is serving a life sentence in prison for espionage. She completed her term in 2015. Covered nationally, the case remains a striking example of bona fide radical activity in the state.[22]

In the context of radicalism in South Dakota, we need also to consider the state's turbulent history in regard to Native Americans. Specifically, the fight for civil rights has generated forceful responses, particularly in terms of political participation and radical protest. Indeed, in 1889 South Dakota had legislated limited voting, jury service, and political candidates to white men only. Later, and despite the federal Indian Citizenship Act of 1924, South Dakota failed to observe this statute. Even into the 1970s and 1980s cases upheld the pattern of disenfranchisement of those South Dakotans living in "unorganized counties" (read: reservations).[23]

Radical responses to the lack of equity for Native Americans surfaced in the 1960s and 1970s. Established in 1968, the American Indian Movement (AIM) initiated several occupations, notably Alcatraz Island in San Francisco and later the Bureau of Indian Affairs building in Washington, D.C. These demonstrated pushback against the wider and longer legacy of historic mistreatment of American Indians, including, but not limited to, violations of 1868 Fort Laramie Treaty, the memory of the 1862 lynching of 38 Dakotas in Minnesota, widespread poverty, and the "Massacre of the Innocents" in 1890.

Russell Means, South Dakotan and Lakota Sioux, emerged as one of the most prominent AIM spokesmen. Along with many other Sioux organizations, AIM grew, to the chagrin of federal officials. FBI agent Joseph Trimbach called Pine Ridge a place "attempting to promote a left-wing agenda." Then on February 27, 1973, AIM members led about 200 Sioux in occupying the town of Wounded Knee. The site of the famed 1890 massacre, it was doubly significant for the economic inequity it represented. The occupation spanned 71 days and during the standoff gunfire between the protestors and government agents left two Sioux men dead. It stood as a powerful reminder of the long and frustrating history of Ameri-Indian relations and the radicalism it has spurred.[24]

Other examples of radicalism and protest have followed in the 1970s and since. Leonard Peltier, an AIM member, shot two FBI agents (Jack Coler and Ron Williams) at Pine Ridge in June 1975. The agents were searching for another AIM member named Jimmy Eagle when they engaged in a firefight with Peltier and others. He has been imprisoned since 1977, following a controversial trial. We have seen even more contemporary expressions of protest from and on behalf of the American Indian community in South Dakota. As the Dakota Access Pipeline was announced and constructed, significant and widely publicized protests occurred at the Standing Rock Reservation, straddling North and South Dakota. In recent years the state's prison population (which grew 500% from 1977-2012) is 1/3rd Native, despite Natives comprising only 9% of the state's population. There is disparity in representation in South Dakota legislation for Native Americans. The state has nine federally recognized tribes, yet the state legislature represents approximately 4% of that body.[25]

There certainly may be labor fights and political ones ahead in the state. South Dakota's demographics point to an 85% white population and only 7% of its workforce is unionized, for example. In addition, the recent culture wars and political battles over our collective history have accelerated. In 2020 South Dakota Governor Kristi Noem commented on historical monuments and reinforced the message from President Trump's speech at Mount Rushmore as "unifying" and "positive," noting the importance of honoring the founders and our traditional understanding. "I think it's important we protect our history. This isn't about equality anymore," Noem told Fox host Neil Cavuto. "This is a radical rewriting of our history to take away our freedoms and liberties. It's really trying to rewrite the foundation of this country and so it's alarming to me," she said.[26]

Examining the historical record, and particularly focusing our attention on moments of agrarian protest, Marxists, female, and Native

American protest, at least some currents of radicalism in South Dakota have been persistent, varied, and important to shaping the modern state.

Notes

[1] BBC News, September 21, 2020, https://www.bbc.com/news/world-us-canada-54238101.

[2] See V.L. Parrington, *Main Currents in American Thought,* 3 vols. (1927).

[3] William C. Pratt, "Rural Radicalism on the Northern Plains, 1912-1950." *Montana: The Magazine of Western History* 42: 1 (1992): 43. There are certainly numerous examples of historians who have chronicled the broader American West's radical past and, most frequently, their work has centered on leftist labor and working class radicalism in the region. Those works include Melvyn Dubofsky's 1966 essay in *Labor History* titled "The Origins of Western Working Class Radicalism, 1890–1905," and Carlos A. Schwantes' 1979 book *Radical Heritage: Labor, Socialism, and Reform in Washington and British Columbia, 1885–1917*; both represent the significant work of this vein. See Jeffrey A. Johnson, "What is Radicalism in the West, Anyway?" *Journal of the West* 53 (Winter 2014): 11.

[4] The Southern Alliance, formed in Texas in 1877, the same year as the Northern Alliance's establishment in New York. Jeffrey A. Johnson, "'Equal Opportunity For All. That's All': South Dakota's H.L. Loucks and the Fight for Reform, 1885-1928," *South Dakota History* 46:1 (Spring 2016): 1-2. For a concise and helpful discussion of the Farmers' Alliances, since their 1877 founding, see Robert McMath, *American Populism: A Social History, 1877-1898* (New York: Hill & Wang, 1993).

[5] Jeffrey A. Johnson, *The 1916 Preparedness Day Bombing: Anarchy and Terrorism in Progressive Era America* (New York & London: Routledge, 2017), 18-19; Alan Dawley, *Struggles for Justice: Social Responsibility and the Liberal State* (Cambridge, MA: Harvard University Press, 1991), 1; Michael McGerr, *A Fierce Discontent: The Rise and Fall of the Progressive Movement in America, 1870–1920* (New York: Oxford, 2003), 24.

[6] See Johnson, "'Equal Opportunity For All.'"

[7] Chris Maier, "The Farmers' Fight for Representation: Third-Party Politics in South Dakota, 1889-1918." *Great Plains Quarterly* 34:2 (Spring 2014): 143.

[8] Johnson, "'Equal Opportunity For All," 10-11.

[9] Brian J. Weed, "Populist thought in North and South Dakota, 1890-1900" (Theses and dissertations, University of North Dakota, 1970), 17, 24; *The Iowa Official Register for 1909-1910* (Des Moines, 1909), 365.

[10] Steven Plott, "The Origins of the Initiative and Referendum in South Dakota: The Political Context." *Great Plains Quarterly* (1992): 185; Katie Hunhoff, "Credit or Blame the Aberdeen Priest," *South Dakota Magazine,* February 21, 2017; Sister Anna Marie Weinreis," Robert W. Haire–Dakota Images," *South Dakota History* (1988): 116-17.

[11] *Appeal to Reason* (Girard, KS), March 23, 1912.

[12] *International Socialist Review* 3 (December 1902): 363-64; *International Socialist Review* 4 (October 1903): 207, 226.

[13] Tom Lawrence, *Black Hills Pioneer*, June 16, 2015; *The Bad River News* (Philip, Stanley County, SD), August 27, 1908; *International Socialist Review* 4 (June 1904): 775. These early socialist electoral returns in gubernatorial races were as follows: In 1902 John C. Crawford received 2,511 votes of 73,939 cast. In 1904 Freeman Knowles received 3,028 of 100,391 cast. In 1906 Freeman Knowles received 2,542 of 74,572 cast. In 1904, it is worth noting, four Presidential Electors were socialists (Christopher Gross, G.A. Grant, D.G. Stewart, and Edward Anderson). SD Election Results 1901-1910. Historic Election Archive, Center for the Study of Politics and Governance, Humphrey Institute of Public Affairs, www.politicsandgovernance.org, adapted from SD Secretary of State, South Dakota Legislative Manual.

[14] The congressional candidates were S.A. Cochrane and H.W. Smith (1904) and Henry Adolph Berg and James Kirwan (1906). South Dakota's socialist candidates for governor and their respective vote percentages were Samuel Lovett (1912 - 3.0%), John Knapp (1914 - 2.7%), and Fred Fairchild (1916 - 2.8%); Maier, "The Farmers' Fight," 157. SD Election Results 1901-1910. *The Daily Capital Journal* (Salem, OR), September 1, 1906.

[15] John Andrews, "Pettigrew's Redemption," *South Dakota Magazine* (September/October 2010); R. F. Pettigrew to Loucks, May 16, 1916, H. L. Loucks Correspondence with R. F. Pettigrew, South Dakota State University Archives and Special Collections, Hilton M. Briggs Library, MA 23, F7. Johnson, "'Equal Opportunity For All"; Letter to R. F. Pettigrew, April 19, 1915, Loucks Correspondence, SDSU, MA 23, F2.

[16] Jeffrey A. Johnson, "Why is There No Socialism in the U.S.?–100 Years Later," in *U.S. History in Global Perspective*, Cathy Gorn, ed. (Santa Barbara, CA: ABC-Clio, 2013), 5. Now, according to Stock, there has been a post-WWII shift: "Today, despite continued misgivings about the power of the federal government in general, and surging interest in the neo-isolationist views of Ron and Rand Paul, few voters in these rural red states have anything but high regard for and close physical ties to the military. They volunteer, serve, and fall in war at much higher numbers per capita than do residents of states on either coast." Catherine McNicol Stock, "Making War Their Business: The Short History of Populist Anti-Militarism," *The Journal of the Gilded Age and Progressive Era*, 13:3 (2014): 389-92. See also Ahrar Ahmad, "War and Peace in South Dakota," in *The Plains Political Tradition: Essays on South Dakota Political Culture*, Jon K. Lauck, John E. Miller, and Donald C. Simmons Jr., eds. (Pierre: South Dakota Historical Society Press, 2011), 186-210.

[17] See Angelica Shirley Carpenter, *Born Criminal: Matilda Joslyn Gage, Radical Suffragist* (Pierre: South Dakota Historical Society Press, 2018) and Sara

Egge, *Woman Suffrage and Citizenship in the Midwest, 1870-1920* (Iowa City: University of Iowa Press, 2018).

[18] See also Aristophanes' *Lysistrata*. Dennis A. Norlin, "The Suffrage Movement and South Dakota Churches: Radicals and the Status Quo, 1890." *South Dakota History* 14 (December 1984): 308-10, 322-33.

[19] See John L. Shover, "The Farmers' Holiday Association Strike, August 1932." *Agricultural History* 39 (October 1965): 196-203; John E. Miller, "Restrained, Respectable Radicals: The South Dakota Farm Holiday," *Agricultural History* 59: 3 (1985): 429, 447.

[20] More conventional political demands/positions, such as cash relief for workers and school fee freezes, were also included. Allan Mathews, "Agrarian Radicals: The United Farmers League of South Dakota." *South Dakota History* 3 (1973): 408, 411, 414, 416; Pratt, "Rural Radicalism," 48-49, 51. *Capital Journal* (Pierre, SD), June 19, 2014. Beginning in 1915, in Montana's northeastern corner, Sheridan County radicals published the *Producers News* in Plentywood. The paper existed until 1937 and represented a number of political perspectives, including those of the Non-Partisan League, the Farmer-Labor Party, and the United Farmers League. In the paper's earliest years, though, its editor was "Red Flag" Charles ("Charlie") Taylor, later a two-term senator in the Montana legislature. See Jeffrey A. Johnson, *"They Are All Red Out Here": Socialist Politics in the Pacific Northwest, 1895-*1925 (Norman: University of Oklahoma Press, 2008).

[21] John E. Miller, "McCarthyism Before McCarthy: The 1938 Election in South Dakota," unpublished manuscript at Emporia State University, 3-4, 7, www.spacep01.emporia.edu.

[22] *New York Times*, June 18, 2009. See also David S. Mills, "Politics, Piety, and Patriotism: Early Cold War Politics in South Dakota," in Lauck et al., *The Plains Political Tradition* (2011).

[23] Jean Reith Schroedel and Artour Aslanian, "A Case Study of Descriptive Representation: The Experience of Native American Elected Officials in South Dakota." *American Indian Quarterly* 41:3 (2017): 255.

[24] AIM organizers initiated the 1972 Trail of Broken Treaties and the "Longest Walk" in 1978. Elizabeth Cook-Lynn, "Twentieth-Century American Indian Political Dissent and Russell Means," *Wicazo Sa Review* 29:1 (2014): 15.

[25] Joseph Ezzo, *"The Leonard Peltier Case: An Argument in Support of Executive Clemency Based on Norms of International Human Rights," American Indian Law Review* 38 (2013): 37-38; Nick Estes, "Fighting for Our Lives: #NoDAPL in Historical Context"; *Wicazo Sa Review* 32: 2 (2017): 118; Darren Thompson, "South Dakota's Election Has Significant Impact on Tribes," *Native News Online*, November 4, 2020; Schroedel and Aslanian, "A Case Study of Descriptive Representation," 254.

[26] "South Dakota Gov. Noem decries 'radical agenda, which is a political agenda designed to destroy this country," "The Future of Labor Is Growing in South Dakota," *New Republic*, September 7, 2020; FoxNews.com, July 7, 2020.

8

The German-Language Press in South Dakota

Samantha M. Litty
Europa-Universität Flensburg

Introduction[1]

When (im)migration to South Dakota peaked around 1910, the number of foreign-born reached just over 100,000 with German-speaking (im)migrants among the largest group between 1890-1930.[2] Previous research on Germans in South Dakota has focused on German-speaking immigrants from Russia and on sectarian religious groups such as the Mennonites and Hutterites,[3] but little considers the German-language press. Anton H. Richter[4] notes that only one publication has been described in any detail (*Dakota Freie Presse*[5]). While Istvan Gombocz' recent piece on the *Eureka Rundschau*[6] adds another publication to that list, major works on German publications in the United States rarely mention South Dakota. Carl Frederick Wittke[7] notes the German-language press in South Dakota only twice and Karl J. R. Arndt and Mary E. Olson suggest "A complete study of the history of the German-Americans in South Dakota ought to be undertaken [. . .] before more records are destroyed or lost."[8] The lack of mentions of South Dakota newspapers shows that the German-language press in this region has been drastically understudied.

In the decade before the Civil War, the German press in the United States expanded greatly. By 1850, some Midwestern cities had a more robust German-language press than in European German cities[9] with several cities including Milwaukee, Chicago, and St. Louis offering multiple daily papers.[10] Despite beginning well after the Civil War, following German immigration to the region, South Dakota developed a strong German-language press central to the formation of a regional German-American identity.

Like the German-language presses in other regions, those in South Dakota printed on a broad range of topics, reporting local, national, and international news, often from the "homeland." Despite local and regional differences, the German-language press in South Dakota regularly included tales of murder, robbery, or great fires,[11] but also literary elements such as poetry, *Humoristisches* "comedic elements," and serialized novels.

This chapter takes an introductory look at the history and variation in German-language publications in South Dakota, focusing on newspapers. After a brief description of German immigration to the region, this chapter describes the history of the German-language press in South Dakota, examines several trends in German-language publication types, and closes with a case study showing how one of these papers used direct address to its readership to create and foster a German identity based on language rather than origin or nationality.

German Immigration to Dakota Territory and South Dakota[12]

(Im)migration to the Dakota Territory began in the first half of the nineteenth century, slowly at first by riverboats and covered wagons with Yankees–English-speakers, primarily Americans born on the east coast–as initial settlers of towns such as Sioux Falls and Yankton.[13] By the 1870s many societal institutions–churches, public schools, social organizations, and English-language press–were already founded by Yankee settlers,[14] paving the way for a shift to institutions dominated by the foreign-born population in the last two decades of the nineteenth century.[15]

A variety of factors encouraged German (im)migration to the Dakota Territory (and later South Dakota), often paralleling (im) migration to other states in the Midwest (cf. Litty forthcoming). The Dakota Territory provided immigrants with a place where they could settle in groups "drawn together by their common history, language, and religion."[16] The earliest German-speaking settlers to the Dakota Territory are those referred to as Germans from Russia, sometimes called "German-Russians." Most came from near the Black Sea, where they had been for several generations prior to immigration. The Germans from Russia, belonging to several religions, including Catholics, Lutherans, Jews, Mennonites, and Hutterites,[17] began settling in the Dakota Territory as early as 1873.[18]

From 1890 to 1910, immigrants from Norway, Germany, and Russia made up at least half of all foreign-born immigrants in South Dakota. Norwegian immigrants made up the largest group from any one country, but as over 80% of the immigrants from Austria, Germany, Rumania, Russia, and Switzerland indicated their first language as German, linguistically, the "German" group made up over 30% of all foreign-born immigrants,[19] making them the largest immigrant group. In 1930 immigrants who identified as German speaking frequently comprised substantial percentages of the total immigrant population from Austria (89.1%), Czechoslovakia (4.5%), Germany (99.5%), Poland (35%), Rumania (73.4%), Russia (88.1%), and Switzerland (90%).[20] Distinguishing between groups based on language rather than origin is therefore necessary as the "mother tongue of the immigrant indicates his cultural or ethnic origin; the country of birth indicates his geographical and political origin" and "persons of German language and culture [. . .] come from other countries than Germany itself."[21] If we consider nation of origin alone, many thousands of German-speaking immigrants throughout the state would not be identified. Given the large numbers of German-speaking settlers, largely German-speaking communities with their social networks in place were frequently becoming the norm, highlighting both a need and a market for a German-language press.

German-language Press in South Dakota

The total number of German-language publications in the U.S. from its inception is estimated at around 5,000, the first founded by Benjamin Franklin.[22] Arndt and Olson assert that the large number of German-language publications shows "the wide range of the German language as a native language."[23] Although initially written over forty years ago, it bears repeating "that English was not the only native American language"[24] nor is it today.

While English-language papers were established in (now) South Dakota as early as 1859 with *The Democrat* in Sioux Falls,[25] the German-language press arose later, as the demand for news in the German language increased. The foreign-language press in the nineteenth century was generally seen as performing the same function as American press, albeit "published in a foreign tongue."[26] While operating in a minority or foreign language, the news and views published therein were locally owned and operated and descriptive of the American(-German) perspective. Nineteenth-century foreign-language press is often credited with playing a substantial role in the transition of immigrants into their new environment, allowing them to retain ties to their places of origin, but also integrating them into the customs and culture of their new residence.[27] Richter goes so far as to describe the foreign-language press as a "linguistic lifeline" for new immigrants, but also calls it "an agent of Americanization, providing instruction in the history, ideals and procedures of the new country, printing local and national news, giving advice in its editorials, and acquainting the newcomer with the American standard of living."[28]

Thirty-seven publications using German as a print language have been published in South Dakota.[29] The earliest and longest running was the *Dakota Freie Presse*, which began in Yankton in 1874 and ran until 1954.[30] The last founded came into existence in 1915 (*Eureka Rundschau*). Previous research identifies only twenty-five German-language publications in South Dakota.[31] Given recent digitalization efforts by the South Dakota State Historical Society and the Library of Congress, it is likely that more publications have been unearthed or distinguished as separate publications since Arndt and Olson conducted their bibliographic work in the mid-twentieth century. The classification "German-language publication" considers any publication which used German as a print language at any time during its publication run. As some publications existed only briefly, frequently changed owners or locations, or simply due to the passage of time, it is likely that some publications have been lost or have no known record.

Publications at this time often underwent name changes which may cause variation in overall publication counts. Where one publication has undergone a name change, these are considered one publication. For example, the *Süd-Dakota Nachrichten*,[32] was also known under the names *Süd-Dakota Nachrichten und Herold*, the *Nachrichten-Herold*, and the *Deutscher Herold*. The German-language press encompasses publications almost entirely published in German, but also primarily English publications which sometimes had German-language sections or articles. Unsurprisingly, some initially German-language publications shifted to include English alongside German. Many of the English-language publications with German-language sections were published for only a brief period of time, generally in the early twentieth century, ending around the end of World War I.

This decline of German as a print language is generally attributed to section nineteen of the Trading with the Enemy Act of 1917, which required "true and complete translations" of any foreign-language print, newspaper, or publication regarding the war to be filed with the local postmaster until they had proven their loyalty to the U.S. and received a permit to continue printing without supervision.[33] Yet, of fifteen publications in South Dakota printing in German in 1916, three had already ceased publication in German by the end of 1916, but ten were still publishing in German after 1918. This indicates that the 1917 law, which has previously been given so much weight as the main reason the German-language press stopped existing,[34] does not appear to hold true in South Dakota.

The "Americanization" or loss of the German language and German-language institutions is a natural process that began prior to World War I, not appearing suddenly or unexpectedly.[35] By the beginning of the twentieth century, the consolidation of newspapers and publishers was well underway as it was only through the adaptation and merging of business endeavors that they could remain in business. The trend toward a rapid decline in numbers of papers and their circulation was evident and "unmistakable before World War I."[36] Across the U.S., many publications suspended business, hoping to revive publication after the war ended, but many never resumed publication.[37] Estimates of German-language publications in 1918 dropped and many remaining publications were not newspapers, but lodge, church, or trade publications, many of which became bilingual or shifted entirely to English at this time.[38] While there were no newly founded German-language publications in South Dakota in 1917, five were founded 1922-1935, four of which were religious bulletins, and one was a manual for a youth organization.

Variation in German-language Use

There are several variants of what is categorized as German-language press. Some are nearly entirely printed in German, others are a mix of German and English, and there are predominantly English-language papers, which also include some German. While the German-language press has been described as among the institutions making up the "backbone" of German cultural institutions in the U.S.,[39] previous research acknowledges but fails to examine publications that underwent name changes or mergers, and little has shown the variety in these text types.

Among the thirty-seven publications from South Dakota, it is possible to identify three types based on print language, as shown in Table 1.

Table 1. South Dakota Newspaper Types based on print language

Type	Specs	Example(s)
Majority German	Published almost entirely in German, occasional English-language advertisements, rarely English language articles.	Dakota Freie Presse Süd-Dakota Nachrichten
German and English parallel editions	German and English papers published under the same or a very similar name or from the same publishing house/location.	Die Eureka Post/Eureka Post
Majority English	Published almost entirely in English, but with specific sections or columns designated for German language news. These differ from Majority German papers in that there are few to no non-English language advertisements to be found.	Reporter and Farmer
	German only during WWI (1914-1918)	Dakota Farmer's Leader

Even the "most" German of these newspapers included some English, which is why it is difficult to create a "German only" category. It is possible, however, that some of the German-language publications other than newspapers (church or club bulletins, for example) were published entirely in German.

While a progression from a Majority German to Majority English publication may seem like a natural step in the shift from German to English in the U.S., this is not the case for German-language publications in South Dakota. Rather, German-language publications remained true to their original publication language. Although they may have increased in the amount of English used over time (especially in advertisements),[40] none appear to shift directly from German to English.

Majority German-language Publications

Most German-language newspapers in South Dakota belong to this category. The best-known is the *Dakota Freie Presse*, which was both the earliest and longest running (1874-1954). The weekly paper was considered the "organ of all Russian-Germans" and called "the bible of the Russian-Germans" because it "provided them with a feeling of community and common identity.[41] It is given a great weight of importance as creating a "sense of community" and for being the reason Germans from Russia were joined together by "lasting, tight-knit feelings of community and identity."[42]

The contents of many German-language papers were very similar; besides news from the Dakotas, they often included regional, national, and international news, focusing on Germany, Russia, and Austria-Hungary. These papers printed letters and correspondence articles (sometimes from abroad), a serialized novel, a variety of articles and advice columns on health and farming, and the market report.[43] Beyond the commonalities they share with other publications at this time–most German publications were printed in Fraktur, a common gothic typeface previously used in German publications, characterized by "fractured" lines and angles–almost all articles were published in German, and most advertisements were printed in German (Image 1). There is some variation in language and typeface in advertisements, with English words and phrases generally appearing in the roman typeface. Some exhibited mixed languages and/or typeface, especially product names and company locations (Image 2). Very rarely an advertisement printed in German would appear in the roman typeface (Image 3).

Image 1. H. Billion, *Leichenbestatter* "undertaker," *Süd-Dakota Nachrichten*, February 6, 1896, p. 8.

Image 2. Santa Claus Soap, *Süd-Dakota Nachrichten*, May 21, 1896, p. 7.

Image 3. Hood's Sarsaparilla (Partial). *Süd-Dakota Nachrichten*, April 16, 1896, p. 4.

German and English Parallel Editions

Majority German and majority English publications also existed parallel to one another, either according to name, publication location, or both, for example, *Die Eureka Post* and *Eureka Post*, both in the town of Eureka. The German version appeared in 1889 and was followed in 1896 by an English version. Both continued publication until a sale in 1907 led to the discontinuation of the English version. The German paper continued until 1912 and was later consolidated into the *Eureka Rundschau*.[44]

The English version was considered a supplement to the German, as articles were rarely published in both. Comparing two randomly selected editions from June 1904, a major difference is immediately evident. The German edition begins with international news, paying special attention to fighting between Russia and Japan, where the English edition begins with local and regional news and advertisements. This initial difference is carried throughout with the German edition focusing heavily on international news and the English covering more local and regional news. The English version has advertisements on every page, sometimes covering as much as half a page, but the German version has four pages with no advertisements present at all, making the paper appear almost more official and literary due to the large blocks of text. Although they do not appear to include any of the same articles, both include several of the same advertisements that appear in the language of the overall publication. The schedule for the Artas-Eureka Stage Line appears in both, with the German version printed in Fraktur (Images 4 and 5).

Image 4. *Die Eureka Post*, June 22, 1904, Artas-Eureka Stage Linie, p. 3

Image 5. *Eureka Post*, June 24, 1904, Artas-Eureka Stage Line, p. 1

Particularly notable for these two parallel papers is a farewell address to the readership (March 27, 1907), wherein longtime owner and publisher O. J. Roe self-describes as a "Vermont-Yankee" who can neither read, write, nor speak German. The English edition from the same week includes an almost identical notice to the readership, minus the "Vermont-Yankee" line.

This is the first time in this publication that announcements or addresses to the readership regarding the fate of the publication emerge, despite the paper having changed ownership in the past. The announcements appear as an attempt from the editorial board to reassure the readership of the quality of the publication to retain them as loyal consumers.

Unlike the brief English announcement, the German announcement focuses on the future of the paper, promising to remain Republican leaning and expressing intent at growing the readership to be in every home where German is read. The German edition continued publication with an emphasis on international news, especially from Russia, until June 6, 1912, when the *Eureka Post* was sold to the Volkszeitung Publishing Company.

Majority English

Finally, perhaps the most interesting and surprising of the German-language types is that of the Majority English papers with some German. In all instances, these publications were published first as English only papers, and then added German segments or columns later.

A prime example of this phenomenon is the *Reporter and Farmer*, first published in Webster in 1881. It was entirely English until 1904, when the paper expanded from a nine-column, four-page paper to a six-column, eight-page paper adding more international news "to satisfy the recent European immigrants of Day County."[45] The *Reporter and Farmer* published German segments semi-regularly from November 1906 to January 1910. The German segments or columns–generally encompassing only two of forty-eight columns–were printed in Fraktur, while the rest of the paper was printed in roman typeface. Attention paid to these two columns seems rather haphazard, occasionally occurring with major errors such as the second column of the German-language news appearing entirely upside-down (Image 6).

Unlike the papers where a Majority German and Majority English paper were published parallel to one another, the *Reporter and Farmer* published similar articles in German and in English, such as in the August 1, 1907, edition which lengthily published the tale of a murderer in Berlin in German and an abbreviated English version on the same page.

While it is unsurprising that an English paper in a heavily German-settled area might have German-language segments of the

Trennung von Kirche und Staat.

Französische Regierung ist fest entschlossen, das Trennungsgesetz rücksichtslos durchzuführen.

Der berühmte „Hauptmann von Köpenick" erhält vier Jahre.

Großbritannien sieht Gespenster.

Deutschland.

Berlin, 6. Dez. — Alle Welt, Presse und Publikum, beschäftigt sich in der eingehendsten Weise mit dem zur cause celèbre gewordenen Prozeß des Schuhmachers und früheren Zuchthäuslers Wilhelm Voigt, der als „Hauptmann von Köpenick" Weltberühmtheit erlangt hat. Die Blät-

Image 6. *Reporter and Farmer*, December 13, 1906, p. 2, top portion of columns 2-3.

paper, it is noteworthy that there are numerous publications which only published in German during World War I after having been entirely English for decades prior, a part of the history of the German-language press which is often overlooked. The common idea, perpetrated in previous work, is that WWI served as the death knell to the German-language press in the United States. Majority English papers introducing German-language segments near the beginning of WWI runs contrary to this declaration by Wittke: "World War I struck the German-language press a blow from which it has never recovered. The number of papers and their circulation had been declining for some years because of falling immigration and the normal processes of Americanization, but it was the war and the hysterical reaction to all things German which precipitated a unique crisis in the history of American's foreign-language press."[46]

While there are repeated stories of newspaper editors who failed to submit translations of German articles to their local postmasters, and who were fined or imprisoned because of this, and while there was indeed anti-German sentiment by the end of the war negatively impacting some publishers and publications, the German-speaking population of this state was important and numerous enough that four Majority English papers only ever printed anything in German during WWI. All four Majority English-language papers that began publishing segments in German in 1915-1916 had returned to English-only by the end of 1917, but that they considered it important enough to do so at all is telling.

The *Dakota Farmer's Leader*, published in Canton, 1890-1919, is one such paper. It only included one German-language segment, *Diese Abteilung ist für die Familienglieder, welche am liebsten Deutsch lessen* ("This section is for the family members, who prefer to read German") from March 12, 1915, to October 22, 1915. In each edition only two columns are devoted to news in German, generally war related, but occasionally covering other topics. The editorial staff gave no introduction or explanation of the new column coming or going. Given the title of the segment, specifically mentioning family members, it was perhaps seen as an explanation itself, or perhaps it was not considered necessary to give an explanation at all.

As there were only six Majority German-language papers in press at this time (*Dakota Freie Presse*, *Neue Deutsche Presse*, *Dakota Volkszeitung*, *Eureka Rundschau*, *Java Herald*, and the *Süd-Dakota Nachrichten*), it is remarkable that four papers added a German segment. This overview shows a preliminary step in the process of unearthing the diversity of the German-language press and how individual publications chose to engage with bilingual audiences as a group.

Sioux Falls: From *Süd-Dakota Nachrichten* to *Deutscher Herold*

Unlike the Majority English papers which included no explanation of their choice to include a German-language segment, German papers were more likely to directly address their readership. This direct communication from the editorial staff can be seen as bringing the readers into the publishing world. Although they do not have a say, the transparency the editorial builds by keeping them informed brings them closer on a personal level, a tactic which was common in the German-language press of South Dakota.

The *Süd-Dakota Nachrichten*, the second longest running of any German-language publication, was founded by Hermann Butikofer and Paul B. Meyer in 1890 in Mitchell where it remained until 1896 when it moved to Sioux Falls. The paper underwent many changes in publication location, title, editorial staff and/or ownership during its publishing run from 1890-1918, beginning as the *Süd Dakota Nachrichten* (henceforth SDN) from 1890-1900, transitioning to the *Süd Dakota Nachrichten und Herold* from 1900-1901, thereafter published as *Nachrichten-Herold* from 1901-1907, and finally from 1907-1918 as *Deutscher Herold.* Each of these changes came with its own set of challenges of retaining previous readers and attempting to expand readership and circulation. With each major change, the editorial staff printed announcements not only to assure readers of the quality of the paper's content but generally keeping them apprised of the paper's internal goings on. These announcements show how the editorial staff interact with their readership, sharing the paper's development. In doing so they are making the paper relatable and creating a connection between the identity of the paper and tying it to that of the German readership and their Germanness.[47] Many of these announcements are framed in a way that make changes appear not to be just about the financial aspects of a sale or merger, but about how the change is good for the preservation of the German language and heritage, and are used to unify German speakers in South Dakota (and later across the region) based on language and shared characteristics rather than origin.

Süd-Dakota Nachrichten: 1890-1900

When the SDN moved from Mitchell to Sioux Falls in 1896, the editorial staff began a tradition of semi-regular announcements to the readership, thus indirectly involving them in the success and identity of the paper. This tradition began in the January 23, 1896, Sioux Falls edition, with a brief address reassuring that the change of location would be a positive development. This first address does not distinguish a particular readership or explain the paper's goals, rather it is left "up to the new readers to decide" (*den neuen Lesern selbst überlassen, sich* [. . .] *selbst darüber genaue Auskunft zu verschaffen*) and describes only what can be found in the supplement (*Beilage*), namely a mixture of reading materials, short stories, and *Humoristisches*. A second address to the old readership (*unsere alten Leser*) also lists the topics generally covered in the paper but names its primary goal as building a paper which every German of South Dakota can call their own. The SDN Mitchell edition only briefly acknowledges a change in location in the previous week's edition. The two papers continued appearing under the same name parallel to another until May 14, 1896, when the Mitchell edition was renamed *Dakota Post*, in order to distinguish itself from the Sioux Falls edition.

Süd-Dakota Nachrichten und Herold: 1900-1901

In 1900 the SDN's new owner, Hans Demuth, stepped in as publisher and editor. The April 26, 1900, edition announces the paper will thereafter be called the *Süd-Dakota Nachrichten und Herold* (henceforth *Nachrichten*).[48] This shift in title is due to the consolidation of the SDN with the *Dakota Herold*, both published weekly in Minnehaha County. In his opening address to the readership, Demuth describes what he assumes to be the readership's concerns, namely the political leaning of the consolidated papers, and assures them that the *Nachrichten* will remain entirely politically independent, reiterating that this is more important than ever because the *Dakota Herold* subscribers included *eine ganze Reihe von republikanisch gesinnten deutschen Lesern* ("a good number of republican-minded German readers"). Demuth declares that the *Nachrichten* will not try to reconcile different political opinions, but rather will publish impartially so readers can form their own opinions. He goes on in a complimentary tone, that Germans are intelligent and will find the right way without long-winded leading editorials (*Der Deutsche ist intelligent und weiß auch ohne langathmige Leitartikel das Rechte zu finden*).

The announcement impresses upon the readers how important it is for Germans to support a local newspaper, not just for local news, but because of the shoddy workmanship of some of the mass-produced newspapers from cities like New York, Milwaukee, and Chicago. Particularly notable from this announcement is the strong play to the German group identity, setting the German-language paper on the same level as the German heritage of the region, suggesting that only if the readers remain loyal and bring in new readers will they be able to fight on behalf of the honor of the newspaper, the protection and strengthening of German-American interests ([. . .] *damit wir zusammen noch manche Schlacht schlagen können zur Ehre der Zeitung, zum Schutz und zur Stärkung der deutsch-amerikanischen Interessen*). Demuth not only uses militaristic imagery (as in the previous quote), but he also appeals to the emotions of the readers, suggesting,

> Und speziell in Sioux Falls soll uns die Hebung und Einigung des Deutschthums am Herzen liegen. Es sollen im Sommer gemeinschaftliche Pic-Nics gefeiert werden, in der Germania-Halle interessante Vorträge, Unterhaltungen usw. stattfinden und das Motto soll heißen: Einer für Alle, Alle für Einen! Darum bitte ich im eigenen Interesse und Ansehen des Deutschthums um das so nöthige und durch die Verhältnisse der Vergangenheit leider theilweise geschwundene Vertrauen und Eure Hülfe.
>
> "And especially in Sioux Falls, the elevation and unification of Germanness must be close to our hearts. In the summer there shall be picnics celebrated together, interesting lectures, entertainment, etc. shall take place at Germania Hall and our motto shall be: One for all and all for one! Therefore, in my own interest and the respect of Germanness, I ask for

> the trust and your help, which is so necessary and unfortunately partly lost due to past circumstances."

The overt chauvinistic tone here plays to the emotions of the German group identity, singling out German-Americanness as core to the reader's cultural and linguistic heritage based on shared language and values rather than nation or origin, and tying them to the success of the newspaper. The same announcement is published in the following week's *Nachrichten*, along with a repetition and emphasis of the paper's intent to be a German family newspaper, not the mouthpiece of politicians (*sollen ein deutsches Familienblatt, kein Organ für Politiker sein*).

The final issues of the *Nachrichten* from August 1901 show no indication of a coming change in title or editorial team. The lack of announcement to the readership may indicate the editorial staff did not consider the upcoming change to be of significance to the readership, or as there was no change in ownership or editorial staff, it may have been decided rather at the last minute.

Nachrichten-Herold: 1901-1907

The first edition with the name *Nachrichten-Herold* appeared August 29, 1901. An explanation of the change appears on the first page: the decision to drop "South Dakota" was due to much of the readership being from outside the state. In an attempt to gain more correspondents outside of the regular area, the editor thanks former correspondents for writing in the interests of the German newspaper and of all Germanness/German heritage (*im Interesse der deutschen Zeitung und des Deutschthums)*. The call for new correspondents is particularly striking due to its linguistic open-endedness. If the correspondent is unable to write German correctly enough for publication, they will polish it. English-language correspondences will be translated by the paper as long as they are upholding the interests of Germanness (*im Interesse des Deutschthums)*. These appeals for news correspondents regardless of language ability, and the paper's willingness to refine the pieces, shows an expectation for standard

German-language use at the official, publication level, but acceptance of variation at the personal, individual level.

Although not as a specific address to the reader, this section also includes an advertisement of a book the publishing office has to sell. The ad notes the book has been published in German and English and if the order does not specifically request the book in English, they will be sent the German version, implying the expected preferred reading language of all readers of this German-language paper is German in other mediums as well.

The final edition of the *Nachrichten-Herold*, August 29, 1907, opens with an announcement informing the reader that the paper has been completely reorganized and reformed as a corporation under the name "Herold Publishing Company." It declares the German element of South Dakota has "suffered" more than Germans in other states due to there being no impartial paper representing the entirety of German interests. In fact, the author considers only two German-language papers in South Dakota to be of any consequence, namely the *Dakota Freie Presse* and the *Nachrichten-Herold*. However, they feel that the *Dakota Freie Presse* has long been under the control of "professional politicians" (*professionellen Politkern*)–although it is unclear who exactly is meant, the previous owners or outsiders with some sway at the *Dakota Freie Presse*–and therefore more likely to lead new German immigrants astray than to inform/educate them.

The author is not content with disparaging other South Dakota papers, but also declares the German press in North Dakota to be no better, perhaps worse because some are half English, half German which the author claims has done more to hurt the German-language press than to help it. Overall, this announcement goes beyond previous readership addresses by not only tying the German readership to the paper as part of an in-group, but by denigrating other German papers locally and regionally, the editors are emphasizing the us-vs.-them mentality which strengthens the connection of the German readership to the success of the paper.

Because of this perceived lack of decent German-language press in the Dakotas, the author declares much of the potential German readership finds its news elsewhere, namely from other major Midwestern cities. These papers are shown with their circulation numbers from 1890-1915 (where available) in Table 2.

Table 2. Major German-language press (weeklies) deemed most read by the Herold Publishing Company editorial, August 29, 1907.

Location	Paper	Years active	Circulation numbers[49]				
			1890	1900	1905	1910	1915
Milwaukee, Wisconsin	Germania	1873-1924	81,220 (1891)	91,450	104,642	108,166 (1911)	100,000 (1916)
	Herold	1861-1910	21,000	22,000	n/a[50]	17,500	--[51]
St. Paul, Minnesota	Volkszeitung	1877-1921	800 (1878)	26,200 (1901)	29,249 (1903)	14,706 (1913)	13,464 (1921)
Chicago, Illinois	Illinois Staatszeitung	1848-1922	34,600	38,000	n/a	n/a	15,000
Winona, Minnesota	(Nord) westlicher Herold	1881-1924	1,600 (1885)	n/a	n/a	21,858	80,725 (1921)
Lincoln, Nebraska	Lincoln Freie Presse	1884-1924	n/a	5,500 (1897)	158,594	142,440	121,749 (1920)
St. Louis, Missouri	Anzeiger des Westens	1835-1912	14,800	28,500	31,740	30,000	--
Eureka, South Dakota	Die Eureka Post	1890-1912	n/a	650	1,400	1,000	--
Sioux Falls, South Dakota	Deutscher Herold	1890-1918	n/a	1,425	2,585	1,500	3,750

No circulation numbers were found for the *Dakota Freie Presse*, but the next two major papers (according to length in existence) were added to show how different the circulation was. The editorial author argues that many Germans in South Dakota are drawing on these other publications from out of state but neglects to contextualize this. Those publications all began earlier (6-65 years earlier) and apart from the (*Nord*) *Westlicher Herold*[52] had circulation numbers 3.85 to 64 times that of the *Deutscher Herold* in 1900. They were very simply in another league entirely according to circulation numbers.

Beyond this, the circulation data show another central indicator of the German-language press more broadly, namely that the peak of each of these publications regardless of location is 1905 with circulation numbers declining after that. However, without context, circulation numbers still fail to show the whole picture. From the data presented here, it seems that the *Westlicher Herold* experienced rapid growth between 1910 and 1921. This large increase in circulation numbers is due to several mergers under the Westlicher Herold Publishing Company (especially in the period 1917-1925). Beginning in 1912, the *Germania* (Milwaukee) merged with the *Milwaukee Herold* to become the *Germania-Herold* until 1918 when it changed titles and became the *Milwaukee America.* The *Milwaukee America*, having already attracted the audience of several local papers, merged with the *Westlicher Herold.* These (among other) combined publications took on the name *America-Herold*, positioning itself as a national weekly, rather than the regional or state specific weeklies from which it was built.

Deutscher Herold: 1907-1918

With the first edition of the newly dubbed *Deutscher Herold* appearing September 5, 1907, the same announcement again appears, but is directly followed by a second editorial signed by editor and publisher F. W. Sallet, in which he addresses his "old friends," readers of the *Dakota Freie Presse*. Sallet acknowledges he left the editorial staff of the *Dakota Freie Presse* in 1906 and suggests that his successors have besmirched his good reputation and dragged his honest name in the mud (*die meinen guten Ruf besudeln und meiner, ehrlichen Namen in den Schmutz zerren*), again delineating a clear outgroup. He goes on to use his position as new editor of the *Deutscher Herold* to draw the readers and correspondents together. For the first time in this paper, Germans from Russia are specifically addressed (*Meinen lieben Rußländer*, "my dear Russians") as Sallet pledges to bring news and correspondence from South Russia and incorporate them with the rest of the news for the entire German population. Sallet writes,

> Alle sind wir Kinder des großen deutschen Volksstammes, ob unsere Wiege in Preußen, Bayern, der Schweiz, in Rußland oder sonstwo gestanden. Dieselben Charaktereigenschaften vereinigen uns und so soll auch der „Deutsche Herold" dem Gesammtinteresse [sic] unserer deutschen Stammesgenossen gewidmet sein!
>
> "We are all children of the great German tribe, whether our cradles were in Prussia, Bavaria, Switzerland, Russia or somewhere else. The same characteristics unite us and so, too, shall the *Deutsche Herold* pursue the overall interests of our German tribesmen."

Sallet reiterates this combining of the interests of the German-language press as being a core aspect of the Germanness of the readership, where the German language is a key characteristic of the German identity in South Dakota and beyond.

In the September 15, 1910, issue the editorial staff makes an announcement regarding an expansion from 10 to 12 pages, but more importantly reassures the readers that the *Deutscher Herold* "will hold to the principle of banding together all Germania's sons under one banner and that the German heritage will not be segregated according to narrow political borders" (*weiterhin an dem Princip festhalten, alle Söhne Germanias unter ein Banner zu schaaren und das Deutschtum nicht nach engen Landesgrenzen abzusondern*).

Beginning as early as September 1910 and continuing through 1914, the *Deutscher Herold* semi-regularly runs a blurb, *Aus welchem Grunde man den "Deutscher Herold" halten sollte* "for which reasons one should subscribe to the *Deutscher Herold*," which not only describes their intended audience, but declares its reason for existing:

> die deutsche Sprache wach zu erhalten und durch belehrende und unterhaltende Artikel das Publikum zu interessiren, ihnen immer wieder den hohen Wert des Deutschtums vor Augen zu führen, sie immer wieder daran zu erinnern, daß ohne die deutsche Presse das Deutschtum in diesem Lande bald zu den gewesenen Dingen gehören würde.
>
> "to keep the German language alive and to interest the audience through instructive and entertaining articles, to repeatedly make them aware of the high value of Germanness, to repeatedly remind them that without the German press Germanness in this country would soon be a thing of the past."

This tradition of addressing and keeping the readership apprised of even minor changes affecting the publication grew and developed over time. Initially used to indicate larger changes, this example shows how even just a two-page expansion is used as an opportunity to remind the readership of their shared group identity as German speakers. This example is extreme in that it specifically ties the success of the German-language press to that of the existence of Germanness in the United States.

These are just some examples of announcements to the German readership of this paper, but this tradition continues, for example, in November 1911 editions: describing a sale of shares in the publishing company, suggestions of bringing all the German papers of the state together as long as the interests of Germanness would be a priority ([. . .] *in erster Linie die Interessen des Deutschtums in Auge gefaßt würden*), using Thanksgiving Day as an opportunity to thank the German readership for their loyalty and repeating affiliative terminology (*ganz gleich wo ihre Wiege stand*, "no matter where their cradles stood"; *die Einigung aller Kinder Germanias*, "the unification of all children of Germania"; etc.), creating a feeling of unity and grouping all German speakers together. In July 1914 a self-promoting advertisement declares the paper as a bearer of more than just important news: it brings *deutsche Kultur* "German culture." A March 1915 edition beseeches readers to send the names of other Germans who might enjoy a sample of the *Deutscher Herold* "in honor of Germanness" (*zur Ehre des Deutschthums*). Later editions regularly include a statement declaring its perspective and objective, asserting "The *Deutscher Herold* is politically independent; honestly and selflessly it has always stood up for German interests" (*Der „Deutscher Herold" ist politisch unabhängig; ehrlich und uneigennützig ist er stets für die deutschen Interessen eingetreten*). This self-published statement of identity and purpose summarizes the trajectory and tradition of the paper's development throughout its nearly thirty-year existence. Regardless of ownership or title, the publication attempted to join German speakers together, focusing more on commonalities than ethnic or national origin.

Naturally, the *Deutscher Herold* addressed its readership regarding changes in publication language due to the Trading with the Enemy Act of 1917. The act was passed on October 6, 1917, and went into effect on October 16, 1917. According to the October 11 edition, however, the local postmaster had not yet received official news of the law and suggested that it would likely not be followed through on. An announcement to the readership the following week declares it was still unclear what was allowed to be published in German, so they would publish a reduced amount of war news in German, but they hoped to receive a license from the postmaster general to return to publication as normal. In the meantime, the *Deutscher Herold* reprinted an article from *The Chicago Tribune* regarding the mission of the German-language press and asks the readership to share it with their monolingual English neighbors. They also began publishing a note regarding the "aim of the foreign language newspapers of America," which can only be described as profusely placative, declaring the press' intent:

> to help preserve the ideals and sacred traditions of this, our adopted country, the United States of

> America. To revere its laws and inspire others to respect and obey them. To strive unceasingly to quicken the public's sense of civic duty. In all ways to aid in making this country greater and better than we found it.

By the third week's address to the readership (October 25, 1917), the editorial staff apologizes to the readers for the *Lesemischmasch*, "reading hodgepodge," created by the confusion regarding allowed publishing language, which they also find "abhorrent" (*zuwider*). Two weeks later (November 8, 1917), the *Deutscher Herold* had still not received permission to publish entirely in German but takes the opportunity to affirm that the one enduring stance of the publication has been printing from the American perspective, indicating once again that the editorial staff does not tie language to nationality.

After purchasing the *Deutscher Herold* at the end of 1917, Conrad Kornmann brings up the importance of the German-language press for the preservation of Germanness and German citizens of America in a year's end address. He posits German churches, German schools, and the German-language press as the pillars of Germanness in America, which he believes will endure long into the future. Unlike at previous changes in management, Hans Demuth, former owner and editor, bids farewell to the readership in a lengthy editorial, where he affirms the goal of the paper was to bring together the Germans/Germanness of the state as one indivisible unit.

The position of German language in schools and press, as well as of German-Americans in the U.S., remain hot topics through the final year of the *Deutscher Herold.* It is then perhaps rather unsurprising that the lead article of the final edition of the *Deutscher Herold* is titled *Die Schicksalsstunde der Deutschamerikaner*, "The hour of destiny of German-Americans." While there is no final farewell from the editorial staff, the lead article seems, perhaps unknowingly, to take on this role, projecting an image of German-Americans as stuck between two identities, too American to be German and too German to be American. The article suggests that this is a unique situation for the immigrant generation, and that their children and grandchildren will be saved this "between" existence, as they will have known only one country. Even from the despair expressed in this article at not really being accepted as American due to their German heritage, language is never a named factor. Being German vs. being American is tied to origin, family, and loyalty, not language use.

Conclusion

Despite getting a later start than the English-language press in South Dakota or even in other areas of the Midwest, the German-language press in South Dakota was built to last. By adapting to the needs of its readership, the German-language press evolved and remained in existence for over eighty years, surpassing expectations of only serving the purpose of a transitionary aid to new immigrants. The German-language press in South Dakota held an important enough role to force multiple English-only publications to print news in German during World War I. The editorial staffs of several German papers used their position and their pen to form a connection to the German speakers of the state and beyond. Rather than focusing on individual heritage or ethnic groups, the German-language press as a whole considered their shared language to be their uniting characteristic, creating a bond between the press and its readership unparalleled by their English-language counterparts, likely adding to their success and durability as a pillar of Germanness in South Dakota.

Notes

1 This research is supported by a Postdoctoral Research Fellowship through the Alexander von Humboldt Foundation. I thank the following for comments, suggestions and discussions on this topic: Temmo Bosse, Jan Niklas Heinrich, David Natvig, Joe Salmons, and the editor of this volume. All remaining shortcomings are my own.

2 John P. Johansen, "Immigrants and their Children in South Dakota," *Bulletins*, Paper 302 (1936): 5.

3 Anthony H. Richter, "A Heritage of Faith: Religion and the German Settlers of South Dakota," *South Dakota History* 21 (1991): 155-72.

4 Anton H. Richter, "'Gebt ihr den Vorzug': The German-Language Press of North and South Dakota," *South Dakota History* 10 (1980): 190.

[5] While I refrained from translating newspaper titles, all other translations are my own.

[6] Istvan Gombocz, "'Whatever our language, we have the same flag': The German Weekly Newspaper *Eureka Rundschau*, 1915-1927," *South Dakota History* 51:3 (2021).

[7] Carl Frederick Wittke, *The German-language Press in America* (Lexington, KY: University of Kentucky Press, 1957), 196, 204, 250.

[8] Karl J.R. Arndt and Mary E. Olson, *Die Deutschsprachige Presse der Amerikas 1732-1968: Geschichte und Bibliographie*, vol. 1, 3d ed. (München: Verlag Dokumentation, 1976), 608.

[9] Samantha M. Litty, "The German Midwest," in *The Oxford Handbook of Midwestern History*, ed. Jon K. Lauck (Oxford: Oxford University Press, forthcoming).

[10] Wittke, *Press*, 76-77.

[11] Compare from Russell's description of the German-language press in Michigan. John Andrew Russell, *The Germanic Influence in the Making of Michigan* (Detroit: Herold Press, 1927).

[12] For detailed description of the settlement of South Dakota, see Gary D. Olson, "Yankee and European Settlement," in *A New South Dakota History*, ed. Harry F. Thompson (Sioux Falls, SD: Center for Western Studies, 2005), 117-42.

[13] Olson, 117, 120-22.

[14] Olson, 122-23.

[15] Olson, 117.

[16] Richter, *Faith*, 156.

[17] For a detailed discussion of German religious denominations in South Dakota, see Lynwood E. Oyos, "Protestant Faith and Learning," in *A New South Dakota History*, ed. Harry F. Thompson (Sioux Falls: Center for Western Studies, 2005), 331-55.

[18] Olson, 135.

[19] Johansen, *Children*, 10.

[20] Johansen, *Children*, 19.

[21] Johansen, *Children*, 17-18.

[22] Arndt and Olson, vol. 1, 9.

[23] Arndt and Olson, vol. 1, 9.

[24] Arndt and Olson, vol. 1, 10. This was, however, referring to other European languages, excluding Native American languages.

[25] "About the Democrat," Library of Congress: Chronicling America, July 23, 2021, https://chroniclingamerica.loc.gov/lccn/sn91066738/.

[26] Wittke, *Press*, 1-6.

[27] Cf. Wittke, *Press*, 1-6; Arndt and Olson, 8-9; Richter, *Press*, 193-94; Olson, 136; Litty, forthcoming.

[28] Richter, *Press*, 194.

[29] Arndt and Olson, vol. 1, 608-11; Vol 2., 556. “US Newspaper Directory,” Library of Congress: Chronicling America, July 23, 2021, https://chroniclingamerica.loc.gov/search/titles/.

[30] For a detailed description of the *Dakota Freie Presse* and its downfall, see La Vern J. Rippley, “A History of the Dakota Freie Presse,” *North Dakota Society of Germans from Russia Heritage Review* 7 (1973): 9-17; Rippley, “The Dakota Freie Presse: Its Brightest and Its Darkest Hour,” *North Dakota Society of Germans from Russia Heritage Review* 9 (1974):15-20.

[31] Arndt and Olson, vol. 1, 608-11; Richter, *Press*, 192; Olson, 136.

[32] Where original publications used “=” to indicate a hyphen, I have replaced these with a dash “-“ for ease of readability.

[33] Wittke, *Press*, 264-65.

[34] Carl Wittke, *German Americans and the World War*, (Columbus, OH: Ohio State Archaeological and Historical Society, 1936; repr., 1974), 33-34; Richter, *Press*, 197; Olson, 136.

[35] Joseph Salmons, “The Shift from German to English, World War I and the German Language Press in Wisconsin,” *Menschen zwischen zwei Welten: Auswanderung, Ansiedlung, Akkulturation* (2002): 179-93; Michael T. Putnam and Joseph Salmons, “Multilingualism in the Midwest: How German Has Shaped (and Still Shapes) the Midwest,” *Middle West Review* 1:2 (2015): 33.

[36] Wittke, *Press*, 231-34.

[37] Litty, forthcoming.

[38] Wittke, *Press*, 273.

[39] Wittke, *Press*, 7.

[40] Richter, *Press*, 198-203.

[41] Richter, *Press*, 196-97.

[42] Richter, *Press*, 197; Rippley, “The Dakota Freie Presse,” 15.

[43] Richter, *Press*, 197.

[44] “About Die Eureka Post,”, Library of Congress: Chronicling America, July 23, 2021, https://chroniclingamerica.loc.gov/lccn/sn99062854/.

[45] “About Reporter and Farmer,” Library of Congress: Chronicling America, July 23, 2021, https://chroniclingamerica.loc.gov/lccn/sn99068116/. Detailed paper specs based on issues from March 10, 1892, and November 29, 1906.

[46] Wittke, *Press*, 274.

[47] I use “Germanness” to encompass the terms *Deutschtum* (“German culture / nationality”) and *deutsch sein* (“being German or Germanic”) and the linguistic and ethnic heritage associated with the German language and / or culture. While at this time, “Germanness” is largely connected to the language, proficiency in the German language is not a necessary factor in the social and cultural constructs associated with Germanness. Especially as time passes, a greater emphasis is put on social and cultural factors such as music, foods, holidays and events, in effect anything that the particular

group identifying as "German" collectively decides (explicitly or implicitly) belongs to their "Germanness."

[48] *Nachrichten* is the shortened form of the title also used by the editorial staff to refer to the paper.

[49] From Arndt and Olson, vol. 1, 608-11.

[50] "n/a" indicates circulation numbers are unknown, but the paper was still publishing at that time.

[51] "--" indicates the paper had ceased publishing.

[52] The editorial author names the *Nordwestlicher Herold*; however, no other records indicate this title, rather all other sources list the *Westlicher Herold*, for which I have included data.

9

Bread, Berries, and Butter: Challenging South Dakota's History through Changing Foodways

Sara Egge
Centre College

In 1985 the American Lutheran Church Women (ALCW) of the Bergen Lutheran Church, a rural church located near Bristol in Day County, South Dakota, published a community cookbook entitled "Bergen Centennial Cookbook." Its bright yellow cover featured an image of the church front surrounded by trees and pillowy clouds.[1] Inside its pages, the members of the ALCW had collected over two-hundred pages of recipes, organizing them under twelve headings, including "Meat and Casseroles," "Jams, Jellies, and Pickles," and "Salads, Dressings, and Dips." Four of the twelve sections emphasized sweets or baked goods—"Cookies and Bars," "Cakes, Frostings, and Candy," "Pastries and Desserts," and "Bread and Rolls."[2] The cookbook was a commemorative expression, created to mark a milestone anniversary in the life of the congregation. While some commemorative cookbooks explained the history of the town, church, hospital, school, or other such institution, the Bergen women did not offer any information about themselves or the church to which they belonged. Instead, they opened with a section entitled "Foreign" and placed recipes in it that revealed a great deal about how they viewed themselves and their community. Other than one recipe for kuchen, a German custard-filled pastry, and another for kottbollar, or Swedish meatballs, the recipes featured Norwegian dishes like lefsa, a thin potato-based flatbread, rosettes, crispy, cookie-like fritters made with iron molds in lacy patterns, and sandbakkelse, an almond-flavored shortbread tart made in tin molds.[3]

That the women of the Bergen ALCW began their cookbook with a section devoted to "foreign" or ethnic dishes was striking. Most of the recipes were not "foreign" but cherished favorites prepared for special occasions by the Norwegian-American families who had settled in the area. Introducing the cookbook with this category was intentional, and it undoubtedly resonated with many South Dakotans who by the mid-twentieth century had noted that expressions of ethnicity were diminishing.[4] Generational change and uneven, but steady adoption of American culture had worked over decades to promote homogeneity. English had largely replaced heritage languages in churches by World War II as congregations sought to "retain or keep their young people."[5] Lakota struggled against federal policies that forced children into boarding schools and government commodities into their stomachs.[6] These transformations occurred against a backdrop of economic and cultural change in South Dakota as population decline, economic challenges, and agricultural consolidations upended farming as a widely shared livelihood. When home cooks placed foods that were ubiquitous only a generation or so earlier into separate categories like "foreign" and "heritage," they were signaling an ending or loss. But highlighting these recipes was also an act of defiance. Sections like these testified to the ways South Dakota's home cooks resisted the prescriptions of domestic scientists, processed foods of food companies, and nutritional standards of the federal government. The "Bergen Centennial Cookbook," one of hundreds of community cookbooks produced in South Dakota in the twentieth century, revealed that while attempts to standardize the American diet were powerful, they were also contested and incomplete.

Women enjoyed substantial economic, political, and social power in South Dakota because of their control over the production, preparation, and consumption of food. Curating recipes, writing their own histories, and selling them in a cookbook showcased how women could simultaneously uphold and bend domestic norms. They challenged assumptions that drudgery was the only outcome of female household labor, proving that knowledge about food had an appeal and economic value. That they organized around food was no accident. Not only was food at the center of family survival, but it was also essential to forging the relationships that sustained communities, especially small towns and rural neighborhoods that struggled during periods of upheaval. In those moments, women often gathered people together to share a meal, a practice scholars call commensality.[7] When they relied on established collective networks in this way, they accrued formidable economic and political authority. Controlling how people ate together, what they consumed, and what it meant countered declensionist narratives that focused on population decreases and economic challenges in South Dakota in the twentieth century.[8]

Women from a variety of backgrounds had ritualized food production and consumption in South Dakota before the twentieth-century proliferation of community cookbooks like the one from the Bergen Lutheran Church. They held tremendous sway because the gender division of labor almost always assigned food to the domestic sphere.[9] They followed patterns established for generations by their foremothers, relying on knowledge typically passed down a matrilineal line and years of experience in the kitchen to hone their craft. They adapted to seasonal rhythms and employed techniques and evolving technologies to process, preserve, and prepare what they and other members of their families and communities either raised, farmed, foraged, or hunted. Their household productive capabilities often determined the quantities and kinds of the ingredients they used in their recipes. Not only did they feed the members of their households, but they were also members of communities who fed each other through complex social networks that promoted collective eating at large gatherings.[10]

Before twentieth-century grocery stores or federal food programs provided the bulk of their food options, South Dakotans largely raised, grew, or hunted what they ate. Domestic gardens provided vegetables and fruits while wild plants offered variety. Some of the first photographic evidence from the early twentieth century shows sprawling yards full of potatoes, corn, pumpkins, beans, cabbages, and peas.[11] While growers planted an assortment of foodstuffs, they prioritized vegetables and fruits that either stored well for long periods or could be dried, crushed, ground, or otherwise preserved. Hunting and fishing also provided vital sources of protein, and South Dakotans pursued large game such as buffalo, elk, and deer, small game including squirrel, prairie dog, and rabbit, and many avian species like pheasant, goose, and duck.[12] For indigenous groups like the Dakota, buffalo was an essential part of their diets. In addition, nuts like hickory, berries like chokecherries, and plants like wild potatoes and turnips, as well as garden produce like corn, squash, beans, and sunflowers, offered important nutrients.[13] As white people, both American and foreign-born, arrived in the area, they also raised staples like corn, beans, and potatoes, but they also brought new ingredients, recipes, and knowledge about food to the state. Dairy and poultry products, including milk, butter, and eggs, as well as domesticated animal products such as chicken, pork, and beef featured prominently in their recipes. South Dakota's shorter growing season and harsh winters sometimes made substitutions necessary, and cooks adapted familiar dishes to the ingredients they had on hand. Preserving perishable foods was difficult until refrigeration and canning technologies, along with household electrification, became more widespread in the twentieth century.[14]

By the early twentieth century, dramatic transformations to South Dakota's culinary landscapes were on the horizon. Technological innovations related to preserving and storing food, such as canning, as well as scientific interventions into ideas about diet and nutrition, influenced South Dakota's food cultures. Research about vitamins, among other elements, spurred the United States Department of Agriculture (USDA) to separate foods into groups, recommending daily servings of each category.[15] Emerging national grocery markets and improved transportation networks in the early twentieth century slowly added ingredients grown or raised outside of the state. By the early-to-mid-twentieth century, national food corporations further transformed the practices of sharing a meal when factory-processed foods and restaurant meals began to replace the from-scratch recipes that comprised many South Dakota diets. Culinary expectations were rapidly homogenizing by the close of World War II as federal food programs consolidated and grocery stores expanded.[16] Many women began purchasing store-bought ingredients rather than raising the foodstuffs themselves, although rural households typically had less access to grocery stores than urban ones.

Not only did technological and economic changes influence what South Dakotans could eat, but also national efforts by domestic scientists to standardize the American diet prescribed how they should cook. Inspired by the growth of industrial and technological invention, domestic scientists created a field of study and experimentation that sought to improve what Americans ate. In the late nineteenth century, reformers mostly from New England engaged in a broad exploration of domestic economy and public anxieties about sanitation, health, safety, nutrition, and disease. Within this movement, groups of women with interests in food founded schools to investigate a scientific approach to cooking. Their work modernized the meals made by American cooks by stressing precise measurements, standard ingredients, and a meal planning logic that emphasized a rudimentary understanding of a balanced diet rather than taste. Their menus encouraged specific ratios of carbohydrates, proteins, and fats, and they produced recipes with these specifications in cookbooks they published in the 1880s and 1890s.[17]

The work of domestic scientists to create cookbooks for a national audience reshaped the country's culinary expectations. These reformers were mostly white, middle-class, and Anglo-Saxon, and they prioritized foods that aided the digestive process rather than satisfied appetites and cravings. They believed that spices, herbs, and sweets caused health problems while savory dishes of boiled meats and vegetables, usually topped with a white sauce, were the most salubrious. Class, race, and region shaped their work, and they admonished poor, nonwhite, rural, and foreign-born cooks for cooking with too much sugar, fat, or other ingredients they considered unhealthy.[18] Their recommendations often conflicted with home cooks who learned how to command a kitchen from their mothers or grandmothers. Their recipes, often skewed toward fats and sweets, rarely contained detailed instructions; they often left out cooking times, oven temperatures, or precise measurements, assuming a great deal of knowledge on the part of the cook. While domestic scientists championed precision, believing a scientific model in the kitchen made for better food, home cooks built their culinary skills with informal practice, learning when food was ready by sight, smell, sound, taste, and touch.[19]

Unlike the cookbooks produced by national reformers in the late nineteenth century, the aim of community cookbooks created by women in South Dakota was not to improve diets by applying scientific principles. Community cookbooks appeared across the United States soon after women in the nineteenth century organized collectively into societies or clubs with shared goals or interests. Groups including church societies, social clubs, women's auxiliaries, and suffrage organizations all created cookbooks, and most designed them as fundraisers. Scholars have largely overlooked cookbooks as historical sources, but they reveal how women from different backgrounds joined together to support a particular cause or institution. Contributing a recipe signaled to the community where women stood on an issue or with whom they affiliated, which invited public scrutiny and personal risk. Focusing on food helped to mitigate potential threats, amplifying the ideal of domesticity while actively subverting its alleged confines. When included in the host of literary practices with which women in the twentieth century engaged, including writing news articles, poetry, and songs as well as signing petitions, endorsing resolutions, and participating in letter-writing campaigns, cookbooks revealed how women leveraged economic and political power out of the resources, social networks, and knowledge they had. Finally, because community cookbooks feature recipes directly from the home cooks who prepared them, they reveal what and how South Dakotans ate.[20]

There is little historical analysis of South Dakota's foodways. No systematic study of the topic appears among scholarship in the relatively new field of food studies, and historians of South Dakota have failed to pay it much attention. Herbert Schell's *History of South Dakota* nodded to subjects like droughts in the 1890s and 1930s and rationing in the 1940s that offered brief glimpses at the state's food cultures.[21] Schell's intent in these discussions, however, was to introduce federal policies aimed to alleviate drought conditions or note how wartime mobilization shaped the home front, respectively, not to explore food itself in greater detail. The second edition of *A New South Dakota History* also mentioned topics related to food in the context of other themes, like the fur-trading era or the rise of the ranching industry.[22] In both accounts, historians most often assessed food as an agricultural commodity, framing it as a marketable good produced by male farmers whose goal was surplus and profit, not familial sustenance. Most treatments on agriculture in South Dakota take this view, leaving out the foods produced and eaten and focusing on mechanization, technological and scientific innovations, or commodities and markets.[23]

While community cookbooks in South Dakota appeared throughout the twentieth century, the majority were published after World War II. By then, a handful of small printers located in states like Minnesota, Iowa, and Kansas produced most of the community cookbooks.[24] The Special Collections and Archives Department at South Dakota State University has the most comprehensive collection of community cookbooks to date, with over five hundred items. The collection boasts examples from across the state, but it contains more from east of the Missouri River. Because ethnicity and religion organized white settlement in South Dakota, they played outsized roles in shaping the institutions—libraries, schools, churches, hospitals, and businesses—that came to dominate South Dakota's hamlets, towns, and cities.[25] Many cookbooks created to support these entities featured recipes that reflected these ethnic and religious identities. There were few cookbooks authored by nonwhite people in the collection. Most named a few members of a group who served as a "cookbook committee" responsible for tasks including soliciting, typing, and proofing recipes as well as illustrating the pages and distributing the final printed product. Several cookbooks represented the recipes of a single cook, with titles like "From Dorothy's Kitchen: 90 Years of Recipes and Family History" and "Grandma Jenny's Favorite Recipes: 80 Years of Home Cooking."[26]

South Dakotans experienced radical change in terms of what they ate during the twentieth century, and the cookbooks they produced captured these transformations. Some of the earliest cookbooks from the 1920s demonstrated how South Dakota's home cooks, particularly American and foreign-born, largely adopted recipes prescribed by domestic scientists within white, Northern European foodways. They believed these reformers when they claimed a scientific approach to cooking saved money while reducing labor requirements and making food healthier. They welcomed canning into their household work to aid in preserving foods that otherwise spoiled. Even though South Dakotans, particularly immigrants and their children, continued to serve ethnic foods that retained distinct flavor profiles, preparations, and ingredients, these recipes were relatively rare in the earliest twentieth-century cookbooks. For indigenous peoples like the Lakota, the earliest community cookbooks reveal the toll of attacks by government officials and white settlers on their foodways. Centuries of hunting, fishing, farming, and foraging practices, and staples such as berries, wild plants, and buffalo had created numerous and distinct indigenous foodways, but in the nineteenth century, government agencies and white reformers sought to eliminate indigenous foods as sources of spiritual and tribal identity. They targeted the buffalo, and the near extinction of that species created perilous conditions for the Lakota. The violent removal from their hunting, foraging, and fishing lands and waters and onto federally controlled reservations aimed to upend generations of indigenous food practices. Government-issued commodities, administered by officials who seldom worked for the best interests of the Lakota, were erratically distributed if they were at all.

The result was that recipes for Lakota dishes did not appear in early twentieth-century community cookbooks.[27]

Most of the earliest community cookbooks demonstrated the profound influence of domestic scientists from the northeast to standardize American diets. In 1925 the Ladies' Aid Society of the American Lutheran Church in Huron published a cookbook entitled "Tested Recipes with Practical References."[28] The women raised funds by featuring advertisements from a wide variety of local businesses like the Sanitary Barber Shop, the Osborn Clothing Company, and the Fair City Paint and Glass Company.[29] Most of the recipes adhered closely to the standardized menus prescribed by the northeastern cooking schools. Hedvig Melum, a naturalized immigrant from Norway, contributed a recipe for a "New England Boiled Dinner." After boiling two pounds each of corned beef and salt pork, Melum instructed cooks to boil "1 small head of cabbage, 6 small carrots, beets, potatoes, onions, and turnips," garnishing the dish with pickles.[30] Other recipes featuring boiled fish with white sauce, vegetable-based cream soups, or "Boston Baked Beans" reflected the sway of New England domestic scientists.[31] A few of the recipes did not follow the dictates of the scientific approach to cooking. Below the "Boiled Dinner" recipe was one for "Lute Fisk," a dish common in Scandinavian countries in which fish, usually dried cod, soaked in lye and water to tenderize it before skinning, boning, and boiling the fish to create a gelatinous texture. The recipe came from Caroline Gunderson, who, like Melum, was a naturalized Norwegian immigrant, but Gunderson was seventy-nine years old in 1925, almost thirty years older than Melum was.[32] Gunderson's recipe was simple and left out a great deal, directing cooks merely to "cook the fish in boiling salted water. Do not cook too long. Serve with cream sauce, or hot melted butter."[33]

The "Tested Recipes" cookbook joined others produced in the 1920s and 1930s that showcased how South Dakota's cuisine was multifaceted in the early twentieth century as home cooks incorporated scientific cookery while attempting to maintain ethnic culinary traditions. In a 1920s coverless cookbook from Mitchell, one of the first pages listed the standard weights, measurements, cooking times, and abbreviations. It also instructed home cooks to test their oven with a piece of white paper left inside for three minutes. A golden-brown color indicated a moderate temperature; dark brown meant it was hot.[34] Scientific tests coexisted with the handful of ethnic recipes found in these cookbooks. The "Tested Recipes" cookbook from Huron included recipes for lefse, a potato-based Norwegian flatbread, rommegrod, a Norwegian dairy-rich pudding, and "Klump," or "Danish Dumplings," which made a stiff batter of boiled butter, flour, and milk followed by an unbeaten egg. According to the contributor, Katrine Nelson, a thirty-seven-year-old housewife born in South Dakota to German parents but married to a Swede, the Danish dumplings were excellent for soups.[35] The ethnic mix in this one recipe was striking.

The cookbooks from Mitchell and Huron also showcased how home cooks both adapted to local food resources and adopted technological innovations. The "Tested Recipes" book from Huron offered seven recipes for nut bread, which was the most for the same dish in the "Bread" section, and almost all called for chopped walnuts or "walnut meats." The prominence of walnut bread was notable because black walnut trees were native to the state.[36] Both cookbooks featured extensive sections with labels like "Pickles and Relishes," "Puddings," "Pies," and "Jellies and Conserves." That two of the four largest sections featured the relatively new technique of home canning showcased its appeal to South Dakotans with large gardens, small iceboxes, and no electricity. South Dakotans canned vegetables produced in their gardens, including tomatoes, peppers, cucumbers, beets, and carrots, but recipes for jellies called for fruits like pineapples, figs, and strawberries. Only urban and well-to-do home cooks had access to those ingredients. Many rural women found ready substitutes from fruits such as mulberries, chokecherries, and plums that often grew wild on the prairies. While there were no recipes that featured fresh game or buffalo, there was one—the final recipe in the "Tested Recipes" cookbook—for pheasant, entitled "Canned Pheasant or Fowl." After cleaning, seasoning, and frying the bird until about 75 percent done, the meat and all the frying oil went into a sterilized jar. After sealing partially, the jar went into a hot water bath for ninety minutes, after which the cook had to "seal [it] immediately."[37]

By midcentury, community cookbooks transformed as South Dakotans responded to dramatic economic and cultural changes. Population declines precipitated by larger farms and a smaller number of farmers, along with new household technological innovations, coincided with rising rates of women's employment outside the home.[38] Food corporations and the brands of processed foods they advertised shifted South Dakota's culinary expectations yet again. These convenient options appealed to South Dakota's home cooks who by that time were raising fewer garden staples and incorporating more convenient grocery-store options that required less time, skill, and knowledge of food. Some cookbooks published after 1980 even added a "Microwave" section.[39] But South Dakotans did not reject home cooking, and community cookbooks published after about 1950 reveal resistance to national culinary trends. Even though their recipes took the form of national ones, with precise ingredients, measurements, and directions listed in a specific order, the nutritional ratio skewed heavily toward sweets, fats, and carbohydrates. Their choice of titles like "Favorites from the Country," "Home Cookin' is a Family Affair," and "Butter 'n Love Recipes" confirmed that offering familiar or comforting foods, not healthy ones, was the goal.[40] And despite their use of store-bought items, their recipes were as much from-scratch as possible. When women contributed recipes to or spearheaded the creation of community cookbooks, they were not always following the scientific standards of domestic scientists or the nutritional principles of the USDA. Unlike earlier cookbooks, many post-midcentury cookbooks contained full sections labeled "foreign" or "heritage," and they included more recipes for cherished ethnic dishes than ones from the 1920s. Recipes for Lakota dishes also became featured in some cookbooks created by white South Dakotans in the 1960s and 1970s. Since the

1990s, Lakota cooks have reclaimed their foodways, producing cookbooks as a testament to the strength of indigenous foodways.[41]

Community cookbooks created in the second half of the twentieth century demonstrated the power accrued by women's collective networks when they used food to commemorate institutional milestones and recast narratives of decline. Many opened with remarks of appreciation or dedication in which whoever compiled the recipes explained their intent. The Bethel Lutheran Ladies of Marvin, a town in Grant County, South Dakota, explained that their 1980 community cookbook marked the "occasion of the 100th Anniversary of the town."[42] They celebrated the opportunity to "gather regularly" and enjoy the "great feast of the Christian encounter," one the Bethel Lutheran Ladies claimed was alive and well in Marvin, a town they noted had only fifty-one residents in 1980, a drop from ninety-three people in 1960 and sixty-five in 1970.[43] Despite the decrease, the women boasted a full social calendar of suppers, bazaars, ice cream socials, waffle lunches, holiday programs, teas, banquets, and camping trips, which brought "special blessings and memories for many."[44] They also listed the names of the 127 people who contributed a recipe, more than double Marvin's population.[45] Of the fourteen categories, five were for sweets like bars, cookies, candy, pies, puddings, frostings, and pastries. They also included a ten-page section entitled "Canning, Freezing, and Preserves," a twenty-four-page section for "Foreign" recipes, and a twelve-page section for "Quantity Recipes," which featured dishes that could feed crowds as large as fifty to one hundred people.[46]

Community cookbooks that appeared in the 1970s and 1980s were often for centennial commemorations. Like the Bethel Lutheran Ladies in Marvin, the Mothers' Club of Bowdle, in Edmunds County, South Dakota, compiled a community cookbook to mark the town's centennial in 1986. The Mothers' Club formed in 1948 when its members built Meakins Park to give their children a place to play. Their cookbook offered categories like those in Marvin's cookbook—seven of the fifteen sections were for baked sweet items—but no single ethnic tradition dominated the recipes in the

"Foreign" section. Instead, the Mothers' Club had divided the recipes into "Chinese," "German," "Italian," "Mexican," and "Miscellaneous."[47] Unlike Marvin, whose white settlers were primarily Norwegian, Bowdle's earliest residents were Germans from Russia, an immigrant group who had lived for about a century in southern Russia near the Volga River before settling across the Dakotas.[48] Perhaps the Mothers' Club cookbook committee chose these designations to capture the diversity of submissions they received from Bowdle's home cooks. Maybe they wanted the cookbook to appeal to a variety of tastes. Whatever the case, they made clear that they saw a bright future for their community. The last page featured two photographs of Meakins Park, complete with swings, slides, seesaws, a merry-go-round, and picnic shelters that continued to entice its children and community to gather.[49] The cookbook and the park stemmed from a well of civic optimism fostered by the members of the Mothers' Club.

Community cookbooks also revealed the tightknit social networks that shaped South Dakota's culinary traditions. A few cookbooks had a single author, but most were collaborations among several contributors. The women of the Pleasant Study Club, a federated women's club formed in 1920, created a community cookbook to celebrate their sixtieth anniversary. The group organized during World War I as a local chapter of the American Red Cross. Most were Norwegian American farmers and neighbors from Pleasant Township, located just outside Beresford in Lincoln County, South Dakota. When the war ended, they "missed being together," so they began to meet.[50] While their primary focus was to study "current problems, world issues, art, music, literature, as well as domestic interests," they also planned local art festivals and served the Beresford Meals on Wheels program.[51] For six decades, they held teas, suppers, and parties during which they raised funds for institutions like South Dakota Public Television and the Bethesda Home, a senior-living facility. One of their "greatest thrills" was donating one thousand dollars to the Memorial Art Center at South Dakota State University.[52] One member captured the club's vitality when she explained that she could not reduce their accomplishments to a single initiative. "We have worked hard; we have enjoyed much; we have learned from each other. Our women have been strong and dedicated," she declared.[53]

The Pleasant Study Club offered more than just recipes in their cookbook. They included photographs of the group as well as poetry and short stories written by members. These creative pieces at times overshadowed the recipes, which pivoted the focus of the cookbook away from food and toward the close friendships enjoyed by members of the club. The structure of the cookbook itself, then, with quotes, poems, and other sayings interspersed among the recipes, revealed how social ties gave meaning to the foods they prepared and consumed. How they enjoyed a meal—together, in shared fellowship and friendship—was sometimes more important than what was on the table. They also maintained close friendships even when distance separated them. When Florence Gubbrud's husband, Archie, became the twenty-second governor of South Dakota in 1960, members held a "First Lady" Tea to honor her before her departure. The club also visited her twice in Pierre during her husband's two terms.[54] Their close ties lasted until their deaths. Obituaries for Geraldine Bovill, Bertyne Birkland, Ruth B. Eneboe Kittelson, Marie O'Connor Muhlenkort, Florence Gubbrud, and Tilda Sophia Ringsrud Johnson all prominently mentioned their longstanding devotion to the club.[55]

Most of South Dakota's community cookbooks came from groups like the Pleasant Study Club, groups of "strong and dedicated" women whose commitment to each other and their communities carried them through changing and difficult times. Collecting and publishing recipes gave them power not only over the foods they ate but also over the stories people told about themselves and their communities. Memorializing the past through reminiscence was a frequent way that cookbooks engaged in community storytelling, which emphasized commensality as a significant community-building act. While the tone of these stories was often nostalgic, with a tinge of sadness and loss, they formed an important bridge to recall meaningful civic and communal experiences. Reminiscing operated the same way that "foreign" or "heritage" recipes did but with overt aims. It connected daily meals to the places and people who prepared them, underlining boundaries of belonging in the process.[56]

Pairing the recipes with the reminisces that appeared in South Dakota's community cookbooks highlights the multifaceted ways commensality functioned. The act of reminiscing took a variety of forms, with some people offering minute details that served as a documentation of past work while others shared sentimental memories. A community cookbook created in 1994 for the eightieth anniversary of the founding of Bethesda Home in Beresford provided recipes in categories like "Large Quantity," "Scandinavian," "Canning, Freezing, and Miscellaneous," and "Bethesda Favorites." Five of the fifteen sections were for sweets, including muffins, candies, cookies, and pies.[57] The cookbook allowed staff to recall cherished memories. Nurses Diane Landon, Kaye Bergman, Betty Fizgerald, and Maye Fahlberg spoke highly of the original Bethesda Home location, describing it as "nestled in a grove of evergreen trees which provided a beautiful, tranquil setting."[58] Residents also offered memories from their lives, including Agnes Quinn, who loved to dance to bandmaster Lawrence Welk, a well-known performer on WNAX radio who later had a television show, and Milda Haugland, who "loved [her] little white stove."[59] She explained that on Sunday mornings, she baked cookies for visitors who came every Sunday afternoon.[60] The cookbook committee not only featured these memories, but they also listed specific details about the labor required to run the facility, including the people who served on the board of directors and names of all staff and their respective departments. Finally, each section heading featured a vignette from Bethesda Home's history, documenting the completion of the first addition to the original building in 1932 and the installation of an elevator in 1951.[61] By 1985 Bethesda Home had reached its capacity, and additional fundraising allowed contractors to break ground on a new facility. Including these details allowed the cookbook committee to construct a story that linked past accomplishments to present work. Even the cookbook title, "80

Years and Still Cookin',” was an intentional choice meant to reflect the continued vibrancy of this longstanding community institution.[62]

Cover of the 1954 edition of the *Your Neighbor Lady* book series from WNAX. *The Center for Western Studies.*

Memories abounded in community cookbooks created largely by women's collective networks. The Swedona Ladies' Aid Society of the Swedona Evangelical Covenant Church, a rural church founded by Swedish settlers located outside Brandon, in Minnehaha County, South Dakota, published a cookbook in 1977 to mark the church's one hundredth anniversary. The women wrote their own history, and it did not include typical items, like the names of the pastors or church elders or a chronological listing of construction projects, found in church histories. Instead, they documented the many “money-raising projects,” including “birthday socials, suppers, lunches at farm sales . . . bazaars, collecting coffee coupons, [and] bringing sewing, cooking, and canning exhibits to the fair” that they enjoyed.[63] They also described in detail the preparations for the annual chicken supper, which included catching, killing, and cleaning the chickens, frying them in large pots, peeling, cooking and mashing “huge amounts of potatoes,” boiling beans in “every available kettle preparatory to cooking,” and making dozens of homemade pies, breads, and pickles.[64] With the money they raised, they furnished the church and parsonage and covered expenses "when funds were low." Considering the frequency with which these women held fundraising events, the funds they raised were critical, not supplemental, to the church's budget. In the 1940s the women noted that a single meal often netted about two hundred dollars.[65]

Native American students preparing meals at St. Mary's Episcopal School for Indian Girls, Springfield, c. 1945. *The Center for Western Studies.*

The absence of Lakota recipes in South Dakota's community cookbooks was glaring. A few white-authored cookbooks produced after the mid-twentieth century featured short sections often entitled "Indian Foods" or "Indian Dishes." The recipes regularly substituted other ingredients, especially commodities, for traditional Lakota ones. In a 1963 cookbook produced by the St. Mary's Episcopal School for Indian Girls, located in Springfield, South Dakota, a recipe for *wasna*, or pemmican, a sacred food made with dried, pounded buffalo and mixed with berries and fat, contained none of these ingredients. Instead, the dish called for corn meal, butter, sugar, raisins, and salt cooked together.[66] The cookbook indicated that the school's version incorporated cornmeal and butter because they were "some of the most useful commodities supplied through the school lunch program," a federal social welfare program administered by the USDA.[67] Including cornmeal was in line with early-twentieth-century efforts by the federal government to intervenc in Lakota foodways, especially after the decimation of the buffalo as a food source and shift toward government commodity programs.[68] Cornmeal *wasna* was the result of decades of federal assimilationist policies.[69]

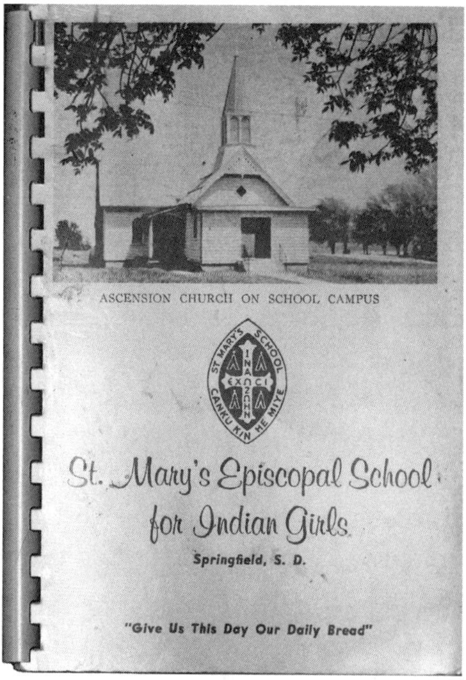

Cover of St. Mary's Episcopal School for Indian Girls cookbook. *The Center for Western Studies.*

By the late 1990s, Lakota cooks began to reclaim their deep food heritage, producing cookbooks that reflected the intimate connection they had with the land and its resources. These community compilations were more than recipes; they challenged ideas about food in South Dakota that overlooked its indigenous and spiritual dimensions. In 1999 Spuka Sni Win gathered recipes from friends and family who lived on the Pine Ridge Reservation. Not only did she list ingredients and directions, but she also explained the preservation techniques, healthful benefits, and typical meal combinations. For example, Lakota women sliced deer, beef, or buffalo meat thinly and used an oven, dehydration machine, or clothesline to dry it, creating a foodstuff called *papa*. The process took about two days, leaving a nutrient-rich dehydrated meat that retained 90 percent of its vitamins and minerals.[70] Another section featured breads, including one called *Gabubu Bread*, a pan-fried bread Lakota cooks adapted from white settlers. She instructed cooks to serve it either with *wahanpi*, or soup, or *wajopi*, a berry sauce made with frozen, canned, or fresh berries or dried wild berries.[71]

Like many of her white counterparts, Sni Win also wrote her own history, one of Lakota foodways that counterbalanced declensionist narratives. She explained the spiritual relationship between the Lakota and their lands, emphasizing that hunters and gatherers left offerings and gave thanks because "kinship is one of the most essential beliefs to the Lakota way of life."[72] She admitted that the loss of the "sacred buffalo" to the "white man's gun and intent" removed them to reservations, "starving and at the mercy of the U.S. Government."[73] While government-issued foods like beef, cornmeal, and flour replaced wild sources, Sni Win argued that the foods they developed, including *Gabubu* and other fried breads, became like buffalo to them, playing "the same role" in helping her "people survive throughout the toughest times of struggle."[74] She ended her history by explaining that Lakota gatherings continued to feature traditional and contemporary foods, including fried bread, menudo, and Indian tacos. In other words, Lakota foodways had endured against federal policies because Lakota cooks were resourceful during difficult times while remaining committed to preserving traditional foodways.

The presence of ethnic recipes in community cookbooks published after midcentury was not meant as an amusing, but fleeting glimpse at a bygone era. Their inclusion was part of a reaction by South Dakota home cooks to recall the state's culinary past at a critical moment. They were countering declensionist narratives that claimed that South Dakotans were losing their heritage, and they were reemphasizing the vibrancy of the state and its institutions. Creating Lakota cookbooks in the 1990s acted in a similar way, offering powerful evidence of the endurance of indigenous foodways even after decades of federal government policies designed to eradicate Lakota foods. Commemorating anniversaries, like the centennial celebration of the Bergen Lutheran Church in 1985, was a simple but powerful signal to the community of persistence and commitment. And, because these recipes appeared within cookbooks created by women, it earned them economic clout and reinforced the idea that women were not only the authorities of food in their communities but also central figures to fostering social and civic life in a state that, as they told it, was full of cultural vitality.

Notes

[1] "Standard Atlas of Day County: Including a Plat Book of the Villages, Cities, and Townships of the County," (Chicago: Brock & Company, 1929), 22.

[2] American Lutheran Church Women, Bergen Lutheran Church, Bergen Centennial Cookbook 1885-1985, "Table of Contents" page, South Dakota Community Cookbook Collection, Special Collections and Archives, Hilton Briggs Library, South Dakota State University, Brookings, South Dakota [hereafter SDSU].

[3] Ibid., 4-12.

[4] Jon Gjerde, *The Minds of the West: Ethnocultural Evolution in the Rural Middle West, 1830-1917* (Chapel Hill: University of North Carolina, 1997); Jon Gjerde, *From Peasants to Farmers: The Migration from Balestrand, Norway, to the Upper Middle West* (New York: Cambridge University Press, 1985).

[5] Maynnard F. Brass, "German Presbyterians and the Synod of the West," *Journal of Presbyterian History* 56 (Fall 1978): 241-43.

[6] David Wallace Adams, *Education for Extinction: American Indians and the Boarding School Experience, 1875-1928* (Lawrence: University Press of Kansas, 2020); Dana Vantrease, "Commod Bods and Frybread Power: Government Food Aid in American Indian Culture" *The Journal of American Folklore* 126 (Winter 2013): 55-69.

[7] Meredith Abarca, "Commensality: Networks of Personal, Family, and Community Social Transformation," *The Sociological Review* 69 (2021): 664-80; Claude Fischler, "Commensality, Society, and Culture," *Social Science Information* 50 (2011): 528-48; Melinda Mills, "'Cooking with Love,': Food, Gender, and Power," (Master's Thesis: Georgia State University, 2010); Debbie A. Hanson, "Home on the Range: How Community Cookbooks Define the Middle Border," in *The Interior Borderlands: Regional Identity in the Midwest and Great Plains,* ed. Jon K. Lauck (Sioux Falls: Center for Western Studies, 2019), 140-48.

[8] Herbert Schell, *History of South Dakota* (Pierre: South Dakota State Historical Society, 2004 [Fourth Edition]), 320-49; Jon Lauck, *American Agriculture and the Problem of Monopoly: The Political Economy of Grain Belt Farming, 1953-1980* (Lincoln: University of Nebraska Press, 2000).

[9] Tracey Deutsch, "Labor Histories of Food," in *The Oxford Handbook of Food History,* Jeffrey M. Pilcher, ed. (New York: Oxford University Press, 2012), 61-80.

[10] As Tom Isern explains, women were responsible for cooking meals for threshing crews, and he noted that while the crews desired quality foods—fried chicken was a common staple—cooks knew that "bulk was imperative." Observers noted that workers needed "plenty of potatoes and bread and foods containing starch and sugars to furnish the necessary energy for their work." See Tom Isern, "Folklife of the Threshing Outfit," *South Dakota History* 16:1 (1986): 18-34.

[11] Gustav Johnson, "Vegetable Garden, Philip, SD, Haakon County," Gustav M. Johnson Plate Collection, South Dakota State Historical Society, Pierre, South Dakota [hereafter SDSHS] https://sddigitalarchives.contentdm.oclc.org/digital/collection/photos/id/38353; "House with a Garden," Todd (Bystrom) Family Collection, SDSHS, https://sddigitalarchives.contentdm.oclc.org/digital/collection/photos/id/76896; "Della Todd" Todd (Bystrom) Family Collection, SDSHS, https://sddigitalarchives.contentdm.oclc.org/digital/collection/photos/id/76893; "Indian Agency and Garden, Rosebud, SD, Todd County," Rosebud Agency Collection, SDSHS, https://sddigitalarchives.contentdm.oclc.org/digital/collection/photos/id/14629; Henry M. Reed, "My Potato Patch by Saint Charles Hotel, Pierre SD, Hughes County," 1917, Pierre—Public Buildings, SDSHS, https://sddigitalarchives.contentdm.oclc.org/digital/collection/photos/id/75615.

[12] Lonnie Shafer, *The South Dakota Pheasant Hunting Seasons Data Book: 100th Anniversary Edition* (Pierre: South Dakota Department of Game, Fish, and Parks, 2019).

[13] For an in-depth look at early-twentieth-century riverine gardening techniques practiced by the Hidatsa in North Dakota, see, Gilbert L. Wilson, *Buffalo Bird Woman's Garden: The Classic Account of Hidatsa American Indian Gardening Techniques* (St. Paul: Minnesota Historical Society Press, 1987); Herbert T. Hoover, "Arikara, Sioux, and Government Farmers: Three American Indian Agricultural Legacies," *South Dakota History* 13:1-2 (1983): 22-48; James H. Howard, *The Dakota or Sioux Indians: A Study in Human Ecology,* (Vermillion, S. Dak.: Dakota Museum, 1966); Linda S. Black Elk, *Culturally Important Plants of the Lakota: Based on Interviews, Research, and a Comprehensive Review of Historical Documents* (Fort Yates, N. Dak.: Sitting Bull College, 1998).

[14] Doane Robinson estimated that egg and poultry production was worth five million dollars in 1904. See, Doane Robinson, *South Dakota Historical Collections, Illustrated with Maps and Engravings,* vol. 3 (Pierre: State Historical Society, 1906).

[15] S. Welsh, C. Davis, and A. Shaw, "A Brief History of Food Guides in the United States," *Nutrition Today* (Nov./Dec. 1992): 6-11; S. Welsh, C. Davis, and A. Shaw, "Development of the Food Guide Pyramid," *Nutrition Today* (Nov./Dec. 1992: 12-23).

[16] Tracey Deutsch, *Building a Housewife's Paradise: Gender, Government and American Grocery Stores in the Twentieth Century* (Chapel Hill: University

of North Carolina Press, 2010); Jennifer Jensen Wallach, *How America Eats: A Social History of U. S. Food and Culture* (Lanham, Md.: Rowan and Littlefield, 2013).

[17] Laura Shapiro, *Perfection Salad: Women and Cooking at the Turn of the Century* (Berkeley: University of California Press, 2009), 44-119.

[18] Shapiro, *Perfection Salad,* 73-76.

[19] Alice L. McLean, *Cooking in America, 1840-1945* (Westport, Conn.: Greenwood Press, 2006); Susan Williams, *Food in the United States, 1820-1890* (Westport, Conn.: Greenwood Press, 2006).

[20] Hanson, "Home on the Range," 140-42; Anne Bower, "Our Sisters' Recipes: Exploring 'Community' in a Community Cookbook," *Journal of Popular Culture* 31 (Winter 1997): 137-51; Anne Bower, "Cooking Up Stories: Narrative Elements in Community Cookbooks," *Recipes for Reading: Community Cookbooks, Stories, Histories* (Amherst: University of Massachusetts Press, 1997), 29-50; Traci Nathans-Kelly, "Embracing Compiled Cookbooks as Historical Documents," in *The State We're In: Reflections on Minnesota History,* ed. Annette Atkins and Deborah L. Miller (St. Paul: Minnesota Historical Society Press, 2010), 271-80; Mary Anna DuSablon, *America's Collectible Cookbooks: The History, the Politics, the Recipes* (Athens, Ohio: Ohio University Press, 1994); Barbara Epstein, *The Politics of Domesticity* (Middletown, Conn.: Wesleyan University Press, 1986); Laurel Foster, "Liberating the Recipe: A Study of Food and Feminism in the early 1970s," *The Recipe Reader: Narratives, Contexts, Traditions* (Burlington, Vermont: Ashgate, 2003), 147-68; Lynne Ireland, "The Compiled Cookbook as Foodways Autobiography," *The Taste of American Place,* edited by Barbara Shortridge and James Shortridge (New York: Rowman and Littlefield, 1998), 111-17; Rebecca Sharpless, "Cookbooks as Resources for Rural Research," *Agricultural History* (Spring 2016): 195-208; Jessica Derleth, "'Kneading Politics': Cookery and the American Woman Suffrage Movement," *The Journal of the Gilded Age and Progressive Era* 17 (July 2018): 450-74; Rosalyn Collings Eves, "A Recipe for Remembrance: Memory and Identity in African-American Women's Cookbooks," *Rhetoric Review* 24 (2005): 280-97; Kennan Ferguson, "Intensifying Taste, Intensifying Identity: Collectivity through Community Cookbooks," *Signs: Journal of Women in Culture and Society* 27 (2012): 695-717; Megan Elias, *Stir It Up: Home Economics in American Culture* (Philadelphia: University of Pennsylvania Press, 2008), 6-7, 20-22, 30-40; Janice Longone, "'The Old Girl Network': Charity Cookbooks and the Empowerment of Women," Lecture, William Clements Library, University of Michigan, Ann Arbor, Michigan, http://lecb.physics.lsa.umich.edu/CWIS/browser.php?Resourceld=1179. The Janice Bluestein Longone Culinary Archive at the University of Michigan Library has a number of suffrage cookbooks. See Janice Bluestein Longone Culinary Archive, Special Collection Research Center, Hatcher Graduate Library, University of

Michigan Library, Ann Arbor, Michigan, https://www.lib.umich.edu/janice-bluestein-longone-culinary-archive-0.

[21] Schell, *History of South Dakota,* 223-24, 283-94, 319-20.

[22] Harry F. Thompson, ed., *A New South Dakota History,* 2d ed. (Sioux Falls: Center for Western Studies, 2009).

[23] South Dakota State Historical Society, *Homesteading and Agricultural Development Context* (Vermillion, S. Dak.: South Dakota State Historical Preservation Center, 1994); Thomas Witt, Kathleen Corbett, Holly Norton, and James Steely, *The History of Agriculture in South Dakota: Components for a Fully Developed Historic Context* (Pierre, S. Dak.: South Dakota State Historical Society, 2013); Gilbert C. Fite, "Agricultural Pioneering in Dakota: A Case Study," *Great Plains Quarterly* 1 (1981): 169-80; Gilbert C. Fite, "The Transformation of South Dakota Agriculture: The Effects of Mechanization, 1939-1964," *South Dakota History* 19 (Fall 1989): 278-305. In his chronicle of the Gist family, James Marten mentions the garden Gladys, the matriarch, grew, but does so within a discussion of technological changes on the farms they occupied. See James Marten, "Continuity and Change on the Twentieth-Century Farm: The Gists of South Dakota, 1921-71." *Great Plains Quarterly* 11:1 (Winter 1991): 37-52. For books on midwestern foodways, see Oliver B. Pollak, "Recent Books on Midwestern Foodways," *Middle West Review* 3:2 (Spring 2017): 161-68.

[24] Some of the printers of the community cookbooks found most often in the South Dakota Community Cookbook Collection in the Special Collections and Archives at South Dakota State University were Crescent Publishing, Inc. of Garretson, South Dakota, and Hills, Minnesota, Circulation Service of Shawnee, Kansas, Morris Press Cookbooks of Kearney, Nebraska, Jumbo Jack's Cookbooks of Audubon, Iowa, and General Publishing and Binding of Iowa Falls, Iowa.

[25] Gjerde, *The Minds of the West.*

[26] Dorothy Deethardt, "From Dorothy's Kitchen: 90 Years of Recipes and Family History," 1990, Box 4, SDSU; "Grandma Jenny's Favorite Recipes: 80 Years of home Cooking," 2016, Box 2, SDSU.

[27] Vantrease, "Commod Bods and Frybread Power," 55-69.

[28] Ladies' Aid Society, American Lutheran Church, "Tested Recipes with Practical References," 1925, Box 9, SDSU.

[29] Ibid.

[30] Ladies' Aid Society, American Lutheran Church, "Tested Recipes with Practical References," 1925, page 20, Box 9, SDSU; Hedvig Melum, Huron Ward 1, Beadle County, South Dakota, page 9B, Fourteenth Census of the United States, 1920, Records of the Bureau of the Census, Record Group 29 (Provo, UT: Ancestry.com, 2010).

[31] Ladies' Aid Society, American Lutheran Church, "Tested Recipes with Practical References," 1925, page 20, Box 9, SDSU, 4, 20, 32.

[32] Caroline Gunderson, Huron Ward 1, Beadle County, South Dakota, page 8B, Fourteenth Census of the United States, 1920, Records of the Bureau of the Census, Record Group 29 (Provo, UT: Ancestry.com, 2010).

[33] Ladies' Aid Society, American Lutheran Church, "Tested Recipes with Practical References," 1925, page 20, Box 9, SDSU.

[34] [No Cover Page], Mitchell, South Dakota, ca. 1920s, introduction, Box 4, SDSU.

[35] Ladies' Aid Society, American Lutheran Church, "Tested Recipes with Practical References," 1925, p. 36, Box 9, SDSU; Katrine Nelson, Huron Ward 1, Beadle County, South Dakota, p. 5B, Fourteenth Census of the United States, 1920, Records of the Bureau of the Census, Record Group 29 (Provo, UT: Ancestry.com, 2010).

[36] Ladies' Aid Society, American Lutheran Church, "Tested Recipes with Practical References," 1925, pp. 8-18, Box 9, SDSU; South Dakota Department of Agriculture, "South Dakota Native Trees," 2012, https://sdda.sd.gov/conservation-forestry/forest-woodlands-trees/south-dakota-native-trees/.

[37] Ladies' Aid Society, American Lutheran Church, "Tested Recipes with Practical References," 1925, p. 112, Box 9, SDSU.

[38] Marvin P. Riley, "South Dakota's Population in Perspective, 1960-70: Selected Population Data for South Dakota, the North Central States, Regions of the United States, and the United States," (Brookings, S. Dak.: Agricultural Experiment Station, South Dakota State University, May 1974); Schell, *History of South Dakota,* 320-49; Deanna Pucciarelli and Adrienne Thomas, "Determinates That Influence Food Consumption among Older Members of a Midwest Community," *Food and Nutrition Sciences* 2 (2011): 1018-26.

[39] American Lutheran Church Women, Bergen Lutheran Church, Bergen Centennial Cookbook 1885-1985, "Table of Contents" page, SDSU.

[40] Putney Ladies Aid, "Favorites from the Country," Groton, S. Dak., 2008, Box 5, SDSU; St. John's Lutheran Church of Hosmer, "Home Cookin' is a Family Affair," Hosmer, S. Dak., 1994, Box 2, SDSU; Zion Lutheran Church, "Butter 'n Love Recipes," Sioux Falls, S. Dak., 1978, Box 3, SDSU.

[41] One of the most well-known Lakota chefs is Sean Sherman, whose mission is to not only produce Lakota recipes but also to revitalize Native American cuisine. See Sean Sherman, *The Sioux Chef's Indigenous Kitchen* (St. Paul: University of Minnesota Press, 2017).

[42] Bethel Lutheran Church, "Bethel Lutheran Church Cookbook, Members—Friends 1880-1980, 100th Anniversary of Marvin, South Dakota," Marvin, S. Dak., 1980, p. i, Box 2, SDSU.

[43] Ibid., i-iv; Eighteenth Census of the United States, 1960, Census of Population: 1960—V1—Part 43, Characteristics of Population, South Dakota, Section 2, "Number of Inhabitants," p. 17, United States

Bureau of the Census, https://www2.census.gov/prod2/decennial/documents/40393331v1p43ch2.pdf.

[44] Bethel Lutheran Church, "Bethel Lutheran Church Cookbook," iv.

[45] Ibid., v-vii.

[46] Ibid., 10, 1-12.

[47] Mothers' Club, "Mothers' Club Cookbook, Bowdle Centennial, June 27-28-29, 1886-1986," Bowdle, S. Dak., Box 2, SDSU.

[48] Brosz, Allyn, Alex Herzog, and Thomas Stangl, eds. *A Reference Book for Russian German and German Russian History and Culture, With Place Name Listings of Former German Settlement Areas by Ulrich Mertens,* Brigitte von Budde and Alex Herzog, trans. (Fargo, N. Dak.: Germans from Russia Heritage Collection, North Dakota State University Libraries, 2010).

[49] Mothers' Club, "Mothers' Club Cookbook, Bowdle Centennial," 325.

[50] Pleasant Study Club, "Pleasant Study Club 60th Anniversary Cookbook, 1920-1980," Beresford, S. Dak., p. 6, Box 8, SDSU; Lincoln County History Committee, *The History of Lincoln County, South Dakota* (Pierre: South Dakota Committee on the Humanities, 1985).

[51] Pleasant Study Club, "Pleasant Study Club 60th Anniversary Cookbook, 1920-1980," p. 6.

[52] Ibid., 6-7.

[53] Ibid., 8.

[54] Pleasant Study Club, "Pleasant Study Club 60th Anniversary Cookbook, 1920-1980," p. 6-8; "Ex-Governor Gubbrud of South Dakota Dies," *The New York Times,* April 28, 1987.

[55] Geraldine Bovill, Obituary, Wass Funeral Home, April 30, 2011, https://www.wassfuneralhome.com/obituary/5919854; "Champion of Excellence: Bertyne Birkland," South Dakota Hall of Fame, Programs Directory Site, 1998, https://sdexcellence.org/Bertyne_Birkland_1998; Ruth B. (Eneboe) Kittelson, Obituary, Heritage Funeral Home and Cremation Services, Aug. 25, 2016, https://www.legacy.com/obituaries/name/ruth-eneboe-kittelson-obituary?pid=181240113; Marie O'Connor Muhlenkort, Obituary, Doeppenschmidt Funeral Home, Dec. 18, 2013, https://www.doeppenschmidtfuneralhome.com/obituaries/print?o_id=2361297; Florence Gubbrud, Obituary, Wass Funeral Home, May 9, 2006, https://www.wassfuneralhome.com/obituary/5920097; Tilda S. Ringsrud Johnson, Memorial Inscription, Zion Methodist Church, Find a Grave, https://www.findagrave.com/memorial/15102845/tilda-sophia-johnson.

[56] Anita Mannur, "Culinary Nostalgia: Authenticity, Nationalism, and Diaspora," *MELUS* 32 (Winter 2007): 11-31; R. I. M. Dunbar, "Breaking Bread: The Functions of Social Eating," *Adaptive Human Behavior and Physiology* 3 (2017) 198-211; Karen Metheny, "Modeling Communities Through Food: Connecting the Daily Meal to the Construction of Place and Identity," *Northeast Historical Archeology* 42 (2013): 147-83; Hakan Jonsson, "One Hundred Years of Solitude and Commensality: A Study of Cooking and

Meals in Swedish Households," in *Places of Food Production: Origin, Identity, Imagination,* S. Bartsch and P. Lysaght, eds. (Bern, Switzerland: Peter Lang Publishing Group, 2017), 259-72; Banu Bargu, "The Politics of Commensality," in *The Anarchist Turn,* Jacob Blumenfeld, Chiara Bottici, and Simon Critchley, eds. (New York: Palgrave Macmillan, 2013); Alexandra Vignolles and Paul-Emmanuel Pichon, "A Taste of Nostalgia: Links between Nostalgia and Food Consumption," *Qualitative Market Research* (June 2014): 1-17.

[57] "Bethesda Home 80 Years…and Still Cookin'," pp. 13-14, Box 2, SDSU.

[58] Ibid., 8.

[59] Ibid., 8-11; John Miller, *Small Town Dreams: Stories of Midwestern Boys Who Shaped America* (Lawrence: University of Kansas Press, 2014), 335-66.

[60] "Bethesda Home 80 Years…and Still Cookin'," pp. 8-11, Box 2, SDSU.

[61] Ibid., 3-6, 13-14, 101, 241.

[62] Ibid., 5.

[63] Swedona Ladies' Aid Society, "Swedona Centennial Cookbook, 1877-1977," Brandon, S. Dak., 1977, pp. 4-5, Box 3, SDSU.

[64] Ibid.

[65] Ibid.

[66] "St. Mary's Episcopal School for Indian Girls, Springfield, S. D.," Cookbook, 1963, p. 16, Box 8, SDSU. The Bicentennial Cookbook produced by the South Dakota State Extension Clubs Organization had a section entitled "Indian Culture Recipes." It also included a recipe called "corn wasna" which featured cornmeal, sugar, non-fat dry milk, salt, raisins or cooked prunes, and hot tallow. See, South Dakota State Extension Clubs, "Bicentennial Heritage Recipes: Eat Drink and Be Merry," Cookbook, 1975, p. 54, Box 2, SDSU.

[67] "St. Mary's Episcopal School for Indian Girls, Springfield, S.D.," p. 16; Susan Levine, *School Lunch Politics: The Surprising History of America's Favorite Welfare Program* (Princeton: Princeton University Press, 2008).

[68] Janice Goodwin and Judy Hall, *Healthy Traditions: Recipes of Our Ancestors,* Cookbook (Grand Forks: National Center for Native American Aging at the Center for Rural Health, University of North Dakota.

[69] Some Lakota cooks are on a mission to promote traditional foods like wasna, including Jerry Goes In Center, who is encouraging Lakota to move away from "reservation comfort foods" developed from government-run commodity food programs and back to their heritage recipes. See Mary Garrigan, "Wasna Woman," *Rapid City Journal,* Oct. 5, 2004.

[70] Spuka Sni Win, *Lakota Recipes,* Cookbook, 1999, Box 1, SDSU.

[71] Ibid.

[72] Ibid.

[73] Ibid.

[74] Ibid.

10

South Dakota Sports: Building Individual Integrity and Community Identity

Paul Higbee

There are few better examples of a community's enthusiasm for its school sports than what Yankton demonstrated in April 1924. Other South Dakota towns took note, too. The *Sioux Falls Argus Leader* wrote, "Everybody who loves real spirit and superior athletics, and whose heart warms at the success of a real he-fighter, will take off his hat to the Yankton high school basketball team." Coached by Clement Letich, Yankton won the state high school championship and then accepted an invitation to a Chicago tournament featuring 39 of the country's best prep teams. In Chicago Yankton beat teams from much bigger cities including Dallas, Texas, and Chattanooga, Tennessee. When news of each triumph reached Yankton via telegraph, impromptu celebrations broke out across town, complete with bonfires. But what appeared to be a run to a mythical "national championship" became instead the "near-miss of 1924," analyzed by Yanktonians for years, with most fans agreeing that guard John McDonough's tournament-ending neck injury in game three was the deflating factor. Without McDonough, Yankton lost the finale to another small school, Windsor, Colorado. Yet that didn't dampen Yankton's pride. The team was greeted at Sioux City and Vermillion railroad depots and players received word that 3,000 people awaited them down the tracks at Yankton. Thus warned, Coach Letich dropped off the train just outside Yankton to avoid the crush and allow his players to bask in adulation. But admirers quickly found him and carried him to the celebration.[1]

The 1924 Yankton fan base reflected unprecedented interest in spectator sports seen nationally that decade, from prep games to professional leagues. South Dakota has always taken pleasure in watching its athletes take down "big city" opponents. Of course, for most South Dakota towns, Sioux Falls and Rapid City are urban, and defeating their teams produces no less of a thrill.

Semantics have often complicated discussion of South Dakota sport because, for a large percentage of the state's population, the term chiefly means hunting and fishing. For some outsiders, pheasant hunting largely defines South Dakota, and the state's hills and plains attract residents and out-of-state hunters seeking other game, too. From the start the Pick-Sloan Plan that dammed the Missouri River in the 1950s and '60s stressed that sport fishing would be a central goal, not merely a by-product of power generation and irrigation projects.[2] South Dakotans have proven themselves inventive in adding elements of human competition to hunting and fishing, establishing tournaments based on harvesting by volume and weight. An example is the Harding County Coyote Callers which, in addition to advancing wildlife management, draws hunters to compete for bounty and then enjoy food, drink, "and tales of the hunt," as one news writer reported.[3]

While acknowledging the significance of that form of sport in South Dakota, this chapter will explore athletic games as they evolved across the state and shaped the overall culture. Perhaps the most difficult aspect of this exploration, from a twenty-first-century perspective, is grasping how nineteenth-century sports—even those that looked very much like modern versions—were played when the concept of leisure time for adults was alien. For an adult to "play" was an absurd notion. Very young children played because that's where their capabilities lay. Adults could participate in athletics if there was a practical connection to work or community well-being. For example, daring and physical agility might reveal leadership potential in military or business circles, while hook-and-ladder competitions between fire departments (well attended as a spectator sport in territorial days) provided insight into how well protected communities were against disaster.[4] In Lakota culture, contests helped tribal elders identify the next generation of likely leaders. Games on horseback created the foundation for powerful Lakota equestrian forces, while *napeoglece* was a system for developing strong and accurate spear-throwing.[5]

Baseball

As South Dakota approached statehood in 1889, an up-and-coming sport was moving past hook-and-ladder contests in demonstrating admirable "manly" qualities, to use terminology of the times. Ironically, it was essentially an English game for children, rounders. Americanized as baseball, the main difference between versions was a defensive rule: in rounders a batter was called out when a fielder grabbed a fly ball on the first or second bounce and held on. Baseball rules dictated that an out would be recorded only if the fielder caught the fly (or line drive) before it hit the ground—a feat that demonstrated a good eye, quick reflexes, and true daring in the era before fielders wore mitts.[6] Industries organized teams to advertise the caliber of men who made up their workforce, and communities formed baseball clubs that made statements about local youthful energy. Games often combined spectator picnicking and wagering, played out on fields midway between tiny towns or in the heart of big ones, and on reservations. Typically, athletes were men in their teens, 20s, and 30s. By the twentieth century baseball was indisputably the national pastime and South Dakota newspapers carried news of professional players—some familiar. Jim Scott, born in Deadwood, was a big and often dominating pitcher for the early Chicago White Sox.[7] Charles "Deacon" Phillippe, another pitcher, grew up in the Redfield area and played on town teams there before making history with the Pittsburgh Pirates by winning the first-ever World Series game in 1903 (against Cy Young).[8] The best known pro player then was Detroit Tiger Ty Cobb—no South Dakota connection until he hunted pheasants there late in life—who displayed remarkable hitting prowess and a penchant for on-field fights. His fights were often contrived to produce a Detroit edge. South Dakota claimed lots of Cobb imitators when it came to diamond fisticuffs; brothers Earl and Lee Morford of Deadwood, for example, earned reputations as fine players and baseball promoters (they brought Babe Ruth to the Black Hills to play an exhibition game in 1922) and as fighters on Deadwood's town team. "When the ball team played you could bet there would be one or more fights during the game started by the Morford brothers," wrote historian George Moses, who grew up attending those games. He added, "I cannot remember either of the Morfords ever losing a fight as they were well experienced."[9]

Why is baseball's two-fisted era in South Dakota worth remembering? Because given its culture in the 1920s, baseball seemed an unlikely vehicle for promoting personal integrity, sportsmanship, and respectful citizenship. Yet that's what happened after members of South Dakota American Legion posts gathered at Milbank for a convention in 1925. They listened to a speech by guest John Griffith, commissioner of the Big Ten college athletic conference. He urged them to initiate a statewide baseball league for teenaged boys that would stress commitment to community, fair play, and quality competition. Within a year Legion posts in South Dakota were sponsoring teams and calling for other states to follow their lead. A year after that, Legion teams played in 15 states and there was a national tournament. Today American Legion baseball is played in all 50 states, and half of current major league ballplayers were members of Legion teams.[10] There can be little argument that Legion baseball is South Dakota's foremost contribution to the sport nationally.

Still, other baseball contributions have not been insignificant. South Dakota produced the first major league manager to win World Series titles in both the American and National leagues (Bridgewater's Sparky Anderson) and the only big leaguer to pinch hit for Ted Williams (Sturgis's Carroll Hardy).[11] What's more, for minor leaguers everywhere, South Dakota came to epitomize the idea of summers spent honing skills in small towns (homes to Western, Northern and Basin league teams) and long post-game bus rides through the night. Within the state, baseball led to the popularity of softball, played widely by both sexes and all ages.[12]

Football

The sport that generated the most criticism related to violence early in the twentieth century was, not surprisingly, football. The game was mostly one of running, blocking and tackling then, with protective padding virtually nonexistent. Helmets, not universally used, were leather, effective against head lacerations but worthless in preventing concussions and skull fractures. Among game fatalities that alarmed the nation was Harry Jordan of Sioux Falls College in 1902.[13] University of South Dakota president Garrett Droppers believed that the extreme exertion football demanded was as injurious as hard hits and tackles, writing, "The question may be fairly asked whether football does not wear out the student rather than develop him."[14] In 1905 the state legislature passed a law to disqualify any player who intentionally hurt an opponent, and behind the scenes President Theodore Roosevelt urged for implementation of new rules to prevent injuries. Mostly Roosevelt addressed college presidents and coaches because post-secondary schools drove football's development.[15] That was particularly true in South Dakota; college leaders saw football as a means for connecting with other Midwestern institutions of higher education. The strategy worked, with the University of South Dakota and South Dakota State squaring off against the University of Minnesota, Iowa State, University of Nebraska, and Notre Dame early on.[16]

In 1906, in response to Roosevelt's plea for safer football, college rules were changed to allow for forward passes, opening the door to moving the ball through the air. The rule did, indeed, reduce injuries and from perspectives of most fans, made the game more interesting. But it took teams a few seasons to execute pass strategies well. Among the first to do so was Notre Dame in 1913, a season when it went undefeated and had the University of South Dakota on its schedule. The Coyotes got a first-hand look at Notre Dame's passing game but nonetheless played the Fighting Irish perhaps as tough as any opponent that year, falling 20-7 after Notre Dame surged late.[17] On the Notre Dame squad that day was right end Fred Gushurst of Lead, soon to return to South Dakota where he became South Dakota School of Mines' first paid football coach in 1917 and established a strong passing game.[18]

Years before the National Football League gained a wide audience, the college game was where national football writers focused their attention, and they did not overlook South Dakota. In 1935 coach Paul Rose led his Black Hills Teachers College team to an undefeated, untied season (one of seven colleges nationally to do so). Twenty sports writers from across the country voted unsuccessfully to send the Spearfish college to the Rose Bowl.[19] The sports scribes likely were hoping for something along the lines of the 1922 Rose Bowl that won wide attention by matching tiny powerhouse Washington and Jefferson College of Pennsylvania against the University of California, resulting in a thrilling scoreless tie.

South Dakota newspapers developed sportswriters who were observant and frank in their reporting, and not necessarily inclined to make excuses for local teams. Although Augustana won its 1925 homecoming contest against Huron College, J. D. Ashley of the *Sioux Falls Argus Leader* cast a critical eye, feeling that Augie should have played better. He wrote, "Steeped to the gills in fight and determination, Huron College's football team battled Augustana, top heavy favorite to win, leading the local eleven until the final three minutes . . . the Huron team stole the Vikings' thunder, for the homecoming fight was not that of the local team but carried by the invaders." Papers were not hesitant about drumming up attendance, sometimes reminding readers that those invading teams would come to town with "enthusiastic boosters," and in the case of the *Argus Leader* in 1912, flat out asserting that "everybody ought to be there to boost one of the best football teams Sioux Falls school has ever turned out. They are worthy of your support and expect you to turn out and see them deliver the goods."[20]

Augustana College's Viking Days homecoming game against Huron College, October 17, 1925. Huron led throughout the game, until the last few minutes, when Augustana pulled ahead, winning 7-6. *The Center for Western Studies.*

Sportswriters advanced (and sometimes invented) college team names that, in many cases, reflected South Dakotans' natural surroundings. There were the University of South Dakota Coyotes, South Dakota State Jackrabbits, and the Northern State Wolves when that predator was still being driven off the Great Plains. High schools followed suit with the Provo Rattlers, Waverly Wood-Chucks, and Claremont Honkers, and they put imagination to work in inventing the Monroe Wooden-Shoed Canaries. Agriculture was honored with the Buffalo Ranchers, Newell Irrigators, and Vale Beetdiggers.[21]

Those team names were applied to all sports teams within a school. "The snarl of a fighting Coyote pack echoed and re-echoed upon the hardwood courts of both home and foreign basketball floors," wrote a University of South Dakota student reporter.[22] But when it came to pomp, football was hard to top. College homecomings, especially the first half of the century, delivered unsurpassed entertainment to small town South Dakota. Black Hills Teachers College's Swarm Day, November 3, 1928, featured an opera, Mardi Gras, parade, dinner, dance and, of course, a football game. South Dakota State students invited former world heavyweight boxing champion Max Baer to campus to emcee Hobo Day 1939, and he accepted.[23]

High school football's development mirrored the college game although small schools struggled to find enough athletes to fill rosters. In order to make certain all schools could play, the state High School Athletics Association approved versions of football modified for fewer than eleven players per team. Stephen Epler in Nebraska invented six-man football, played on fields 80 yards long and 40 yards wide, with liberal substitution rules that brought about an emphasis on diverse skills rather than specialty players. Beginning in the 1930s, the six-man game was played widely in rural regions of the United States. South Dakotan Bill Welsh, former teammate of Red Grange at the University of Illinois, came home to coach, and became perhaps Epler's most successful disciple. He formed a six-man team at Claremont High School and won a national record 61 straight games, 1947-53.[24] Nine-man football is played by nearly half of the state's high schools in the 2020s.[25]

The early state Athletics Association (it became the Activities Association in 1961) knew football to be an expensive sport. As safety equipment improved, costs per player rose significantly. Not wanting to further burden successful teams with costs related to postseason tournaments, the Association in 1926 ruled that high school teams were forbidden to participate in after-season games "to determine a high school football champion."[26]

By the middle of the twentieth century, South Dakotans were contributing to major college and professional football, not only as players but as coaches and executives. Miller's Weert Engelmann played on Green Bay Packers teams that won two National Football League titles in the 1930s.[27] The 1940s and '50s saw Winner's Frank Leahy coach Notre Dame to an 87-11-9 record,[28] and Mitchell's Ordell Braase began a career as defensive end on powerful Baltimore Colts teams and became NFL Players Association president.[29] In the 1960s Sioux Falls' Joe Foss served as commissioner of the American Football League,[30] soon to merge with the NFL, while Sisseton's Joe Robbie was principal founding owner of the NFL's Miami Dolphins.[31]

It was an era of exploding interest and TV coverage for the NFL and its personalities, and South Dakotans rolled their eyes as broadcasters routinely asked variations on this question about the state's athletes: "How on earth did he make the jump from that little place to the big time?" For local residents the answer was this: good coaches who prefer small communities and schools to big ones, emphasis on playing multiple sports that develop well-rounded athletic skills, environments where no talent slips through the cracks unnoticed, and opponents who offer stiff competition.

In the 1970s South Dakotans began expressing hope that the state might better showcase its high school football talent by finding a way around the 1926 playoff ban. A perfect venue was in the works on the University of South Dakota campus, the DakotaDome, so that the final games could be played indoors in November. But the ban seemed ironclad because the Athletics Association had stipulated that only a two-thirds vote by its board could overturn it. In 1981 Tony Weisensee, Sioux Falls attorney and father of an O'Gorman High School football player, expressed the view that the two-thirds vote was the chief problem and that it should be overturned in court so that a simple majority vote could lift the ban. Weisensee won his argument in court early in 1981, the Activities Association dropped appeals and voted to approve playoffs, and announced a system would be in place for those games that fall.[32]

Soon after, South Dakotans first heard that the state's public colleges and universities hoped to upgrade from National Collegiate Athletics Association (NCAA) Division II to NCAA Division I, and from National Association of Intercollegiate Athletics (NAIA) to NCAA Division II. Moving up would impact student-athlete standards, physical facilities, and scholarships. Of the state's two biggest universities, South Dakota State reached NCAA Division I status in 2004, and the University of South Dakota in 2008.[33]

By then it was becoming obvious that kicker Adam Vinatieri was enjoying an NFL career unparalleled among South Dakotans. A product of Rapid City Central and South Dakota State, he joined the New England Patriots in 1996, stayed in the league for 24 seasons, scored 2,673 points, and was part of four Super Bowl championships with New England and Indianapolis.[34]

Basketball

It can be argued that basketball holds the state's attention more than any other sport and shines most brightly in South Dakota as a high school game. Less than a decade after James Naismith invented the game in Massachusetts in 1891, South Dakotans were singing its merits and repurposing hardwood floors anywhere as courts (for example, Hitchcock's Murphy's Store saw contests played upstairs, and Spearfish's Matthews Opera House featured an inviting flat auditorium floor).[35] Tight venues with low ceilings led to "line drive" shooting with little arc on the ball.

As high schools were built across the state, gyms were usually part of the architectural design, often small but seldom lacking character. For generations coaches visiting Humboldt had to determine how to position players on a floor where support pillars were in play. By contrast, Mitchell's municipal Corn Palace felt palatial indeed in size and opulence (the current building took form in 1921 and hosted its first state high school basketball tournament in 1922).[36]

Just a couple hundred fans could fill those small gyms with ear-piercing noise.[37] Cramped and noisy or not, school gyms were often the most comfortable spots in town on cold winter nights. Sometimes gyms were where the public first heard about and saw evidence of issues that included school district consolidation, ending a ban that kept Catholic schools out of post-season state tournaments ("Tough, bitter religious fight," remembered a lobbyist who worked successfully to overturn the ban in the 1960s),[38] Title IX, and open enrollment.

The state's school landscape shifted in the middle of the twentieth century as small communities struggled with declining enrollments. One hundred schools or entire school districts closed permanently between 1950 and 1975,[39] and the matter was often reported in the media through a sports lens. Students from eliminated schools transferred to neighboring ones, often schools that had been sports rivals. Some administrators and teachers worried that mergers would prompt memories of elbows and other dirty plays, and trigger hallway fights. To no great extent, it turned out. School reorganization seemed more difficult for some parents who felt deprived by not seeing their children wearing their old school colors, and for business people in affected towns who lost game day revenues.[40]

At the same time that Yankton thrilled South Dakotans in the Chicago tournament of 1924, girls played varsity basketball in the state. But then South Dakota (and other states) heeded medical advice that basketball was too strenuous for girls, likely to result in permanent injury, and the game for girls was relegated to mostly intramural status for decades.[41] Track and golf would gain popularity as girls' varsity sports before girls' basketball regained that status.

High school and college women's sports are popular in South Dakota. Here, South Dakota State University battles Augustana University. *The Center for Western Studies.*

Girls played sanctioned high school varsity basketball, and women played college ball, after President Richard Nixon signed Title IX into law in 1972. The federal mandate prohibited sex-based discrimination in schools receiving federal funding and was challenged in Congress and the courts for years,[42] but South Dakota complied quickly. The first few seasons of girls' basketball were played in fall because of schools' concerns about allotting sufficient gym time for two varsity teams. August practices and September games in non-air-conditioned gyms sometimes left players, refs, and fans feeling wilted. "And there were people who asked, 'Why do girls have to have all the same things boys do?'" recalled Randy Parry, who coached the first girls' teams at Howard High School. "Statewide, attendance wasn't good at first. You had to build it up, and players did that by working hard and improving so that people noticed."

Watertown's Kay Stormo was a player fans couldn't help but notice, and she led her high school to the 1976 state championship.[43] At Wakonda Becky Flynn played six seasons of high school basketball, scored 3,268 points, and led her team to three Class B state championships and 101 consecutive wins, 1988-91.[44] "Wakonda is such a tiny town and that team's success helped, and in fact really put it on the map," observed Parry.

There were high school tournaments for determining state boys' champions as early as 1912, under the auspices of the State Athletics Association after 1916,[45] and now for girls, too. Tournaments were sometimes bedeviled by March snow storms and the legend of Basketball Tournament Blizzards grew. Blowing snow and icy roads affected teams and fans alike, some of whom drove hundreds of miles for district and state finals play. Clear Lake boys' coach Warner Williamson believed the shared adventure could create a bond between teams and their communities—especially when games went well. A series of severe blizzards in 1952 left South Dakotans exhausted and hungry for a diversion, but a storm district week buried Clear Lake and left the team short on practice and wondering how to cut a path to Watertown, site of the games. The town pitched in, and the team and fans made the 27-mile trip where the boys "went on to win the district tournament," Williamson remembered. "This important victory for the team generated a tremendous amount of interest and pride."[46]

Twenty-four years later, an invitational high school basketball tournament (also no stranger to snowy and icy conditions) was established in Rapid City and grew into a nationally unique event.

The Lakota Nation Invitational, scheduled annually a few days before Christmas, brought reservation teams and invited off-reservation schools together, beginning with a grand opening to the beat of traditional drumming. Over the years other athletic competitions and academic games were added to the Invitational schedule.[47] The tournament was where many South Dakotans first became aware of the gifted SuAnne Big Crow of Pine Ridge High. She captured still more attention when she clinched the Class A state basketball championship in 1989 by nabbing an offensive rebound and hitting the winning basket with just seconds left on the clock. In her senior year, Big Crow averaged 30 points per game. Tragically, she died in a car crash at age 17, and today the South Dakota High School Activities Association presents its Spirit of Su Award at state basketball tournaments to players exemplifying Big Crow's qualities of athletic and academic excellence, sportsmanship, and leadership.[48]

A contemporary of Big Crow, Becky Hammon at Rapid City Stevens High School demonstrated leadership on the court and off, and went on to stand as a true pioneer in women's athletics nationally. She played for the New York Liberty and San Antonio Stars of the Women's National Basketball Association, was a six-time WNBA all-star, then moved to coach in the National Basketball Association and became the league's first woman to step up as acting head coach (with the San Antonio Spurs). After seven NBA seasons, Hammon returned to the WNBA as the Las Vegas Aces head coach.[49]

Along with football, South Dakota colleges and universities made basketball central to their athletic culture. In the early years, casual fans almost needed a glossary at times to fully understand newspaper game accounts. For example, "The tall visitors were unable to head off the speedy Youngworthmen, once they got started on the scoring rampage, the locals breaking up their passes and carrying the ball down the floor with bewildering floor work." Translation: an Iowa team with height was no match for Yankton College, coached by Carl Youngworth, in a game played in Yankton.[50]

All college fans across the state turned their attention to Aberdeen in 2009 when Northern State University's Don Meyer coached the Wolves to his 903rd win, becoming the all-time winningest men's college basketball coach in the nation. *New York Times* writer Richard Goldstein appreciated Meyer's emphasis on developing players with smarts about the game in addition to competitive grit.[51]

Basketball players from South Dakota made the NBA and exhibited smarts that led to long careers, most notably Rapid City's Eric Piatkowski and Mitchell's Mike Miller. Piatkowski came up as a Los Angeles Clippers standout in 1994,[52] and Miller started his 17-year career (eight teams) by winning league Rookie of the Year in 2001.[53] Meanwhile, back home, South Dakotans were witnessing minor league pro basketball. By 2022 the Sioux Falls Skyforce, affiliated with the NBA's Miami Heat, was the longest running minor league basketball team in the United States (since 1989).[54]

Track

It stands as one of TV's iconic moments in sports play-by-play: Pine Ridge's Billy Mills running 10,000 meters at the 1964 summer Olympics in Tokyo. Mills wasn't expected to be a factor, NBC's Bud Palmer told his audience early in the race. But nearly half an hour later, in the last lap, Mills, Australia's Ron Clarke (the event's world record holder), and Tunisia's Mohammed Gammoudi were in the lead. In the final seconds Mills veered right and burst ahead as NBC analyst Dick Bank screamed, "Look at Mills! Look at Mills!" Mills won gold, breaking the tape at 28:24.4 to set a new world record.[55]

Years later Mills stressed that the Tokyo win was only part of his story. He remembered, "as a kid coming to race at the School of Mines track and finishing dead last." It's important for youth to understand, he added, "that a dead last finish now and then shouldn't terminate big dreams."[56]

In the 1930s and '40s, Charles Lindbergh Feeney ran daily to school from his family's ranch outside Pierre, and in high school excelled as a 100-yard and 220-yard sprinter, never losing to another South Dakotan in those races. Steve Heidenreich, a generation later, was credited as South Dakota's top miler by the time he graduated from Watertown High School in 1971. He beat the four-minute-mile barrier eight times.[57] Names like Feeney and Heidenreich built excitement among running fans in Sioux Falls in spring as the annual Howard Wood Dakota Relays approached. The huge meet, established in 1923, became a staple of Midwestern athletics.[58]

Wilmot's Cindy Grenier and Huron's Rod DeHaven were names South Dakotans knew, too, and they followed Billy Mills to the Olympics, Grenier in 1984, '88 and '92, and DeHaven in 2000. Teaming with Olympics great Jackie Joyner-Kersee, Grenier competed in the seven-event track and field heptathlon, and at the Sydney Olympics, 2000, DeHaven made up the entire U.S. marathon team.[59]

In the 1970s the state's colleges and universities, through their physical education curriculums, began emphasizing lifetime sports—gentle activities graduates could enjoy as adults, even into their golden years. No one anticipated that 50 years later a favorite participatory sport for middle-aged South Dakotans would be cross-country marathon running, anything but gentle. Annual races took root in Brookings, Sioux Falls, Deadwood, Custer, and elsewhere. The most rigorous, Sturgis's Black Hills 100 Ultramarathon with courses of up to 100 miles over steep terrain, began in 2011. Over its first decade, the race saw a great increase in South Dakota runners (the national ultramarathon community discovered it first), and typically more than half were men and women in the 40-59 age range.[60]

Wrestling

The state School for the Blind at Gary first organized a wrestling team in 1953. Other schools—high schools and colleges—liked the sport because it matched athletes evenly in weight classes and could produce individual champions as well as team winners. Some football coaches saw wrestling as excellent conditioning for their sport.[61] Less enthused, though, were residents in towns with good TV reception, where the public tended to associate the sport with televised wrestling of the '50s. Whether that bizarre spectacle was even legitimate competition—with its emphasis on strutting and posing, costumes, and what appeared to some as staged choreography—was open to debate. In the late '50s coaches Warner Williamson of South Dakota State and Tony Schavone of Black Hills Teachers College took their college wrestlers on the road[62] for exhibition matches, explaining freestyle wrestling rules and scoring. The exhibition squads appeared at schools and sometimes before civic organizations.

Wrestler Roger Denker graduated from South Dakota State and coached a first-time Spearfish High School wrestling team in 1957-58. Pictured in the school yearbook, Denker's young men somewhat resembled TV wrestlers, shirtless and wearing trunks because their school supplied no uniforms (Denker quickly learned that long underwear dyed team colors would suffice as tights). "Only this year did wrestling become an 'A' sport in the Spearfish High School athletic program," the yearbook noted, "but the peppy newcomers proved themselves by capturing the state wrestling crown."[63] In 1964 the state high school tournament at Watertown drew 3,000 spectators, while the same spring Spearfish hosted the National Association of Intercollegiate Athletics (NAIA) wrestling tournament, featuring 51 colleges from coast to coast and 210 athletes. Tony Schavone, one of the coaches who had traveled to introduce the sport the previous decade, shouldered responsibility for the big meet and watched 2,500 fans file in for the championship round.[64]

Within a few years, South Dakotans watched their wrestlers compete in the Olympics. Rapid City's Randy Lewis won gold at the 1984 Los Angeles games.[65] Doland's Dennis Koslowski had twice placed third in the state class B tournament, then surprised former teammates and opponents by winning bronze and silver at the Olympics (1988 and 1992) after switching from freestyle to Greco-Roman (emphasis on the upper body). Also at the 1988 Seoul Olympics were Mobridge twin brothers Bill and Jim Scherr; Bill moved up in weight class to give Jim a shot at making the U.S. team[66] and won bronze in freestyle, 220 pounds. Lincoln McIlravy won five individual high school championships for Philip and won bronze at the 2000 Sydney Olympics.[67]

Wrestling, in about 40 years, proved it could motivate quality athletes and draw fans, and eventually girls were brought onto school teams. For schools with declining enrollments, it was perhaps the easiest sport for coaches to consider blending with a neighboring school. Strangely, though, it was a sport high schools and universities could justify eliminating if budgets demanded drastic action.

Boxing, Rodeo, and Other Sports

Boxing, rodeo, competitive skiing, and hockey are not sports South Dakotans necessarily associate with their high schools and universities (rodeo made inroads well after its firm establishment in South Dakota culture). Credit for the presence of these sports goes to independent athletes and associations, and to South Dakota entrepreneurs who saw certain sports as forms of profitable town building.

Riding a bucking bronco at the Frontier Days Rodeo, in existence since 1912, in White River. *The Center for Western Studies.*

Before the turn of the twentieth century, Huron people couldn't help noticing Oscar Nelson, as the young man moved with a confident bearing running errands for Edler's meat market. That confidence led him to the lightweight boxing championship of the world (1905-06 and 1908-10). In the ring he was known as Battling Nelson. His punchcs didn't pack tremendous power, but Nelson was consistently aggressive, plunging back into a fight after taking punishing blows.[68] He said, "I want to get in as many punches on the other fellow in places where they will do the most good, and in order to do this, I'm willing to take a few hard raps myself. I know I can stand them."[69]

Boxing gyms and coaches appeared in even the tiniest South Dakota towns but the business and promotion of boxing was centered in cities. When *Chicago Tribune* sportswriter Arch Ward first proposed the Golden Gloves program for developing boxers, he was mostly thinking of urban fighters and especially envisioned tournaments involving Chicago and New York teams. In 1962, however, Golden Gloves restructured itself nationally so that all young adults (ages 17-34) could learn to fight.[70] South Dakota embraced Golden Gloves. Rapid City's Pat Jefferson won a base of local fans as a Golden Glover who was three-time state amateur Boxer of the Year in the 1970s. He competed against international fighters through AAU and seemed Olympics-bound until the United States boycott of 1980. Then the light-weight turned pro, 1980-85, and recorded a 21-6 record.[71]

Residents and out-of-state visitors alike had to wonder whether they were reading promotion for an athletic competition or a wild west show in 1923, when Belle Fourche's Tri-State Roundup (today the Black Hills Roundup) was described as featuring "real cowhands, whose first recollection of life was being surrounded by cactus, rattlesnakes and tarantulas—their mothers gave them a stalk of cactus to chew when they cried for candy—are they wild? You ask 'em."[72]

Russ Madison, owner of a ranch west of Rapid City, with spirited livestock, can be credited as the South Dakotan who moved rodeo from informal contests where working cowboys established bragging rights among themselves to a spectacle that packed grandstands.[73] Competitors went up against not only broncs and bulls but one another. Belle Fourche staged its first Roundup as a World War I benefit for the Red Cross, then incorporated the event and made it a regular Fourth of July feature that continues today. From the beginning, women competed, including steer wrestler Fox Hastings and saddle bronc rider Mildred Douglas.[74] On the men's side, Belvidere's world saddle bronc champion Earl Thode and a strong bucking horse named Tipperary gained the state a reputation as saddle bronc country. Competitors must stay atop a bucking bronc for eight seconds, gripping the reins with one hand; they lose qualification by dropping the reins or losing a stirrup or touching the horse or themselves with their free hand. They gain points for riding style and inducing the bronc to buck hard. Other South Dakotans who won multiple world saddle bronc titles were Spearfish's Clint Johnson, Ree Heights' Billy Etbauer, and the state's most famous rodeo cowboy, Fort Pierre's Casey Tibbs.[75] Huron-born Marvin Garrett did something similar in bareback riding, winning five world championships.[76]

Rodeos, ranging from big-time pro events to little jack-pot shows, spread across South Dakota—on the reservations, in White River, Deadwood, Rapid City, Watertown, Sioux Falls, and in a natural bowl at Clear Lake. Critics took aim at many of them. C. I. Hunt of Chicago's Anti-Rodeo League wrote to the Belle Fourche's commercial club just as the town was gearing up for the 1926 Roundup, claiming 150,000 Americans condemned "this form of commercialized cruelty, and are making a strenuous effort to prohibit it in the U.S." Commercial club chairman R. L. Bronson replied that it was easy for outsiders to think of westerners as brutes, but "we are infants when it comes to rough-stuff and cruelty." Bronson cited press reports about gang murders in Chicago and advised that the city's residents should "clean up their own barnyard . . . when this is done you may rest assured we will help you protect the outlaw steers."[77]

The next year President Calvin Coolidge helped legitimize rodeo by attending both Belle Fourche's Roundup and Deadwood's Days of '76 rodeos[78] and in 1928 the new Pine Ridge Rodeo's success represented a step toward the sport gaining a reputation as a

"Lakota National Pastime."[79] In the 1930s professional competitors organized, leading the way to a points system based on winnings that qualifies them for the National Finals Rodeo each December. South Dakota fans who attend the Finals or watch it on TV always recognize cowboys and cowgirls who rode through South Dakota to accumulate points. Schools caught up with rodeo in 1949 with both the South Dakota High School Rodeo Association[80] and National Intercollegiate Rodeo Association forming.

Visiting Norwegians in 1912 fascinated Augustana College, then located in Canton, South Dakota, with accounts of ski jumping competitions back home. So much so, in fact, that students and faculty enlisted the help of Canton residents to help build a wooden jump structure—two, as it turned out, because they weren't satisfied with the first. The second was a 60-foot tower that, when combined with the hill on which it stood, made for a 275-foot vertical drop. The Sioux Valley Ski Club formed, welcoming anyone wanting to learn, and the club made the jump available for major competitions, including the U.S. Nationals of 1925, '30 and '35, and the U.S. Olympics trials of 1932. But in 1944 winds toppled the tower and it was not rebuilt.[81]

By that time Homestake Gold Mine and the community of Lead—365 miles west of Canton—had a plan for enhancing Black Hills lifestyles by transforming 7,000-foot Terry Peak into a ski area bigger than anything else in the Midwest, with a 1,000-foot natural vertical drop. A mountain of that size, in the days before detachable ski bindings especially, demanded quality ski instructors. One who stepped up was Walter Kussy, former member of the Czech Olympic ski team, who escaped communism and rebuilt his life in the United States. The Terry Peak Ski Club had a ski jumping team ready for national competition at Steamboat Springs, Colorado, in 1951.[82]

Lead took great pride in both the evolving development at Terry Peak and local competitive skiers. Former team member Bob Morcum recalled that "we had jumping, downhill, slalom, giant slalom, and cross-country. There were skiers hoping Terry Peak would help them get into universities that have ski teams." Many did.[83]

Watertown tennis phenom Phyllis Hunter, while still in high school in 1941, made it through regional amateur tournaments all the way to the precursor of the U.S. Open in New York City. She got there again in 1946. The national press found her fascinating because she couldn't find a tennis instructor in Watertown and taught herself by swatting balls off her family's home, and by acquiring tennis books and somehow translating written descriptions of technique into action.[84] Sportswriters intended for Hunter's story to inspire, but South Dakotans felt some chagrin for not meeting Hunter's training needs. Decades before pro golfer Kris Tschetter and the Sanford International golf tournament called Sioux Falls home, Aberdeen sisters Alice and Marlene Bauer became two of thirteen charter members of the Ladies Professional Golf Association in 1950, and some people wondered whether they could have excelled except for the fact that while growing up they lived in an Aberdeen golf course's clubhouse.[85] Golf and tennis were not sanctioned as girls' high school sports when Hunter and the Bauers were students (not until the 1968-69 academic year).[86] Into the twenty-first century certain sports with facilities fees and high equipment costs were out of reach for most South Dakota schools and families. That was true not only in tiny towns, but sometimes in the state's biggest. Walker Duehr is a case in point.

Duehr notched eight minutes, forty-seven seconds on the ice for the Calgary Flames, November 14, 2021, becoming the first South Dakotan ever in the National Hockey League (NHL).[87] That late date surprised fans because South Dakota is the western neighbor of the self-proclaimed "State of Hockey," Minnesota. After his NHL debut, Duehr told a Calgary sportswriter that hockey in his home state is much more prominent now than in his youth.[88] He recalled that, as a Sioux Falls kid early in the 2000s, he played a version of the sport with no ice involved, on a concrete pad wearing shoes or roller blades, and relishing hard contact.

South Dakota is one of only a few states that has never sanctioned high school swimming as a varsity sport. Yet through clubs organized by parents, coaches have been recruited and meets organized so that young South Dakotans are prepared for swim teams at South Dakota universities. "Swimmers swim because they're swimmers, not for any public glory," said Jim Phillips, former club coach at Deadwood. "I consider them a cut above."[89]

Gymnastics equipment is expensive, and private centers bore that cost and recouped it through lessons and coaching before sanctioned high school meets began in 1974.[90] Parents and community volunteers coached girls' volleyball clubs in the 1970s and early '80s, and the Parker Jaycees organized a volleyball tournament between schools just before the Activities Association sanctioned the first state meet in 1982.[91] Simultaneously, knowledgeable volunteer coaches introduced soccer statewide, including Spearfish's Ronnie Theisz, a former pro player in Europe who advanced the sport in South Dakota for young children, high school and university athletes, and adults.[92] Soccer exploded in popularity, making its status as a sanctioned sport for both sexes inevitable at South Dakota high schools and universities.

For all sports, South Dakotans celebrate victories and yet are fatalistic enough to understand winning streaks end—even those of the Claremont six-man football and Wakonda girls' basketball squads. An overriding value fans and participants alike express is exhibiting grace in victory as well as in defeat.[93]

Notes

1 Robert F. Karolevitz, *Yankton: A Pioneer Past* (Aberdeen, SD: North Plains Press, 1972) 168-71.

2 Sean Flynn, *Without Reservation, Benjamin Reifel and American Indian Acculturation* (Pierre: South Dakota Historical Society Press, 2018) 152

3 "Harding County Coyote Callers have another successful year," Nancy Johnson, *Nation's Center News*, Dec. 23, 2021, 3-4.

4 Ye Tang led a Chinese fire company in Deadwood that won a national championship for hose cart racing in 1888. *Some History of Lawrence County* (Deadwood: Lawrence County Historical Society, 1981), 572.

5 "Lakota Games on Ice," Steve Kinsella, *South Dakota Magazine*, January-February 2017, 59-61.

6 "Early baseball in America" en.m.wikipedia.org/wiki/Origins_of_baseball.

7 South Dakota Sports Hall of Fame, www.sdshof.com/inductees/charles.phillippe.

[8] Ibid., www.sdshof.com/inductees/jim.scott.

[9] George Moses, *Those Good Old Days in the Black Hills* (Rapid City: Rapid City Journal publication, 1991), 69-70.

[10] Andy Romey, "History of American Legion Baseball," www.legion.org, 2009.

[11] South Dakota Hall of Fame, www.sdexcellence.org, George Anderson video; South Dakota Sports Hall of Fame, www.sdshof.com/inductees/carroll.hardy.

[12] After the 1960s minor league baseball, especially in rural regions, faded as TV brought major league baseball into living rooms regularly, and big league teams were less willing to subsidize far-flung developmental leagues. But that form of baseball made a comeback in the 1990s and beyond through independent leagues and short-season college developmental leagues, featuring family friendly environments and local foods and beers in Sioux Falls, Pierre, and Spearfish.

[13] David Kemp and Tamra Zastrow, *One Hundred Years of South Dakota High School Activities and Athletics* (Sioux Falls: Mariah Press, 2006), 33.

[14] "Modify Old Game or Play New One," *Sioux Falls Argus Leader*, Dec. 30, 1905, 3.

[15] John J. Miller, *The Big Scrum—How Teddy Roosevelt Saved Football* (New York: Harper Perennial, 2012) 181, 191, 205-22.

[16] Printed schedules, and gophersports.com, "Football History vs. South Dakota State University from Oct. 7, 1916-Aug. 29, 2019," and archives.nd.edu, "Notre Dame Football 1913."

[17] Ibid.

[18] South Dakota Sports Hall of Fame, www.sdshof.com/inductees/fred.gushurst.

[19] Paul Haivala, *The Friendly College: The First 100 Years of Black Hills State College* (Spearfish: Black Hills State College, 1983) 71-72.

[20] Scalpers Give Auggie Scare," *Sioux Falls Argus Leader*, Oct. 19, 1925, 9; "Tomorrow's Football Game Will Be Close," *Deadwood Weekly Pioneer Times*," October 29, 1925, 1; "Real Live Football is Promised for Next Saturday Afternoon," *Sioux Falls Argus Leader*, October 30, 1912, 10.

[21] "Dakotiana: Go, Beetdiggers Go!", staff column, *South Dakota Magazine*, January-February 2001, 60-62.

[22] 1930 Coyote yearbook, University of South Dakota, 91.

[23] Swarm Day announcement printed in *The Black Hills Historian*, Black Hills State University, Fall 2021, 8. Hobo Day described in 1940 *Jack Rabbit* yearbook, South Dakota State University, 31

[24] Marc Rasmussen, *Six, A Football Coach's Journey To a National Record* (Pierre: South Dakota State Historical Society Press, 2011), 81-127.

[25] "Here's how the South Dakota 11-man football classes align," Brian Haenchen, *Sioux Falls Argus Leader*, Jan. 19, 2021 (retrieved online).

[26] "Lawsuit was the Hail Mary that brought playoff football to South Dakota," Travis Fossing, posted online by KELO TV, November 10, 2021.

[27] South Dakota Sports Hall of Fame, www.sdshof.com/inductees/weert.engelman.

[28] "Notre Dame Fighting Irish Football Record by Year," www.swports-reference.com.

[29] South Dakota Sports Hall of Fame, www.sdshof.com/inductees/ordell.braase.

[30] Joe Foss with Donna Wild Foss, *A Proud American, The Autobiography of Joe Foss* (New York: Pocket Books, 1992) 235-304.

[31] South Dakota Sports Hall of Fame, sdexcellence.org, "Joseph Robbie."

[32] "Lawsuit was the Hail Mary."

[33] "SDSU Football History," gojacks.com and "South Dakota Coyotes football," en.m.wikipedia.org.

[34] Wikipedia.org/wiki/Adam_Vinatieri.

[35] Hitchcock centennial publication, unpublished; interview with opera house historian Louise Smock, Sept. 25, 2005.

[36] Randy Parry, December 14, 2021, and "Corn Palace History," cornpalace.com.

[37] Parry; interviews with longtime South Dakota sports officials Bob and Jim Phillips, Nov. 22, 2021.

[38] Jon Lauck, "'You Can't Mix Wheat and Potatoes in the Same Bin': Anti-Catholicism in South Dakota," *South Dakota History*, 38:1 (2008): 1-46.

[39] "History of School District Reorganization, 1950 to Present," South Dakota Department of Education, doe.sd.gov.

[40] Parry; Phillips and Phillips.

[41] Kemp and Zastrow, 74.

[42] Women's Sports Foundation, www.womanssportsfoundation.org.

[43] South Dakota Sports Hall of Fame, sdshof.com/inductees/kay.stormo.freund. A remarkable athlete in multiple sports, Stormo once scored 25 points and grabbed 13 rebounds on the same day she won a cross country race in record time.

[44] Kemp and Zastrow, 30.

[45] Ibid., 21.

[46] *A Precious Legacy* (Clear Lake Centennial Committee, Ted Burges editor, 1984), 361-62.

[47] www.lakotanationinvitational.com.

[48] South Dakota High School Basketball Hall of Fame, sdbbhof.com/2017-inductees/suanne-big-crow.

[49] "Hammon continues to reach for the stars," Matt Case, *Rapid City Journal*, January 19, 2022, 1, 3.

[50] "Greyhounds Play Brilliantly in Defeating Rangy Telegrapher Cagers," *Sioux Falls Argus Leader*, December 21, 1927, 9.

[51] "Don Meyer, a Coach With 923 Victories, Is Dead at 69," Richard Goldstein, *New York Times*, May 18, 2014 (retrieved online).

[52] South Dakota Sports Hall of Fame, sdshof.com/inductees/eric.piatkowski.

[53] "Mike Miller NBA," en.m.wikipedia.org

[54] Siouxfalls.gleague.nba.com.

[55] "Watch Billy Mills' upset in 1964 Tokyo Olympics," nbcsports.com.

[56] Interview with Billy Mills, March 12, 2004.

[57] South Dakota Sports Hall of Fame, www.sdshof.com/inductees/charles.lindbergh.feeney and www.sdshof.com/inductees/steve.heidenreich.

[58] "Howard Wood Dakota Relays," www.dakotarelays.com. The event is named for Howard Wood, Sioux Falls educator and coach for 40 years.

[59] South Dakota Sports Hall of Fame, www.sdshof.com/inductees/cindy.grenier, and www.sdshof.com/inductees/rod.dehaven.

[60] Interview, Ryan Phillips (Black Hills 100 Ultramarathon owner), February 7, 2022.

[61] Kemp and Zastrow, 53-58.

[62] Ibid, and interview with Alyce Schavone, January 31, 2022.

[63] 1958 *Spearfish Spartan Yearbook*, 17.

[64] "Spearfish Tops As Wrestler Host," *Rapid City Daily Journal*, March 26, 1964, 17.

[65] National Wrestling Hall of Fame, nwhof.org.

[66] Scherr and Scherr Alike," Craig Neff, *Sports Illustrated*, September 14, 1988 (retrieved online); www.sdshof.com/induction/dennis.koslowski.

[67] South Dakota Sports Hall of Fame, sdshof.com/inductees/lincoln.mcilravy.

[68] Huss, Kuni, Lampe and Moxon, *Huron Revisited* (Huron: East Eagle Company, 1988) 259-60; South Dakota Sports Hall of Fame, www.sdshof.com/inductees/battling.nelson.

[69] "Remembering Battling Nelson and his greatest fight," Pete Ehrmann, OnMilwaukee.com, 2017.

[70] "Golden Gloves boxing competition," www.britannica.com.

[71] South Dakota Sports Hall of Fame, www.sdshof.com/inductees/pat.jefferson.

[72] Ad in the Black Hills Roundup exhibit, Tri-State Museum, Belle Fourche.

[73] National Cowboy and Western Heritage Museum, Oklahoma City, nationalcowboymuseum.org.

[74] Tri-State Museum.

[75] Interview with Jim Thompson, pro rodeo announcer, November 15, 2008.

[76] South Dakota Sports Hall of Fame, www.sdshof.com/inductees/billy.etbauer.

[77] Hunt and Bronson letters on exhibit at the Tri-State Museum.

[78] Seth Tupper, *Calvin Coolidge in the Black Hills* (Charleston, SC: The History Press, 2017) 84-86, 92-94.

[79] "*Cowboys on the Reservation*," Allison Fuss, *South Dakota History*, 29:3 (Fall 1999); *"Rodeo Organizations,"* ProRodeo Hall of Fame, prorodeohalloffame.com.

[80] "South Dakota High School Rodeo," sdhsra.com.

[81] South Dakota State Historical Society marker on U.S. Highway 18, Canton.

[82] Interview with Jack Morcom, early Terry Peak Ski Club member, October 14, 2013.

[83] Interview with Bob Morcom, former ski team member, February 2, 2022.

[84] South Dakota Sports Hall of Fame, sdshof.com/inductees/phyllis.hunter.

[85] South Dakota Sports Hall of Fame, www.sdshof.com/inductees/marlene.bauer.hagge.

[86] Kemp and Zastrow, 60, 81.

[87] "Flames forward Walker Duehr makes home-state history in NHL debut," Wes Gilbertson, *Calgary Herald*, November 15, 2021 (retrieved online).

[88] Today South Dakota is home to youth developmental teams supported by professional leagues, a minor league with NHL affiliations, and will see its first university team at Augustana University in 2023.

[89] Interview with Jim Phillips, November 22, 2021.

[90] Interview with Pam Junek, Rapid City Central/Stevens gymnastics coach, April 27, 2022.

[91] Kemp and Zastrow, 83-89.

[92] "Ballfield renamed Ronnie Theisz Soccer Field," Brad Blume, *Black Hills Pioneer*, July 24, 2002 (retrieved online).

[93] Rasmussen, 125-26; interview with former Wakonda basketball player Sarah Carlson, December 17, 2021.

11

The Perils of Abundance: Hunting and Fishing in South Dakota's History

Lance Nixon

It is a little-known fact of South Dakota history that the abundance and easy taking of big game at the fur trade post that would become modern-day Fort Pierre prompted one of the most far-sighted proposals in American history—the idea of the national park. It happened when a famous visitor to that post saw what the trade in hides and delicacies was doing to that great game animal of the Plains, the bison. For the painter George Catlin saw more than form and color with his artist's eye, and he wrote tirelessly of the life he experienced among the Plains Indian tribes during the years 1832 to 1839. That is why he later recalls so vividly his visit to that trading post at the junction of the Bad River and the Missouri in May 1832. Chief trader William Laidlaw and clerk Jacob Halsey, some other traders at the fort and some Native Americans informed Catlin that there had been a buffalo hunt just days before his arrival, when an immense herd of bison showed themselves on the other side of the river—that is, on the east shore of the Missouri, where the present-day capital city of South Dakota, Pierre, is located. The herd was so large that it nearly turned the plain above the river black for a great distance. A party of 500 to 600 Sioux Indians forded the Missouri River about midday, hunted until near sunset and returned to the fort on the west side of the river that evening. They brought back no hides and not a pound of meat except for 1,400 fresh buffalo tongues, "for which they required but a few gallons of whiskey."[1]

The "profligate waste of the lives of these noble and useful animals" in that incident is what prompts Catlin to foresee the extinction of the bison within years if the destruction continued.[2] The solution Catlin suggests is probably the clearest early formulation of what is now taken for granted as an essential part of conservation. He imagines that the bison "might in future be seen, (by some great protecting policy of government), preserved in their pristine beauty and wildness, in a magnificent park, where the world could see for ages to come, the native Indian in his classic attire, galloping his wild horse, with sinewy bow, and shield and lance, amid the fleeting herds of elks and buffaloes. . . . A nation's Park, containing man and beast, in all the wild and freshness of their nature's beauty!" Catlin would wish for no other monument to his memory than the honor of having founded such an institution, he muses.[3]

Clearly Catlin was ahead of his time in seeing both the crisis and the solution. More than a decade later, in 1843, the naturalist and painter John James Audubon, on a trip up the Missouri, meets four boats traveling from the fur trade post at Fort Pierre to Saint Louis with 10,000 buffalo robes—evidence that the harvesting of buffalo is continuing without restriction.[4] Audubon records the number of hides moving down river, but doesn't seem to share Catlin's concern about the effect on bison populations; after all, he is still able to count 2,000 buffalo in a single forenoon within thirty miles of Fort Pierre on that journey.[5]

Catlin's idea comes about in time, but not for decades, and not first of all on the Great Plains, where he envisions it. The national park as we know it today doesn't include Native Americans living their traditional lifestyles and following the wild game. Yet Catlin's far-sighted proposal continues to preserve the bison at, among other places, Wind Cave National Park and Badlands National Park in South Dakota. Perhaps just as important, a powerful idea that is implied in Catlin's plan, the "protecting policy of government," continues to be essential in places such as South Dakota for managing wildlife as a resource for hunters, anglers, and others who simply enjoy the wild. For the same vexing problem that troubled George Catlin—the reckless harvesting of a vast but finite resource—has been a defining theme in the history of wildlife in South Dakota.

The issues surrounding wildlife harvesting and ultimately, wildlife management, may have been particularly important in South Dakota because it remains to this day the state that is arguably most devoted to hunting as a part of its culture, with some of the greatest opportunities. No less an arbiter than Pheasants Forever counted four South Dakota communities among its list of the Top 25 destinations for bird hunting in its April 2013 ranking, placing Pierre at No. 1, Huron at No. 4, Eureka at No. 13, and Redfield at No. 15. No other state had more than two locations on that list.[6] What is even more striking is that on the previous year's list, in which Pheasants Forever listed only top pheasant-hunting destinations, South Dakota had six communities on the list: Chamberlain at No. 1, Aberdeen at No. 6, Lemmon at No. 14, Mobridge at No. 17, Mitchell at No. 19, and Winner at No. 24. Since the organization tries not to repeat communities on its lists from year to year, it seems clear that South Dakota is the premier place for hunting upland game birds in the past decade. As a Pheasants Forever staffer said then, the reality is that South Dakota could field twenty-five locations on that list.[7]

By the most meaningful measure of all—the share of its population that buys hunting licenses—one recent study of the data ranks South Dakota first among the states in its passion for hunting, followed by three of its neighbors. The news service Stacker released its study of hunting license data in October 2021, finding that 24.1 percent of South Dakotans had bought hunting licenses, followed by Wyoming (22.7 percent), Montana (21.1 percent), and North Dakota (17.2 percent).[8]

Of course the large-scale harvesting of animals started long before the fur trade era. Researchers for the South Dakota State Historical Society say there are more than thirty recorded bison kill sites in the state, dating from about 9,000 B.C. to A.D. 1875.[9] At one of the sites explored most recently—one of several locations along a ridge near Ree Heights, where prehistoric Indian people are known to have trapped bison along the ridge or perhaps driven them over it—archaeologists are exploring the possibility that the hunters may have been doing more than supplying their own needs, perhaps processing meat they don't need for their own use to make a meat product for trade. The prehistoric Indian village at Mitchell, about 100 miles away and inhabited about 1,100 years ago, or roughly the same time as the latest Ree Heights bison kill site, is known to have been "processing bison on an industrial scale to extract bone grease for the manufacture of pemmican."[10]

Because a bison kill was indiscriminate, it would have harvested young and old animals, bulls and cows, suggesting Native Americans could have affected bison populations even in prehistoric days. Catlin, ever the careful observer, credits both Indian and whites for the crisis of depopulation he sees looming for bison in fur trade days, noting that "not only the red men, but red men and white, have aimed destruction at the race of these animals."[11] Catlin finds fault, in particular, with the trade in whiskey. Priced at $16 a gallon in Catlin's day, it soon impoverished the natives who acquired a taste for it and "must soon strip the skin from the last buffalo's back that lives in their country."[12] The problem is perhaps more complex than Catlin painted it, but he was right about the commodity that hunters were after. Economist M. Scott Taylor notes that there were an estimated 25 to 30 million bison in the sixteenth century but fewer than 100 remained by the late nineteenth century. Taylor argues that European demand for industrial leather and American policy failure together drove the slaughter of bison on the Great Plains.[13]

For South Dakotans, the unavoidable fact is that during the fur trade era, a huge portion of that trade in bison hides funneled through the area that would become South Dakota. Fort Pierre Chouteau, at the site of modern Fort Pierre, was the largest fur trading post ever built in the United States,[14] and the confluence of the Bad River with the Missouri River in central South Dakota saw such a succession of fur trade posts greater than any other area.[15]

Yet it is testament to George Catlin's vision for saving the buffalo that in South Dakota, a few hunters annually at Custer State Park now are allowed to harvest both non-trophy buffalo—mostly two-year-old bulls[16]—and trophy buffalo, usually bulls of 10 years or older.[17] It would doubtless please Catlin to learn that 2017 data from the U.S. Department of Agriculture's Census of Agriculture shows South Dakota—the place where Catlin feared the extinction of the bison—currently has more bison than any other state, with more than 30,000 in private herds. That figure doesn't include some 2,000 head in public herds in places such as Wind Cave National Park, Badlands National Park, and Custer State Park.[18]

Because settlement days in South Dakota were marked by conflict with Native Americans over hunting and dwindling populations of game, it's not surprising to see that whites arriving in the region attributed the disappearance of bison and then other species to the activities of Native Americans. Evadna Cochrane Burba, in writing about the experience of Deuel County settler B. J. Cochrane, for whom Lake Cochrane is named, noted that the last buffalo in the county was killed a few years before Cochrane arrived in 1872, adding that the Indians "drove most of those great prairie beasts west of the Missouri River after 1869."[19] In Harding County, at the northwest corner of South Dakota, rancher W. H. Hamilton recalled that Native Americans from the reservations came hunting and gathering plums on multiple occasions, traveling in wagons and sometimes trading meat for groceries.[20] On one occasion in about 1889 Sitting Bull himself led a party of thirteen wagons, he notes.[21] But the Indians were poor marksmen, Hamilton wrote in his memoir, and "they go in such droves and shoot so much they scare everything out of the country."[22] In Custer, where deer and elk carcasses that didn't sell for the going rate of $3 to $5 were left to rot by early settlers, some white residents blamed Indians for excessive hunting, ostensibly while making trips into the mountains to cut tipi poles.[23]

Indian hunting rights were also the point of contention in perhaps the most serious incident of its kind in regional history in October 1903, when a sheriff's posse of 13 men in what is now Niobrara County, Wyoming, fought a group of 41 Oglala adults and their children from South Dakota. Seven people died in the gun battle, including Sheriff William Miller and Oglala leader Eagle Feather. The posse was trying to arrest some of the Oglalas—made up of two separate groups that had been issued permits by the Indian agent at Pine Ridge to gather plants in the Black Hills—for allegedly violating the game laws of Wyoming. In the investigation that followed the gun battle, several of the Oglalas denied killing antelope in Wyoming, but did admit to taking big game in the Black Hills in South Dakota.[24] The Oglalas cited the Fort Laramie Treaty of 1868 and the Black Hills Agreement of 1876, asserting that these documents guaranteed their rights to hunt in either South Dakota or Wyoming.[25] Native Americans' loss of hunting rights and the vast reserves of habitat in the Black Hills was only one of the ways white settlement hurt the tribes. The building of the Missouri River dams took rich bottomland away from the Crow Creek, Lower Brule, Cheyenne River, and Standing Rock Sioux tribes, and the new recreational opportunities for pursuits such as swimming, fishing, and boating were not culturally important to Indians, at least at that time. As historian Michael Lee Lawson noted in regard to the Cheyenne River Sioux, "If anything, the recreational activities of the tribal members have declined as a result of the Oahe project since the flooding of the bottomlands has drastically reduced the game population in the reservation and has led to the subsequent decline in hunting, which was previously the favorite sport of the Indians."[26]

Species by species, the rapid settlement of South Dakota has forced changes in wildlife populations and ranges, with negative consequences for some species but also some benefits for others. The pronghorn antelope has a special place in South Dakota history because although it had been observed earlier, the first specimen collected by the science-minded Lewis and Clark Expedition was near Ball Creek in what is now South Dakota in September 1804. The members of the expedition feasted on its meat but sent the hide and skeleton back to President Thomas Jefferson.[27] William Clark's hasty description for science on that occasion is still a good first glance at one of the more interesting animals of the Great Plains: "I killed a Buck Goat of this Countrey, about the hight of the Grown Deer, its body Shorter, the horns which is not very hard and forks 2/3 up one prong . . . he is more like the Antilope or Gazelle of Africa than any other Species of Goat."[28]

Biologists estimate that pronghorn numbered more than 700,000 in the area that is now South Dakota prior to 1800, but increased settlement drove them nearly to extinction. In 1911 the South Dakota Legislature responded to the decline in pronghorn numbers by passing legislation that made it unlawful to kill, wound, or capture the animals. More than three decades later, in 1942, the state again allowed hunting of pronghorns, issuing 500 licenses that year.[29] Archery and firearm seasons for antelope in South Dakota continue under careful management, with populations of the animals greatest in the state's western rangelands.[30]

South Dakota has more than 6,000 Rocky Mountain elk in the Black Hills, with a scattering elsewhere, and the state holds both firearm and archery seasons.[31] However, this is a vast change from the time whites were first entering the country. The Lewis and Clark party killed an elk on Bonhomme Island in what is now southeastern South Dakota on September 1, 1806. Decades later, in 1843, John James Audubon was presented by a fur trader with an Indian-dressed elk skin and the enormous antlers of the largest such animal taken in the region—perhaps an indication that already hunters were aware of trophy animals and gunning for them.[32] Biologists believe the last native elk in South Dakota was killed in 1888, leading to a reintroduction effort that brought Rocky Mountain elk from Yellowstone National Park to the Black Hills from 1911 to 1920.[33] South Dakota's first carefully managed season for elk, based on that reintroduced population, was in 1952.[34] Now, under careful management, there is fierce competition for elk licenses in the state. From 2002 to 2007, for example, 94,977 hunters applied for 11,821 elk hunting licenses in South Dakota.[35]

Elk hunting in the Black Hills is popular, with the number of applications far exceeding the number of licenses granted. *The Center for Western Studies.*

Though historically not as numerous as bison or antelope, both whitetail deer and mule deer today are plentiful in South Dakota, but that is largely due to regulations established by the South Dakota Department of Game, Fish and Parks (SDGFP) in the early 1900s to help deer populations recover from historic lows. Black Hills newspapers were lamenting the slaughter of deer in the 1890s, and in Custer, elk and venison sold for $3 to $5 a carcass, while animals that didn't sell were left to rot.[36] Historical records suggest deer east of the Missouri disappeared between 1875 and 1880, and all but disappeared in West River counties outside of the Black Hills by 1900.[37] In 1883 the territorial government prohibited deer hunting from January 1 to September 1 annually to reduce market hunting, but populations didn't begin to recover until passage of a buck law in 1911 and 1921 (amended in 1925 to prohibit all deer hunting in counties outside the Black Hills).[38] Hunting seasons have occurred regularly since the 1950s, and in 2010, a record year, hunters in the state harvested 95,000 deer.[39] However, as with the state's elk population, chronic wasting disease is a concern. This fatal brain disease of deer, elk, and moose has been found in eighteen counties of central and western South Dakota as of November 2021. South Dakota has implemented regulations to try to keep the disease from spreading.[40]

There is anecdotal evidence that settlement may have pushed or lured some species into new areas, either because of encroaching settlement or perhaps because cultivated crops offered an easy source of nutrient-rich forage. In Harding County, for example, at the far northwest corner of South Dakota, pioneer W. H. Hamilton, who ranched in the area in the 1880s and 1890s, wrote in his memoir that he had shot the first white-tail deer taken in the Cave Hills country.[41] Elsewhere Hamilton notes the presence of "black-tail" deer—probably mule deer, which are even today far more common in western South Dakota—in a way that suggests they were common in the area.[42]

Bighorn sheep didn't fare as well in South Dakota history as deer. W. H. Hamilton, the Harding County pioneer, missed his one shot at what he called a "mountain sheep," lamenting afterward that it had "horns that looked as big as stove pipes."[43] It seems plausible that the animal Hamilton was shooting at may have been a now-extinct subspecies of bighorn called Audubon's bighorn sheep that inhabited the Black Hills and surrounding areas. "A herd of 200 Audubon's bighorn sheep was reported in the White River Badlands in 1909, but this subspecies is believed to have gone extinct a few years later," a study of South Dakota mammals noted in 2000.[44] South Dakota Governor Peter Norbeck obtained eight Rocky Mountain bighorn sheep from Alberta and released them in Custer State Park in 1922 to try to replace this lost native population, but the herd had died out by the late 1950s.[45] There have been other introductions since then, chiefly in 1964 and 1991, of bighorn sheep brought in from Colorado, Alberta, and Wyoming.[46] With the success of those efforts, South Dakota has issued eight licenses for bighorn sheep in recent years, seven in a drawing for residents only, and one sold at auction to the highest bidder to raise money for the bighorn sheep program and other wildlife work within the department.[47]

Mountain goats have a curious history in South Dakota. Though not a native species, the state introduced a few animals from Alberta, Canada, in 1924. Some escaped Custer State Park in 1929 and began multiplying in the wild after a tree fell on one of the fences that was confining them. A 2000 study estimated the range of the animals extended to Custer, Lawrence, and Pennington counties.[48] South Dakota has allowed some hunting of mountain goats since 1967, but has closed the season for several years at a time when populations fell too low. Since 2015 the population has again rebounded enough to allow two licenses to be issued.[49]

William Clark makes a curious observation in his journal about wild turkeys on September 2, 1806, as the Lewis and Clark Expedition was descending the Missouri. On the same day the party passes the mouth of the James River, or near present-day Yankton, South Dakota, Clark observes there have been "two turkys killed to day of which the Indians very much admired being the first which they ever saw."[50] Very likely the Indians to whom he refers are the small delegation of Mandans who had agreed to accompany the Lewis and Clark party on their return trip to visit Washington.[51] That would suggest that the wild turkey was present at the start of the nineteenth century in the southern reaches of what is now South Dakota but was unknown to the Mandans of present-day North Dakota.

More evidence of the native range of wild turkeys lies in the place names of Turkey Creek, in Yankton County, and the Turkey Ridge and Turkey Ridge Creek in Turner County. A 1940 guide to South Dakota place names notes that Turkey Creek takes its name from turkeys that "in the early days were to be found along its heavily wooded banks"–probably a commentary on the lack of turkeys in 1940.[52] Biologist E. H. Smith noted in 1953 that in addition to woodland areas in southeastern South Dakota, native turkey range extended along the Missouri to the mouth of the Cheyenne River.[53] However, market hunting and destruction of forest habitat probably meant there were no more wild turkeys in the state by 1920. All the wild turkeys in the state today are the result of introduction or reintroductions.[54] "The South Dakota Department of Game, Fish and Parks released over 5,400 wild turkeys from 1930 through 2004 from sources both within and outside the state's borders," researchers note, as successful introductions in the Black Hills were used to seed other locations for release of wild turkeys.[55] Hunting began in 1954 in the Black Hills and in 1957 in some prairie regions, while the first spring gobbler seasons started in 1962 and 1964, respectively, in the Black Hills and prairie regions.[56] A 2003 estimate indicated that spring turkey hunters alone spent $6,458,070 in South Dakota.[57]

Lewis and Clark also find the greater prairie chicken on their descent of the Missouri River, on the same day on which they encounter wild turkeys. Clark notes on September 2, 1806, the same day on which they passed the mouth of "the River Jacque" (the James), "I saw 4 prarie fowls Common to the Illinois, those are the highest up which have been Seen."[58] Clark is right to associate them with country along the Illinois River in what is now the state of Illinois, for biologists say the birds were originally a tallgrass species once centered in the area where the present-day states of Missouri, Illinois, and Iowa come together.[59] During his 1843 journey up the Missouri River, Audubon, too, records a sighting of greater prairie chickens in present-day South Dakota, quite far north from where Lewis and Clark saw them, just south of the Great Bend of the Missouri—"we started the first and only Prairie Hen we have seen since our departure from St. Louis."[60] These anecdotes seem to suggest that while the greater prairie chicken surely was present at the time those early naturalists recorded their observations, the country that would become South Dakota must have been near the western limit of its range. Because the prairie chicken thrived when cropland made up 20 to 30 percent of its range, the species increased in the first years after settlement in the Midwest, then declined as native grass lost place to crops.[61] Even as late as the 1920s, flights of prairie chickens filled almost the whole width of the Big Sioux River bottomlands west of Brookings.[62] However, biologists say more than 50 percent of the landscape must be in tallgrass prairie, mixed-grass prairie, or a transition of those types of grassland to support prairie chickens.[63] Because western South Dakota still has vast tracts of rangeland, much of it native grass, the prairie chicken still thrives in South Dakota, along with the sharp-tailed grouse—the "pointed tail" prairie hens that Lewis and Clark observed near the mouth of the Grand River.[64] In particular, the Fort Pierre National Grassland, within thirty miles of where Audubon observed prairie chickens, is now one of the premier places in the United States to hunt them.

In South Dakota hunting parlance, a "grand slam" is when a hunter bags those two native birds—the sharp-tailed grouse and the prairie chicken—as part of the same hunt in which he or she also brings home the two introduced species that have been wildly successful in South Dakota: the gray partridge and the ring-necked pheasant. South Dakota became synonymous with pheasant hunting in the middle decades of the twentieth century, partly through marketing efforts that included attracting celebrity hunters such as the great novelist Ernest Hemingway—an effort that didn't pay off, in that case, since Hemingway demanded strict secrecy about his hunt in Wentworth, South Dakota, during the drought year 1936.[65] Individual South Dakotans began importing Chinese ring-necked pheasants and releasing them in the 1890s, and the first hunting season for pheasants was a one-day affair in Spink County in 1919 that allowed hunters no more than two cock pheasants each.[66] By 1929, 2,760 non-residents bought licenses to hunt pheasants in South Dakota, and the longest season in the state was 1944, when it lasted 163 days, from late September to the end of February, with a limit of ten birds, of which five could be hens.[67] South Dakota got word-of-mouth advertising about its amazing pheasant resource when some 20,000 soldiers a month passing through Aberdeen on the Chicago, Milwaukee & St. Paul Railway were served pheasant sandwiches by the Aberdeen canteen during the heart of World War II.[68]

Biologists say South Dakota's pheasant population has peaked four times when massive changes or disruptions on the landscape increased pheasant cover: the Great Depression of the 1930s, the World War II years of the early and mid-1940s, the Soil Bank era of the late 1950s and early 1960s, and the Conservation Reserve Program years that began in 1986.[69] The pheasant population in South

Dakota reached an all-time high of between 16 million and 17 million birds in the mid-1940s, reached 11 million in Soil Bank days, and reached about 12 million between 2003 and 2008 during the CRP years.[70]

Pheasant hunters spent an estimated $231 million in South Dakota in 2010.[71] One fairly recent trend away from public hunting is reflected in the data that suggest residents spent 12 percent of their pheasant hunting time and non-residents spent 36 percent of their pheasant-hunting time on private, fee-access areas (excluding licensed shooting preserves, which accounted for 2 percent or less of their time for both residents and non-residents).[72]

Because of its cultural and economic significance, pheasant hunting and pheasant populations remain important topics of public policy in South Dakota. Former Governor Dennis Daugaard held a pheasant habitat summit in December 2013 that subsequently led to a state-sponsored Habitat Pays Initiative to help landowners maintain or improve wildlife habitat.[73] More controversially, Governor Kristi Noem's administration put in place a Nest Predator Bounty Program that tries to protect pheasant and duck populations by paying a bounty for killing predators such as raccoons that raid nests. Although the program had resulted in the deaths of 134,000 predators shot or trapped as of October 2021, former Game, Fish and Parks secretary and commissioner John Cooper said the program was created as a political act rather than a sound wildlife management strategy to enhance pheasant numbers.[74] Interestingly, the idea of paying a bounty for predators that prey on pheasants and ducks is replaying a theme from 1966, when a group called Pheasants Unlimited organized, calling itself "a citizens' program for restoring our pheasant population." It advocated a three-pronged approach that included habitat improvement, predator control, and restocking when necessary.[75]

Addressing land use to protect habitat, not fighting predators, may be the key issue to assuring South Dakota's pheasant populations in the future—especially as Conservation Reserve Program contracts expire that had paid farmers to sow fragile lands to cover crops. Biologists who authored a publication some years ago called "Life after CRP: Maintaining Ring-Necked Pheasants in a Changing Landscape," noted that pheasants thrive in a mix of about 70 percent cropland (ideally about 30 percent row crop and 40 percent small grains) and 30 percent hay or grassland (of which 10-15 percent would be undisturbed nesting cover).[76]

Waterfowl hunting in South Dakota has been famous since the end of the nineteenth century, when well-off gentlemen from urban areas farther east traveled by train to both Dakotas to hunt ducks and geese in the wetlands that make up the Prairie Pothole Region—hunts they wrote about in a slew of articles in hunting magazines.[77] North Dakota attracted more attention, judging by hunting articles of the time, but a writer from Milwaukee who called himself "Greenhead" clearly found much to like about hunting the marshes of northeast South Dakota.[78] About forty species of waterfowl occur annually or periodically in South Dakota, biologists say, and seventeen species nest in the state.[79] Archaeological evidence shows that the Arikara people made use of at least thirteen species of waterfowl.[80] South Dakota became a well-known hunting destination for waterfowlers by 1895, when railroads reached into every part of the state's East River country,[81] although newspapers such as the Volga Tribune noted as early as 1884 that waterfowl hunters from eastern cities were arriving by train to hunt in local marshes, where they were "slaughtering . . . at wholesale" ducks and geese.[82] Codington County pioneer Flora Spicer, who kept house for her brother on a claim near the Rauville elevator, recalls the wild geese were so thick they looked like snowdrifts. Hunters would ride to within shooting distance, and later discovered they could stalk the geese by driving a horse or ox along, letting it eat as it went, and following along behind—hidden by the animal, apparently—until within shooting distance.[83] There was market hunting in South Dakota in the late nineteenth and early twentieth century, on Sand Lake and elsewhere, but the influential Migratory Bird Treaty Act of 1918 signaled a huge change as countries such as the United States began to recognize waterfowl as a resource to be conserved.[84] However, drainage continued for decades, eventually eliminating about 35 percent of the original, natural surface wetlands that provide key habitat for waterfowl–an ongoing challenge for waterfowl management in the future.[85]

Oddly enough for a state that welcomes nonresident pheasant hunters in droves, South Dakota has been far less welcoming of nonresident waterfowl hunters. The state actually banned nonresident hunters after World War II but allowed some back into the state after 1969 when it became a condition of receiving some federal money. Nevertheless, that controversy of some seven decades remains "nothing short of a firestorm in the state's hunting politics" in the eyes of some wildlife watchers, even after the legislature ceded oversight of nonresident waterfowl licenses to the Game, Fish and Parks Commission in 2014.[86]

It is worth noting that South Dakota's long history of hunting includes conflict with predator species taken as trophies or adversaries, among them the bear, the wolf, the mountain lion, and the coyote. The mountain man Hugh Glass nearly died in an encounter with a grizzly bear, now the stuff of novels and films, and that real-life encounter took place in 1823 near the forks of the Grand River in the northern part of present-day South Dakota.[87] That same year, the mountain man Jedediah Smith had his scalp nearly torn off by a grizzly in or near the Black Hills, either in South Dakota or Wyoming.[88] George Armstrong Custer famously shot a grizzly while exploring the Black Hills in 1874 and posed for a photograph.[89] Yet not only the grizzly bear, but the less aggressive black bear was extirpated from South Dakota's river valleys and Black Hills by the end of the nineteenth century. Fred W. Whitley, the historian of early Custer City, notes that four bears were killed by trophy hunters in the Hell's Canyon area west of Custer in 1888. "Two species, bears and Audubon sheep, disappeared completely from the Custer area, and eventually from the Hills," he writes.[90]

Wolves and coyotes were such devastating adversaries that local governments began offering bounties—Custer County offered $5 for a wolf and $1.50 for a coyote in 1893. Custer County reduced the bounties by 1896 to $1.50 for wolves, nothing for coyotes.[91]

Nevertheless, wolves continued to be a threat to livestock, and the cleverest of them achieved legendary status. The U.S. Department of Agriculture Yearbook for 1920 includes an item about the so-called Custer wolf that patrolled an area of 40 miles by 60, causing at least $25,000 in cattle losses before a government trapper caught it, then tracked it for three miles in order to get a shot at it as the animal was getting away with the trap.[92] One writer's book-length attempt at a biography of the wolf says the animal was killed in October 1920.[93] In Harding County, the famous wolf Three Toes hunted the area where South Dakota, North Dakota, and Montana meet from about 1912 until 1925, when a trapper caught him near Buffalo, South Dakota. He's said to have caused at least $50,000 in livestock losses.[94] A 2000 study concluded the gray wolf is likely found nowhere in South Dakota.[95]

Less devastating than the wolf but also a historic predator in South Dakota is the mountain lion, now hunted as a trophy animal. South Dakota has had a resident-only season since 2005, and in 2015, hunters took 43 mountain lions (22 females, 21 males).[96]

Fishing has a considerably different trajectory in South Dakota history in the sense that settlement has had, in general, a more positive effect on fishing resources thanks in part to stocking efforts that introduced fish to many prairie lakes and potholes where they were not present previously. In addition the building of the four Missouri River dams in South Dakota created Lake Oahe, Lake Sharpe, Lake Francis Case, and Lewis and Clark Lake—home to world-class walleye fisheries and, in Lake Oahe, even a salmon fishery.[97] The dams have not been wholly positive in that at least one species that was listed as endangered in 1990, the pallid sturgeon, may be affected by loss of habitat and changes in river flow brought about by the dams.[98] Those who lived with the river before the dams relied on it as a fishery for such species as catfish and sturgeon, as well as walleye.[99]

Aided by such hatcheries as the D. C. Booth Historic National Fish Hatchery and Archives, in Spearfish, fishing is a productive activity for sports enthusiasts throughout the state, as seen here near Sioux Falls. *The Center for Western Studies.*

Archaeology shows that even on lesser waterways, Native Americans in present-day South Dakota were catching fish for food at least 10,000 years ago during the Paleo-Indian Period. For example, minnows have been found along with mammoth bones at a site in southwestern South Dakota.[100] Cache pits at a site on the Big Sioux River in Lincoln County show that not only fish, but also frogs and turtles were food sources in the period from A.D. 500 to 1500.[101] Fish identified from archaeological sites in the state include gar, bowfin, pike, mooneye, minnow, sucker, catfish, temperate bass, sunfish, perch, and drum.[102]

White settlers in Dakota, too, were making good use of the native fish species, as the *Dakota Democrat* of Sioux Falls is noting already in 1859 when it observes "our piscatorial friends are just at the present time enjoying rare sport in hauling out catfish, perch, wall-eyed pike, &c., from the Big Sioux. The river, below the Falls, is filled with them."[103] Evadna Cochrane Burba's memoir about early Deuel County mentions catching bullheads by the barrel in spring.[104] In Custer Township south of Huron, Frank Bloodgood's memoir records that his family and about six others owned a fish net in common and strung it across the river—probably the James?—and drove fish into it, beating the water with willow wands and sometimes catching a bushel of fish at a time. "I do not know if there was a law against fishing with a net, but we were never molested."[105] The July 13, 1885, minutes of the Codington County Commission indicate that local government officials in what was to be South Dakota already were worrying about what was fair play for taking fish, noting that complaints had been received "that fish at the outlet of Lake Kampeska were being taken unlawfully."[106]

Perhaps the biggest change for fisheries in South Dakota came from the growing realization in the earliest days of statehood that—as with pheasants later in the state's uplands—species could be introduced to the state's waters to improve fishing opportunities. C. C. Crary of Custer convinced Wyoming officials to release a "can" of trout in French Creek in spring 1889, where 3,000 trout were stocked two years later; Riley Miller stocked trout fingerlings in his private ponds in 1890; Rapid City pioneer Sam Scott, who later moved to Custer, persuaded Colorado officials to send trout to the Black Hills in 1892.[107] Arguably, this is the impulse that led eventually to South Dakota's Cleghorn Springs, McNenny, Blue Dog and Whitlock Bay fish hatcheries that continue to maintain the state's fish resources to this day.[108]

In sum, it would seem that South Dakota, while it is first among states in the percentage of residents who hunt and is consistently ranked first by hunting organizations for the quality of its hunts for some kinds of game, can only remain a hunting and fishing paradise if wildlife resources are carefully managed. The available records in South Dakota history suggest a pattern or weave of trends from the fur trade era onward, sometimes happening concurrently: harvesting and sometimes overharvesting of a seemingly abundant resource; movement of game populations into new areas and away from old territories; depletion of game populations due to hunting or conversion of habitat for uses such as farming and ranching; blame and blame-shifting for the depletion or extirpation of some species of game in some areas; outright extinction in at least one case; a recognition early in the twentieth century of the need for rules to govern the taking of game; introductions of desirable new species, or reintroductions of native species, under careful management; and ongoing concerns about dwindling habitat. The state's recognition of hunting and fishing as a valuable part of its culture and the need to protect habitat and hunting and fishing opportunities for future generations will be ongoing topics of public discussion in South Dakota.

Notes

[1] George Catlin, *Letters and Notes on the Manners, Customs, and Conditions of North American Indians Written during Eight Years' Travel (1832-1839) amongst the Wildest Tribes of Indians in North America*, vol. 1, (New York: Dover Publications, 1973), 256.

[2] Ibid, 256-57.

[3] Ibid, 261-62.

[4] Maria R. Audubon, *Audubon and his Journals*, vol. 1 (New York: Dover Publications Inc., 1986), 499.

[5] Ibid., 519-20.

[6] David Rookhuyzen, "Hunt Pierre? A Capital Idea." *South Dakota Outdoors* 1 (Fall 2013): 32.

[7] Ibid, 34.

[8] Meagan Drillinger, "States with the Most Registered Hunters," https://stacker.com/stories/4268/states-most-registered-hunters (accessed Nov. 7, 2021).

[9] Carlson Dietmeier, Jenna, and Michael Fosha and Chris Nelson, "Bison Kill Sites in South Dakota, 9,000 B.C.– A.D. 1875: A National Register of Historic Places Multiple Property Listing." Presented at the 84th Annual Meeting of the Society for American Archaeology, Albuquerque, N.M., 2019. (tDAR id: 450301)

[10] Mitchell Indian Village, "About the museum," https://www.mitchellindianvillage.org/about-the-museum (accessed Jan. 5, 2022).

[11] George Catlin, *Letters and Notes on the Manners, Customs, and Conditions of North American Indians*, 257.

[12] Ibid.

[13] M. Scott Taylor, "Buffalo Hunt: International Trade and the Virtual Extinction of the North American Bison," *American Economic Review* 101:7 (2011): 3162-95.

[14] James A. Hanson, Foreword, *Fort Tecumseh and Fort Pierre Chouteau: Journal and Letter Books 1830–1850* (Pierre: South Dakota Historical Society Press, 2017), ix.

[15] Ibid., map by Brian R. Austin, page facing xiv.

[16] South Dakota Department of Game, Fish and Parks, "Non-Trophy Buffalo," https://gfp.sd.gov/nontrophy-buffalo/ (accessed Jan. 17, 2022).

[17] South Dakota Dcpartment of Game, Fish and Parks, "Trophy Buffalo," https://gfp.sd.gov/trophy-buffalo/, (accessed Jan. 17, 2022).

[18] Assistant Director Jim Matheson, National Bison Association, e-mail message to author, Jan. 21, 2022.

[19] Evadna Cochrane Burba, "B. J. Cochrane, Dakota Pioneer 1849-1949," *South Dakota Historical Collections* 34 (1968): 408.

[20] W. H. Hamilton, "Dakota: An Autobiography of a Cowman," *South Dakota Historical Collections* 19 (1938): 612.

[21] Ibid., 536.

[22] Ibid.

[23] Fred W. Whitley, "A History of Custer City, South Dakota 1874-1900," *South Dakota Historical Collections* 37 (1974): 324.

[24] Lee R. Boyer, "Conflict over Hunting Rights: Lightning Creek, 1903," *South Dakota History* 23:4 (Winter 1993): 301-20.

[25] Ibid., 309.

[26] Michael Lee Lawson, "Reservoir and Reservation: The Oahe Dam and the Cheyenne River Sioux," *South Dakota Historical Collections* 37 (1974): 209.

[27] Robert McCracken Peck, "To acquire what knolege you can": The Scientific Contributions of Lewis and Clark, *South Dakota History* 34:1 (Spring 2004): 21.

[28] Gary E. Moulton and Thomas W. Dunlay, eds.,*The Journals of the Lewis and Clark Expedition,* vol. 3 (Lincoln: University of Nebraska Press, 1987), 71.

[29] Mary C. Gibbs, Jonathan A. Jenks, and Bok F. Sowell, *Pronghorn and Agriculture: Maintaining a Balance* (Brookings: South Dakota State University Extension fact sheet 886, 1993), 1.

[30] South Dakota Department of Game, Fish and Parks, "Antelope," https://gfp.sd.gov/antelope/ (accessed Jan. 17, 2022).

[31] South Dakota Department of Game, Fish and Parks, "Elk," https://gfp.sd.gov/elk/ (accessed Jan. 17, 2022).

[32] John Francis McDermott, ed., *Up the Missouri with Audubon: The Journal of Edward Harris* (Norman: University of Oklahoma Press, 1951), 25.

[33] Kenneth F. Higgins, Eileen Dowd Stukel, Judyann M. Goulet, and Douglas C. Backlund, *Wild Mammals of South Dakota* (Pierre: South Dakota Department of Game, Fish and Parks, 2000), 227.

[34] Cited in Benjamin D. Simpson, "Population Ecology of Rocky Mountain Elk in the Black Hills, South Dakota and Wyoming (Master's thesis, South Dakota State University, 2015), 3.

[35] Benjamin D. Simpson, "Population Ecology of Rocky Mountain Elk in the Black Hills, South Dakota and Wyoming (Master's thesis, South Dakota State University, 2015), 3.

[36] Whitley, *A History of Custer City*, 324.

[37] Arthur H. Richardson and Lyle E. Petersen, "History and Management of South Dakota Deer," Bulletin No. 5 (Pierre: South Dakota Department of Game, Fish and Parks, 1974), 1.

[38] Ibid., 2.

[39] South Dakota Department of Game, Fish and Parks, "Deer," https://gfp.sd.gov/deer/ (accessed Jan. 19, 2022).

[40] South Dakota Department of Game, Fish and Parks, "Chronic Wasting Disease Detected in New Area," news release, November 16, 2021.

[41] Hamilton, *Dakota*, 618-19.

[42] Ibid., 534.

[43] Ibid., 611.

[44] Kenneth F. Higgins, Eileen Dowd Stukel, Judyann M. Goulet, and Douglas C. Backlund, *Wild Mammals of South Dakota* (Pierre: South Dakota Department of Game, Fish and Parks, 2000), 249.

[45] South Dakota Department of Game, Fish and Parks, "Bighorn Sheep," https://gfp.sd.gov/bighorn-sheep/ (accessed Jan. 19, 2022).

[46] Higgins, *Wild Mammals of South Dakota*, 611.

[47] KELO Capitol News Bureau, "SD tag to kill a bighorn brought big bucks again," https://www.keloland.com/news/capitol-news-bureau/s-d-tag-to-kill-a-bighorn-brought-big-bucks-again/, June 9, 2021 (accessed January 19, 2022).

[48] Higgins, *Wild Mammals of South Dakota*, 244-46.

[49] South Dakota Department of Game, Fish and Parks, South Dakota Mountain Goat Management Plan, 2018-2022, draft, https://gfp.sd.gov/UserDocs/nav/mountaingoat_draft.pdf (accessed January 19, 2022).

[50] Moulton,*The Journals of the Lewis & Clark Expedition,* vol. 8 (Lincoln: University of Nebraska Press, 1993), 345.

[51] Ibid., 302-06.

[52] *South Dakota Place Names*, workers of the Writers' Program of the Work Projects Administration in South Dakota, compilers. (Vermillion, University of South Dakota, 1940), 65-66.

[53] E. H. Smith, "Turkey Talk," *South Dakota Conservation Digest* 20 (1953): 2-5.

[54] South Dakota Department of Game, Fish and Parks, "South Dakota Wild Turkey Management Plan 2016–2020, https://gfp.sd.gov/UserDocs/nav/WildTurkeyPlan.pdf (accessed Jan. 21, 2022), 2.

[55] L. D. Flake, C. P. Lehman, A. P. Leif, M. A. Rumble, and D. J. Thompson, *The Wild Turkey in South Dakota* (Pierre: South Dakota Department of Game, Fish and Parks/Brookings: South Dakota Agricultural Experiment Station, 2006), 4.

[56] Ibid., 134-35.

[57] Ibid., 145.

[58] Moulton, *The Journals of the Lewis & Clark Expedition,* vol. 8, 345.

[59] W. Daniel Svedarsky, Ronald L. Westemeier, Robert J. Robel, Sharon Gough, and John E. Toepher, "Status and management of the great prairie-chicken *Tympanuchus cupido pinnatus* in North America,"Wildlife Biology 6:4 (December 2000): 277-84.

[60] Marie R. Audubon, *Audubon and his Journals, vol. 1*, 514.

[61] W. Daniel Svedarsky, Ronald L. Westemeier, Robert J. Robel, Sharon Gough, and John E. Toepher, "Status and management of the great prairie-chicken *Tympanuchus cupido pinnatus* in North America," 277.

[62] L. D. Flake, J. W. Connelly, T. R. Kirschenmann, and A. J. Lindbloom, Grouse of the Plains and Mountains: The South Dakota Story (Pierre: South Dakota Department of Game, Fish and Parks, 2010), 13.

[63] Ibid.

[64] Ibid., 16.

[65] Local historian Ardyce Habeger Samp, cited in Lance Nixon, "The Hunting Story They Couldn't Tell," *South Dakota Outdoors*, 1 (Fall 2013): 36-41.

[66] James Marten, "'We Always Looked Forward to the Hunters Coming': The Culture of Pheasant Hunting in South Dakota," *South Dakota History* 29 (Summer 1999): 88-89.

[67] Ibid., 89-91.

[68] Helen J. Bergh, "Troop Trains and Pheasant Sandwiches: The Aberdeen Canteen in World War II," *South Dakota History* 23 (Summer 1993): 133-41.

[69] L. D. Flake, A. E. Gabbert, T. R. Kirschenmann, A. P. Leif, and C. T. Switzer, *Ring-Necked Pheasants: Thriving in South Dakota* (Pierre: South Dakota Department of Game, Fish and Parks, 2012), 10.

[70] Ibid., 11-13.

[71] Ibid., 233.

[72] Ibid., 232.

[73] Pheasants Forever, "South Dakota Introduces Habitat Pays Initiative," https://pheasantsforever.org/BlogLanding/Blogs/Field-Notes/South-Dakota-Introduces-Habitat-Pays-Initiative.aspx?feed=articles (accessed March 7, 2022).

[74] Danielle Ferguson, South Dakota News Watch, "Gov. Noem's bounty program 'not doing anything for pheasant management,' former wildlife official says," https://rapidcityjournal.com/news/local/gov-noems-bounty-program-not-doing-anything-for-pheasant-management-former-wildlife-official-says/article_fec871d2-0c73-5a9c-bd90-1a43359d8c6b.html (accessed March 7, 2022).

[75] Al Schock, *Upland Game: The History and Activities of Pheasants Unlimited in South Dakota, plus The Impact of Predation on Duck Populations*. Excerpted from Al Schock's *Autobiography*. (Sioux Falls: Nordica Enterprises Inc., 1996), 7-16.

[76] U.S. Department of Agriculture's Natural Resources Conservation Service, North Dakota Game and Fish Department, North Dakota State University

Hettinger Research Extension Center, Pheasants Forever/Quail Forever, *Life after CRP: Maintaining Ring-Necked Pheasants in a Changing Landscape. A guide for Landowners and Pheasant Enthusiasts*, https://gf.nd.gov/gnf/private-lands/docs/life-after-crp.pdf (accessed April 13, 2022).

[77] Harold F. Duebbert, ed., *Wildfowling in Dakota, 1873–1903: Old-Time Duck and Goose Shooting on the Dakota Prairies* (Bismarck: Windfeather Press, 2003).

[78] Lance Nixon, "Waterfowl Hunting in a Golden Age: A gentleman hunter visits South Dakota, 1897–1902," *Capital Journal*, Jan. 9, 2015.

[79] K. C. Jensen, K. F. Higgins, and S. J. Vaa, compilers, *A History of Waterfowl Management, Research, and Hunting in South Dakota* (Pierre: South Dakota Department of Game, Fish and Parks, 2014), 1.

[80] Ibid., 5, 9.

[81] Ibid., 159.

[82] *Volga Tribune*, Nov. 13, 1884, cited in K. C. Jensen, K. F. Higgins, and S. J. Vaa, compilers, *A History of Waterfowl Management, Research, and Hunting in South Dakota*, 160.

[83] Flora Spicer, "A Woman Pioneer Tells of her Experiences," in Wright Tarbell, *The Early and Territorial History of Codington County* (Pierre: South Dakota Historical Collections 24: 1949), 348-49.

[84] U.S. Fish and Wildlife Service, "Digest of Federal Resource Laws of Interest to the U.S. Fish and Wildlife Service: Migratory Bird Treaty Act of 1918," https://www.fws.gov/laws/lawsdigest/migtrea.html (accessed Jan. 31, 2022).

[85] K. C. Jensen, K. F. Higgins, and S. J. Vaa, compilers, *A History of Waterfowl Management, Research, and Hunting in South Dakota,* 352.

[86] Nick Lowrey, "Non-resident waterfowl hunting remains hot topic," *Capital Journal*, May 12, 2015, updated September 24, 2019, https://www.capjournal.com/news/non-resident-waterfowl-hunting-remains-hot-topic/article_2580d098-f925-11e4-93fc-0325fdcc0907.html (accessed March 29, 2022).

[87] John R. Milton, Foreword to Frederick Manfred, *Lord Grizzly* (Lincoln: University of Nebraska Press, 1983), viii.

[88] Dale L. Morgan, *Jedediah Smith and the Opening of the West* (Lincoln: University of Nebraska Press, 1953), 83-84.

[89] Photo, "Our first Grizzly, killed by General Custer." In Ernest Grafe and Paul Horsted,"Dakota Resources: In Illingsworth's Footsteps: Rediscovering the First Photographs of the Black Hills," *South Dakota History* 31 (Fall/Winter 2001): 289.

[90] Fred. W. Whitley, *A History of Custer City*, 324.

[91] Ibid.

[92] United States Department of Agriculture Yearbook 1920 (Washington: Government Printing Office, 1921), 297.

[93] Roger A. Caras, *The Custer Wolf: The Biography of an American Renegade* (Boston: Little, Brown and Co., 1966), 172.

[94] Archer B. Gilfillan, *Sheep: Life on the South Dakota Range* (Minneapolis: University of Minnesota Press, 1928, 1929), 181-96. It is worth adding that W. H. Hamilton's *Dakota: An Autobiography of a Cowman* reports hunting wolves in Harding County with dogs (605-20) and notes that his pioneer family also roped wolves from horseback when the wolves were full from feeding (586-87).

[95] Kenneth F. Higgins, Eileen Dowd Stukel, Judyann M. Goulet, and Douglas C. Backlund, *Wild Mammals of South Dakota,* 169.

[96] Cynthia L. Longmire, "2015 Black Hills Mt. Lion Season: Hunter Survey Results," (Pierre: South Dakota Department of Game, Fish and Parks, 2015), iii.

[97] South Dakota Missouri River Tourism, "The Four Lakes and Dams," https://sdmissouririver.com/follow-the-river/the-four-lakes-and-dams/ (accessed February 1, 2022).

[98] U.S. Army Corps of Engineers, "Missouri River Recovery Program," https://www.nwo.usace.army.mil/MRRP/ (accessed Feb. 1, 2022).

[99] Lance Nixon, "Tending his lines: James Pollock's watercolor art," *South Dakota Outdoors* 2 (Spring 2014): 16-17.

[100] C. Berry, K. Higgins, D. Willis, and S. Chipps, eds., *History of Fisheries and Fishing in South Dakota* (Pierre: South Dakota Department of Game, Fish and Parks, 2007), 28.

[101] Ibid., 29.

[102] Ibid., 32-35.

[103] *Dakota Democrat*, no. 3, August 26, 1859, in "Newspapers of South Dakota," *South Dakota Historical Collections* 11 (1922): 434.

[104] Evadna Cochrane Burba, "B. J. Cochrane, Dakota Pioneer 1849-1949," 408.

[105] Steven J. Bucklin, ed., "Pioneer Days in South Dakota: The Memoir of Frank Bloodgood," *South Dakota History* 29 (Summer 1999): 137-38.

[106] Wright Tarbell, *The Early and Territorial History of Codington County*, 371.

[107] Whitley, *A History of Custer City*, 325.

[108] "Hatcheries," South Dakota Department of Game, Fish and Parks, https://gfp.sd.gov/fish/ (accessed February 3, 2022).

12

The American Indian Movement: A Half-Century Assessment

Carson Walker

The American Indian Movement (AIM) burst onto the national scene in the early 1970s with its occupation and ransacking of the Bureau of Indian Affairs (BIA) headquarters in Washington, D.C., and 71-day standoff at the Pine Ridge Indian Reservation village of Wounded Knee in South Dakota. While attracting the sympathies and financial support of many non-Indian groups, churches and individuals, its efforts also drew the ire of the Federal Bureau of Investigation (FBI), as well as many non-Indians and other native people who did not agree with the violence that often accompanied the demonstrations intended to focus attention on broken treaties with the United States government, the plight of Native Americans and their mistreatment.

Tribal members Clyde Bellecourt, Dennis Banks, Eddie Benton Banai, and George Mitchell formed an organization that became the American Indian Movement in the late 1960s. It was a response to a higher-than-normal incarceration rate of Native people who had been relocated to urban settings, including in Minneapolis, where AIM's headquarters remains. AIM also boasts numerous local chapters around the country. Its priorities initially were finding people jobs, housing, and education. It also set up street patrols to film arrests and attempt to protect Indians from police abuse and violence, and then remind them of their rights when they were taken into custody. AIM adopted the upside-down American flag as its symbol, the international distress signal for people in trouble.[1]

(In 2020 Minneapolis also became the epicenter of riots in response to police brutality against Blacks after George Floyd was killed when a white officer placed him face-down on the pavement with a knee on Floyd's back for more than nine minutes.)

By November 1972, AIM said it had taken part in more than 150 demonstrations.[2] As its support grew, it drew more prominent members, including Russell Means, a Lakota who was born on the Pine Ridge Reservation but grew up in California, Leonard Crow Dog, another Lakota and the first spiritual leader to endorse the organization, and John Trudell, a Santee Sioux who served as AIM's spokesman and later as its chairman, as well as support from Hollywood stars like Marlon Brando and Jane Fonda.[3] None of the original AIM leaders is still alive.

All of this happened a century after the federal government's relocation of Indian tribes onto reservations that ultimately shrank farther as the U.S. grew westward. On a parallel track to AIM's rise, author Dee Brown published the narrative *Bury My Heart at Wounded Knee* in 1970 based on Indian oral history records.[4] It recounted in great detail how Indians died from starvation and battles with government troops. The book, which sold nearly five million copies, challenged the perception many people had about the American West and the role the federal government played in its expansion.[5]

> *Bury My Heart* touched a raw nerve and became a surprise national bestseller. It was a magnificent book—forcefully written, exhaustively researched, clarion in its tone of moral outrage. But more than that, it came along at the precise moment when the public was ready to receive the full plangency of its message. *Bury My Heart* landed on America's doorstep in the anguished midst of the Vietnam War, shortly after revelations of the My Lai massacre had plunged the nation into gnawing self-doubt. Here

> was a book filled with a hundred My Lais, a book that explored the dark roots of American arrogance while dealing a near-deathblow to our fondest folk myth. The main idea behind Brown's book was so obvious it was radical: If Anglo-Americans had "won" the West, why not tell the story from the vantage point of those who "lost" it—the Apaches, the Nez Perces, the Utes, the Cheyennes, the Sioux, the Navahos?[6]

The publication of that history provided the backdrop for AIM's support from many non-Indians and its ascension as the go-to group for many Native people who believed they had nowhere else to turn for help. At a 1976 trial for two members, John Trudell, AIM national chairman at the time, summed up the organization's purpose as it related to Native Americans.

> We are statistics that everyone has heard about, the unemployed, uneducated, alcoholics, welfare recipients. We have been the study of many Congressional studies and investigations, all types of studies, but yet we as statistics still remain—our situation has remained the same for a century. So we have grouped together behind our religious beliefs, our respect for human rights, our beliefs that we are entitled to human rights as well as everybody else. Our functions have been to educate our own people and to try and educate the white Americans as to the fact that we exist yet today. I mean when you look at AIM, [this is] who we are. We are the descendants of Geronimo, Crazy Horse. We are the indigenous people. We are concerned about what is happening to our people now, because, you know, we don't like to be a statistic.[7]

Three years later, in 1979, Trudell burned an upside-down American flag during a rally for imprisoned AIM member Leonard Peltier outside the FBI building in Washington, D.C. Early the next morning at his in-law's house on the Duck Valley Reservation, in Nevada, his wife, three young children, and mother-in-law died in a fire that started in a fireplace clean-out.[8] There's no evidence Trudell's protest and the fire were connected, but the FBI also never investigated.[9]

The American Indian Movement's heyday largely ended in the 1970s. Most recently, AIM's focus has included urging sports teams to abandon Native American mascots[10] and protesting projects such as the Dakota Access Pipeline, which the group said threatened Native lands and the Missouri River.[11] The organization also has maintained its support for Leonard Peltier, Dennis Banks' former bodyguard, who is serving two life prison sentences for the 1975 murders of two FBI agents on the Pine Ridge Indian Reservation.

Reservation Murders

On June 26, 1975, while looking for a young Indian man wanted on robbery and assault with a deadly weapon charges, FBI Special Agents Jack Coler and Ron Williams and AIM member Joe Stuntz were fatally shot during a shootout at the Jumping Bull ranch near Oglala. The event became known as the Reservation Murders, or ResMurs. The two agents were wounded and then shot at close range with a high-powered rifle. Stuntz, who was found wearing one of the agents' FBI jackets, also was shot in the head. His grave at a nearby cemetery reads "Incident at Oglala Warrior, American Indian Movement Patriot."[12] It was later determined that a Bureau of Indian Affairs officer shot Stuntz as he fired at an FBI agent.[13] Two AIM members, Bob Robideau and Dino Butler, were acquitted on charges of killing the agents during a trial in Cedar Rapids, Iowa. A third, Leonard Peltier, eventually was apprehended in Canada and extradited to the United States, tried in Fargo, North Dakota, and convicted in 1977 of two counts of first-degree murder for which he was sentenced to consecutive life prison sentences. He maintains his innocence and has drawn support from human rights groups and people around the world, despite numerous courts and U.S. presidents that have rejected his appeals and commutation pleas.

When the shooting started, Jack Coler got out of his car to get his unloaded rifle from the trunk and got hit in the arm by a heavy-caliber bullet that pierced his trunk, leaving his arm hanging from the elbow. Ron Williams, who was by his car and wounded in his shooting arm and one leg, ran over to Coler, took off his shirt and made a tourniquet. Three to five men soon after walked up to the two wounded agents. Williams was shot in the face with a .223-caliber bullet while holding his hand in front of his face, which blew off four fingers.[14]

Robideau, Butler, and Peltier acknowledged going through the agents' cars after the gunfight.[15] Those who question whether Peltier was the final triggerman point to the fact that other AIM members present at the ranch that day said dozens of Indians took part in the gunfight.[16] A 1976 FBI memo stated that "numerous individuals, some of which have not yet been positively identified, were involved in the deaths of Coler and Williams."[17]

Peltier's case was the foundation of another national bestseller, published in 1983, *In the Spirit of Crazy Horse* by Peter Matthiessen, which alleged that the FBI framed Peltier. Matthiessen later acknowledged being an agent for the Central Intelligence Agency during the 1950s in Paris. "The only adventure I regret was the CIA," he was quoted in his 2014 obituary, adding that he left the agency because his evolving left-leaning political beliefs made him no longer trustworthy and he was not on the CIA's side.[18] Most other subsequent books and movies generally were sympathetic to AIM and Peltier.

Annie Mae Pictou-Aquash

Besides Peltier, there also has been considerable attention paid to another AIM worker, Anna "Annie" Mae Pictou, whose unsolved slaying lingered as a mystery for decades after the intense AIM activities of the 1970s. The Mi'kmaq from Nova Scotia, Canada, had been active in Native issues in her home country and was inspired to join AIM's efforts in the United States, so she responded to support AIM at Wounded Knee in 1973, leaving two young daughters at home. During the Wounded Knee standoff, she married Ojibwa artist Nogeeshik Aquash.[19]

Pictou-Aquash quickly became a trusted member of the inner circle of AIM leadership but over time drew suspicions that she was an FBI informant. Wanblee, South Dakota, rancher Roger Amiotte found her unidentified, frozen body on February 24, 1976, in a ravine near the Badlands. An initial autopsy by the local coroner concluded she died of exposure and she was buried in an Oglala cemetery. But because of questions surrounding her death, the body was exhumed and an independent coroner ruled she died of a gunshot wound to the back of the head with a .38-caliber handgun. In 1999 Russell Means accused senior AIM members of ordering her killing because Aquash knew which of them were government informants.

Several grand juries met over the years to explore the case, including a 2003 inquiry in South Dakota that led to the first criminal charges in the case.[20] In March 2003 a federal grand jury indicted two AIM members on charges of first-degree murder committed in the perpetration of a kidnapping for Pictou-Aquash's killing. Arlo Looking Cloud, a Lakota who grew up on the Pine Ridge Reservation, was arrested in Denver, Colorado. Authorities said they also were looking for a Canadian man, John Graham, also known as John Boy Patton, who acknowledged in a 2000 interview that he was with Pictou-Aquash before she died but denied any involvement in her killing. Graham was later arrested in Vancouver, Canada, and extradited.[21]

Investigators said AIM leaders ordered Looking Cloud and Graham to kill Pictou-Aquash, which all AIM leaders denied. At Looking Cloud's February 2004 trial in Rapid City, prosecutors said Looking Cloud, Graham, and another AIM member, Theda Clarke, in December 1975 drove Aquash-Pictou from Denver in Clarke's red Ford Pinto to a remote location near the Badlands and walked her to a cliff where Graham shot her in the back of her head as she begged for her life and prayed.[22]

Though Pictou-Aquash's killing was the subject of the trial, one of the first prosecution witnesses put into the record sworn testimony that challenged Leonard Peltier's claims of innocence. Darlene "Ka-Mook" Nichols, the former common-law wife of Dennis Banks, told jurors she was with Pictou-Aquash when Peltier bragged about killing the two FBI agents, indicating that one of them begged for his life. Nichols said Peltier also previously put a gun to Pictou-Aquash's head and wanted to know if she was an informant. Nichols testified that Pictou-Aquash was not a government informant but Banks and Peltier probably thought she was. Pictou-Aquash started talking to Nichols in the fall of 1975 when they shared a jail cell, and she made it clear she was scared of Peltier and Banks, with whom she previously had an affair. Nichols said Banks called to let her know Pictou-Aquash's body was found on the day it was discovered but weeks before it was positively identified. The fact that he had such knowledge prompted her suspicions that AIM was responsible, so after separating from Banks, she cooperated with the investigation.[23]

Paul DeMain, a Native American journalist who has written extensively about AIM, called Nichols' testimony a bombshell. "What it did was take both the cases, Aquash and the Peltier case, and turned them on their head," he said.[24]

The Rapid City jury convicted Looking Cloud in 2004 and he was sentenced to life in prison, which was reduced to 20 years because he later testified against Graham.[25] In 2010 a jury in South Dakota state court convicted Graham of felony murder committed during the kidnapping of Annie Mae Pictou-Aquash.[26] Graham is serving a life prison sentence at the penitentiary in Sioux Falls. While the government convicted him as the triggerman, what remains legally undetermined is who ordered her killing, though AIM members have said leader Vernon Bellecourt, who died in 2007, gave the order, which he denied.[27]

In 2004 Pictou Aquash's two daughters had her body exhumed again and taken back to her native Canada and buried on the Indian Brook Reserve outside of Halifax, Nova Scotia. "It was about bringing her back to her own territory and where she came from," said her older daughter, Denise Maloney Pictou. "That was sacred. You get to return to where you were born." AIM leaders made themselves out to be warriors who followed traditional values but were not, she said:

> I call it a legacy of destruction that has perpetuated itself well past the events of that era that now impact the future generations because we have youths looking up to these individuals as the fathers of resistance for indigenous values. . . . The kids look up to these guys and when you realize how twisted and corrupted they are, it's like losing their religion.... I still talk to people about what happened to my mother and they find out who was responsible. The narrative that is put out there, unfortunately, is very different from the reality of the facts. . . . They relied on the dysfunction of oppression to justify the taking of a woman's life. And it's happening still today. . . . The misogyny that they've adopted goes against everything our traditional culture represents.[28]

FBI Counterpunch

Four years after the Arlo Looking Cloud trial, Joseph Trimbach, the FBI Special Agent in Charge at the Wounded Knee standoff and Reservation Murders, published *American Indian Mafia.* It challenged many of Matthiessen's theories from *In the Spirit of Crazy Horse,* refuted allegations the FBI had anything to do with Pictou-Aquash's slaying and placed blame on AIM leaders, and defended the agency's handling of the Peltier case and Wounded Knee. Trimbach concluded that AIM ultimately did more harm than good in South Dakota:

> Pine Ridge Indians were particularly harmed by AIM's destructive influence. When the leadership was not exploiting tragedies on the reservation, they were actively engaging in them. Especially with regard to their core constituents, Lakota Indians, it

> is hard to see how any lasting benefits resulted from a movement whose principle mission was to destroy. Pine Ridge Indians have started to fight back, as more and more reservation residents speak out against the old Movement leadership. They know the sad truth: that AIM never lived up to its ideals. Today, more than any other reservation in the country, Pine Ridge is still awash in poverty, despair, and the damaging after effects of AIM's calamitous rule and subsequent abandonment of the people. The Movement's present day organization, though mostly benign, often defends AIM's violent past, while the leaders of old occasionally favor the reservations with patronizing visits.[29]

In addition to general criticism at AIM and most of what's been written about it, Trimbach included examples to argue that much of what many people have believed about Leonard Peltier is wrong. As Jack Coler lay seriously wounded and in shock, Ron Williams took off his shirt and apparently waved it as a surrender flag before making a tourniquet for Coler. Rather than continue the firefight, Williams, who was wounded but could still speak, opted to wait for the shooters to approach and reason with them, in hopes of saving his partner. Forensics from the scene indicated that the two agents fired relatively few shots compared to well over a hundred from the surrounding AIM members. After less than ten minutes, the gunfire ended. Peltier and others walked down the hill and found the wounded agents next to one of their vehicles. A credible witness put Peltier's red-and-white Chevrolet Suburban in the fork of the road from where the firing started. Then in the rush to leave the scene, Peltier and the men with him recovered just two of the three spent .223- caliber shell casings from Peltier's AR-15 used to shoot the agents. The third landed in the open trunk of Coler's car.[30] "Peltier has never overcome court testimony that placed him at the scene of the executions and with the murder weapon in hand."[31]

Peltier's extensive court file includes a summary of factual conclusions by the 8th Circuit U.S. Court of Appeals that no one has refuted. Among the conclusions are thc following: Peltier was in the vehicle the agents followed onto the Jumping Bull ranch; Peltier could well have believed that the two agents were after him, since there was a federal warrant out for his arrest; Peltier was seen holding an AR-15 near the agents' bodies before authorities arrived; the agents were killed with a high-velocity, small-caliber gun like the AR-15 and no other gunman was using that weapon; a shell casing that matched the AR-15 was found in the open trunk of Coler's car; Peltier was heard discussing details of the killings that evening; and Coler's handgun was found in a bag that had Peltier's thumb print on it, which was found in a motor home Peltier was riding in before being stopped by a trooper in Oregon.[32] Trimbach writes,

> The idea that the FBI wanted to frame Peltier because he was an emerging AIM leader is, of course, pure hogwash. Prior to June 26, 1975, Dennis Banks' aspiring bodyguard had no credentials as a leader. Peltier was a follower, a misguided wannabe. On that fateful day when he took matters into his own hands, he became *less* of a symbol of the Indian struggle. . . . The FBI pursued him vigorously not because he was an Indian, and not because he wielded political power, and not because he was an AIM rising star. They pursued him for one simple reason: they believed him to be a murderous thug.[33]

AIM's Rise

While the American Indian Movement started in Minnesota, it was the February 1972 killing of Raymond Yellow Thunder, an Oglala Lakota from the Pine Ridge Indian Reservation, that gave rise to its stature in South Dakota and nationally. Two white brothers in near-by Gordon, Nebraska, humiliated and assaulted Yellow Thunder, who later died of his injuries. Yellow Thunder's family called AIM leaders, who were meeting a few hours away in Omaha, Nebraska. They organized a caravan that headed to Gordon in a show of force over alleged racism.[34]

But opposition to AIM also grew. One of its most vocal critics was Richard "Dick" Wilson, who in the spring of 1972 was elected tribal council president on Pine Ridge. Wilson opposed AIM, banned all of its activities on the reservation and beefed up the local BIA police force with locals dubbed the "GOON (Guardians of the Oglala Nation) squad." Wilson's opposition of AIM earned him the support of the BIA and FBI, which established the battle lines for the standoff between federal agents and AIM members a year later.[35]

BIA Headquarters

Later that year, on November 1, 1972, a cross-country caravan with carloads and busloads of Indians associated with AIM and other native groups from around the country arrived in Washington, D.C., days before election day. Plans for the event, called the Trail of Broken Treaties, included presenting a 20-point proposal on Indian rights. Among its demands was that the U.S. government treat Indians according to treaties that were signed in exchange for the land they gave up.[36]

When the promised lodging for the group turned out to be a rat-infested church, the group went to BIA headquarters to complain, which led to the occupation that lasted five days and resulted in considerable damage to the building. The U.S. government ultimately paid $66,000 to the Indians for their transportation out of town, but it was not without fallout. The federal government ended its financial support of AIM through the Office of Economic Opportunity, the FBI classified AIM as "an extremist organization," its leaders were added to the list of "key extremists," and the White House rejected the Trail of Broken Treaties' 20-point proposal.[37]

The effort was doomed from the start. President Richard Nixon, whose attention the Indians hoped to draw with a march around the

White House, was out of town campaigning for a second term (which he won by defeating South Dakota Senator George McGovern). A former tribal chairman who was helping to organize the event failed to secure the housing and food. Priceless Indian artifacts and crafts were destroyed. And deed books for the Chippewas of Minnesota and the Oneida tribe of Wisconsin disappeared.[38]

Custer and Wounded Knee

If there is a single event that etched the American Indian Movement's place in history, it is the group's 71-day takeover of Wounded Knee, a small village on South Dakota's Pine Ridge Indian Reservation because of its historic significance. On December 29, 1890, hundreds of Lakota men, women and children were killed in what would be the last major conflict between the United States Cavalry and Native American tribes.

In January 1973 a white businessman stabbed to death an Indian named Wesley Bad Heart Bull in a Buffalo Gap, South Dakota, bar and was charged with involuntary manslaughter, despite indicating "he was going to kill an Indian." Bad Heart Bull's mother, Sarah Bad Heart Bull, called in AIM to make sure justice was served by state authorities prosecuting the case. When more than 200 Indians showed up at the Custer, South Dakota, courthouse on February 6, 1973, a confrontation between them and police sparked a riot that ended with two destroyed police cars and the burning of an adjacent abandoned building. The clash and another a few weeks later fueled AIM's plans for something larger. "For their part, AIM leaders were eager for more confrontations, persuading themselves that militancy (and publicity) could accomplish what traditional patience and stoicism had not."[39] AIM leader Russell Means, who was born on the Pine Ridge Reservation, had been pondering a spot for a military encounter for some time and believed that nearby Wounded Knee would be ideal.[40]

On February 27, 1973, local Lakota Indians and outside members of AIM traveled to Wounded Knee for a meeting at which they demanded an investigation of the BIA and hearings over the Fort

Laramie Treaty of 1868 that established the Great Sioux Reservation. Ellen Moves Camp, one of the local women who joined the protest, said the decision came at a community gathering a day earlier and with the blessing of tribal chiefs.

> We decided that we did need the American Indian Movement in here because our men were scared, they hung to the back. It was mostly the women that went forward and spoke out. … All of our older people from the reservation helped us make the decision. … And when we kept talking about it then the chiefs said, "Go ahead and do it, go to Wounded Knee. … So take your brothers from the American Indian Movement and go to Wounded Knee and make your stand there." … With our brothers and sisters of the American Indian Movement, we feel stronger.[41]

A day later, on February 28, 1973, agents from the FBI, BIA, and U.S. Marshals Service surrounded the village and the assembled locals and AIM members, who said later they did not plan for a long-term takeover. However, when it happened, they seized control of the Catholic church building and other structures, including the trading post, which they emptied of guns, ammunition, food, and clothing. While some residents left, others stayed to protect their property.[42] The FBI's account is that AIM members and supporters triggered the event and were not peaceful but rather seized the village, took hostages, set fires, looted homes and businesses, and fired weapons at authorities who responded.[43] Agnes Gildersleeve, a 68-year-old Chippewa who owned and operated the Wounded Knee Trading Post and Museum with her husband, Clive, described how it was looted and destroyed:

> (AIM) members arrived and started shooting. … We heard shooting and observed people entering the Trading Post. … My husband and I estimated approximately 60 vehicles were on the streets and in

> the area of the Trading Post. Two armed guards were placed at the entrance of the Trading Post as soon as entrance was made. My husband, myself, and my sister Mrs. Clark, got down on the floor and were afraid that we would be shot. I went to the phone and called (the BIA, FBI, US Marshals and the fire department). I observed Indians going in and out of the Trading Post with armloads of merchandise and loading vans which were parked outside. This merchandise consisted of guns, food, Indian artifacts, pottery (worth approximately $150,000). … At approximately 11:00 p.m. a knock on the door was heard, and members of AIM came in and stated, "You are to consider yourself a political prisoner and hostage."[44]

What followed was 71 days of gunfights between the encircled federal agents and the entrenched AIM members and sympathizers from dozens of tribes and many other non-Indians, numerous ceasefires, roadblocks that forced deliveries of supplies and the movement of people into and out of Wounded Knee at night, and on-again, off-again negotiations.[45] On April 17 a Cherokee, Frank Clearwater, was struck and killed by a stray bullet.[46] On or around April 21 a Black activist from Alabama named Ray Robinson was shot during an argument, bled to death, and was buried (along with six other people rumored to have been killed during the standoff).[47] On April 26 Buddy Lamont, a Lakota who had served in Vietnam voluntarily, was hit by a sniper's bullet and killed. The standoff ended May 9, 1973, when the remaining fighters laid down their arms and surrendered.[48]

AIM leaders (l. to r.) Russell Means, Dennis Banks, and Clyde Bellecourt pose with former U.S. Senator James Abourezk (2d from r.) at the 44th Annual Dakota Conference on the Northern Plains (2012), hosted by the Center for Western Studies. *The Center for Western Studies.*

Though several AIM members were indicted, leaders Dennis Banks and Russell Means were tried separately. U.S. District Court Judge Fred Nichol from Sioux Falls moved the trial to Saint Paul, Minnesota, after concluding they couldn't receive a fair trial in South Dakota. It opened January 8, 1974, and lasted more than eight months. The defense attempted to show Banks and Means as political prisoners. The prosecution argued they were criminals who took over, terrorized, and harmed an innocent community.[49] Trimbach's assessment leaves no room for doubt:

> There was never any doubt that Dennis Banks and Russell Means led the assault and sustained occupation of the village. It would require stupefying logic, creative legalistic maneuvering, and a series of faltering judgments from the bench to ignore the mountain of incriminating evidence. … The totality

> of evidence placed the defendants at the scene, in charge, and deeply involved. There was no logical reason or basis in fact to find them innocent. The defense team, nonetheless, assembled an impressive number of motions intended to suggest the prosecution intentionally withheld exculpatory evidence. What that evidence might have been was never made clear. No genuine exhibit produced at anytime during trial pointed to the defendants' innocence or their non-participation in the village takeover.[50]

When the prosecution finished its case in July, Judge Nichol dismissed most of the charges against Banks and Means. When a member of the jury became ill on September 17, the judge dismissed the other four counts, saying the prosecution acted in bad faith several times during the trial.[51] Ultimately, Leonard Crow Dog was the only AIM leader to spend a day in prison on charges stemming from Wounded Knee, and he served just a few months.[52]

After Dennis Banks' chief lieutenant, Douglas Durham, announced publicly in March 1975 that he was an FBI informant who had infiltrated the American Indian Movement, he testified before Congress that Judge Nichol had hosted a tea party for him, Banks, and Banks' lawyer at Nichol's home two months before the start of the trial. Despite the clear ethical concern, the Eighth U.S. Circuit Court of Appeals later ruled that the verdict could not be appealed.[53] Nichol recused himself from hearing any other Wounded Knee cases.[54]

On the 30th anniversary of the standoff, Warren Littlemoon walked the spot in Wounded Knee where his late mother's house stood, one of those destroyed during the occupation. Still visible was a trench that the occupiers used to crawl in when moving to and from their bunker up the hill to avoid the sight of federal agents on the surrounding hills. Littlemoon, who later wrote about the experience and others in a book entitled *They Called Me Uncivilized: The Memory of an Everyday Lakota Man from Wounded Knee*, said AIM gave nothing back to the community and took much. "This is where I grew up. (There's) nothing left after the occupation," he said. "They have killed us psychologically and the memories we grew up with. They scattered families all over the country with their so-called acts of bravery. They killed families and friendships and replaced that whole thing with a great big devastated life."[55]

Augustana Dorm Takeover

Much of AIM's funding came from federal government programs intended to help the poor, but the Congressional report on AIM said its leaders also coerced church leaders and community organizations into contributing significant money.[56] In July 1970 Lutheran Social Services held a conference at Augustana College in Sioux Falls to discuss Indian self-determination and ministry. It was organized by the American Lutheran Church, the Lutheran Church in America, and the Lutheran Church-Missouri Synod. Dennis Banks, one of more than 100 Indians who attended, called the meeting "a complete farce" because the groups failed to pay AIM the $750,000 it had requested the year before.[57]

In protest the following weekend, on August 3, 1970, about 40 Indians took over the Bergsaker Hall dormitory at Augustana, vowing not to leave until their demands were met. It ended three days later when Clyde Bellecourt said one of the three Lutheran organizations promised his group's $250,000 share of AIM's request. Bellecourt also said a Minneapolis lawyer for AIM would file a $1 billion breach-of-promise lawsuit against the Lutheran Council of the USA for punitive damages, gross violations of the Ten Commandments, and alienation of ecumenical affections.[58]

Lutheran Influence

AIM's connection to Lutherans goes back to its founding. Paul Boe, executive director of the American Lutheran Church (ALC) Division of Social Service, in Minneapolis, received a visit at his office in late 1968 by AIM leaders Clyde Bellecourt and Dennis Banks to discuss their plan for the organization. With Boe's support and financial assistance from the ALC, AIM was incorporated the following year.[59]

Rev. Paul Boe (l.) speaks with Oglala Chief Frank Fools Crow, a nephew of Black Elk. Both Boe and Fools Crow were supporters of AIM and present at the occupation of Wounded Knee in 1973. *The Center for Western Studies.*

Boe's relationship with both AIM leaders grew and he became a confidant, which led to his presence at the Wounded Knee occupation. In a March 7, 1973, memorandum to his board and president, Boe wrote that Clyde Bellecourt invited him on March 1 to attend as an observer and possibly a mediator for the local Indians and AIM members. He said during his time there from the morning of March 2 through the evening of March 5, a number of Indians carried small guns, and the group had taken over the museum and trading post, having looted it of food, guns, and ammunition. They had also taken over two nearby houses owned by people who were held hostage for a time and by that time were free to leave but chose to stay to protect their homes. Around the local Catholic church and hillside were trenches from which the Indians exchanged gunfire with government agents at least five times. "There was, throughout, a seriousness of purpose regarding the attainment of their objectives and a stated willingness to even die to achieve them," he wrote. Boe's memo included the fact that since he helped Banks and Clyde Bellecourt incorporate the American Indian Movement, the Division of Social Service had given AIM $37,000 toward basic expenses.[60]

Boe's visit to Wounded Knee and acknowledgment of the church's financial support to AIM ignited an intense debate among church clergy and members. Though many leaders and congregants supported the effort and wrote encouraging letters, Boe received numerous personal notes among the approximately 300 letters he received that expressed disapproval from many who thought he and the American Lutheran Church had no business personally and financially supporting what they believed was a violent organization that openly defied the United States government. Many people indicated they were withholding further financial support in protest.

In asking for more information, a Rapid City pastor wrote Boe, "Some of our 'solid citizens' are uptight about their benevolence money being used to support 'those who threaten and terrorize us.'" A month later, the pastor told Boe, "I don't have to tell you that some of your brothers and sisters here are hot under the collar. This includes both pastors and lay people."[61]

A member of a Sturgis, South Dakota, congregation suggested ALC enabled the Wounded Knee occupation, and Indians already had enough financial support from the government: "I was deeply hurt to learn we had given contributions to the AIM Indians. If we church people of different churches hadn't given to them we sure wouldn't have had that militant gang here in South Dakota. Look! What are they doing to our South Dakota Indians at Wounded

Knee today? It's terrible. This looks like a good example—churches should stay within their field instead of trying to run the U.S.A."[62]

In some of his responses, Boe explained the rationale behind the church support, such as this to a Rapid City pastor: "Minority people have frequently not had opportunities for advancement in our society similar to those of other groups of people. This is especially true of Indians." Boe said support for AIM was vital in order to live out the Christian faith. "Jesus stood with the poor and outcast from society in his day. If the church is to be true to the spirit of Christ it must also stand alongside those who suffer injustice and deprivation." However, while defending the support, Boe did acknowledge reservations: "I am sure that I can say that very few persons including myself would condone some of the destructive activities Indians have used in their efforts to achieve their objectives."[63]

One letter echoed what other locals around the Pine Ridge Indian Reservation indicated, that not everyone was happy with AIM taking over Wounded Knee. "We live near the Pine Ridge and Wounded Knee areas and see Indians every day. Many are our friends and they tell us that the Oglala Sioux Tribal Council is interested in their needs and they do not need AIM meddling in their affairs."[64]

While most of the opposition came from South Dakota churches, Boe did receive numerous letters of support, mainly from other places, especially the Twin Cities: "Noted your pipe was present at Wounded Knee, no doubt a peace pipe! Anyway—just wanted to say thank you for what you are doing in this and other areas of service. Power to you," wrote the pastor of Central Lutheran Church in Minneapolis.[65] The president of the Iowa district of the American Lutheran Church in Des Moines also sent his support: "I want to compliment you for sticking your neck in this instance, taking the risk necessary to be there trying to be an arbitrator and counselor, and in offering the help you have provided. I have gotten some flak on this and I am sure you will get some more."[66]

After learning of the ALC's support for AIM, a Rapid City motel owner sent a bill to Boe for $2,252.46 for rooms and meals, $1,836.50 in damages and $15,000 in lost business in the motel and lounge, saying its leaders, among them Clyde Bellecourt, Vernon Bellecourt, Bill Means, and William War Soldier "registered under the guise of National Lutheran Board."[67] In a response to the motel owner, Boe said neither the ALC nor its congregation would pay because they were not responsible for AIM.[68]

Boe's letters included similar responses, such as this to a woman in Ronan, Montana, who wrote to inform him that she was withholding financial support:

> I am not sure you and I are reading the same Bible. If we are we must be reading different parts of it. . . . While we have a responsibility to those who are members of the Christian church it seems to me that we have an even greater responsibility to reach out with hands of love and concern for all men who are suffering. . . . Jesus usually identified himself more with the poor and the outcast than he did with the church people of his day. I believe that it is the responsibility of his church to identify with the poor and the outcast in our day as Jesus did in his.[69]

And just as Jesus faced judicial proceedings, Boe's relationship with AIM also landed him in court and nearly in jail. After the Wounded Knee standoff, Boe assumed responsibility to ensure that Clyde Bellecourt met the conditions of his release.[70] Then federal prosecutors charged Boe with contempt of court for refusing to testify about what he observed. Boe argued that as a member of the clergy, his observations and communications were protected by law and under the religious clause of the First Amendment to the U.S. Constitution. His resistance gained support from several other religious organizations, which filed friend-of-court briefs to affirm Boe's belief that he was not obligated to share privileged information that the government could gather from the hundreds of other people present during the Wounded Knee occupation. Those groups included the National Council of Churches and the United States Catholic Conference, as well as "the Lutheran Church-Missouri Synod, the Lutheran Church in America, the United Presbyterian Church in the U.S.A., the Right Rev. John E. Hines, Presiding Bishop of thc Episcopal Church; the Center for Social Action of the United Church of Christ; the Board of Church and Society of the United Methodist Church; Monsignor John Egan, executive director of the Catholic Committee on Urban Ministry; and the Department of Church and Society of the Division of Homeland Ministries of the Christian Church (Disciples of Christ)."[71]

Boe was sentenced for up to 14 months in jail but could have been set free had he answered what the prosecutors wanted to know: which AIM leaders he saw carrying guns. In January 1974, an hour before he was to turn himself in to serve his time, the Eighth Circuit U.S. Court of Appeals reversed the court order and he was set free. "I feel like I've had a cannonball lifted off my head," Boe said.[72]

Ray Robinson

One of the non-Indians to take part in Wounded Knee was a Black civil rights activist named Ray Robinson. He made the trek to South Dakota to support the Indians but never came out, and his body has not been found. His widow, Cheryl Buswell-Robinson, said multiple sources indicated he was shot in the leg and then bled to death after he refused to put down a bowl of oatmeal and immediately meet with one of AIM's leaders.[73]

Ray Robinson's participation in the civil rights movement was well documented. He was in Washington for Martin Luther King Jr.'s *I Have a Dream* speech, attended the 1964 funeral of three white civil rights workers in Mississippi, and was among those who set up the Resurrection City camp at the Washington Mall in 1968. After King's assassination that year, Robinson moved his family to Alabama and began a communal farm. Cheryl Robinson said she didn't want him to go to South Dakota because it was spring planting time and he was needed there. He went anyway.[74] In 2014 the FBI said it suspected militant AIM members were to blame, but AIM leaders denied knowledge of Robinson's death.[75] Robinson's disappearance at Wounded Knee was kept secret for years because his death would

Civil rights worker Ray Robinson left his home in Alabama to participate in the occupation of Wounded Knee but never returned. *Photo courtesy Cheryl Buswell. The Center for Western Studies.*

have hurt AIM's growing association with Blacks.[76]

Buswell-Robinson, who is white, said she was left to raise their three young children and respond to acts of racism herself, which included the Ku Klux Klan burning crosses in the yard, burning their house and engaging in a firefight. "I was left to deal with that by myself and three little kids," she said.· She eventually moved to Detroit, studied and worked in nursing, and also worked the line at a diesel plant. She continues to pursue the location of her husband's grave in the hope for closure. Her children, grandchildren, and great-grandchildren also want to know what happened to Ray Robinson. "For a long time, I never said much. It was too painful. And that was the wrong thing to do," she said. "It was wrong because it made the kids think I was keeping something from them or didn't want to talk about him." For her, AIM will be remembered for its lost opportunities. "I think it's a mixed legacy. And the missed potential. They had so much potential that they failed to realize because of their inability to deal with internal conflict like sexism, like racism. Ray died because of the racism, I do believe," she said. "Ray went out there in the spirit of solidarity and it just wasn't to be."[77]

"Too Many Pieces"

Paul DeMain, the Indian journalist who has written extensively about the American Indian Movement, said its legacy is simple: "It's good, it's bad and it's ugly. There's good stuff. There's bad stuff. And then there's murder and crime." Among the good things was the reawakening of people's Native heritage. "They helped build identity among thousands of American Indians who didn't have or felt they had lost their identity," he said. The bad included all the people wounded or killed. "The AIM situation is a puzzle with a thousand pieces. The only trouble is it has one thousand, one-hundred pieces because of the lies. There's too many pieces. There's not missing pieces."[78]

Notes

1 Peter Matthiessen, *In the Spirit of Crazy Horse* (New York: Penguin Books, 1983), 34-36.

2 American Indian Movement (AIM), https://www.aimovement.org/peltier.

3 Matthiessen, 38-40.

4 Dee Brown, *Bury My Heart at Wounded Knee* (New York: Holt Paperbacks, 1970), xxiv.

5 Ibid, xvii.

6 Ibid, xvi.

7 Matthiessen, 299.

8 Associated Press, "Funeral for fire victims Tuesday," *Reno Gazette-Journal*, February 19, 1979, 39.

9 Matthiessen, 518.

10 AIM, http://aimovement.org/ncrsm/index.html.

11 AIM, http://aimovement.org/moipr/DAPL.html.

12 Carson Walker, Associated Press, "Issues linger 30 years after shootout," *Sioux Falls Argus Leader*, June 25, 2005, 3B.

13 Joseph H. Trimbach, *American Indian Mafia: An FBI Agent's True Story About Wounded Knee, Leonard Peltier, and the American Indian Movement (AIM)* (Denver: Outskirts Press, Inc., 2009), 332.

14 Matthiessen, 456-57.

15 Ibid, 549.

16 Ibid, 157.

17 Ibid, 476.

18 "Peter Matthiessen-obituary," *The Telegraph* (London), June 24, 2014, https://www.telegraph.co.uk/news/obituaries/10923119/Peter-Matthiessen-obituary.html.

[19] Matthiessen, 110.

[20] Carson Walker, Associated Press, "Grand jury examines AIM case," *Rapid City Journal*, January 25, 2003, 1.

[21] Carson Walker, Associated Press, "One man held, second sought in Indian activist's '70s slaying," *Daily Oklahoman,* April 4, 2003, 17A.

[22] Carson Walker, Associated Press, "Trial opens in AIM activist's murder," *Sioux Falls Argus Leader*, February 4, 2004, 1B.

[23] Carson Walker, Associated Press, "Witness: Peltier admitted FBI killing," *Sioux Falls Argus Leader*, February 5, 2004, 1A.

[24] Interview with Paul DeMain, July 16, 2021.

[25] Associated Press, "Sentence reduced in 1975 South Dakota AIM slaying," *Great Falls Tribune*, September 27, 2011, 2A.

[26] Heidi Bell Gease, "Graham Guilty in Aquash Murder," *Rapid City Journal*, December 11, 2010, 1.

[27] Trimbach, 16.

[28] Interview with Denise Maloney Pictou, July 19, 2021.

[29] Trimbach, 9-10.

[30] Ibid, 422-26.

[31] Ibid, 443.

[32] Ibid, 444.

[33] Ibid, 461.

[34] Matthiessen, 59-60.

[35] Ibid, 60-61.

[36] AIM, http://www.aimovement.org/archives/index.html.

[37] Matthiessen, 52-56.

[38] Trimbach, 63-65.

[39] Matthiessen, 62-64.

[40] Paul Chaat Smith and Robert Allen Warrior, *Like a Hurricane* (New York: The New Press, 1996), 100.

[41] Matthiessen, 64-66.

[42] Ibid, 66-68.

[43] Trimbach, 73.

[44] Ibid, 86-87.

[45] Matthiessen, 80-82.

[46] Ibid, 77.

[47] Trimbach, 513.

[48] Matthiessen, 78-80.

[49] Ibid, 87-88.

[50] Trimbach, 204.

[51] Matthiessen, 97-98.

[52] Ibid, 99.

[53] Trimbach, 276-278.

[54] Ibid, 514.

[55] Carson Walker, Associated Press, "Wounded Knee still aching," *Rapid City Journal*, February 24, 2003, B1.

[56] Trimbach, 10.

[57] Associated Press, "Lutheran-Indian conference praised, blasted," *Rapid City Journal*, August 3, 1970, 2.

[58] Thomas Brettingen, Associated Press, "Indians Leave Dormitory at Augustana College," *Sioux Falls Argus Leader*, August 6, 1970, 1.

[59] Paul Boe affidavit, Paul Boe Collection, Center for Western Studies Archives, Augustana University, Sioux Falls, South Dakota, undated.

[60] Memorandum, Paul Boe Collection, March 7, 1973.

[61] Jonathan Preus letters, Paul Boe Collection, February 23, 1973, and March 23, 1973.

[62] Letter, Paul Boe Collection, March 3, 1973.

[63] Paul Boe to Pastor Burnell Lund, Paul Boe Collection, February 28, 1973.

[64] Letter from Immanuel Lutheran Church women, Rushville, Nebraska, Paul Boe Collection, March 15, 1973.

[65] Letter, Paul Boe Collection, March 13, 1973.

[66] Bruno Schlachtenhaufen letter, Paul Boe Collection, March 19, 1973.

[67] Imperial Motel bill, Paul Boe Collection, March 26, 1973.

[68] Paul Boe letter to R. Kurylas, Paul Boe Collection, March 29, 1973.

[69] Letter, Paul Boe Collection, February 23, 1973.

[70] Paul Boe letter to James Wilson, Paul Boe Collection, April 13, 1973.

[71] Staff, "Protestant and Catholic Groups Support Silence by Clergyman," *The New York Times*, January 11, 1974, 61, https://www.nytimes.com/1974/01/11/archives/protestant-and-catholic-groups-support-silence-by-a-clergyman.html.

[72] Chuck Offenburger, "'Crucifixion' Missing; Boe Wins in Case," *The Des Moines Register*, January 17, 1974, 4.

[73] Interview with Cheryl Buswell-Robinson, July 16, 2021.

[74] Carson Walker, Associated Press, "Civil rights leader lost pursuing peace," *Sioux Falls Argus Leader*, January 19, 2004, 1A.

[75] Associated Press, "FBI confirms activist was killed in SD in 1973," *The Black Hills Pioneer*, Feb. 20, 2014, 3.

[76] Trimbach, 465.

[77] Buswell-Robinson, July 16, 2021.

[78] DeMain, July 16, 2021.

13

From Deadwood to Hollywood: South Dakota on Screen

Jon D. Schaff
Northern State University

There are many ways to study a people's political culture. A typical manner is through the gathering of data. Social scientists are fond of describing people through numbers as quantification gives the impression of objectivity. So if one wants to know the culture of a particular people, one consults survey data on voting patterns, family structure, religious belief, education level, etc. Those numbers are the snapshot of a culture.

One does not wish to dismiss the utility of quantitative evidence, but when it comes to really knowing a people, as opposed to merely describing them, one must avoid the abstraction from actual human life that mere numerical data provides. If you want someone to really know a friend, you tell stories that illustrate your friend's character. Human beings are narrative creatures. If we wish to know the culture of a particular community, we might consult data, but we'd better attend closely to the stories they tell.

Today our most widely told stories are on film.[1] Whether in feature-length movies or television shows, video is contemporary America's primary narrative form. Seldom do people gather around the proverbial water cooler to discuss a "must read" book.[2] To the contrary, discussion often turns to the latest streaming television series the group is watching or what they thought of the newest Marvel super-hero movie. One does not want to make too much of popular culture; as its driving force is money rather than meaning, however, pop culture is often a window into society's hopes and anxieties.

In the video age, starting roughly a century ago, there have been instances of South Dakota on film. In some cases the story takes place outside of South Dakota, but the filmmaker wants to make use of South Dakota geography to tell the tale. The two most prominent instances of this phenomenon are the Academy Award winning film *Dances with Wolves* (1990), shot largely in South Dakota, and the Alfred Hitchcock film *North By Northwest* (1959), which famously concludes at Mount Rushmore. The climax of *National Treasure: Book of Secrets* (2007) also takes place at Mount Rushmore. Another example is the science fiction film *Starship Troopers* (1997), which made use of the stark geography of South Dakota's Badlands in the southwestern part of the state to create the illusion of an alien world.

Then there are films that are actually set in South Dakota. With some exceptions, films about South Dakota tend to center around Native American themes (of course *Dances with Wolves* also centers around this theme, but does not take place in South Dakota). These films include the major studio release *Thunderheart* (1992), as well as independent films such as those of the contemporary filmmaker Chloé Zhao, whose first two films, *Songs My Brother Taught Me* (2015) and *The Rider* (2017) both take place and were shot on Pine Ridge Reservation, near the Badlands. Zhao's breakthrough film, the Academy Award winning film *Nomadland* (2020), also contains various scenes shot and set in South Dakota, once again near the Badlands region, but does not consider Native themes. There is also the HBO film *Bury My Heart at Wounded Knee* (2007), based on the famous book by Dee Brown that tells the history of the "Indian Wars" of the late nineteenth century, with both film and book culminating in the massacre of Natives by United States cavalry at Wounded Knee, South Dakota, in December 1890. Also of note here is the major studio film *Hidalgo* (2004), which begins in South Dakota, indeed with the Wounded Knee massacre, and whose main character is part Lakota. While the film largely takes place in North

Africa, these South Dakota ties are important to the film's themes. It should be noted that three of these films, *Thunderheart*, *Hidalgo*, and naturally *Bury My Heart at Wounded Knee*, either depict or feature the Wounded Knee event as part of the plot.

The Badlands in western South Dakota provide a backdrop for directors who seek an "otherworldly" setting for their films. *The Center for Western Studies.*

There are a number of films that tell a South Dakota story without Native themes. While not devoid of Native characters and plot points, *The Revenant* (2015), with an Academy winning performance by Leonardo DiCaprio, tells the story of the historical figure Hugh Glass, who was mauled by a bear and left for dead just south of present-day Lemmon, South Dakota. In an entirely different vein is the 1968 Disney film *The One and Only, Genuine, Original Family Band.* This film presents the tale of the Bower Family Band who help settle Dakota Territory. The independent film *Tater Tot and Patton* (2017) is notable for a number of reasons. First, it is the only film discussed in this essay made by an actual South Dakotan, the filmmaker Andrew Kightlinger who hails from Pierre, South Dakota.[3] The film is also noteworthy for ignoring the physically iconographic areas of South Dakota, the Badlands and Black Hills, as the film was shot just outside of Pierre, almost exactly in the center of the state. Like Zhao, Kightlinger's film eschews grand narratives, telling a more modest, character-driven story.

There are also a couple instances of television shows being set—but not shot—in South Dakota.[4] One such show is the recent science fiction series *Warehouse 13* (2009-2014). However, while the titular warehouse actually resides in South Dakota the characters in the show, field agents who hunt down artifacts with supernatural powers, are typically in action somewhere else. In contrast, a true South Dakota television series is the critically acclaimed HBO series *Deadwood* (2004-2006, 2019). Made up of three seasons and a feature-length film to wrap up the show, *Deadwood* is a fictionalized version of the early days of the mining camp of Deadwood in the northern Black Hills. The film uses the founding of Deadwood to explore the Machiavellian notion that all regimes are founded in injustice and violence. To this end *Deadwood* touches upon historical circumstances surrounding the founding of actual Deadwood.

The list of films and television shows is not meant to be exhaustive. There are other films either shot or set in South Dakota. *Return of a Man Called Horse* (1976), *Pow Wow Highway* (1989), *Into the Wild* (2007), Terrance Malick's first film *Badlands* (1973), even the old Doris Day film *Calamity Jane* (1953) touch upon South Dakota either in setting or plot. One should also mention the African American silent film director Oscar Micheaux. Micheaux homesteaded for a while in South Dakota, and his first film, *The Homesteader* (1919), is based on his experience. Sadly, there is no existing copy of *The Homesteader*. This discussion will be limited to films that hit most directly upon the themes one sees across South Dakota related films. While the plot of *Dances with Wolves* does not take the viewer to South Dakota, it was shot almost entirely in the state and does consider the state's predominant Native population, the Lakota Sioux. We'll also consider other films with Native themes: *Thunderheart*, the first two films of Chloé Zhao, and *Bury My Heart at Wounded*

Knee. We'll then turn to non-Native themed films that take place largely in South Dakota, including *The Revenant*, *The One and Only, Genuine, Original Family Band,* and *Tater Tot and Patton*. Finally, we'll consider the one television show with major South Dakota themes, *Deadwood*. In each case we will consider the films in their own right, but also how they use South Dakota to advance the themes of the individual narratives.

Native Themes in South Dakota Film

It is not surprising that Native themes should loom large when the film community turns its eyes to South Dakota. The state is home to nine reservations, the most of any state, including Pine Ridge Reservation, which as one of the nation's poorest regions sadly serves as a poster child for Native poverty and failures of America toward Native peoples. This is heightened by the fact that the Lakota people, who populate most of the reservations in the state, are prominent in the tale of Native peoples in America. Bands of Lakota who were trying to maintain a traditional way of life, especially those led by the legendary Sitting Bull, were among the last to move to a reservation. Add to this the duplicitous nature of the government's dealings with the Lakota and there is much here with which to form a compelling narrative. The films we will consider here either depict or harken back to the ultimate defeat of the Lakota by the United States government or emphasize the plight of the Native in modern America.

While the classic Western typically depicted Native peoples in a negative light, this has changed in more modern stories. Starting roughly with the rise of a discernable American Indian political activism in the 1960s and 1970s, film began to portray Natives in a largely positive light with the United States military more likely portrayed as villains rather than heroes. The 1990 film *Dances with Wolves* is indicative of this tendency in the portrayal of Native people in American film.[5]

South Dakota is typically divided into what locals call East River and West River, river here meaning the Missouri River that roughly bisects the state.[6] East River South Dakota is generally flatter and has richer soil with which to engage in crop farming. West River is geographically more rolling grassland hills and buttes, also including the rocky outcroppings of the Badlands and the Black Hills. Notably, the Black Hills represents the only region of the state that is substantially forested. Typically in South Dakota tree belts are unnatural, planted by farmers to shelter their fields from the driving prairie winds. Films shot in South Dakota are almost exclusively shot near the Missouri River or places west, as this is where there is undulation in the terrain that most people find more visually interesting. *Dances with Wolves* is no exception, shot near the state capital of Pierre, which is on the Missouri River, and parts west.

Dances with Wolves is a Civil War era film. The main character, Union Lieutenant Dunbar, played by Kevin Costner, fighting in the war, makes a literal suicidal dash on horseback toward Confederate lines. While he miraculously survives, his antics distract the enemy, leading to a Union victory in battle. Dunbar is wrongly considered a hero. Given his choice of assignments due to his "heroism," Dunbar declares he wants to go West. "I always wanted to see the frontier. Before it's gone," he says. He is seeking the romance of the West.

One thing the film gets right is that during the war and even afterwards, the Western military was largely filled with officers who had failed elsewhere and with troops of dubious quality, usually quite green. During the war, naturally the best troops were in the East fighting the war. After the war the military was divided between enforcing Reconstruction in the South and fighting Indian Wars in the West. With Reconstruction taking precedence, the West did not exactly get the cream of the military crop.[7] This is depicted in the film in the obviously demented officer who directs Dunbar at this first outpost and an almost caricatured sadism of many members of the military. The relatively passive Dunbar is the exception.

Rather than the heroic cowboy tale of the traditional Western, *Dances with Wolves* is a story of a white man slowly coming to identify with his Lakota neighbors, eventually seeing their ways as superior to those of his own civilization. Mistakenly left alone at his small dilapidated outpost, Dunbar hesitantly befriends the Lakota who live near the fort. An early distrust on each side evolves into friendship. Seeking some sort of companionship on the wide-open plains, Dunbar more and more integrates himself into the Lakota community, eventually marrying a white woman, Stands with Fist, who was raised by the tribe from a young age after her family was slaughtered by the rival Pawnee tribe.[8] In the film, Dunbar lends aid to the Lakota both in fighting the Pawnee and hunting buffalo. His befriending of a local wolf leads the Lakota to give him his own Indian moniker, "Dances with Wolves."

When military support finally arrives at Dunbar's small fort, they find him largely assimilated into Lakota culture and, Dunbar having taken to living with the tribe, they determine he's abandoned his post. Captured by his former military comrades, Dunbar is abused and taken prisoner. The cruelty of the soldiers is exemplified in their killing of Dunbar's beloved horse, Cisco, and the wolf Dunbar has befriended. Rescued by his new Lakota brethren, Dunbar leaves to live his life as a Native.

Although the actual events of the film take place near the confluence of Kansas, Colorado, and Nebraska (the film doesn't provide a precise location for most of the film's action), it is western South Dakota's rolling grassy prairie that gives the film its visual power. This is especially true early in the film where Dunbar's isolation is a key plot point. The vast, open prairie, seldom even broken by a tree, allows for this visual impression of remoteness. In addition, the story centers around interactions between the American military and the Lakota people, a story with deep South Dakota antecedents as South Dakota is where a majority of Lakota now reside. In fact, much of the dialogue in the film is in Lakota.[9]

Themes of Native identity undergird the story of *Thunderheart*.[10] This film tells the story of Ray Levoi, an FBI agent of partial Sioux descent, who is sent by the FBI to help investigate a murder on Pine Ridge Reservation. The film makes obvious references to battles between the FBI and the American Indian Movement (AIM) in the 1970s. In the film it is the Aboriginal Rights Movement (ARM) that exists as a militant expression of Native discontent, much as AIM did in the 1970s. The film also alludes to actual conflicts between AIM activists and tribal leader Dick Wilson and Wilson's use of a private security group that called themselves the Guardians of the Oglala Nation (GOONs). This was a conflict, in part, between AIM as the voice of traditionalism and Wilson and others who preached modernization. Wilson was accused of misdeeds as chairman of the reservation.[11] In *Thunderheart*, this role is performed by the character Jack Milton, a corrupt tribal leader with his own band of enforcers. A suspicious murder brings Levoi to Pine Ridge, partnered with the cynical Frank "Cooch" Coutelle.

The film opens with a depiction of native dancers fading away to the Badlands and then cuts to the instigating murder. There is then a quick cut to Levoi in Washington, D.C., in a car with Bruce Springsteen's "Badlands" playing on the radio. He gets his orders to go to South Dakota from an FBI official named William Dawes, clearly referencing the nineteenth-century Senator Henry Dawes who sponsored the 1887 legislation commonly called the Dawes Act. The Dawes Act encouraged private land ownership by Natives on reservation and had as its goal the assimilation of Native peoples into the larger economy and society. Levoi is informed by the film's Dawes that his job is to persuade Natives to get over their illusions of the past. He's assured, "No one's gonna ask you to weave any baskets or make it rain."

Upon arrival in South Dakota, Levoi sees the poverty of Pine Ridge, described as "the third world right here in America." While the Native used to own all this land right up to Canada, it is explained, reservation land is all they are left with. Cooch prods Levoi to make necessary relationships with the Pine Ridge residents to solve the case. "They're your own people," says Cooch. "These are *not* my people," insists Levoi.

Initial skepticism by Levoi slowly begins to break down through experience. Levoi witnesses the poverty and violence of Pine Ridge, well depicted in the film, along with vulgar racial epithets slung at the Natives by white citizens. Under the guidance of tribal policeman Walter Crow Horse and Pine Ridge activist Maggie Eagle Bear, Levoi begins to question his assumptions. Various interactions with tribal elder Grandpa Sam Reaches unsettle Levoi who begins to have visions and is introduced to various tribal traditions. Crow Horse tells Levoi that at one point he didn't want to be Indian either, the government boarding school making sure of that. These are a "proud people but a conquered people," says Crow Horse. "Their future is dictated by the nation that conquered them." Levoi's visions draw him to his native ancestry, including having visions of the massacre at Wounded Knee. Initially assuming that the problems on reservation, including the murder he's investigating, are the work of ARM, Levoi starts to see that it is Jack Milton and his goons that are behind much of the violence, ultimately with the corrupt cooperation of Cooch. A final standoff occurs in the Badlands with the ARM militants coming to Crow Horse's and Levoi's rescue from Cooch and Milton's gang.

In some ways *Thunderheart* is the quintessential South Dakota film. It is shot on location and uses the Badlands to show some of the most stark and beautiful geography in the state. In addition, the film tackles familiar Native themes. While set in the modern day, through Levoi's visions and his education by Crow Heart and others, the film directly references the past by invoking Wounded Knee, the attempts to stifle Native culture through educational institutions, and, by invoking the Dawes name, attempts to get Natives to assimilate. Levoi at first resists his Native heritage, but upon experience and reflection, he learns to embrace that heritage. By film's end Levoi has left the FBI, disgusted by yet another example of the federal government mistreating Native peoples. Where he goes from there is anyone's guess, but it doesn't take much imagination to conclude that Levoi will be living out his Native heritage in some significant way. South Dakota has changed Levoi.

Another film with Native themes is the HBO film *Bury My Heart at Wounded Knee*, borrowing its title and its overall themes from the book of that title by Dee Brown.[12] Brown's book made an immediate mark upon its release in 1970 for telling the history of the Indian

Wars from the Native perspective. While some have argued that this univocal take on that part of American history subtracts from the book's accuracy, its influence cannot be denied.[13]

Historically, the Wounded Knee massacre stems from attempts to bring a band of Miniconjou Sioux under the Chief Spotted Elk to the Pine Ridge agency in late December 1890. Tensions were already high as earlier that month Sitting Bull had been killed under disputed circumstances while being arrested on Standing Rock Reservation. While there is some confusion about the actual instigation of the Wounded Knee event, what is clear is that the military was under orders to disarm the Sioux. They did not immediately do this, and the retinue of Natives and cavalry, coincidently Custer's former Seventh Cavalry, camped near Wounded Knee Creek on December 28, 1890. The next morning the military renewed its effort to gather up all firearms from the Natives, who were reluctant to hand them over. One might dispute the wisdom or even justice of the order, thus the desultory manner in which Natives complied is understandable. Soldiers became more aggressive, searching individual teepees for weapons. It seems likely that some small number of Natives began a Ghost Dance, a dance associated with an emerging spiritual movement among Natives that prophesized a time when whites would be defeated and Natives would return to former glory. This dance had been interpreted by many whites as a call for renewed warfare against white settlers. The commencement of the dance only raised tensions. At some point a soldier tried to wrestle a rifle away from a Miniconjou man. There is evidence that the man was deaf and did not understand the orders. Whatever the case, the gun went off. This set off a flurry of panicked, close-range gunfire from both sides. What could conceivably have remained as a small, albeit tragic, battle quickly, however, became a massacre. As Natives attempted to run away from the scene, including women and children, cavalry soldiers opened fire, using the four Hotchkiss guns with which they had encircled the camp the previous day. In the end, 250 Natives were killed and left to freeze in the blustery winter conditions. One of those killed early in the melee was Spotted Elk, whose frozen body was captured in an infamous photograph. Thus does a tragic misunderstanding regarding an accidently fired weapon become a legendary catastrophe.[14]

The film can be said more to follow the book's ethos rather than its narrative. While Brown tells the story of the Indian Wars in various parts of the country, the film focuses on the battle between the government and the Sioux, with Sitting Bull, playing a prominent role. The film features a young Native, Beach, who as a young boy is sent to an Indian school, encouraged to take a Christian name, and have his hair cut short. Sent East, this child takes the name Charles Eastman, goes to college, and becomes a doctor. This is done under the patronage of the aforementioned Senator Henry Dawes. Dawes sees Charles as a model for what the Native can become: educated, Christian, assimilated.

The film often consists less of conversational dialogue than speeches from characters. There is a distinct lack of nuance, with military personnel consistently leering and cynical, white teachers condescending, and the Sioux not a strong warrior people in persistent conflict with Pawnee, Crow, and other tribes, but a quaint, passive people. As such the film is more a political harangue than an attempt to give an accurate depiction of the Indian wars. Still, the film takes the viewer through central events in this time period regarding relations between Natives and governments. It shows attempts to use boarding schools to limit the passing on of Native traditions, efforts by the government to cut deals trading land, money, and goods in exchange for railroad access to the Black Hills. On this matter, early in the film Dawes is portrayed relatively positively as someone who seeks to protect Natives against the violent predilections of the military. However, as the story unfolds, Dawes becomes increasingly condescending and paternalistic. He becomes angry with Charles when Charles starts taking the Native side in land disputes. Dawes thinks Charles is the model Indian, namely one who is assimilated. He feels betrayed by Charles. Charles, on the other hand, comes to regret going East as a child and getting educated. As the Ghost Dance arises on the reservation, Charles is at first skeptical, but becomes more and more conflicted. Finally, the events of the Wounded Knee massacre bring scores of wounded to Charles's clinic. He breaks with Dawes and comes to identify more closely with his Native roots.

Perhaps the most complex character in the film is Sitting Bull. A fierce defender of his peoples' ways, after coming back from Canada to America and reservation, he is disappointed in the ways reservation life has emasculated his people. Hunting for food is reduced to shooting a cow in a pen. People wear conventional American clothes. Some Natives become enforcers for the government, including those who ultimately kill Sitting Bull while trying to arrest him. But Sitting Bull also sells out. While not shown in the film, it is discussed how Sitting Bull periodically joins Bill Cody's western show to make money by play-acting. He sells his autograph for money. He has bought into the celebrity of being Sitting Bull. If it is true that a traditional life of hunting and gathering is no longer viable, what is there for the Native to do other than take up white ways? For Sitting Bull, it is his celebrity status that allows him to reject the accommodations to white life that others feel forced to make for survival.

Each film discussed so far has in some way dealt with Indian identity. Dunbar, Levoi, and Charles Eastman all find themselves caught between white and Native worlds, uncertain of where they belong. It is notable that all three of them chose Native life in the end. The Native seems to be in a different position than other minority groups in America, or even immigrant groups who typically begin poor and underprivileged. In those cases there is usually a desire to become successful like Charles Eastman. What immigrant or minority would not be overjoyed that their son became an Ivy League educated doctor? Here we might think of Frederick Douglass's famous address of 1847 where he asks, "What country have I?"[15] This is his query: can the slave or former slave really call the United States his country? Over the course of Douglass's career he ultimately answers that question, "Yes," even if it can only be as a step-child.[16] The promise of America's founding, that all are created equal and a regime dedicated to the principle of natural rights, however poorly the country lives up to these ideals, is worth the Black man's patriotism. This is a question these films also ask. Given the way of life of the Native people, especially for the Lakota, and the history of violence and duplicity coming from the U.S. government, ultimately, what country have they? Can they live in the broader society and assimilate into American economic, educational, and social life while remaining Native? The answer of all three films seems to be, "No."[17]

Contrast this with the first two films from the remarkable young filmmaker Chloé Zhao. Zhao was well-known as an independent filmmaker, but broke through in 2020 with the Academy Award winning *Nomadland.* Here we will focus on her first two films, *Songs My Brothers Taught Me* and *The Rider*. These films are extraordinary for a number of reasons. First, they are shot almost entirely on Pine Ridge Reservation. But what is more, Zhao cast the films with locals, most of whom had little to no acting experience. The characters' first names are usually those of the actors. This gives Zhao's films a feeling of verisimilitude. Zhao is clearly drawn to the people of Pine Ridge and South Dakota in general, since each of her three films has been filmed in part or in whole in the state. While her films do show some of South Dakota's natural beauty, the land is somewhat incidental to her films. Her stories tend to be close character studies where the focus literally and figuratively is on the people.

Of the two films considered here, *Songs My Brother Taught Me* is more specifically a Native-themed film.[18] The film commences with a scene of breaking (i.e., taming) horses. A character says, "Anything that runs wild got something bad in them; you wanna leave some of that in there because they need that to survive out here." That sets up the theme for the film, namely how much badness, or to put it in terms the film ultimately develops, toughness it takes to live on reservation.

The main character, Johnny, wishes to leave reservation to live in Los Angeles with his girlfriend, who is moving there for college. Johnny makes his money by driving across the state line to Nebraska to buy alcohol, which he then sells illegally on reservation. Here Zhao witnesses to the problem of alcoholism on reservation. Meanwhile, at school one of Johnny's teachers asks the students what they want to do when they leave school. Almost to a person they want to ranch or be involved in rodeo. Their life options seem quite limited.

Johnny has a brother in prison. He urges Johnny, "Just get off this rez." As Johnny continues his illegal alcohol bootlegging, he and his friends debate whether the reservation should legalize alcohol. Won't it bring jobs and money onto the reservation? But it will also harm children and cripple families, others claim. But that happens already is the retort. There seems to be no good choice.

Meanwhile Johnny's sister, Jashaun, has decided to help Travis, an artist recently released from prison. He sells artwork and clothes. Her proficiency in math and record keeping help him run his business efficiently. Travis relates to her a belief that the seventh generation after Wounded Knee will represent renewal of the Native people. This is young Jashaun's generation.

Johnny remains committed to going out to California, although he withholds this decision from Jashaun, knowing how it will hurt her for him to leave. Johnny faces opposition to his plans when his girlfriend's family openly questions how he will make a living in Los Angeles with no job and no place to live. Meanwhile, Johnny's illegal activity gets him in trouble as rivals start to harass him, ultimately burning his car. In the end, Johnny walks to his girlfriend's home for her high school graduation party. As he approaches the driveway he stops, ponders, turns around and heads back. He will not leave. Instead he takes the advice of one of his half-brothers and gets a job at an auto-shop, looking to make his living on reservation.

Songs My Brothers Taught Me engages many of the issues that face contemporary life on reservation: alcohol, crime, prison, family break-up, and suicide. It also movingly considers the choices the young Native has to make about getting off reservation to leave these pathologies behind or remaining on reservation to remain closer to one's roots.

The cast of *The Rider*, like *Songs My Brothers Taught Me*, is made of Natives from Pine Ridge and takes place on reservation.[19] The Native angle, however, is largely incidental to the film. The film tells the story of Brady Blackburn, which mirrors that of the man who plays him, Brady Jandreau. Brady, real and fictional, had a promising rodeo career cut short by an accident in competition causing a serious brain injury. This is Brady Blackburn's problem. His brain injury makes it impossible for him to ride a horse. This is difficult for a young man whose dream is to ride rodeo and train horses. Brady chafes at the limitations placed on him, noting that when a horse gets injured and can no longer perform it's euthanized. Brady takes a job at a local supermarket to get money for his family, his father and sister (played by Brady Jandreau's father and sister). Brady attempts to ride, but his brain injury causes serious side-effects. The doctors tell Brady that if he rides anymore he may die. Brady still goes to a rodeo preparing to do the one thing he feels he is meant to do. But seeing his father and sister at the rodeo, Brady decides not to ride, clearly choosing his health over his dream.

The Rider is an outlier among the films featuring Native stories. As stated above, while the film takes place and was filmed in South Dakota, it is really a personal story about a young man overcoming serious injury, facing life-changing choices. As Pekka Hämäläinen notes, "The Lakotas have become the embodiment of the horse-mounted Plains Indians. . . . The mobile, horse-powered hunting way of life in the grasslands was a late development, a culmination of long history that has largely gone unnoticed."[20] It is Brady's attachment to this horse culture that most closely ties the film to Native themes. We saw in *Songs My Brothers Taught Me* that the high school students dreamed of ranching and rodeo, the same dreams Brady has. What will he do when those dreams do not come true?

A Bear, a Band, and a Tater Tot

It is clear that the history of Native Americans in South Dakota has provided fruitful ground for filmmakers. Still, there are other stories, either based in history or fully fictional, that have come out of the state: *The Revenant*, *The One and Only, Genuine, Original Family Band*, and *Tater Tot and Patton*.

The Revenant is the story of the historical figure of frontiersman Hugh Glass.[21] Glass was mauled by a bear in northwestern South Dakota while part of a trapping operation in 1823. The Natives that populate *The Revenant* are Arikara and Pawnee, not any branch of the Sioux. The presence of Native people in the story is not entirely secondary, still, the focus of the story is on the travails of Glass. After Glass's mauling, his companions carry him some distance, but Glass slows them down. Certain he is going to die, they leave him for dead. Glass instead crawled his way to Fort Kiowa, roughly 200 miles from where he was left.

The story of mountain man Hugh Glass is told most famously by Frederick Manfred in his novel *Lord Grizzly*, thought to be the unacknowledged inspiration for the 1971 film *Man in the Wilderness*, starring Richard Harris as Zachary Bass, a Hugh Glass-like character. *Cover art courtesy McGraw-Hill, New York, 1954. The Center for Western Studies.*

The film was not shot in South Dakota, and it shows. Filmed mostly in Canada and Argentina, the scenes are of thick forests, with rapidly flowing rivers surrounded by mountain peaks. The vegetation is a lush green from the obvious plentitude of precipitation.

Anyone familiar with South Dakota will see the problem with this setting. Outside of the Black Hills and the Badlands, South Dakota is a prairie where being a tree means living a lonely life. This is particularly true of the area in which Glass's mauling actually occurred, where rain is sparse. Also, the ironically named Grand River, near the spot of Glass' mauling, is anything but the grand river shown in the film. In short, the actual spot where Glass was attacked looks nothing like it does in the film.

So despite its connection to South Dakota lore, *The Revenant* does little to signify anything Dakota. While the film portrays a figure of South Dakota legend, Hugh Glass, the film takes historical liberties with Glass's story to add to character conflict. Only the broad outlines of the true story are retained.

Another South Dakota story is the Disney musical *The One and Only, Genuine, Original Family Band.*[22] This story depicts the drama of the 1888 presidential contest between Grover Cleveland and Benjamin Harrison. This film proves that, yes, one can write a catchy tune about Grover Cleveland, "Let's Put It Over With Grover." In the film a young John Carder, played by John Davidson, is trying to recruit Republicans to move to Dakota Territory. The idea is that Dakota is about to become a state (actually two states as it turned out), and the Republicans want control. To this end Carder calls a town meeting where he sings the song "Dakota" extolling the virtues of Dakota Territory. The song claims that Dakota is a place "where a man stands tall" and "where there's land for all." It announces that "rolling rivers embrace the plain," which in reality is a bit of an exaggeration. The song closes by referencing the "Black Hills, the blue skies of the shining West." Dakota, concludes the song, is "by the heavens blest."

The song achieves its goal by convincing the Bower family, the titular family band, to move to Rapid City. From there the story takes a turn, mostly dealing with the romance between Carder and the oldest Bower daughter, Alice, and following the high jinks of the family grandfather, played by Walter Brennen. The film becomes less of a Dakota story and more of a typical musical comedy. One thing the film gets right is that Dakota Territory was interested in the 1888 election as Harrison was the pro-statehood candidate with Cleveland in opposition. Harrison won that closely fought election and in 1889 both North and South Dakota entered the Union as states. Also, since its inception, South Dakota has been a Republican state, seldom deviating from the Republican roots depicted in the film.[23]

In a very different vein is the fine independent film *Tater Tot and Patton*, a film written and directed by South Dakota native Andrew Kightlinger.[24] This family drama concerns a young woman, Andie, who, rather than go into drug rehab in her hometown of Los Angeles, takes her mother's suggestion to spend the summer in South Dakota with the mother's sister. When Andie, whose nickname as a child was Tater Tot, arrives in Pierre she is met by her uncle, Erwin. It turns out that her aunt is sick with cancer and is living in Rochester, Minnesota, while getting treatment at the Mayo Clinic. Thus Andie's summer will be spent alone with the mercurial Erwin.

What Zhao's films do for Pine Ridge Kightlinger does for the lives of the typical South Dakotan living off reservation. Erwin lives on a ranch. A good part of his day is spent "riding the line," making sure fence is still up and cattle are contained. Fixing barbed wire is a daily chore. Erwin also lives in a remote area. Like many South Dakotans, Erwin's closest neighbor is likely miles away. Also, Andie's first reaction to South Dakota is sound: "It's kinda flat." And she's not even in the flattest part of South Dakota. Kightlinger is unusual in eschewing what most people think of as the grandeur of South Dakota for showing life in a remote, rural area, in the grasslands, with no mountains or trees to be seen. As in most places in South Dakota, the skyline in *Tater Tot and Patton* is broken by neither trees nor mountains but by haystacks. Kightlinger uses this geography to his advantage. The main theme of the film is two lonely people who happen to be thrown together learning to overcome their respective demons. The barrenness of the land helps highlight the isolation each character feels. Kightlinger succeeds in telling a compelling South Dakota story without using South Dakota iconography of the Black Hills, Badlands, or cowboys and natives.

Deadwood

The movies discussed here have actually had little to do with the most photogenic part of South Dakota, the Black Hills. We've made reference to the use of Mount Rushmore in both *North by Northwest* and *National Treasure 2*. But no films in this essay have been set primarily in the Black Hills. The television show *Deadwood* is unique in this respect, as well as being the only television series to date set primarily in South Dakota (historically, Dakota Territory). *Deadwood* ran for three seasons on HBO, from 2004 to 2006. The first two seasons are generally considered some of the best television ever made. The third season is more uneven. At the conclusion of season three the show's creator, David Milch, unexpectedly shut down production to focus on other projects, leaving many storylines unresolved. Then in 2019 Milch got the band back together and released a *Deadwood* movie on HBO that brought the story to resolution.

The rough-and-tumble mining town of Deadwood, in the Black Hills, was the "setting" for the popular television series *Deadwood* (2004-6), starring Timothy Olyphant as Seth Bullock and Ian McShane as Al Swearengen. *The Center for Western Studies.*

While the show takes place in Deadwood, South Dakota, it was shot on location in California. The setting does, however, bear remarkable resemblance to that of actual Deadwood. The show also features many characters who had historic connections to Deadwood. The most famous of these are Bill Hickok and Jane Cannary, aka Calamity Jane. But other characters are also based on real Deadwood residents, such as Seth Bullock, Sol Star, Al Swearengen, and Preacher Smith, albeit with liberties taken for dramatic effect.

What *Deadwood* accomplishes is placing a compelling story of a political founding amidst the Black Hills of South Dakota. In this case the historical circumstances of the founding of Deadwood are useful for the show's themes. Deadwood was a mining camp, rising in 1876 from the Black Hills gold rush. This was problematic since by treaty whites were forbidden from going into the Hills. The military made some efforts to keep prospectors out of the Hills, but with little success. So while whites were settling the Hills, their claims were of questionable legality. The military at one point dispersed the prospectors, but instructed them to mark their claims for the eventuality that nearly everyone saw coming, the abrogation of the Natives' treaty rights to the land.[25]

As the series starts, the legal position of Deadwood is uncertain. Moreover, the series begins in July 1876, shortly after the Battle of Little Bighorn. Hatred of Natives is at its height and there is the sense that whites need to organize for their own political and physical protection. Enter the series' most compelling character, Al Swearengen, owner of the Gem Saloon. Swearengen is a violent, foul, ruthless man, more than willing to kill to get his way. But he is also very clever, which we might call cunning given the uses to which he puts his intelligence. Swearengen is aware that the camp needs to create political order if it wants to be seen as legitimate. Central to the first two seasons of the show are Swearengen's manipulation of events to impress (and bribe) territorial leaders into advocating for Deadwood's legitimacy. Thus, for example, Swearengen is instrumental in creating a town council, getting a mayor appointed (albeit as a figurehead), and ultimately Bullock appointed as sheriff.

The relationship between Swearengen and Bullock is at the center of Deadwood's main themes. Bullock is a man of strong ideals who wants to do the right thing. He is the typical Western hero in that he wants to use violence to promote order and justice. Swearengen, though, is a schemer, a criminal, who has a much darker view of human nature. From the show's perspective, Swearengen sees things that Bullock doesn't and is willing to do things Bullock is not. As with a Machiavellian prince, Swearengen sees that the act of founding requires getting one's hands dirty. There must be bribery, duplicity, even killing if a political regime is to be founded successfully. Swearengen does the brutal but necessary things behind the scenes while the idealistic Bullock provides a public front of legitimacy. The two want the same ends, the success of Deadwood, for different reasons: Bullock for the good of his family and progress, Swearengen for his own profit.

These themes underlie a variety of literature and films. In that sense there is no particular need to set this story in Deadwood. But the historical roots of Deadwood are useful for such weighty themes. The precariousness of the settler's claims and the remoteness of Deadwood from civilization and thus law lend themselves to telling a founding story. In the typical Western film (think of classics such as *My Darling Clementine*, *Shane*, or *The Man Who Shot Liberty Valance*), there are small farmers or town people who want to bring civilization to a wild land. There is a villain, typically a violent large land owner, who opposes them. There is a hero, who from his own moral code chooses to protect civilization and the rule of law, usually with violence. *Deadwood* is not dissimilar except that it splits the hero role into the traditional hero, Bullock, and an antihero, Swearengen. If Deadwood is victorious against its enemies, that victory will not be pure and noble as in the traditional Western.

Conclusion

South Dakota is not Los Angeles, New York, or Chicago. There will never be as many films set in South Dakota as in these major cities. When South Dakota is a setting for a film it is usually a Western, very broadly defined. Almost all the films discussed have some kind of Western or Native American theme. These stories, especially traditional Westerns, are not as popular as they once were, so South

Dakota will never be a movie-making mecca. But we can see certain themes arise from the films considered.

First, filmmakers are interested in the Native American stories that arise from the South Dakota narrative. Whether historical or contemporary, the Native American story is a compelling one to many Americans. This makes sense narratively. Native history contains strong elements of both tragedy and triumph. In short, the Native story is a dramatic story. The great Lakota culture, the mistreatment of the Lakota by the government, and the persistence of the Lakota people into the twenty-first century represent various narratives that deserve telling.

South Dakota also has unique geography. Most films actually shot in South Dakota focus on the southwestern part of the state, where the Badlands and Black Hills are located. There is a reason thousands of tourists come every year to see this part of South Dakota. It is breathtaking. While for many the prairie is an acquired taste, almost everyone is moved by the beauty of the stark rock formations of the Badlands and lustrous splendor of the Black Hills. Add in Mount Rushmore, and one can see why filmmakers are drawn to these visually compelling places. For these reasons, filmmakers will return for the stories and natural beauty of South Dakota.

Notes

1 Of course, few films are shot on actual film anymore, but I use that nomenclature nonetheless.

2 See Joseph Bottom, *The Decline of the Novel*. (South Bend, IN: St. Augustine's Press, 2019).

3 Kightlinger also shot his post-apocalyptic film *Dust of War* (2013) in South Dakota, but I will not discuss this film in this essay.

4 Oddly, this does not include the iconic Dakota story, namely the *Little House* books of Laura Ingalls Wilder. The plurality of the action in that book series takes place near DeSmet, South Dakota, but when filmed for television the story is set in Minnesota.

5 *Dances With Wolves*, directed by Kevin Costner (Orion Pictures, 1990).

6 The river also follows roughly the geographically significant 100th° meridian. See Harry F. Thompson, ed., *A New South Dakota History*, 2d ed. (Sioux Falls: Center for Western Studies, 2009), 26-29; see also Jon K. Lauck,

ed., *The Interior Borderlands: Regional Identity in the Midwest and Great Plains* (Sioux Falls: Center for Western Studies, 2019).

[7] See Peter Cozzens, *The Earth is Weeping: The Epic Story of the Indian Wars for the American West* (New York: Alfred A. Knopf, 2016), 47-60.

[8] Here the film deviates from the historic record. While it is not impossible that a particular Lakota band could be harassed by Pawnee, in fact Lakota aggression toward the Pawnee was far more typical. See Cozzens, 8, 63, 196 and Pekka Hämäläinen*, Lakota America: A New History of Indigenous Power* (New Haven: Yale University Press, 2019), 188, 239.

[9] "Indian people value their languages for many other reasons as well. They are cornerstones of identity, and their use keeps us recognizable to our ancestors. They are defining features of nationhood. The retention of tribal languages tells the world that we have not been assimilated, in spite of five hundred years of concerted effort to achieve that." Anton Treuer, *Everything You Wanted to Know About Indians But Were Afraid to Ask* (St. Paul, MN: Borealis Books. 2012), 81.

[10] *Thunderheart*, directed by Michael Apted (Tristar Pictures, 1992).

[11] For a brief overview of AIM and the conflicts with the FBI, see David Treuer, *The Heartbeat of Wounded Knee: Native America from 1890 to the Present* (New York: Riverhead Books, 2019), 296-330.

[12] Dee Brown, *Bury My Heart at Wounded Knee: An Indian History of the American West* (New York: Henry Holt and Company, 1970); *Bury My Heart at Wounded Knee*, directed by Yves Simoneau (HBO Film, 2007).

[13] Peter Cozzens says explicitly that he wrote *The Earth is Weeping* in part to correct what he perceives as Brown's scholarly error, namely not researching the subject of the Indian Wars from various perspectives, 8.

[14] For various retellings of the history of the Wounded Knee massacre, see Cozzens, 442-61, Hämäläinen, 378-79, and Brown, 439-45.

[15] Frederick Douglass, "Country, Conscience, and the Anti-Slavery Cause." Yale MacMillan Center: Gilder Lehrman Center for the Study of Slavery, Resistance, and Abolition, accessed June 19, 2021, https://glc.yale.edu/country-conscience-and-anti-slavery-cause.

[16] Frederick Douglass, "Oration in Memory of Abraham Lincoln." Teaching American History, accessed June 19, 2021, https://teachingamericanhistory.org/library/document/oration-in-memory-of-abraham-lincoln/.

[17] While space considerations preclude a discussion of the film *Hidalgo*, that film's main character faces the exact same dilemma as Eastman and Levoi and makes the same choice, to embrace his Native heritage.

[18] *Songs My Brothers Taught Me*, directed by Chloé Zhao (Fortissimo Films, 2015).

[19] *The Rider*, directed by Chloé Zhao (Sony Classic Films, 2017).

[20] Hämäläinen, 4.

[21] *The Revenant*, directed by Alejandro G. Iñárritu (20th Century Fox, 2015). There are various fictional iterations of the Hugh Glass story, recounting

Glass's mauling and his pursuit of revenge against Jim Bridger and John Fitzgerald. Most recent is Michael Punke's *The Revenant: A Novel of Revenge* (New York: Carroll & Graff, 2002), from which the movie takes its title. There is also Frederick Manfred's *Lord Grizzly* (Frederick Feikema Manfred, 1954; reprint, Lincoln, NE: University of Nebraska Press, 1983).

[22] *The One and Only, Genuine, Original Family Band*, directed by Michael O'Herlihy (Walt Disney Productions, 1968).

[23] For example, in the thirty-three presidential elections since South Dakota became a state, only five times has the state not voted Republican (1896, 1912, 1932, 1936, 1964).

[24] *Tater Tot and Patton*, directed by Andrew Kightlinger (Giant Pictures, 2017).

[25] See Harry F. Thompson, ed., *A New South Dakota History*, 2d ed. (Sioux Falls: Center for Western Studies, 2009), 293-307.

Contributors

Sara Egge is the Claude D. Pottinger Professor of History at Centre College in Kentucky. Her first book, *Woman Suffrage and Citizenship in the Midwest, 1870-1920* (2018) won the 2019 Benjamin Shambaugh Award for the best book in Iowa history and the 2019 Gita Chaudhuri Prize for the best book on rural women in any era and any place. She also has published numerous articles in journals such as *Middle West Review*, *Agricultural History*, and *Minnesota History.* While she continues to research about food and gender in the Midwest, she is currently working on a history of the naturalization process. Raised in rural southeastern South Dakota, Egge received undergraduate degrees from North Dakota State University and graduate degrees from Iowa State University.

H. Roger Grant, a native of Albia, Iowa, and graduate of Simpson College in Indianola, Iowa, is the Kathryn and Calhoun Lemon Professor of History at Clemson University in Clemson, South Carolina. Although he has written or edited several non-railroad books, Grant has focused on railroad and transportation topics. Of his more than 35 academic book publications, four have been corporate studies of Midwestern carriers, including the Chicago & North Western; Chicago Great Western; Chicago, Rock Island & Pacific, and Wabash railroads. He has also written *Twilight Rails: The Final Era of Railroad Building in the Midwest* (University of Minnesota Press, 2010). Between 2012 and 2019, Indiana University Press published Grant's trilogy, *Railroads and the American People*, *Electric Interurbans and the American People*, and *Transportation and the American People*. His book manuscript "The Station Agent and the American Railroad

Experience" is currently in production at Indiana University Press. He is at work on a study of five shortline railroads either built or partially built between 1905 and 1915 in western Iowa, "Sunset Cluster: An Iowa Railroad Story." Grant, who began his teaching career in 1970 at the University of Akron, has been at Clemson since 1996. He lives on Lake Hartwell outside Clemson.

Pekka Hämäläinen is the Rhodes Professor of American History at the University of Oxford. His writings have appeared in the *American Historical Review*, *Journal of American History*, *History and Theory*, *William and Mary Quarterly*, *Western Historical Quarterly*, and *Journal of the Civil War Era*. He is the author of *The Comanche Empire* (Yale University Press, 2008), which received twelve book awards, including the Bancroft Prize, the Merle Curti Award, and the Caughey Prize. His second book, *Lakota America: A New History of Indigenous Power*, was named one of the *New York Times* Critics' Top Books of 2019 and one of the 10 Best History Books of 2019 by *Smithsonian Magazine*. It was also the winner of the Utley Book Prize and the MPIBA Reading the West Book Award for narrative nonfiction. His third book, *Indigenous Continent: The Epic Contest for North America*, will be published in the fall of 2022.

John Henris attended Black Hills State University in western South Dakota where he cultivated a lasting appreciation for the natural and human history of the region. After graduating from BHSU he went east for graduate study and eventually became a college professor. He is Associate Professor of History at the University of Arkansas at Monticello. His current academic research and writing is primarily focused on the environmental history of the Black Hills and northern Great Plains. John has written on such topics as the artificial creation of cold-water fisheries, fisheries and mining conflict, and the ecological margins of irrigated apple production in the Black Hills.

Paul Higbee is a Spearfish writer and former educator who authored two book-length biographies of notable South Dakotans: Dust Bowl-era Governor Tom Berry and Doolittle Raid pilot Don

Smith. He holds degrees from Black Hills State University and the University of Notre Dame. Since 1992 Higbee has been a Black Hills feature writer and columnist for *South Dakota Magazine*. He has also scripted documentaries and children's instructional programming for South Dakota Public TV. Higbee earned his first writing paychecks as a 17-year-old sportswriter covering Black Hills Conference high school athletics. At the same age, he won a state journalism award after tracking down future baseball Hall of Famer Catfish Hunter as the pitcher hunted in South Dakota. Higbee and his wife, Janet, raised two daughters in the Black Hills.

Thomas D. Isern is Professor of History and University Distinguished Professor at North Dakota State University, Fargo, where he has served since 1992. He holds a B.A. degree from Bethany College, Lindsborg, Kansas, as well as M.A. and Ph.D. degrees from Oklahoma State University, all in history. His field of specialization is the history and folklore of the Great Plains; he has authored or co-authored seven books, the most recent being *Pacing Dakota* (North Dakota State University Press, 2018). Isern is a five-time grantee of the National Endowment for the Humanities, directing summer seminars for teachers. His weekly radio feature, "Plains Folk," is heard statewide in North Dakota, on Prairie Public.

Jeffrey A. Johnson is Professor of History and Director of the Graduate Program at Providence College, in Rhode Island, where he teaches courses on the Gilded Age/Progressive Era, labor history, and the American West. He is the author of "*They Are All Red Out Here": Socialist Politics in the Pacific Northwest, 1895-1925* (University of Oklahoma Press, 2008), the edited collection *Reforming America: A Thematic Encyclopedia and Document Collection of the Progressive Era* (ABC-Clio, 2017), which received an American Library Association award and placement on its 2018 List of Best Historical Materials, and *The 1916 Preparedness Day Bombing: Anarchists and Terrorism in Progressive Era America* (Routledge, 2018).

Christopher R. Laingen is a Professor of Geography at Eastern Illinois University. He grew up in southern Minnesota near the town of Odin, where much of his interest in the natural environment began. His research focuses on changes in farming and the landscapes of the rural Midwest and Great Plains. He has published in *Great Plains Research*, *Environmental Research Letters*, *The Geographical Review*, and *The Professional Geographer*. He is also the co-author of *American Farms, American Food: A Geography of Agriculture and Food Production in the United States* (Lexington Books), and has contributed chapters for *The Interior Borderlands* and *Heartland River* (both from the Center for Western Studies), and *Finding a New Midwestern History* (UNL Press).

Jon K. Lauck is the author of several books, including *The Lost Region: Toward a Revival of Midwestern History* (University of Iowa Press, 2013) and *From Warm Center to Ragged Edge: The Erosion of Midwestern Regionalism, 1920-1965* (University of Iowa Press, 2017). Lauck has worked as a full-time professor, a part-time professor, and a lawyer and is currently serving as an adjunct professor of history and political science at the University of South Dakota and as Editor-in-Chief of *Middle West Review*. He earned his Ph.D. in history from the University of Iowa and his law degree from the University of Minnesota. Lauck's most recent work is *The Good Country: A History of the American Midwest* (University of Oklahoma Press, 2022).

Samantha M. Litty is a research associate at the Europa-Universität Flensburg, where she recently completed an Alexander von Humboldt Postdoctoral Research Fellow in conjunction with the FAU Erlangen-Nürnberg (2019-2021). She holds a Ph.D. in German Linguistics from the University of Wisconsin-Madison. Her research focuses on language variation and change in the nineteenth century American Midwest and the German-Danish border region of the Southern Jutland Peninsula. She is the author of "The German Midwest" (forthcoming, *The Oxford Handbook of Midwestern History*), "Historical Sociolinguistic Contexts: Networks and feature availability in 19th century German letter collections" (2022, *Selected Proceedings of the 11th Annual Workshop on Immigrant Languages in the Americas (WILA 11)*, "Letters home: German-American Civil War soldiers' letters 1864-1865" (2019, *Journal of Historical Sociolinguistics*), and "A turn of the century courtship: Obstruent variation in personal letters in the Upper Midwest" (2017, *Sociolinguistica*). Other research interests include heritage languages, historical sociolinguistics, and historical multilingualism.

Lance Nixon is a freelance magazine writer based in South Dakota. He spent most of his career as a newspaper and magazine writer and editor in the Dakotas, including at the *Capital Journal* in Pierre, where he co-founded *South Dakota Outdoors* magazine. His fiction about the Sand Lake region in South Dakota has appeared in recent years in Georgia-based *Gray's Sporting Journal*, and in *Dappled Things* magazine, where he was the winner of the 2021 J. F. Powers Prize in Short Fiction. His journalism appears in national magazines such as *Cowboys & Indians*, *Wild West*, and *Pheasants Forever*. He also writes for regional and niche-industry magazines, mainly about the Plains and the West.

Jon D. Schaff is Professor of Political Science at Northern State University in Aberdeen, South Dakota, where he has taught since 2001. He teaches classes in American political thought, American political institutions, as well as politics in literature and film. Prof. Schaff is a regular commentator on South Dakota politics. He is the author of multiple articles and book chapters as well as two books: *Abraham Lincoln and the Limits of Liberal Democracy* and *Age of Anxiety: Meaning, Identity, and Politics in 21st Century Literature and Film* (co-authored with Anthony Wachs). Prof. Schaff received his bachelor's degree from St. John's University (Minnesota), a master's degree from University of Wyoming, and his Ph.D. from Loyola University Chicago.

Frank Van Nuys is Professor of History at South Dakota School of Mines and Technology, where he has taught since 2002. Van Nuys is the author of *Americanizing the West: Race, Immigrants, and Citi-*

zenship, 1890-1930, published by the University Press of Kansas in 2002, and *Varmints and Victims: Predator Control in the American West*, published by the same press in 2015. He teaches courses on the American West, environmental history, and environmental law and policy, along with survey courses in U.S. history and Western Civilization. He and his wife, Janet, live in Rapid City.

Carson Walker was a multi-platform journalist and editor for more than 25 years at KDLT-TV and the *Argus Leader* in Sioux Falls and at The Associated Press in South Dakota and Arizona. He subsequently moved into internal and external communications and video positions at the University of South Dakota, where he also taught journalism, and Sanford Health, where he fosters innovation. His South Dakota story credits include an investigation into unclaimed property owned by a credit-card company, the fatal airplane crash of Gov. George Mickelson, serial killer Robert Leroy Anderson, the criminal and civil cases of Bill Janklow, and the slaying of American Indian Movement activist Anna Mae Pictou-Aquash. He grew up in Iowa, lives in Sioux Falls, studied journalism and political science at Colorado State University, has four adult children, and enjoys running, cycling, hiking, golfing, and downhill and cross-country skiing.

Index

F

G

O

R

Y